Bahrain, Kuwait & Qatar

Gordon Robison
Paul Greenway

LONELY PLANET PUBLICATIONS
Melbourne • Oakland • London • Paris

BAHRAIN, KUWAIT & QATAR

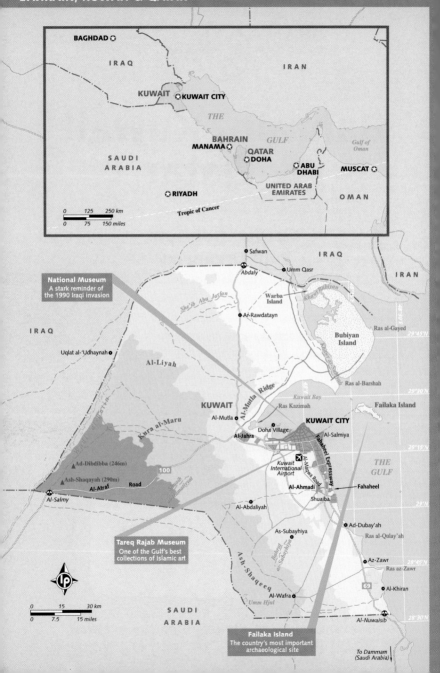

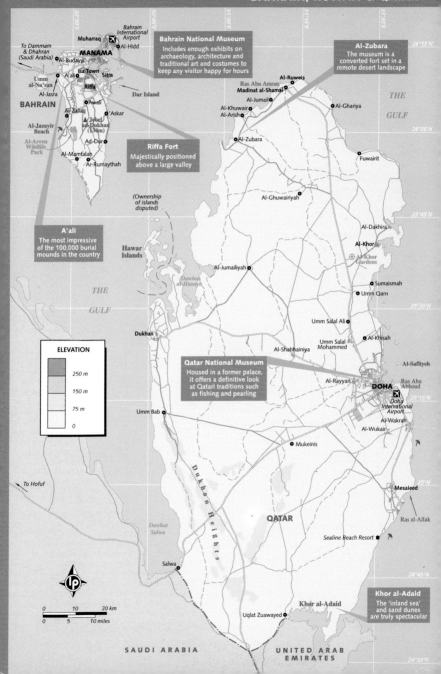

BAHRAIN, KUWAIT & QATAR

Bahrain National Museum
Includes enough exhibits on archaeology, architecture and traditional art and costumes to keep any visitor happy for hours

Al-Zubara
The museum is a converted fort set in a remote desert landscape

Riffa Fort
Majestically positioned above a large valley

A'ali
The most impressive of the 100,000 burial mounds in the country

Qatar National Museum
Housed in a former palace, it offers a definitive look at Qatari traditions such as fishing and pearling

Khor al-Adaid
The 'inland sea' and sand dunes are truly spectacular

ELEVATION

- 250 m
- 150 m
- 75 m
- 0

BAHRAIN

To Dammam & Dhahran (Saudi Arabia)

Bahrain International Airport

Muharraq
MANAMA
Al-Hidd
Al-Budayyi
Umm al-Na'san
A'ali
Isa Town
Sitra
Riffa
Al-Jasra
Dar Island
Awali
Al-Zallaq
'Askar
Jebel ad-Dukhan (134m)
Al-Jazayir Beach
Ad-Dur
Al-Areen Wildlife Park
Al-Mamtalah
Ar-Rumaythath

Hawar Islands

(Ownership of islands disputed)

Dawhat al-Husayn

THE GULF

QATAR

Al-Ruweis
Ras Abu Amran
Madinat al-Shamal
Al-Jumail
Al-Khuwair
Al-Arish
Al-Zubara
Al-Ghariya

THE GULF

Fuwairit

Al-Ghuwairiyah

Al-Dakhira
Al-Khor
Al-Khor Gardens

Al-Jumailiyah

Sumaismah
Umm Qarn

Umm Salal Ali
Al-Khisah
Umm Salal Mohammed
Al-Safliyeh

Dukhan

Al-Shahhainiya
Al-Rayyan
DOHA
Ras Abu Abboud

Umm Bab
Doha International Airport
Al-Wakrah
Al-Wukair

Mukeinis

Dukhan Heights

Mesaieed

Dawhat Salwa

Ras al-Allak

Sealine Beach Resort

Salwa

Khor al-Adaid

Uqlat Zuawayed

To Hofuf

SAUDI ARABIA

UNITED ARAB EMIRATES

0   10   20 km
0 5   10 miles

26°15'N
26°00'N
25°45'N
25°30'N
25°15'N
25°N
24°45'N
24°30'N

Bahrain, Kuwait & Qatar
1st edition – July 2000

Published by
Lonely Planet Publications Pty Ltd A.C.N. 005 607 983
192 Burwood Rd, Hawthorn, Victoria 3122, Australia

Lonely Planet Offices
Australia PO Box 617, Hawthorn, Victoria 3122
USA 150 Linden St, Oakland, CA 94607
UK 10a Spring Place, London NW5 3BH
France 1 rue du Dahomey, 75011 Paris

Photographs
All of the images in this guide are available for licensing from
Lonely Planet Images.
email: lpi@lonelyplanet.com.au

Front cover photograph
Kuwait, the water towers, one of the main landmarks in Kuwait City
(Chris Mellor, Lonely Planet Images)

ISBN 1 86450 132 4

Although the authors
and Lonely Planet try
to make the informa-
tion as accurate as
possible, we accept
no responsibility for
any loss, injury or
inconvenience sus-
tained by anyone
using this book.

Contents – Text

KUWAIT

QATAR

Contents – Maps

MAP LEGEND .... **back page**

METRIC CONVERSION .... **inside back cover**

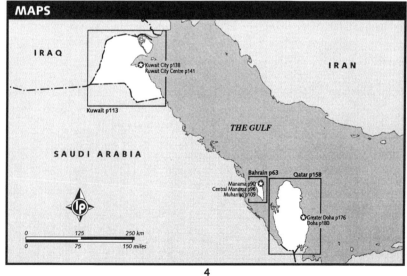

The Authors

Gordon Robison

Gordon Robison was raised in Vermont and Maine in the north-eastern USA. He began to travel extensively while still a student and began writing for Lonely Planet in 1988. For LP, Gordon wrote both editions of *Arab Gulf States*, and has co-authored or contributed material to the *Middle East*, *USA* and *West Asia on a shoestring*.

From 1988 to 1994 Gordon was a freelance journalist based in Cairo where he reported regularly for the American ABC Radio News. Since 1996 he has lived in Atlanta, where he is a producer with CNN International. Gordon is married to Dona Stewart. They have two children: Halle, who frequently accompanies her father on LP research trips, and Mallory, who doesn't know it yet, but will.

Paul Greenway

Gratefully plucked from the blandness and security of the Australian Public Service, Paul has worked on about a dozen Lonely Planet books, including *Mongolia, Iran, Jordan, Middle East, Madagascar* and *Bali & Lombok*. During the rare times that he's not travelling – or writing, reading and dreaming about it – Paul relaxes to (and pretends he can play) heavy rock, eats and breathes Australian Rûles Football, and will go to any lengths (eg, staying in Mongolia and Iran) to avoid settling down.

FROM GORDON

Thank you to Ali Khalil and Sarah Chalabi for their hospitality in Kuwait. Thanks also to Miriam Amie and Ashraf Fouad for their help and friendship over the years in both Egypt and the Gulf.

This Book

This book was based on the Bahrain, Kuwait and Qatar chapters of the 2nd edition of Lonely Planet's *Arab Gulf States*, written by Gordon Robison. Paul Greenway updated the Bahrain and Qatar chapters; Gordon Robison updated and revised the rest.

From the Publisher

This was book edited in Lonely Planet's Melbourne office by Julia Taylor, with assistance from Sarah Mathers and Dan Goldberg. Sonya Brooke coordinated the design and mapping. Quentin Frayne organised the Language chapter, Verity Campbell drew the illustrations and Guillaume Roux designed the cover. Thanks to Peter Ward of Peter Ward Book Exports for his assistance with the bookshop information.

Acknowledgments

Many thanks to the following travellers who used *Arab Gulf States* and wrote to us with helpful hints, useful advice and interesting anecdotes about travelling in the Gulf:

AF Gastaldo, AF Siraa, Abbas Farmand, Alain Morel, Alan Toms, Amy Furtado, Andrew Moss, Andrew Thorburn, Andy Hurst, Anja Nolte, Annie Graham, Ben Samuel, Bert Verversr, Brian Yates, Caroline Williams, Chris Lane, Chris Watts, DF Inglis, Dan Gamber, David Rubin, Dr JV Leonard, Dr Jacques De Ridder, Dr Michael Haisch, Dr Richard Beal, EE Atkins, Eric Hohmann, Ewen Donnelly, GH Peters, Georg Nikolaus Garlichs, George Joachim, George Moore, Giorgia Naccarato, Gokhan Gungor, Graham Egerton, Harry Bonning, Harry Clark, Hope Rodefer, Ilja van Roon, Irmgard Dommel, J Saint, James Wallace, Jason Mountney, Javad Faharzadeh, Jens Baranowski, Jill Stockbridge, Joachim Behrmann, John Jacobs, John Pitman, Joshua Taylor Barnes, Kay McDivitt, Kevin Troy, Klaus & Marion Hempfing, Linda Johnson, Lisa Martin, Luigi Vallero, Kim Gillard, M Carson, Manuel Wedemeyer, Maria Tarrant, Mark Hunt, Maryam Chabastari, Matt Birch, Matthew A Hadlock, Matty Cameron, Maureen Roult, Michael John Brown, Mirjam Coumans, Nicky McLean, Norman Sheppard, P Jerrett, Patric Colquhoun, Patricia Bulat, Paul Sechi, Peter Gray, Pia Kokkarinen, Rainer Sittenthaler, Ralph Lawson, Reinhard Fay, Ritchie Anderson, Robert Maitland, Robert Read, Roger Brand, Ruud Verkerk, Sandie Gustus, Sarah Dewes, Shailendra Shukla, Shona Fisher, Stuart Hales, Steve Rothman, Tamsin Turner, Tim Jessop, Tim Pritchard, Toby Hartnell, Tony Revel, Tony Troughear, Valkan Farkas, Virgil Williams, Warren J Iliff and William Kendrick.

Foreword

ABOUT LONELY PLANET GUIDEBOOKS

The story begins with a classic travel adventure: Tony and Maureen Wheeler's 1972 journey across Europe and Asia to Australia. Useful information about the overland trail did not exist at that time, so Tony and Maureen published the first Lonely Planet guidebook to meet a growing need.

From a kitchen table, then from a tiny office in Melbourne (Australia), Lonely Planet has become the largest independent travel publisher in the world, an international company with offices in Melbourne, Oakland (USA), London (UK) and Paris (France).

Today Lonely Planet guidebooks cover the globe. There is an ever-growing list of books and there's information in a variety of forms and media. Some things haven't changed. The main aim is still to help make it possible for adventurous travellers to get out there – to explore and better understand the world.

At Lonely Planet we believe travellers can make a positive contribution to the countries they visit – if they respect their host communities and spend their money wisely. Since 1986 a percentage of the income from each book has been donated to aid projects and human rights campaigns.

Updates Lonely Planet thoroughly updates each guidebook as often as possible. This usually means there are around two years between editions, although for more unusual or more stable destinations the gap can be longer. Check the imprint page (following the colour map at the beginning of the book) for publication dates.

Between editions up-to-date information is available in two free newsletters – the paper *Planet Talk* and email *Comet* (to subscribe, contact any Lonely Planet office) – and on our Web site at www.lonelyplanet.com. The *Upgrades* section of the Web site covers a number of important and volatile destinations and is regularly updated by Lonely Planet authors. *Scoop* covers news and current affairs relevant to travellers. And, lastly, the *Thorn Tree* bulletin board and *Postcards* section of the site carry unverified, but fascinating, reports from travellers.

Correspondence The process of creating new editions begins with the letters, postcards and emails received from travellers. This correspondence often includes suggestions, criticisms and comments about the current editions. Interesting excerpts are immediately passed on via newsletters and the Web site, and everything goes to our authors to be verified when they're researching on the road. We're keen to get more feedback from organisations or individuals who represent communities visited by travellers.

Lonely Planet gathers information for everyone who's curious about the planet – and especially for those who explore it first-hand. Through guidebooks, phrasebooks, activity guides, maps, literature, newsletters, image library, TV series and Web site we act as an information exchange for a worldwide community of travellers.

Research Authors aim to gather sufficient practical information
to enable travellers to make informed choices and to make the
mechanics of a journey run smoothly. They also research historical and cultural background to help enrich the travel experience
and allow travellers to understand and respond appropriately to
cultural and environmental issues.

Authors don't stay in every hotel because that would mean
spending a couple of months in each medium-sized city and, no,
they don't eat at every restaurant because that would mean
stretching belts beyond capacity. They do visit hotels and restaurants to check standards and prices, but feedback based on
readers' direct experiences can be very helpful.

Many of our authors work undercover, others aren't so secre-
tive. None of them accept freebies in exchange for positive
write-ups. And none of our guidebooks contain any advertising.

Production Authors submit their raw manuscripts and maps to
offices in Australia, USA, UK or France. Editors and cartographers
– all experienced travellers themselves – then begin the process
of assembling the pieces. When the book finally hits the shops,
some things are already out of date, we start getting feedback
from readers and the process begins again …

WARNING & REQUEST

Things change – prices go up, schedules change, good places go bad and bad places go bankrupt – nothing stays the same. So, if you find things better or worse, recently opened or long
since closed, please tell us and help make the next edition even more accurate and useful. We
genuinely value all the feedback we receive. Julie Young coordinates a well travelled team that
reads and acknowledges every letter, postcard and email and ensures that every morsel of information finds its way to the appropriate authors, editors and cartographers for verification.

Everyone who writes to us will find their name in the next edition of the appropriate guidebook. They will also receive the latest issue of *Planet Talk*, our quarterly printed newsletter,
or *Comet*, our monthly email newsletter. Subscriptions to both newsletters are free. The very
best contributions will be rewarded with a free guidebook.

Excerpts from your correspondence may appear in new editions of Lonely Planet guidebooks, the Lonely Planet Web site, *Planet Talk* or *Comet*, so please let us know if you *don't*
want your letter published or your name acknowledged.

Send all correspondence to the Lonely Planet office closest to you:

Australia: PO Box 617, Hawthorn, Victoria 3122
USA: 150 Linden St, Oakland, CA 94607
UK: 10A Spring Place, London NW5 3BH
France: 1 rue du Dahomey, 75011 Paris

Or email us at: talk2us@lonelyplanet.com.au

For news, views and updates see our Web site: www.lonelyplanet.com

HOW TO USE A LONELY PLANET GUIDEBOOK

The best way to use a Lonely Planet guidebook is any way you choose. At Lonely Planet we believe the most memorable travel experiences are often those that are unexpected, and the finest discoveries are those you make yourself. Guidebooks are not intended to be used as if they provide a detailed set of infallible instructions!

Contents All Lonely Planet guidebooks follow roughly the same format. The Facts about the Destination chapters or sections give background information ranging from history to weather. Facts for the Visitor gives practical information on issues like visas and health. Getting There & Away gives a brief starting point for researching travel to and from the destination. Getting Around gives an overview of the transport options when you arrive.

The peculiar demands of each destination determine how subsequent chapters are broken up, but some things remain constant. We always start with background, then proceed to sights, places to stay, places to eat, entertainment, getting there and away, and getting around information – in that order.

Heading Hierarchy Lonely Planet headings are used in a strict hierarchical structure that can be visualised as a set of Russian dolls. Each heading (and its following text) is encompassed by any preceding heading that is higher on the hierarchical ladder.

Entry Points We do not assume guidebooks will be read from beginning to end, but that people will dip into them. The traditional entry points are the list of contents and the index. In addition, however, some books have a complete list of maps and an index map illustrating map coverage.

There may also be a colour map that shows highlights. These highlights are dealt with in greater detail in the Facts for the Visitor chapter, along with planning questions and suggested itineraries. Each chapter covering a geographical region usually begins with a locator map and another list of highlights. Once you find something of interest in a list of highlights, turn to the index.

Maps Maps play a crucial role in Lonely Planet guidebooks and include a huge amount of information. A legend is printed on the back page. We seek to have complete consistency between maps and text, and to have every important place in the text captured on a map. Map key numbers usually start in the top left corner.

Although inclusion in a guidebook usually implies a recommendation we cannot list every good place. Exclusion does not necessarily imply criticism. In fact there are a number of reasons why we might exclude a place – sometimes it is simply inappropriate to encourage an influx of travellers.

Introduction

The term 'oil sheikh' was coined to refer to a Kuwaiti ruler of half a century ago, and is now the one phrase the rulers of the Gulf's microstates would most love to retire. Many of the rather unfortunate images associated with it – gold-lined sinks, expensive cars abandoned in the desert at the first sign of mechanical trouble, garishly painted statues at a Beverly Hills mansion – date from the mid-'70s.

Today's Gulf defies the stereotype and presents the visitor with a set of contradictions. It is both cosmopolitan and insular. It honours ancient tradition amid an overly modern, even plastic society. It professes deep-seated conservatism, while reaching for the products of the liberal, Western world. Its governments often talk as though they are part of the developing world, while their citizens enjoy some of the highest living standards on earth. The Gulf States are clearly, and proudly, Middle Eastern, and yet they are completely unlike anywhere else in the Middle East.

Bahrain, Kuwait and Qatar all played central roles in one of the great stories of the 20th century: the growth of oil and gas as the world's fuel of choice, and the consequent remaking of much of the world in the image of the industrial West.

It is only in recent years that Bahrain Kuwait and Qatar have opened themselves to the outside world as anything other than business centres. Western visitors failing to look beyond the surface have often dismissed these countries as dull and expensive. This is simplistic and fails to do them justice.

Bahrain, Kuwait and Qatar's archaeological and cultural heritage is fascinating. It includes one of the world's oldest known civilisations, Dilmun, and the only ancient Greek settlement in the Gulf. Today, all three countries offer a fascinating blend of tradition and modernity, and all remain off the beaten track. That is sure to change, but for now it makes a visit a special pleasure, offering the traveller the feeling of entering undiscovered territory.

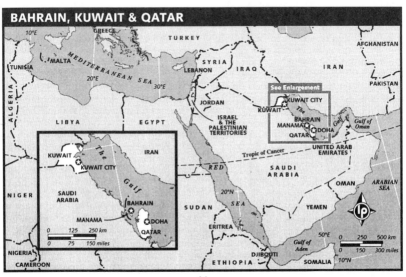

Facts about the Region

HISTORY

While it might seem fair to assume that as Bahrain, Kuwait and Qatar share the region they would also share a great deal of their history, this has only been the case in the broadest terms. What follows is a very general summary of the region's history. Detailed country histories appear in the individual country chapters.

Beginnings

Ten thousand years ago Arabia probably looked much the way East Africa does today, with huge stretches of savanna land and abundant annual rainfall. It is unclear when Arabia was first settled, but the earliest known settlements on or near the Gulf coast date from about 5000 BC.

In Bahrain a civilisation known as Dilmun arose during the 3rd millennium BC. Dilmun eventually became a powerful empire controlling much of the central and northern Gulf. The same period also saw significant settlements in what are now the United Arab Emirates (UAE) and Oman.

The cities of ancient Arabia derived their sometimes considerable wealth from trade. The Gulf lay on the main trade routes linking Mesopotamia with the Indus Valley. In the process of planning an invasion of South Arabia, one of Alexander the Great's admirals, Nearchus, established a colony on Failaka Island, off the coast of Kuwait. The military operation was called off when Alexander died in 323 BC on the eve of his planned departure from Mesopotamia, but the Failaka colony survived to became an important trading centre, and for several centuries maintained trade links with India, Rome and Persia. During the 950 years between Alexander's death and the coming of Islam much of the region came under the sway of a succession of Persian dynasties: the Seleucids, the Parthians and, from the 3rd century AD, the Sassanids. The Gulf was of only marginal political and economic importance to these empires.

Mohammed is Born

The Prophet Mohammed was born at Mecca (in present-day Saudi Arabia) in AD 570, an event that marks the end of one era and the beginning of another in the history of Arabia.

Mohammed received his first revelation in 610 and began to preach publicly three years later. It was only after he and a small band of followers fled Mecca for Medina in 622 that Islam became the established faith of an existing temporal community. From Medina, the new religion preached by Mohammed spread out across the peninsula with remarkable speed. All the peoples living around the Gulf pride themselves on having been among the first to embrace the new faith.

As the Muslim empire grew (it eventually stretched from Spain to India) Arabia itself became increasingly marginalised. Within 30 years of the Prophet's death (in 632) the Muslim capital had been moved from Medina to Damascus.

In global terms, the Gulf soon became the back end of nowhere. From the 9th to the 11th century, during which it was dominated first by the Umayyad and later by the Abbasid Empires, the region was neither wealthy nor important. From the 11th century it became an area of petty sheikhdoms which were constantly at war with one another.

Enter the Europeans

The Portuguese were the first European power to take an interest in the Gulf. In 1498 the explorer Vasco da Gama visited the coasts of modern Oman and the UAE. Within 20 years the Portuguese controlled much of the lower Gulf. Their power eventually extended as far north as Bahrain and lasted until the 1630s. Throughout this time, the Portuguese were trying to build an empire in India and they realised that control of the sea routes linking Lisbon to Bombay and Goa, in other words control of the Gulf, was the key to their success or failure.

The Portuguese gradually gave way to Britain's seemingly omnipresent East India

Company, which had trading links with the Gulf as early as 1616. During the 17th and early 18th centuries the British concentrated on driving their French and Dutch competitors out of the region, a task they had largely accomplished by 1750. It was around this time – the first half of the 18th century – that all of the families which today rule the Gulf States first came to prominence.

The power of these families was entrenched during the 19th century when they signed protection treaties, known as exclusive agreements, with the British. Under these agreements the local rulers gave Britain control of their dealings with the outside world and agreed not to make treaties with, or cede land to, any other foreign power without first receiving Britain's permission. In exchange, the Royal Navy guaranteed their independence from Turkey, Persia and anyone else who might pose a threat.

The British administration in the Gulf fell under the jurisdiction of the British Raj in India. (Until India became independent the rupee was the common currency of all the Gulf States; after 1948 it was replaced by a 'Gulf rupee' which was in circulation until 1971.) The chief British officer in the region was the political resident, who was based in Bushire (on the coast of what is now Iran). The resident supervised the political agents, usually junior officers, stationed in the various sheikhdoms of the Gulf. The system was designed to be discreet while allowing the British to make their presence felt quickly when they wanted to.

In the early years of the 20th century the British were concerned about two main threats to their interests in the Gulf. The first came from the north, where the Ottomans were working to boost their own presence in the region in cooperation with the Germans. The second threat came from within Arabia itself. In 1902 Abdul Aziz bin Abdul Rahman al-Saud, known in the West as Ibn Saud, began a series of conquests which eventually led to the formation of Saudi Arabia. By 1912 the Saudis posed a serious threat to the Gulf sheikhdoms. Had it not been for British promises of protection there is little doubt that Saudi Arabia would today

include most or all of Bahrain, Kuwait, Qatar and the UAE.

Striking Oil

The first commercially viable oil strike in the Gulf was made at Masjid-i-Suleiman, in Persia, in May 1908. At this time, however, the Arab side of the Gulf was of little interest to the oil industry. Masjid-i-Suleiman is around 200km north of the head of the Gulf, and even today many of Iran's major oil fields lie well inland.

The search for oil on the Arab side of the Gulf began shortly after WWI. The most famous prospector was a New Zealander named Frank Holmes, who obtained the first oil concessions in Saudi Arabia and Bahrain in 1923 and 1925, respectively. Holmes let the Saudi concession lapse after failing to find backing for his exploration projects but he eventually secured funding for his Bahrain venture. The British and the local rulers were initially sceptical about the prospects for finding oil in the Gulf. Their interest only picked up after oil was found in commercial quantities in Bahrain in 1932.

This interest was spurred on by the collapse, around 1930, of the pearling industry which had been the mainstay of the Gulf's economy for centuries. The pearl trade fell victim to both the worldwide depression that began in 1929 and to the Japanese discovery, about the same time, of a method by which pearls could be cultured artificially.

Within a few years almost every ruler in the Gulf had given out an oil concession in a desperate attempt to bolster his finances. By the time WWII broke out, a refinery was operating in Bahrain. Kuwaiti operations had to be suspended because of the war, however, by the time the fighting began, the companies were well aware of how valuable their concessions were. Export operations in both countries took off as soon as the war was over.

The first enormous jump in the region's wealth came in the early '50s when Iran's prime minister, Mohammed Mossadiq, nationalised the Anglo-Iranian Oil Company, which was then the world's biggest producer. The oil companies stepped up production in the Gulf, particularly Kuwait, to make up for the supplies they had lost in Iran. By 1960 the Middle East was producing 25% of the non-communist world's oil.

In 1968 Britain announced that it would withdraw from the Gulf by the end of 1971, a move which came as a shock to the rulers of the small sheikhdoms of the middle and lower Gulf. (Kuwait had already become independent in 1961.) In late 1971 Bahrain and Qatar became independent states.

The Embargo

What came to be called the 'oil weapon', ie, the embargo by the Gulf States of oil supplies to the West, was first used during the 1967 Arab-Israeli war. At that time the cut off lasted only a few days and proved ineffective, a result which may have lulled the West into a false sense of security. By the time the Arabs and Israelis went to war again in 1973 things had changed. On 17 October 1973, 11 days after the war began, Arab oil producers, led by Saudi Arabia, cut off oil supplies to the USA and Europe in protest at the West's support for Israel. Within a few days the embargo had been lifted on all countries except the USA and Holland. The embargo was relatively short-lived (supplies were resumed to the USA in March 1974 and to Holland in July 1974) and its effects proved to be more psychological than practical, but if the goal was to get the West's attention then it certainly worked.

Ironically the long-term result was to tie the USA and the Gulf States, particularly Saudi Arabia, more closely to one another. In the final analysis, the West needs the oil and the Gulf States need the revenue that the oil generates. The embargo drove home to both sides the degree to which their economies had become dependent upon each other.

The Oil Boom

With the surge in oil prices that followed the embargo, an enormous building boom began in the Gulf. The mid-'70s and early '80s were a time when almost anything seemed possible. In 1979 the Iranian revolution shook the Gulf States, but it also made them even richer as the oil companies increased their production to fill the gap left first by the revolution and later by the outbreak of the Iran-Iraq war in 1980. This gap caused prices to soar once more, fuelling yet another surge of building.

Obviously this could not go on forever. In 1985 the bottom fell out of the oil market and everything changed. To varying extents all of the Gulf countries had trouble keeping up their building programs while maintaining the generous welfare states which their people had come to expect. The Iran-Iraq war continued to drag on, scaring away potential foreign investors and becoming a constant source of concern throughout the region. This was particularly the case in Kuwait, which was only a few kilometres from the front line.

In May 1981 Saudi Arabia, Kuwait, Bahrain, Qatar, the UAE and Oman formed the Gulf Cooperation Council (GCC) in an effort to increase economic cooperation but also in response to the threat from Iran.

Recent History

When Iran and Iraq grudgingly agreed to a cease-fire in August 1988 the Gulf breathed a collective sigh of relief. After Ayatollah Khomeini, the spiritual leader of Iran's Islamic revolution, died in the summer of 1989 Iran began to seem a bit less foreboding. The economic climate in the Gulf looked reasonably good during late 1989 and the spring and summer of 1990.

In retrospect this period appears to have been the calm before the storm. On 2 August 1990 Iraq invaded Kuwait, which it annexed a few days later. Within days, King Fahd asked the USA to send troops to defend Saudi Arabia against a possible Iraqi attack. The result was Operation Desert Shield, a US-led coalition in Saudi Arabia and the Gulf which eventually numbered over 500,000 troops. On 17 January 1991 the coalition launched Operation Desert Storm to drive Iraq out of Kuwait. This was accomplished after a six-week bombing campaign and a four-day ground offensive. Kuwaitis returned to their country to find hundreds of burning oil wells blackening the sky.

A year after the war, Kuwait's oil fires had been extinguished and the government was working feverishly to erase every trace of Iraq's seven-month occupation. Superficially, the war appeared to have changed little, and trade once again dominated the lives of most of the Gulf's residents – or so everyone said.

That explanation was always a bit too simple. In fact, many things have changed since, and to some extent because of, the war. The most visible of these was the restoration of a limited form of democracy in Kuwait, whose freewheeling parliament stands in marked contrast to the opaque politics of the other Gulf States.

On the broader international stage the region became involved in the Arab-Israeli peace process in ways that would have been unthinkable a few years earlier. The GCC sent an observer to the 1991 Arab-Israeli peace conference in Madrid. In the wake of the 1993 Oslo Accords (the first peace agreement between Israel and the Palestine Liberation Organization), Israeli Prime Minister Yitzhak Rabin visited Oman. In late 1995 Qatar signed an agreement to supply natural gas to Israel, albeit through a third party. Israel later opened a small trade office in Doha – the first official Israeli presence in the region.

There were also internal changes. Bahrain, historically one of the most stable countries in the Middle East, suffered periodic bouts of unrest from 1994 to 1996. The government responded with a crackdown on dissent. The death of the long-reigning emir, Sheikh Isa, in 1999 added a new degree of uncertainty as

Islamic Fundamentalism

Is there a term more excessively used in the Western media these days? Since the Iranian revolution of 1979, the West has been alternately fascinated and appalled by the excesses committed in the name of 'Islamic Fundamentalism'. Yet for most scholars, the term is almost meaningless since it lumps together a wide range of groups and individual believers – some violent, but most not – with little in common save their Islamic faith.

It is intriguing to note that the word is rarely used in the Arab world. In the strict sense, 'fundamentalism' (the term, by the way, originated in the USA in the 1920s and was used almost exclusively to refer to protestant Christians as recently as the late '70s) is an entirely laudable desire to return to the basics of religion, to the essence of Islam as a faith. A handful of Muslim governments, such as Saudi Arabia and Iran, claim to have achieved this; most others say they are working hard at it.

Arab governments tend to refer to religiously based opposition groups or parties they do not like as 'extremists' or 'terrorists', regardless of whether or not the groups in question advocate violence (and most do not). These Islamist parties, as Western scholars usually call them, tend to refer to their governments as 'infidels', 'apostates' or 'secularists'. Each side, in effect, excommunicates the other for the crime of failing to adhere to its own vision of Muslim life.

The problem with the term 'fundamentalist' is that it is essentially undefinable. Members of Egypt's Muslim Brotherhood say that their goal is to build a truly Islamic society. But both Saudi Arabia and Iran, as different as they are, claim to have achieved such a society already, and one thing Egypt's Muslim Brotherhood is at pains to emphasise is that it does not want to remake the country along either Saudi or Iranian lines. That, they will tell you, is overdoing it. Yet in Saudi Arabia itself there are people who believe their society has strayed from the path of Islam and must return to a *more* conservative lifestyle. By Saudi standards, the 'fundamentalist' members of the Kuwaiti parliament are shockingly liberal.

Social trends in a religion as widely spread as Islam cannot be encapsulated in a single word. The academic community has been trying to retire the term 'fundamentalist' for more than a decade, though it seems still very much a part of the Western lexicon.

the island nation entered the 21st century. Another long-serving monarch, Qatar's Sheikh Khalifa, was overthrown by his son, Sheikh Hamad, in 1995. Sheikh Hamad promptly began to open up Qatar's economy and its political system in ways that were not always pleasing to its neighbours. In 1999, the country elected municipal councils with advisory powers. The vote was unique in the Gulf because women participated as both voters and (unsuccessfully) as candidates. Around the same time, Kuwait's emir moved

Oil – A Primer

The modern world is built, more or less, on unlimited access to cheap oil. Oil and its by-products form an integral part of everyday life. Look at the cover of this book. The laminated cover that helps Lonely Planet guides withstand travel is made by applying a thin layer of plastic – one of oil's most visible by-products – over the paper.

Humankind has known about oil since ancient times. Asphalt or bitumen, the residue left behind after oil's liquid and gaseous parts have evaporated, was used in ancient Egypt as a waterproofing agent. Oil gathered from natural springs was used for centuries as insulation, as a building material and as an ingredient in medicines.

Our oil-based society, however, traces its beginnings to the 1850s when scientists in the USA and Canada figured out how to distil crude oil into kerosene. Kerosene rapidly replaced whale oil as the energy source of choice throughout Europe and the Americas – it was cheaper, and burned more efficiently.

At about the same time, oil prospectors in the US state of Pennsylvania attached pumps to drills used to bore for salt, creating the first oil wells. These made it possible to bring vastly larger quantities of crude on to the market. Previously, oil had been gathered from natural springs or dug out of the ground by hand.

Further growth was spurred by the invention, around 1900, of the internal combustion engine. Until that time petrol had been a waste product of the then-primitive refining process. The use of engines on cars and countless other mechanised devices, and the need for oil as a lubricant in those same engines, led to a demand for petrol that far outstripped supply.

The supply problem was solved in 1909 when scientists in the US state of Indiana discovered how to 'crack' oil – heating it under pressure to break down its larger molecules in ways that made the oil easier to refine. Until then only 15% to 20% of a barrel of oil could be turned into anything other than asphalt. Cracking immediately raised that figure to around 45% and subsequent technological advances have brought it to between 80% and 90% today.

Refining essentially breaks oil into its constituent parts. Some of these are sold more or less as is, while others are refined further or go through other processes until they become the range of products we derive from oil today.

The business of oil is divided into upstream and downstream operations. The former refers to exploration and production while the latter includes everything from refining to retail sales in the form of petrol or other products.

Oil as a commodity is traded on the international financial markets. The value of any individual barrel is determined by both the laws of supply and demand, and by the quality of the oil itself. The oil price you hear quoted in daily financial news reports usually refers to one of several 'benchmark' grades of crude such as Dubai Light, Saudi Arabian Light, North Sea Brent or West Texas Intermediate – names that refer to major oilfields where particular grades are dominant.

Oil trades almost exclusively in US dollars and is sold by the barrel. One barrel is equal to 42 US gallons (159 litres). The 42-gallon barrel was established as a standard unit in 1866 in Pennsylvania, though today oil is neither stored nor shipped in barrels of this, or any other, size.

to extend the vote to women. Parliament overturned his decree later in the year, but women's suffrage remains one of the country's most hotly debated issues.

For the visitor all of this generally remains in the background. As far as most people, visitors and residents alike are concerned, the Gulf is still a trade centre of the first order. But it is also an increasingly popular holiday destination. That trend is one thing that is unlikely to change in the short term.

GEOGRAPHY

Bahrain, Kuwait and the adjacent areas of the Saudi coast are sometimes referred to as the 'Upper Gulf', while the 'Lower Gulf' is mainly the UAE. Qatar can wind up in either category. All of these countries have relatively similar geography. They consist almost entirely of low-lying gravelly deserts and salt flats. This is not the part of Arabia to visit if you seek the endless, rolling sand dunes that so dominate Western imaginations.

Bahrain, with an abundance of underground springs, has a lot more natural greenery than either Kuwait or Qatar (which has long had a reputation for being especially bleak). All three of the countries covered in this book have numerous parks and gardens, most of which are the products of modern irrigation and desalinated water. The Gulf itself is extremely shallow in many places.

GEOLOGY

The Arabian peninsula is thought to have originally been part of a larger landmass along with Africa. A split in this ancient continent created both Africa's Great Rift Valley (which extends up through western Yemen and Saudi Arabia into Jordan) and the Red Sea. As Arabia moved away from Africa part of this process involved the peninsula's 'tilting' with the western side rising and the eastern edge dropping in elevation, a process that led to the formation of the Gulf.

Geologists speak of the peninsula in terms of two distinct regions: the Arabian 'shield' and the Arabian 'shelf'. The shield consists of the volcanic and folded, compressed sedi-mentary rocks that make up the western third of today's Arabian penin-

sula. The shelf is made up of the lower-lying areas that slope away from central Arabia to the waters of the Gulf. The rocks beneath the sands of the Arabian shelf are mostly sedimentary.

Hundreds of millions of years ago, as the shelf was being formed, the Gulf (if we can call it that) extended much further west. It was in the waters and, later, marshes of this area that plants, animals and other organic matter died, sank to the bottom and eventually were covered with rock and compressed to form oil (see the boxed text 'The Discovery of Oil' in the Bahrain chapter for further information).

CLIMATE

From April to October much of the Gulf experiences daytime highs of 40°C or more almost daily. The summer is also extremely

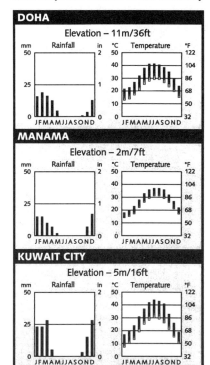

humid and the combination can only be described as stifling. The effect is compounded by the polar levels of air-conditioning commonly used throughout the Gulf. In high summer the indoor/outdoor temperature differential can be as much as 25°C. Stepping outdoors under these circumstances feels not unlike having a large, wet anvil dropped on one's head.

Winter isn't a lot better. From November to early March it is often windy and rainy. None of the Gulf's city streets have storm drains, so when it does rain the water tends to pool up in the road. Except in Kuwait it does not really get cold, but it isn't very pleasant either.

ECOLOGY & ENVIRONMENT

Historically, the Gulf States have not been known for their enthusiasm for environmental protection, but this is changing. Oil and natural gas aside, the Gulf is an area with few natural resources and a fragile ecosystem.

Water is more valuable than oil in the desert, and it is a scarce resource in Arabia. Campaigns to get people to save water, and to be more careful about how they use it, are now common throughout the Gulf.

Governments around the region have also moved to make their people more aware that the desert is a fragile resource. There was a tendency a generation ago, during the region's first rush of wealth, to see the desert as a gigantic rubbish tip. On one level this made sense – for centuries the Bedouin had left their garbage behind them to be consumed by the desert. But that way of life presupposed a society based on very small communities of people who moved around a lot and were in harmony with their surroundings.

The waters of the Gulf are also being treated with greater care today then they were a generation ago. Though the pearl industry collapsed in the 1930s fishing remains a major industry throughout the area. Safety standards in the oil industry are fairly high and, with one exception, there has not been a significant oil spill in the Gulf in many years.

The exception, of course, is the enormous oil slick deliberately released into the Gulf by the Iraqis during the Gulf War in January and February of 1991. The slick is estimated to have reached 11 million barrels in size, making it one of the largest in history. The slick was apparently an attempt by the Iraqis to poison Riyadh's drinking water supply (most of its water is processed at a large desalination plant on the Saudi coast) and to shut down the industrial facilities around Jubail, Saudi Arabia that were supplying fuel to the Allied war effort (these facilities rely on seawater for cooling purposes).

The slick killed untold numbers of fish, birds and marine animals, notably cormorants, and affected the migratory patterns of many others. It did not turn out to be the environmental apocalypse that many predicted at the time, largely due to the major international clean-up effort that was mounted in the months after the war.

In Kuwait itself the Iraqis torched most of the country's oil wells, blackening the sky for months and leaving huge lakes of oil throughout the desert. In these lakes oil saturated the sand to depths of 35cm; the risk of the lakes, up to several metres deep, catching fire, was always high. Astonishingly, the Kuwaitis managed to get the mess cleaned up in about 18 months. The last of the famous oil well fires was extinguished less than a year after the war ended, despite early predictions that putting out the blazes might take up to five years.

FLORA & FAUNA

Although much of the region is desert, there is a wide variety of plant life. But if there is one plant in the region which is ubiquitous, it is the date palm.

If you visit the region in early summer, one of the things you will be struck by is the number of date clusters hanging off the huge number of date palms that line many of the streets and parks. The date palm has always held a vital place in Arabian life. For centuries dates were one of the staple foods of the Bedouin, along with fish, camel meat and camel milk. The reason the date palm can survive in such a harsh climate is because its fruit is roughly 70% sugar. This stops the rot and makes the date edible for a longer period than other tropical fruits.

Apart from providing a major foodstuff, the date palm was also used to make all kinds of useful items. Its trunk was used to make columns and ceilings for houses, while its fronds were used to make roofs and walls (called *areesh*). The date palm provided the only shade available in desert oases. Livestock were fed with its seeds and it was burned as fuel. The palm frond was, and still is, used to make bags, mats, boats (called *shasha*), shelters, brooms and fans. There is no doubt that the Bedouin could not have survived as well as they have without the help of the date palm.

Beyond date palms and some shrubs planted along city roadsides, there is very little greenery in Bahrain, Kuwait and Qatar. Many of the palms and shrubs are, themselves, products of beautification cam-paigns launched during the oil boom (pre-oil Qatar in particular was notorious for being almost completely devoid of vegetation). None of the countries covered here have indulged themselves in the vast (and expensive) crop-growing projects seen in Saudi Arabia.

The average visitor to the Gulf is likely to see little wildlife beyond camels, donkeys and seabirds. The desert teems with other animals, of course, but many of them are nocturnal, some are endangered and all are hard to spot.

A number of species have evolved to meet the demands of life in the desert. Some of the better-known ones include the sand cat, the sand fox and the desert hare. All of these have unusually large ears and tufts of hair on their feet. The large ears allow the animal to hear possible predators from a great distance while the hair on their feet enables them to cross dunes and other areas of loose sand with ease.

An early morning visit to the fish markets around the region will show the Gulf teems with fish life. Diners will be most familiar with the *hamour*, a species of grouper, but the Gulf is also home to an extraordinary range of tropical fish and even several species of sharks, as well as turtles (see the boxed text 'Endangered Species').

GOVERNMENT & POLITICS

All of the Arab Gulf States are monarchies. The three countries covered by this book also have formal systems of outside consultation to advise the ruler on affairs of state. Kuwait has an elected parliament. Bahrain and Qatar have consultative councils whose members are appointed by the ruler and are allowed only to debate such issues as he, or the cabinet, places before them. Qatar also has a popularly elected municipal council. This, too, has only advisory, not legislative, authority.

Arabian culture and tradition allow for – indeed, they require – much more in the way of consultation by the ruler than may at first be apparent. Rulers must always retain the support of both their own family and of the public at large, particularly the powerful

---

Endangered Species

Many of the Gulf's unique species are endangered. Over the last 50 years the hobura bustard, a kind of wild desert chicken that was once plentiful throughout Arabia, has been hunted to the edge of extinction. Other animals, such as sand cats, have been both hunted and sought illegally by foreign collectors. Several species of turtle, notably the green turtle and the hawksbill turtle, nest in the Gulf and have joined the endangered list, too. The turtles can be seen at the Qatar National Museum, though their best-known nesting grounds are on the Omani coast of the Arabian Sea.

The Arabian oryx has long been among the most endangered of the peninsula's native species. It went to the very brink of extinction in the late '70s and early '80s, but has been rescued by breeding programs in a number of countries in the region, including Bahrain.

Indeed, Bahrain is home to the Al-Areen Wildlife Park, one of the region's few conservation areas open to the public.

merchant families that exist in these countries. Throughout the region the rulers and other senior members of the ruling families are accessible to any and all of their subjects in ways that would be unthinkable almost anywhere else in the world. They regularly sit in a *majlis*, or formal meeting room, where any citizen can come and present a petition or discuss a problem.

This constant, if somewhat formalised, consultation is a far cry from Western notions of democratic life, but it does mean that the Gulf's rulers are not as detached from their citizens as many in the West often imagine.

Access, however, should not be confused with activism which, outside of Kuwait politics, is essentially nonexistent in the Gulf. Television and newspaper accounts of cabinet or consultative council meetings never impart any of the substance of whatever discussions may have taken place. Sometimes they do not even mention what decisions, if any, were actually taken.

In all of the Gulf States, members of the ruling family hold several of the key cabinet portfolios (usually defence, foreign affairs and interior and often the labour, information and oil ministries). Nonroyal ministers are usually technocrats who have little clout outside their area of specialisation. Real political authority tends to remain within a small circle of senior members of the ruling family and their advisers.

ECONOMY

Oil, natural gas and petrochemicals dominate the economies of all of the Gulf States either directly or indirectly. Bahrain, for example, produces only a token amount of oil, but it refines a large amount of Saudi oil that arrives via a pipeline under the sea. It also has an extensive oilfield services industry that caters to the entire region. Though oil concessions were originally issued to foreign companies a generation or two ago, the production and refining work is now handled entirely by state-owned companies.

That said, the distribution of oil across the region varies greatly. Kuwait is one of the world's most important oil producers.

Bahrain, as noted above, produces very little oil. Qatar's oil reserves are modest by regional standards, but it sits atop one of the world's largest natural gas fields.

Oil wealth has also made some of the Gulf States, particularly Kuwait, large investors. Prior to the 1990 Iraqi invasion, Kuwait actually made more money from its investments each year than it did from oil.

Beyond oil there is a large financial services industry in Bahrain. Tourism is a small, but growing, part of the economic picture in Bahrain and, to a lesser extent, Qatar.

POPULATION & PEOPLE

The exact population of the three countries is difficult to determine though it is estimated at around 3.5 million. Expatriates outnumber citizens in both Kuwait and Qatar, and are a close match in Bahrain. The figures are uncertain because census data tends to be treated as a state secret. (See the boxed text 'The Expat Existence' later in this chapter.)

Ethnically, the people of the Gulf are Arabs, though many are of Persian or mixed Arab-Persian ancestry. In Bahrain, a few Indian families (the descendants of merchants who arrived generations ago) have been assimilated into the local population.

Although armies of foreign workers are employed throughout the Gulf, these people (be they labourers or investment bankers) are legally regarded as hired help, not immigrants. Even if you work in the Gulf for 30 or 40 years (and many people do), you will be expected to leave once you no longer have a job. It is virtually impossible for a foreigner of any nationality to acquire citizenship in one of the Gulf countries. A handful of foreigners (almost invariably from other Arab countries) may be granted citizenship now and then, but these are usually people who have rendered important services to the ruler or the state over a great many years.

ARTS

The arts scene in the three countries is somewhat limited. There are a few galleries in Kuwait City, Manama and Doha featuring the works of both local and expatriate artists, and government-sponsored programs in all three countries seek to preserve and promote traditional arts and crafts. Large hotels occasionally sponsor exhibitions by foreign artists, usually those who paint or draw on 'Arabian' themes. Qatar has a national theatre.

Traditional Architecture

Wind Towers Called *barjeel* in Arabic, wind towers (preserved or reconstructed at museums) are the Gulf's unique form of non-electrical air-conditioning. In most of the region's cities a handful still exist.

Traditional wind towers rise five or six metres above a house. They are usually built of wood or stone but can also be made from canvas. The tower is open on all four sides and catches even small breezes. These are channelled down around a central shaft and into the room below. In the process the air speeds up and is cooled. The cooler air already in the tower shaft pulls in, and subsequently cools, the hotter air outside through simple convection.

The towers work well. Sitting beneath a wind tower on a day when it is 40°C and humid you will notice a distinct drop in temperature and a consistent breeze even when the air outside feels heavy and still.

Barasti The term *barasti* describes both the traditional Gulf method of building a palm-leaf house and the completed house itself. Barastis consist of a skeleton of wooden poles onto which palm leaves are woven to form a strong structure through which air can still circulate. They were extremely common throughout the Gulf in the centuries before the oil boom, but are now almost nonexistent. The few examples which survive are fishermen's shacks, storage buildings in rural areas and a few examples sitting in the courtyards of museums. For a detailed description of how a barasti house is constructed, see Geoffrey Bibby's book *Looking for Dilmun*.

Coral Coral, quarried from offshore reefs and then cut into stone, has been used as a building material for centuries, sometimes in combination with gypsum. Bahrain's Al-Jasra House is a well-preserved example of a large building construction using a coral-gypsum mixture.

Weaving

Iran, Turkey, Pakistan and Afghanistan are famous for their carpets. Among the Bedouin of Arabia, however, it is weaving that has a time-honoured place in the local culture.

Where carpets are knotted, rugs and other Bedouin work are made on a loom. In settled areas, such as the Bahraini village of Bani Jamrah, these can be quite large, elaborate affairs. Looms used by those Bedouin who still live as nomads are small and can be easily taken apart for transport.

Traditionally, weaving (*sadu* in Arabic) is the job of the women of the household. Bedouin women are responsible for weaving and maintaining the tents in which the family lives, including interior walls and some ground coverings. With time, they may also produce saddlebags and decorative bridles for the family's camels, clothing for other members of the family (woollen vests, for example) and pillows for the family's use. Traditionally, goat hair

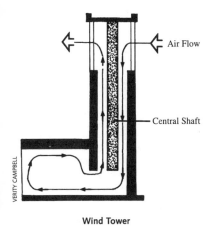

Air Flow

Central Shaft

VERITY CAMPBELL

Wind Tower

Mosque Vocabulary

The Grand Mosque in Mecca and the Prophet's Mosque in Medina, Islam's two holiest sites, can each accommodate hundreds of thousands of worshippers at a time. But throughout the Gulf you can also see small enclosed areas open to the sky – impromptu mosques available to any passing traveller, and capable of holding no more than a handful of people.

A mosque is fundamentally a simple structure, made up of a few basic elements. The most visible of these is the minaret, the tower from which the call to prayer is issued five times every day. Virtually every mosque in the world has a minaret. Many have several. Minarets can be plain or ornate. Some – such as the Giralda at Seville, Spain – are architectural works of great beauty. The first minarets were not built until the early 8th century, some 70 years after the Prophet's death. Prior to that time the *muezzin*, or prayer caller, often stood on a rooftop or some other elevated position so as to be heard as widely as possible. The idea for minarets as we now know them may have originated with the watchtowers that Muslim armies found attached to some of the churches they converted into mosques during the early years of Islam. The

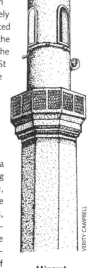

watchtower at the Church of St John the Baptist in Damascus – the building now known as the Umayyad Mosque – is one such example. The minaret at the Mosque of Omar in Domat al-Jandal in northern Saudi Arabia may be another.

A mosque must also have a *mihrab*, a niche in the wall facing Mecca and indicating the *qibla*, the direction believers must face while praying. Like minarets, mihrabs can be simple or elaborate, and they are thought to have been introduced into Islamic architecture around the beginning of the 8th century.

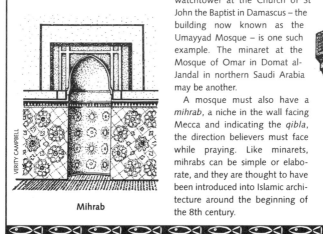

Mihrab

Minaret

was the favoured material for the tents, and camel or goat hair for other purposes.

Today, however, a Bedouin family is more likely to purchase a canvas tent from a tent shop, which may also sell many furnishings for such dwellings. Even in government-run centres designed to preserve the traditional arts (such as those in Kuwait and Bahrain), it is more common to see pillows, saddlebags and other items woven from imported cotton or synthetic fibres.

In most 'traditional' souqs, much of the woven material one sees these days has been produced with Western shoppers in mind. Saddlebags, bridles, runners and tent walls remain popular items among the Bedouin, but few Bedouin have any use for the Western-style bags with shoulder straps that are an increasingly common sight in weaving shops. In the Gulf's cities, many of the woven items one finds for sale are actually imported, usually from Egypt or Syria.

Mosque Vocabulary

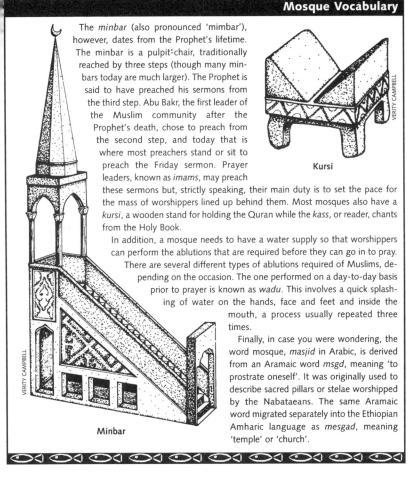

The *minbar* (also pronounced 'mimbar'), however, dates from the Prophet's lifetime. The minbar is a pulpit-chair, traditionally reached by three steps (though many minbars today are much larger). The Prophet is said to have preached his sermons from the third step. Abu Bakr, the first leader of the Muslim community after the Prophet's death, chose to preach from the second step, and today that is where most preachers stand or sit to preach the Friday sermon. Prayer leaders, known as *imams*, may preach

Kursi

these sermons but, strictly speaking, their main duty is to set the pace for the mass of worshippers lined up behind them. Most mosques also have a *kursi*, a wooden stand for holding the Quran while the *kass*, or reader, chants from the Holy Book.

In addition, a mosque needs to have a water supply so that worshippers can perform the ablutions that are required before they can go in to pray. There are several different types of ablutions required of Muslims, depending on the occasion. The one performed on a day-to-day basis prior to prayer is known as *wadu*. This involves a quick splashing of water on the hands, face and feet and inside the mouth, a process usually repeated three times.

Finally, in case you were wondering, the word mosque, *masjid* in Arabic, is derived from an Aramaic word *msgd*, meaning 'to prostrate oneself'. It was originally used to describe sacred pillars or stelae worshipped by the Nabataeans. The same Aramaic word migrated separately into the Ethiopian Amharic language as *mesgad*, meaning 'temple' or 'church'.

Minbar

SOCIETY & CONDUCT
Traditional Dress

The majority of men in the Gulf States wear traditional dress. This consists of a floor-length shirt-dress which is called a *thobe* in Bahrain and Qatar and a *dishdasha* in Kuwait. These are usually white though blue, brown and black ones are common during winter.

Thobes and dishdashas have adopted many of the conventions of Western men's shirts, particularly among wealthier people. Ordinary thobes and dishdashas now routinely have side and breast pockets and more expensive ones may sport Western-style collars and French cuffs.

Men also wear a loose headscarf called a *gutra*. This is usually white, though it may also be red-and-white check. The black headropes used to secure the gutra are called *agal* and are said to have originated with the ropes Bedouin used to hitch their

The Expat Existence

The experience of the Gulf expat varies significantly depending on nationality.

For many Westerners, expat life in the Gulf offers a lifestyle reminiscent of the colonial era. Salaries are relatively high, there are few, if any, taxes to be paid, the fringe benefits (often including housing, a car, regular plane tickets home and school tuition for the kids) can be excellent and maids, nannies and other servants can be hired for a fraction of the cost at home. Add low crime rates to that, including streets that are safe to walk in at night, and it's easy to understand why many Westerners are in no great hurry to leave the Gulf.

For Westerners a typical expat existence is one of near-constant sunny weather, weekend camping and 4WD trips, beach resorts, pubs and restaurants. For most, it just isn't possible to lead that sort of life back home. Ask a Western expat when they're going home for good and you'll find that most won't be able to give you a straight answer.

Most of the Gulf's expats, however, are Asian; and most of them lead lives far removed from those of Westerners. While there are some Indians and Pakistanis working in white-collar jobs around the Gulf, the majority of people from the subcontinent, along with virtually all of the Gulf's East Asians work as labourers, in skilled blue-collar jobs or in service industries. Arab expats can fall into either category – Lebanese and Palestinians are a common sight in the region's financial and media sectors and middle-class Egyptians dominate the ranks of doctors and teachers. Poorer Egyptians, along with Sudanese and Yemenis, work as labourers, security guards, fishermen and in small Arab-style restaurants and coffeehouses.

For those at the bottom of the Gulf's labour pyramid, life is often rough. While it is true that a labourer, taxi driver or shop clerk can earn enough in the Gulf to support a large family or purchase an apartment back home, much of a worker's earnings may be eaten up by debt payments to a labour 'broker' through whom they obtained the job in the first place. Workers employed on building sites toil without proper safety precautions, often working long hours in staggering heat and humidity. Sexual abuse is a danger for women working as nannies or maids.

All that said, there is no shortage of people willing, even eager, to move to the Gulf to take these jobs. Asians' salaries are often one-tenth of those earned by Western expats, but they are still three or four times more than they could expect at home. Anecdotal evidence suggests that Asians are more likely than Westerners to remain in the region for long periods – sometimes 20 years or more – despite seeing their families only once every two years or so.

camels with at night. Men from Qatar often have two long cords hanging from the back of their agals by way of decoration.

Traditional women's dress, at least in public, is little more that an enormous, all-covering black cloak. This may completely obscure the wearer's face, in which case the portion of the cloak which covers the face will be made from a thin black gauze that allows the wearer to look out but prevents the world from looking in. Alternatively, the woman's eyes may be visible between her headscarf and veil. Small masks covering the nose, cheeks and part of the mouth are most often seen in rural areas or among old women in the cities. What a woman wears beneath her cloak may be anything from a traditional caftan to the latest *haute couture* from Paris or Milan.

Though some local women in Kuwait and Bahrain, particularly younger ones, no longer cover their faces, or even their heads, these remain the exception rather than the rule. Arab women walking around a Gulf city with their faces uncovered are much more likely to be Egyptian, Palestinian, Jordanian etc.

Dos & Don'ts

The Gulf is a very conservative place. Even cities like Manama, which are fairly liberal

y Middle Eastern standards, are still very
onservative in comparison with the West.
Given that etiquette is extremely important
n Arab culture, you will find that your time
n the Gulf goes much more smoothly if a
ew simple rules and rituals are followed.

Always stand when someone (other than the coffee boy) enters the room. Upon entering a room yourself shake hands with everyone, touching your heart with the palm of the right hand after each handshake. This goes for both Arab men and women, though men finding themselves in the presence of Arab women should not offer to shake hands unless the woman takes the lead by extending her hand first.

- When two men meet it is considered polite for them to inquire after each other's families but *not* each other's wives.

- Western men should not wear thobes or dishdashas because traditional dress has become an unofficial national uniform throughout the Gulf, visually setting natives of the region apart from the foreign population. Many Gulf Arabs will think that you are making fun of them if you adopt Arabian dress.

- Do not sit in such a way that the soles of your feet are pointing at someone else and do not eat or offer things with your left hand.

- It is considered polite to let your host set the pace in any conversation. Many Gulf Arabs prefer to begin meetings with what, in the West, would be considered an excessive amount of small talk. In such situations you may cause offence if you try to move directly to business.

- It is impolite to photograph people without asking their permission. In most Gulf States it is illegal to photograph police stations, airports, palaces and government buildings.

- Men should never appear bare-chested in public except when at the beach or at a swimming pool. Shorts are generally a bad idea, too, but if you insist on wearing them they should be relatively long – all the way down to the knee, if possible.

- Women should wear loose-fitting clothing that is not revealing. Even in places where a knee-length skirt probably would not be a problem (eg, Manama) you should consider the impression you are making. People will treat you more seriously and with greater respect if you show respect for their culture. One-piece bathing suits are a good idea at the beach (and in some places may be mandatory). All of this goes double for trips to rural areas.

- Throughout the Arab world it is common to attach forms of address to people's given, as op-

posed to their family, names. Just as Arabs refer to each other as 'Mr Mohammed' or 'Mr Abdullah', they will refer to you as 'Mr John', 'Mr Stephen', 'Miss Simone' or 'Mrs Susan'.

- Throughout the Middle East 'sheikh' is usually a term of respect for a scholar or religious leader. You may occasionally encounter this usage in the Gulf, but, in general, the word is used only as a title for members of the ruling family. The rulers themselves carry the formal title of 'Emir' (literally, 'Prince'), but are usually referred to as 'sheikhs', as in 'The Emir of Bahrain, Sheikh Hamad bin Isa al-Khalifa'. The feminine form of sheikh is 'sheikha'. In the Gulf States it applies to all female members of the ruling family.

- It is considered very impolite to refuse an offer of coffee or tea in any social or business setting. If you are the host it is considered equally impolite to fail to make such an offer.

- In cities it is most likely that you will be offered Turkish coffee. This will usually be served *mazboot*, or with medium sugar, unless you specify otherwise. If you only want a little sugar ask to have the coffee *areeha*. *Khafeef* means with a lot of sugar and saada with no sugar at all. Those unfamiliar with Turkish coffee should be aware that it is very thick and strong. You will find a layer of grounds, possibly quite thick, in the bottom of the cup.

- In some places you may be offered Arabian coffee (sometimes called Arabic or Bedouin coffee) and this involves a certain ritual all its own. Arabian coffee is served in tiny handleless cups which hold only two or three sips of coffee. The coffee is flavoured with cardamom which makes it green, or sometimes greenish-brown, in colour. In the city it is fairly tame, but should you ever find yourself out in the desert with Bedouin be prepared for an extremely bitter taste. After finishing your coffee hold out the cup in your right hand for more. If you have had enough rock the cup gently back and forth. It is generally considered impolite to drink more than three cups.

RELIGION
Islam

Life in the Gulf revolves around the Islamic religion. Muslims believe the religion preached in Arabia by the Prophet Mohammed to be God's final revelation to humanity. For them the Quran, God's words revealed through the Prophet, supplements and completes the earlier revelations around which the Christian and

Jewish faiths were built, and corrects human misinterpretations of those earlier revelations. For example, Muslims believe that Jesus was a prophet second only to Mohammed in importance but that his followers later introduced into Christianity the heretical idea that Jesus is the son of God. Islam regards Adam, Abraham, Moses and a number of other Christian and Jewish holy men as prophets. Mohammed, however, was the 'Seal of the Prophets' – the last one who has, or will, come.

The Faith The essence of Islam is the belief that there is only one God and that it is the people's duty to believe in and serve Him in the manner which He has laid out in the Quran. In Arabic, Islam means submission and a Muslim is one who submits to God's will.

In the first instance, one does this by observing the five pillars of the faith:

Shahadah The profession of faith. To become a Muslim one need only state the Islamic creed, 'There is no god but God, and Mohammed is the messenger of God', with conviction.
Sala Prayer. Sometimes written salat. Muslims are required to pray five times every day: at dawn, noon, mid-afternoon, sunset and 1½ hours after sunset. Prayers follow a set ritual pattern which varies slightly depending on the time of day. During prayers a Muslim must perform a series of prostrations while facing in the direction of the Kaaba, the ancient shrine at the centre of the Grand Mosque in Mecca. Before a Muslim can pray, however, he or she must perform a series of ritual ablutions, and if no water is available for this purpose sand or dirt may be substituted.
Zakat Charity or alms. Muslims must give a portion of their income to help those poorer than themselves. How this has operated in practice has varied over the centuries: either it was seen as an individual duty or the state collected zakat as a form of income tax to be redistributed through mosques or religious charities.
Sawm Fasting. It was during the month of Ramadan that Mohammed received his first revelation in AD 610. Muslims mark this event by fasting from sunrise until sunset throughout Ramadan each year. During the fast a Muslim may not take anything into his or her body. This means that not only food and drink but also

smoking and sex are banned. Young children, travellers and those whose health will not permit it are exempt from the fast, though those who are able to do so are supposed to make up the days they missed at a later time.
Haj Pilgrimage. All Muslims who are able to do so are required to make the pilgrimage to Mecca at least once during their lifetime. The pilgrimage must be performed during a specific few days in the first and second weeks of the Muslim month of Zuul-Hijja. Visiting Mecca and performing the prescribed rituals at any other time of the year is considered spiritually desirable, but it is not haj. Such visits are referred to as *umrah*, or 'little pilgrimage'.

Beyond the five pillars of Islam there are many other duties incumbent on Muslims. In the West the best known and least understood of these is *jihad*. This word is usually translated into English as 'holy war', but literally means 'striving in the way of the faith'. Exactly what this means has been a subject of keen debate among Muslim scholars for the last 1400 years. Some scholars have tended to see jihad in spiritual, as opposed to martial, terms.

Muslims are forbidden to eat or drink anything containing pork, alcohol, blood or the meat of any animal which died of natural causes (as opposed to having been slaughtered in the prescribed manner). Muslim women may not marry non-Muslim men, though Muslim men are permitted to marry Christian or Jewish women (but not, for example, Hindus or Buddhists).

The Law The Arabic word 'Sharia'a' is usually translated as 'Islamic Law'. This is misleading. The Sharia'a is not a legal code in the Western sense of the term. It refers to the general body of Islamic legal thought. At the base of this lies the Quran itself, which Muslims believe to be the actual speech of God, revealed to humankind through Mohammed. Where the Quran itself does not provide guidance on a particular subject Muslim scholars turn to the Sunnah, a body of works recording the sayings and doings of the Prophet and, to a lesser extent, his companions as reported by a string of scholarly authorities. There

The Life of the Prophet

Mohammed was born in Mecca, a prosperous centre of trade and pilgrimage, in AD 570. He came from a less well-off branch of the Quraysh, the ruling tribe of Mecca, and his father died before he was born. When Mohammed was seven his mother died and he was subsequently raised first by his grandfather and later by an uncle. As a young man he worked as a shepherd and accompanied caravans to Syria on at least two occasions. At the age of 25 he married a wealthy, and much older, widow named Khadija by whom he had four daughters and two sons (both of the boys died in infancy).

Mohammed received his first revelation in 610 at the age of 40. He was meditating in a cave near Mecca when a voice commanded him to 'Recite'. This first revelation is preserved in the Quran as Sura 96:1-8.

Recite: In the Name of thy Lord who created,
     created Man of a blood-clot.
Recite: And thy Lord is the Most Generous,
     who taught by the Pen,
     taught Man that he knew not.
    No indeed; surely Man waxes insolent,
     for he thinks himself self-sufficient.
     Surely unto thy Lord is the returning.

After an initial period of doubt Mohammed came to believe that this was the actual speech of God, the first of many such revelations he received, conveyed to him through the archangel Gabriel. He had been commanded to preach the religion of the one true God (*Allah* in Arabic) whose messages sent through earlier prophets had been distorted and misunderstood.

Mohammed did not begin to preach in public until 613, three years after this first revelation. When he did reveal himself as God's prophet to the Arabs, the people of Mecca did not exactly rush to embrace the new religion – after four years of preaching Mohammed is said to have had only about 70 followers. The reason for this lay partly in the fact that in attacking the paganism and corruption he saw around him, Mohammed was attacking the foundation of his native city's wealth. Much of Mecca's prosperity was built on its status as a pagan pilgrimage centre.

Eventually Mohammed's verbal assaults on the pagan pilgrim trade so angered the local establishment that they plotted to murder him. Hearing of this, in June 622 the Prophet secretly fled Mecca for Yathrib (present-day Medina) a largely Jewish city in an oasis 360km to the north. This date marks the starting point of the Muslim calendar which also takes its name, Hejira, from the Arabic word *hijrah* meaning 'migration', the term given to the Prophet's journey.

Mohammed quickly established himself in Yathrib, where he already had a substantial following, and the name of the city was changed to Medinat an-Nabi – the City of the Prophet. Medina became the Prophet's model community. Over the next eight years Mohammed's following increased dramatically in Medina and in the rest of Arabia.

The Medina-based Muslims and the still-pagan Meccans fought a series of battles, both military and political, throughout the 620s. Finally, in January 630, the Muslims marched on Mecca with an army of 10,000. The city surrendered without a fight and the next day the Prophet entered the pagan temple (now the Grand Mosque), removed 365 idols from the Kaaba, the shrine at its centre, and declared it cleansed. Later that year he returned to Medina, where he continued to live. In 632 he travelled again to Mecca to perform the pilgrimage and established in their final form the rituals which are still performed by Muslim pilgrims today. After his trip to Mecca, Mohammed returned to Medina where he died later that year.

Ramadan

This month, during which Muslims fast from dawn until dusk, is observed more strictly in the Gulf than in many other parts of the Muslim world. Those Gulf countries in which alcohol is legal usually ban its sale during Ramadan. Discos, where they exist, are closed throughout the month. In all Gulf countries everyone, regardless of their religion, is required to observe the fast in public. That not only means no eating and drinking, but no smoking as well. The few restaurants open during the daytime will invariably be ones that passers-by cannot see into. The penalties for publicly breaking the fast vary: in Saudi Arabia you can go to jail for merely smoking a cigarette while driving in your own car.

Non-Muslims offered coffee or tea when meeting a Muslim during the daytime in Ramadan should initially refuse politely. If your host insists, and repeats the offer several times, you should accept so long as it does not look as though your doing so is going to anger anyone else in the room who may be fasting.

The month of Ramadan varies from year to year as the Islamic calendar is 11 days shorter than the Gregorian calendar. For dates see 'Public Holidays & Special Events' in the Regional Facts for the Visitor chapter.

are many Sunnah authorities and their reliability is determined by the school of Islamic jurisprudence to which one subscribes. There are four main Sunni and two principal Shi'ite schools of Islamic jurisprudence.

The orthodox Sunni schools of jurisprudence are the Shafi'i, Hanbali, Hanafi and Maliki. All but the first of these schools, or rites as they are sometimes known, are found widely in the Gulf though Hanbalis are probably the most numerous. This owes much to the fact that Wahhabism, the predominant Islamic sect in Saudi Arabia and Qatar, follows the Hanbali school. Hanbali Islam is generally regarded as the sternest of the four orthodox Sunni rites. The largest schools of Shi'ite jurisprudence are the Jafari and the Akhbari.

Bahrain's Shi'ite majority mostly subscribe to the Akhbari school.

The Quran and Sunnah together make up the Sharia'a. In some instances the Sharia' is quite specific, such as in the areas of inheritance law and the punishments for certain offences. In many other cases it acts as a series of guidelines. Islam does not recognise a distinction between the secular and religious lives of believers. Thus, a learned scholar or judge can with enough research and if necessary, through use of analogy determine the proper 'Islamic' position on or approach to any problem.

Sunnis & Shi'ites The schism that divided the Muslim world into two broad camps took place only a few years after the death of the Prophet. When Mohammed died, in 632, he left no clear instructions either designating a successor as leader of the Muslim community or setting up a system by which future leaders could be chosen. Some felt the leadership of the community should remain with the Prophet's family, and supported the claim of Ali bin Abi Taleb, Mohammed's cousin and son-in-law and one of the first converts to Islam, to become the *khalif* (caliph) or leader. But the community eventually chose Abu Bakr, the Prophet's closest companion, as leader, and Ali was also passed over in two subsequent leadership contests.

Those who took Ali's side in these disputes became known as the *shi'a*, or 'partisans (of Ali)'. Ali eventually became caliph, the fourth of Mohammed's successors, in 656 but was assassinated five years later by troops loyal to the Governor of Syria, Mu'awiyah bin Abu Sufyan, a distant relative of the Prophet who subsequently set himself up as caliph.

This split the Muslim community into two competing factions. The Sunnis favoured the Umayyads, the dynasty established by Mu'awiyah. As it developed over the succeeding generations Sunni doctrine emphasised the position of the caliph as both the spiritual head of the Muslim community and the temporal ruler of the state in which that community existed. Sunni belief essentially holds that any Muslim who rules with justice and according to the Sharia'a deserves the support of the Muslim community as a whole.

Shi'ites, on the other hand, believe that a descendant of the Prophet through Ali's line should lead the Muslims. Because Shi'ites have rarely held temporal power their doctrine came to emphasise the spiritual position of their leaders, the *imams*.

This split widened and became permanent when Ali's son, Hussein, was killed in brutal circumstances at Karbala (now in southern Iraq) in 680. Over the centuries Sunnism has developed into the 'orthodox' strain of Islam. Today, most of the world's Muslims are Sunnis. In the Gulf, Shi'ites are a majority only in Bahrain (though Bahrain's ruling family are Sunnis). There are significant Shi'ite minorities in Kuwait, the UAE and Saudi Arabia's Eastern Province.

Wahhabis As with any sect embracing about one billion people, Islam has produced many sects, movements and offshoots both within and beyond the traditional Sunni-Shi'ite division. The most important Sunni sect in the Gulf States is the Wahhabis, whose doctrines are the official form of Islam in Saudi Arabia and Qatar.

Wahhabism takes its name from Mohammed bin Abdul Wahhab (1703–92), a preacher and judge who, after seeing an ever-increasing lack of respect for Islam among the Bedouin tribes of central Arabia, preached a return to Islam's origins and traditions as interpreted by the Hanbali school of Islamic jurisprudence. This meant strict adherence to the Quran and the Hadith (accounts of the Prophet's words and actions). Wahhabism is a rather austere form of Islam. Wahhabis reject concepts such as sainthood and forbid the observance of holidays such as the Prophet's birthday. Even the term Wahhabi makes strict followers of the sect uncomfortable because it appears to exalt Mohammed bin Abdul Wahhab over the Prophet. Strict Wahhabis prefer the term *muwahidin*, which roughly translates as 'unitarian' because they profess only the unity of God.

LANGUAGE

Arabic is the official language of Bahrain, Kuwait and Qatar, but English is widely spoken throughout the Gulf. In some cases, English may prove more useful than Arabic. The armies of foreign workers who staff the Gulf's hotels and run its fast-food restaurants generally speak little or no Arabic, and there may be times when a traveller will wonder if a Tagalog, Hindi, Tamil or Urdu phrasebook might not have been a good pre-trip investment. Some basic words of Malayalam (the language of Kerala in India) may also come in handy. If you venture into rural areas you will find that English is not as widespread. Arabic is most useful in dealing with officialdom, taxi drivers, people who work at museums (especially in Kuwait) and with the staff of small restaurants serving Arabic food.

For a grammatical primer and basic vocabulary list, see the Language chapter at the end of this book.

The Perils of Transliteration

Arabic is a non-Western language that does not use the Latin alphabet. It contains several letters whose sounds have no real equivalent in English. We've tried to be consistent, but as TE Lawrence pointed out (see the Language chapter at the end of this book) there are times when flexibility is more important than consistency. For example, while we use the more accepted 'beit' (house) and 'sheikh' throughout the book, in other Gulf States, such as Oman and the United Arab Emirates, 'bait' and 'shaikh' are the spellings any visitors to these countries will find on local maps and road signs.

Wherever possible we have tried to stick with the local usage (ie, what you will actually see on street signs or on locally produced maps). There is bound, however, to be the occasional variation. So just keep in mind that 'beit', 'bait' and 'bayt' are usually the same word. Flexibility, after all, is the hallmark of a good traveller.

Regional Facts for the Visitor

HIGHLIGHTS

Architecture buffs will find a trip to the Gulf interesting. Bahrain has an old-world, semi-colonial feel in places. Kuwait has invested heavily in futuristic buildings, typified by its stock exchange and the Kuwait Towers, and in designs by some of the world's best architects – including the Jorn Utzøn-designed National Assembly building.

Bahrain and Qatar both boast National Museums that should not be missed by any visitor. Kuwait's National Museum is also a must-see: the small collection occupying a corner of the museum complex is at best nondescript, but the ruins of the main part of the museum, preserved as a monument to the 1990 Iraqi invasion, offer lasting insight into the horrors of war. Bahrain's Beit al-Quran offers visitors one of the region's best collections of Islamic art.

The highlights of any Arab country, however, are its streets, alleyways and marketplaces. Prowl the *souqs* (markets), sit in a coffeehouse, or haggle with a shopkeeper over tea. Travel into the desert for a picnic. Try some bitter, green Bedouin coffee. These are the real highlights of a trip to the Gulf – the experiences no visitor should miss.

SUGGESTED ITINERARIES
One week

One Country If you only have one week in which to visit one of the countries covered by this book Bahrain is your best bet. You can see a lot in a very short time.

Two Countries Try splitting your week between Kuwait and Bahrain. Two or three days in Kuwait and three or four in Bahrain will be enough time for most visitors to cover most of the sites listed in this book (bear in mind that a trip to Failaka Island will take most of a day).

Three Countries The Gulf States are small, but they are not *that* small. You can see Bahrain, Kuwait and Qatar all in one

week, but you are going to spend an awful lot of time in airports in the process.

Two weeks

If you want to cover all three countries and not feel too rushed about it, then two weeks will be an ample amount of time. Estimate about five days each for Kuwait and Bahrain and two or three for Qatar (you'll spend the rest of the time going to and from airports and standing in lines at passport control and customs).

PLANNING
When to Go

Avoid the Gulf from April to early October if possible. The tourist season is November to February when the weather is reasonably mild.

You should avoid visiting the Gulf during Ramadan (see the boxed text 'Islamic Holidays' later in this chapter). Bear in mind that Ramadan will overlap with at least part of the November-to-February tourist season until 2006, so plan carefully.

What Kind of Trip

The first thing to be said about any trip to the Gulf is that you should not plan to show up, hang out, maybe pick up a bit of work and then move on. First, it is too expensive a place to hang around for any length of time. Second, the visa rules do not work like that and, in any case, you will not be able to find quasi-legal work teaching English or waiting tables. If you want to work in the Gulf, find a job before you go.

The visa rules for tourists require that you do some advance planning, though you may be able to avoid this by booking a package tour. Package tours have their drawbacks, but they do tend to make it easy for you to cover a lot of territory in a short amount of time. One drawback worth mentioning is that since Kuwait, officially, does not issue tourist visas, packages that include Kuwait are hard (though not impossible) to find.

Many people make the Gulf a stopover on a longer trip from Europe to Asia or vice-versa. Three days in any Gulf city is usually enough to cover most of the things worth seeing. Even if you only have a couple of days, though, you should try to get out of the city. The Gulf States are not big, but some of their most interesting sites are outside the cities.

If time is a factor you should plan to rent a car. You will appreciate the increased mobility. If time is not a factor you are in luck – outside Qatar, most of the places in this book can be reached using some form of public transport.

Those heading out to the Gulf to live have the advantage of time. The air service around the region tends to be very good making the Gulf countries ideally suited to long weekends.

If you want to see something of the desert you should consider booking a half-day, full-day or overnight 4WD trip. These are available out of most of the region's major cities.

Maps

Bartholomew publishes a map of the Gulf. This is somewhat out of date, but is usually adequate for navigation on the ground, especially if used in conjunction with a good locally available map (see the individual country chapters for advice on local maps). Most maps that cover all of Arabia are too large in scale to be of much use in Bahrain and are of only very limited use in Kuwait or Qatar.

What to Bring

A good hat and sunglasses are essential even if you do not plan to spend time travelling in the desert. Long, loose clothing is always the best idea in conservative Islamic countries and the Gulf is no exception.

Almost anything you can get in the West can easily be purchased in any of the Gulf's bigger cities, though voracious readers should note that there are few really good bookshops in the Gulf. Also, most Western works on the history and politics of the Middle East are unavailable in the Gulf States.

RESPONSIBLE TOURISM

After years of breakneck development during which a lot of the Gulf's garbage was simply dumped in the desert, environmental awareness around the region has begun to improve. In places, the desert remains littered with refuse, but governments in the region have launched public education campaigns in a bid to improve things. The Gulf's people traditionally saw the desert as a natural force capable of reclaiming any man-made product. It has taken some time to understand that nature can't cope with either the volume or the type of garbage generated by modern cities.

For the visitor this means that respecting the desert is more important than ever. If you go camping be sure to leave as few traces as possible of your stay. It also means that you should think twice before opting to spend the weekend screaming around the dunes in a 4WD (not to mention the fact that doing so is not particularly safe).

TOURIST OFFICES

Among the three countries covered here only Bahrain has a formal tourist office, and it is of only limited use to independent travellers. Qatar has little formal tourism infrastructure, and none geared to those travelling on the cheap. Kuwait does not issue tourist visas and, hence, makes no effort to promote tourism.

VISAS & DOCUMENTS
Passport

Your passport should be valid for at least six months beyond whenever you plan to leave the region. Make sure there is ample room in the passport for the necessary visas (most visas take up a full page) and bring along a dozen or so extra passport-sized photos. In addition, you should always assume that Israeli stamps will cause problems in any Arab country that has not signed an actual peace treaty with Israel. This remains the case despite the ongoing Arab-Israeli peace process, and despite the fact that most Gulf countries have had some form of official contact with Israel over the last few years.

Visas

The countries covered by this book are among the easiest in the Gulf to visit.

Bahrain issues visas to most native-born Western nationals at the airport and on the causeway connecting Bahrain to Saudi Arabia. Qatar issues both business and tourist visas through its embassies in some countries, but the most common way to get a visa is to arrange it through a hotel and pick the papers up on arrival at Doha airport. Kuwaiti visas, whether for a visit or for transit, must usually be obtained prior to arrival, though it is sometimes possible to pick them up at the airport if arrangements are made in advance (ie, you cannot just show up, as in Bahrain).

If you do not hold a passport from one of the 21 nations who are part of the Organization for Economic Cooperation and Development (OECD), or if you are a naturalised citizen of an OECD country and you originally came from somewhere in the developing world, obtaining a visa to visit any Gulf country can be difficult. Most labour in the Gulf is done by expatriates from the Indian subcontinent, South-East Asia or the poorer parts of the Arab world. Authorities throughout the region are especially sensitive to people from these countries trying to slip into the Gulf to look for work. There is a tendency to assume that anyone from a poor country is a labourer in search of a job, and you may have a hard time convincing the authorities otherwise. Fear of AIDS has also led some Gulf countries to cut back on visas for anyone holding a passport from sub-Saharan Africa.

Inter-Arab political tensions also come into play when applying for a visa. If you are of Palestinian, Iraqi, Libyan, Algerian or Lebanese origin you may have trouble getting a visa even if you hold a Western passport. Obtaining a visa in such circumstances is not impossible, but it generally requires more advance planning. If Americans, Brits or Germans can get a visa through a hotel in a week, a person from any of those countries with a recognisably Palestinian name or whose passport lists, say, Baghdad as their place of birth should probably allow a month to get the paperwork processed.

Visa Sponsorship Outside Bahrain, getting a visa to visit a Gulf country usually requires a sponsor. A sponsor is a national of the country you are visiting who is willing to vouch for your good behaviour while in the country and take responsibility for your departure.

In Kuwait and Qatar most hotels can sponsor visas for travellers. See the individual country chapters for details of the required documentation and processing times. In Bahrain, hotels can arrange sponsorship for those unable to obtain a visa on arrival.

Travel Insurance

A travel insurance policy to cover theft, loss and medical problems is a good idea. A wide variety of policies are available, so check the small print before you commit yourself. Check that the policy covers ambulances or an emergency flight home. In the USA, Council Travel, which has offices in many major American cities, offers affordable policies that cover most contingencies. Similar policies are available in Britain through BUPA.

Driving Licence

You can drive on a Western driving licence in any Gulf country except Bahrain, where an International Driving Permit (IDP) is required. Exactly how long you can drive on your home licence varies from place to place.

In all of the Gulf States you will have to get a local licence if you are coming to the country to live and work. These can usually be issued against your old driving licence from your home country without your having to take a test.

IDPs, while not strictly necessary outside of Bahrain, are a useful document to have. They do not cost much, and are usually issued through travel agents or the automobile association in your home country. Remember that an IDP is only valid when carried in conjunction with your licence from home.

Hostel Card

Bahrain is the only country in this book which has a youth hostel. It is an HI member

The ancient arts of weaving and basket-making are still carried out in some Bahraini villages, and the love of colourful decoration can be seen on the traditional clothing – and the horses.

CHRIS MELLOR

CHRIS MELLOR

CHRISTINE OSBORNE

CHRIS MELLOR

Oil money has paid for high-quality highways throughout the Gulf, including the Sheikh Isa bin Sulman Causeway linking Manama and Muharraq in Bahrain (bottom).

nd HI cards are required. Foreigners can purchase cards at the hostel.

Other Documents

Student, youth and senior's cards are of little use anywhere in the Gulf.

Copies

All important documents (passport data page and visa page, credit cards, travel insurance policy, air/bus/train tickets, driving licence, etc) should be photocopied before you leave home. Leave one copy with someone at home and keep another with you, separate from the originals.

It's also a good idea to store details of your vital travel documents in Lonely Planet's free online Travel Vault just in case you lose the photocopies or can't be bothered with them. Your password-protected Travel Vault is accessible online anywhere in the world – create it at www.ekno.lonelyplanet.com.

EMBASSIES & CONSULATES
Your Own Embassy

It's important to realise what your own embassy – the embassy of the country of which you are a citizen – can and can't do to help you if you get into trouble. Generally speaking, it won't be much help in emergencies if the trouble you're in is remotely your own fault. Remember that you are bound by the laws of the country you are in. Your embassy will not be sympathetic if you end up in jail after committing a crime locally, even if such actions are legal in your own country.

In genuine emergencies you might get some assistance, but only if other channels have been exhausted. For example, if you need to get home urgently, a free ticket home is exceedingly unlikely – the embassy would expect you to have insurance. If you have all your money and documents stolen, it might assist with getting a new passport, but a loan for onward travel is out of the question.

Some embassies used to keep letters for travellers or have a small reading room with home newspapers, but these days the mail holding service has usually been stopped and even newspapers tend to be out of date.

For the addresses and contact details of embassies and consulates, see the individual country chapters.

MONEY
Exchanging Money

Cash With the arguable exception of Kuwait, the Gulf States are still quite cash-oriented societies, particularly at the lowest commercial levels. At cheap restaurants, bus stations and youth hostels, you will need cash for most transactions. Always try to have small bills handy when you travel by taxi. If you get into an argument over the fare it helps not to have to ask for change.

Travellers Cheques Travellers cheques are appealing because they are safe. The problem can be finding someone to change them. When you do find someone the process, in the Gulf, often seems to be unnecessarily complex. Carry either American Express or Thomas Cook cheques as these are the most widely recognised brands. Always have your original purchase receipt with you, as many banks and moneychangers will insist on seeing this before they will change travellers cheques.

ATMs Cash machines can save you a lot of time and hassle. They can also save you money. Withdrawals made at cash machines usually get the interbank exchange rate – a far better rate than you'll get for changing cash or travellers cheques over the counter. The bank that owns the ATM, or your home bank, or both, may charge you a fee for using the machine but this often proves to be less than the commission you would have paid to exchange a similar amount of cash or travellers cheques.

Most of the larger banks in the Gulf have ATMs linked into one of the big global clearing systems: Cirrus, Plus, Global Access or Switch. Most Visa and MasterCards issued in the United States and Western Europe are now coded to operate with at least one of these systems, as are many bank-issued ATM cards. A few of the region's cash machines are also linked with AmEx's Express Cash system.

You will need a personal identification number, or PIN, to operate the machines and if you do not have one you should request one from your card issuer several weeks before travelling.

Credit Cards Credit cards are widely accepted in the Gulf, even by very small hotels and restaurants. American Express is probably the most widely accepted card, but users of Visa and MasterCard should not have too many problems finding someone willing to take their plastic.

International Transfers Unless you have an account at a local bank in the Gulf these are difficult, if not impossible, to arrange.

Moneychangers Moneychangers tend to offer better rates than banks, though they are less likely to take travellers cheques. At both banks and moneychangers you should be careful to ask what sort of commission is being charged on the transaction.

Security
The Gulf is a very safe place and carrying cash around is not really a problem. Indeed, changing money can sometimes be such a hassle that you wind up carrying a lot of cash just to spare yourself the bother.

Costs
These vary greatly from place to place, but it is safe to say that you will find it hard to get around on much less than US$50 per day, a bit less in Bahrain.

Cheap accommodation is often the biggest problem for travellers in the Gulf. Eating cheaply, on the other hand, is rarely a problem and transport costs range from very cheap to reasonable.

Tipping & Bargaining
Tips are not generally expected in the Gulf. Note, however, that the service charge added to most hotel and restaurant bills is not an automatic gratuity that goes to the waiters. It usually goes into the till, and is simply the restaurant's way of making the prices on the menu look 10% to 15%

cheaper than they really are. Waiters in the Gulf tend to be paid appallingly low wages so if the service is good a small tip, while not required, is definitely in order.

As for bargaining, well, this is the Middle East. You can bargain over hotel rates, plane tickets and taxi fares. Some moneychangers will even haggle over the exchange rate. Menu prices are fixed, as are taxi rides when the taxi has a meter. So are the prices in grocery stores. Almost everything else is negotiable. The Gulf is not like Morocco, where shopkeepers will routinely quote prices 10 times higher than what they will settle for. Things rarely come down much below half of the originally offered price, and 25% to 30% off the first quote is more or less the norm. This will vary from place to place and product to product. See the individual country sections for further details.

Taxes & Refunds
By Western standards the Gulf is a very low-tax area. There is often a tax of 5% or so on hotel bills, and sometimes on restaurant bills as well, but the smallest places often simply ignore this.

POST & COMMUNICATIONS
Post
The postal systems in all of the Gulf countries are very good. Sending mail home is never a problem. Incoming mail is a different story. Bahrain is the only country that offers post restante or where American Express will hold clients' mail. In all Gulf countries incoming packages, even fairly small ones, are usually sent to customs for lengthy searches, in the course of which almost any books or magazines that may have been included disappear. Anyone foolish enough to mail you videos has thrown away the cost of the postage.

Telephone
The telephone systems throughout the Gulf are excellent. Home country direct services are available from all Gulf countries, though in some cases the home country direct services only work to the USA. Bahrain has the largest system of these services.

Telephone offices are located in most towns. Cardphone systems in all three of the countries covered here make calling some relatively easy without either going to an office and booking a call or carrying around a small mountain of change.

Fax

Fax machines are now very widespread in the Gulf. Even the smallest hotels often have them. In most countries you can send faxes from the local telephone office. If this does not work, or the service is not available, it is usually possible to send faxes from any medium-size or larger hotel.

Email & Internet Access

Bahrain, Kuwait and Qatar all have a handful of decent Internet cafes. In a pinch you can usually get access to the Web and/or your email via the business centre at any large hotel, though this is likely to be a much more expensive proposition.

In all three countries in this book, direct Internet access is monopolised by the local phone company.

INTERNET RESOURCES

There are several Arab-oriented umbrella sites on the Web, any of which are a good place to start planning a Middle East trip. The main ones are Arab View (www.arab view.net), ArabSites (arabsites.com), and Arab Net (www.arab.net). All of these contain sets of pages covering the history and culture of each country in the Arab world plus links to local businesses and Web sites. None are especially useful if you're looking for a cheap hotel, but all are good for general background information.

Arab Net is run by the same Saudi Arabian marketing company that publishes *Ash-Sharq al-Awsat*, a respected London-based Arabic-language newspaper, and Saudi Arabia's English-language *Arab News*. The site contains a wide variety of opinion pieces, mostly culled from *Arab News*, but some in translation from the Arabic-language press. It is a good place to read up on the 'Arab view' of the region and the outside world.

Also worth a look is the Web site of the University of Texas' Center for Middle Eastern Studies (menic.utexas.edu). They offer a broad range of well-organised links to sites dealing with everything from the oil market to history and culture.

BOOKS

Most books are published in different editions by different publishers in different countries. As a result, a book might be a hardcover rarity in one country while elsewhere it is readily available in paperback. Fortunately, bookshops and libraries search by title or by author, so your local bookshop or library is best placed to advise you on availability of the following titles.

The books listed here contain general information about the Gulf or the Middle East. Some of these books may also be listed in the country chapters.

Lonely Planet

LP's *Middle East* provides abbreviated coverage of the Gulf, in addition to Egypt, Iran, Iraq, Israel, Jordan, Lebanon, Libya, Syria, Turkey and Yemen. LP also publishes an *Oman & the UAE* guide and a *Dubai* city guide.

Guidebooks

If you walk into a bookshop in the Gulf and ask to see the local guidebooks you will be shown either a shelf of glossy coffee-table books or a local commercial directory with a title like 'Kuwait Business & Tourism Guide'. The former might be a nice souvenir; the latter will mainly be advertising.

There are few good travel guides to the Gulf and fewer still that are updated as often as they ought to be. Most of what is available could generously be described as sketchy and far too much of it is, essentially, advertising. Most books cover only one of the Gulf countries and many, the few available regional guides included, are aimed exclusively at upscale business travellers.

If you need a guidebook that also covers things like commercial law in detail your best bet is *The Economist Business Traveller's Guide to the Arabian Peninsula*. This is an excellent reference tool for those looking for a commercial licence, but it tells you precious little about what to do in your spare time, where to stay (if you can't afford a five-star hotel) or where to eat (aside from the restaurants in those same big hotels).

The London-based *Middle East Economic Digest* publishes the *MEED Practical Guides*, a series of country-by-country guides to the Gulf. These were originally issued in the late 1970s and a few have hardly been updated since then. MEED Guides have their good points. They, too, cover commercial law in depth but are aimed mainly at expatriate residents. Their coverage of things like archaeological sites and museums is sketchy and the descriptions of hotels and restaurants appear to be written by the establishments themselves. They are also expensive – US$30 to US$40 a copy.

Travel

Even after 20 years Jonathan Raban's *Arabia Through the Looking Glass* remains the Gulf's essential travel narrative. Raban's observations on expatriate life in the region are as valid today as they were during the oil boom (he visited in early 1979) and, unlike many travel writers, he found the time to speak with a lot of Gulf Arabs in addition to the expats. Another good read is Christopher Dickey's *Expats*, which explores the interaction between Arabs and Westerners in the Middle East.

History & Politics

Most books on the history of the Gulf tend to be either heavy academic works or propagandist in tone. Books on the broader history of the Middle East pass only fleetingly over the Gulf. An exception is Peter Mansfield's *The Arabs*, which is also one of the better books with that particular catch-all title. In addition to a broad-brush history of the Middle East, Mansfield comments on the individual countries in the region. Dilip Hiro's *Inside the Middle East* is also quite good on the Gulf. Neither of these, however, has been seriously updated since the late-'80s. *The Persian Gulf at the Millennium* is a collection of essays that is far

more detailed and up to date than either Mansfield or Hiro, but its very heavy, semi-academic prose can be pretty slow going.

If you want to understand the region's history, politics and economics (and you like books that are heavy on statistical charts), there's the *Area Handbook for the Persian Gulf States* by Richard Nyrop, et al. This is a manual compiled by a team of researchers at American University in Washington DC and published by the US Government Printing Office. It is used for training US diplomats and soldiers headed for the region. It covers Kuwait, Bahrain, Qatar, the United Arab Emirates (UAE) and Oman. You will almost certainly have to go to a specialist bookshop to find it, or order a copy directly from the USGPO. The handbooks are available only in hard cover.

Daniel Yergin's *The Prize*, a history of the oil industry, is essential reading for anyone headed to the Gulf, though it's scope is world wide rather than strictly Middle Eastern.

There have been dozens, maybe hundreds, of books written on the Gulf War. These run the gamut from breathless glorifications of the military aspects of the conflict to furious polemics against one side or the other. The war also produced an extraordinary number of self-serving memoirs by everyone from the politicians and generals at the top of the chain of command to the journalists who covered the fighting. One of the few really good books on the subject is *Guardians of the Gulf* by Michael A Palmer. It is particularly useful because it traces the American and British involvement in the region's security arrangements back to the late 18th century, rather than acting as though the events of 1990–91 emerged out of nowhere (Iraq does not invade Kuwait until you are more than halfway through the book).

Among the best general histories of the Middle East is Albert Hourani's *A History of the Arab Peoples*. It does not have a lot of information specifically on the Gulf, but as a general introduction to the region's history and philosophy you could hardly do better. Among the old-line Orientalists John

Bagot Glubb's *A Short History of the Arab Peoples* is still worth reading today.

Women

Women's role in Middle Eastern society is a topic often discussed, and often misunderstood, in the West. Over the last few years a number of books addressing the subject have come out, helping to take the discussion of women and their role in the Muslim world beyond old stereotypes.

Fatima Mernissi, a Moroccan scholar, and Nawal el-Saadawi, an Egyptian physician and novelist, are probably the female Arab writers best known to Western readers. Mernissi's *Beyond the Veil – Male/Female Dynamics in Modern Muslim Society* and El-Saadawi's *The Hidden Face of Eve* are among the best places you could start an exploration of the subject of women in the Muslim world. *She Has No Place in Paradise*, a collection of El-Saadawi's short fiction, is another widely available work.

On an academic level the work of the Norwegian scholar Unni Wikan has been groundbreaking. Her book *Behind the Veil in Arabia – Women in Oman* may take a bit of looking to find, but is well worth the effort. Wikan's focus is primarily on rural society. For a historical and pictorial look at women in the more urban parts of the Middle East see *Images of Women – The Portrayal of Women in Photography in the Middle East 1860–1950* by Sarah Graham-Brown.

A more recent addition to this genre of literature is *Nine Parts of Desire – The Hidden World of Islamic Women* by Geraldine Brooks.

Be warned that, aside from Wikan, few of these books have much to say about the Gulf countries per se. You should also know that none of them find much favour with the (all-male) powers that be in the Gulf States.

Islam

You cannot hope to understand the Gulf without some understanding of Islam and its history. If you are looking for a relatively short book on Islamic beliefs and practices which is aimed at the general reader, one of the best is *Mohammedanism – An Historical*

Survey by HAR Gibb. If, on the other hand, you want to immerse yourself in the minutiae of Islamic history, culture and civilisation the best work on the subject in English is Marshall GS Hodgson's *The Venture of Islam*. Even if you have no intention of wading through three volumes of Hodgson totalling some 1500 pages, the first 100 pages of volume one (the 'Introduction to the Study of Islamic Civilization' and the 'General Prologue') is required reading for anyone headed for the Middle East.

The Quran itself is notoriously difficult to translate. Pious Muslims insist that it cannot be translated, only rendered or interpreted, into other languages. AJ Arberry's *The Koran Interpreted* is generally believed to be the best version available in English.

Those interested in Islamic literature should try another of Arberry's works, *Aspects of Islamic Civilization*, or James Kritzeck's *Anthology of Islamic Literature*.

The idea that the West is locked in some sort of death struggle with the Islamic world has captured the imaginations of many scholars, journalists and politicians in both the West and the Middle East in recent years. This struggle is usually seen as taking place on a variety of levels – security, immigration and economics, to name but a few – and there is a growing cottage industry in books on the subject. *The Clash of Civilizations* by Samuel Huntington has, for better or worse, set the tone for much of this debate. *The Closed Circle – An Interpretation of the Arabs* by David Pryce-Jones covers much of the same territory but is a bit less alarmist in its conclusions, and more narrowly focused on the Middle East.

Other noteworthy contributions to the literature include *Islam and the West* by the respected American scholar Bernard Lewis and *The Failure of Political Islam* by Olivier Roy.

General

Possibly the best single overview of life, business and culture in the Gulf is *The Merchants* by Michael Field. While ostensibly focusing on the rise of nine of the Gulf's prominent merchant families it is really a book about Arabian society, how it works and how it has changed since the discovery of oil. *The New Arabians* by Peter Mansfield is an introduction to both the history and society of the Gulf, though the focus is mostly on Saudi Arabia and the general tone of the book is fairly uncontroversial. It might also be noted that *The New Arabians* was published in 1981, so it only carries the history of the region up to about late 1979/early 1980.

Peter Theroux gives a witty, candid portrait of culture and politics in the Middle East in his book *Sandstorms – Days and Nights in Arabia*.

NEWSPAPERS & MAGAZINES

All of the Gulf countries have local English-language newspapers. Of these Kuwait's *Arab Times* is probably the best. *Gulf News*, published in Dubai in the UAE, is also quite good and is widely available in Bahrain, Kuwait and Qatar. Both provide adequate coverage of overseas news though coverage of the Gulf itself is sketchy-to-nonexistent in all of the region's papers outside Kuwait.

Foreign publications such as the *International Herald Tribune*, the *Financial Times*, the *Daily Telegraph*, the *Independent*, *Le Monde* and the major German papers are all widely available in the Gulf. These arrive between one and three days late, depending on the country.

RADIO & TV

English-language radio can be heard throughout the region. All three countries have their own English-language services. The US military's AFRTS (Armed Forces Radio & Television Service) can also be heard in Kuwait.

BBC broadcasts can be received on a number of shortwave frequencies including 12.095 MHz, 11.760 MHz, 9.410 MHz and 15.070 MHz, 15.575 MHz throughout the day. You can also get the BBC on 1323 MW in some places. Rental cars often come equipped with shortwave radios.

All of the Gulf countries have English-language TV stations, as well. These usually broadcast in the evening and carry a mix of old American, British and Australian shows and the occasional locally produced magazine program. Most hotels, including the small ones, have satellite TV.

For Arabic-speakers Qatar's Al-Jazeera television has become notorious around the Gulf for airing opposition opinions (in 1999 its correspondent in Kuwait was expelled from the country after a broadcast angered the Kuwaiti government). But even Al-Jazeera airs criticism of other governments, not of Qatar's own rulers.

VIDEO SYSTEMS

All of the Gulf States use the PAL video system. This has limited compatibility with the SECAM system in use in France and is not compatible with the NTSC systems in use in the USA and Australia. Videos sent out from the USA will not work on Gulf TV sets unless the set and video player are both 'multisystem' units that accept NTSC.

PHOTOGRAPHY & VIDEO
Film & Equipment

Kodak and Fuji film are both widely available throughout the Gulf. Camera equipment is also easy to find, but anything fancier than a disposable camera is likely to be very expensive.

Getting colour prints processed is always easy and cheap. Slide or B&W film is another story. It's probably a better idea to hold on to these types of film and get them processed somewhere else.

Restrictions

The basic rules in the Gulf are simple – do not photograph anything even vaguely military in nature (this always includes airports), do not photograph people without their permission, and never photograph women.

Few officials in the Gulf will be pleased by photographs of tents, run-down houses or anything suggestive of poverty, as the tendency is to emphasise what the country has achieved in the last few decades.

TIME

Kuwait, Bahrain and Qatar are four hours ahead of GMT. Summer time, or daylight saving, is not observed. When it's noon in

Manama, Kuwait City and Doha the time elsewhere is:

city	time
Auckland	9 pm
London	9 am
Los Angeles	1 am
New York	4 am
Paris, Rome	10 am
Perth, Hong Kong	5 pm
Sydney	7 pm

ELECTRICITY

Electric voltage in Bahrain and Qatar is 230V using 3-pin UK-style plugs. In Kuwait voltage is 220V or 240V using 2- and 3-pin UK style plugs. Bring along an adapter and transformer if necessary because these sorts of things are hard to find locally.

WEIGHTS & MEASURES

The metric system is in use throughout the Gulf. There is a standard conversion table at the back of this book.

LAUNDRY

There are no laundrettes in the Gulf but most countries have small (usually Indian-run) laundry shops throughout their larger cities. These places generally take about 24 hours to wash and iron your laundry, and their prices are usually very low. See the individual city entries for further details.

HEALTH

Travel health depends on your predeparture preparations, your daily health care while travelling and how you handle any medical problem that does develop. While the potential dangers can seem quite frightening, in reality few travellers experience anything more than an upset stomach.

If you do get sick or have an accident, medical care in Bahrain, Kuwait and Qatar is either free or very reasonably priced by Western standards. Throughout the Gulf, the quality of health care is very high. When the Gulf States began to prosper, their rulers invested huge sums of money in hospitals, clinics and long-term health programs. The result is that countries which only a gener-

ation or two ago were ridden by famines and epidemics (which the Bedouin traditionally used as a way of marking time – for example, a child would be said to have been born 'in the year after the year of measles') now enjoy a standard of health

Medical Kit Check List

Following is a list of items you should consider including in your medical kit – consult your pharmacist for brands available in your country.

☐ **Aspirin or paracetamol (acetaminophen in the USA)** – for pain or fever

☐ **Antihistamine** – for allergies, eg, hay fever; to ease the itch from insect bites or stings; and to prevent motion sickness

☐ **Cold and flu tablets, throat lozenges and nasal decongestant**

☐ **Multivitamins** – consider for long trips, when dietary vitamin intake may be inadequate

☐ **Antibiotics** – consider including these if you're travelling well off the beaten track; see your doctor, as they must be prescribed, and carry the prescription with you

☐ **Loperamide or diphenoxylate** – 'blockers' for diarrhoea

☐ **Prochlorperazine or metaclopramide** – for nausea and vomiting

☐ **Rehydration mixture** – to prevent dehydration, which may occur, for example, during bouts of diarrhoea; particularly important when travelling with children

☐ **Insect repellent, sunscreen, lip balm and eye drops**

☐ **Calamine lotion, sting relief spray or aloe vera** – to ease irritation from sunburn and insect bites or stings

☐ **Antifungal cream or powder** – for fungal skin infections and thrush

☐ **Antiseptic (such as povidone-iodine)** – for cuts and grazes

☐ **Bandages, Band-Aids (plasters) and other wound dressings**

☐ **Water purification tablets or iodine**

☐ **Scissors, tweezers and a thermometer** – note that mercury thermometers are prohibited by airlines care which equals that of the richest countries in the West. For details, see the Health section in the individual country chapters.

Predeparture planning

Immunisations Plan ahead for getting your vaccinations: some of them require more than one injection, while some vaccinations should not be given together. It is recommended you seek medical advice at least six weeks before travel. Note that some vaccinations should not be given during pregnancy or in people with allergies – discuss with your doctor. Discuss your requirements with your doctor, but vaccinations you should consider for this trip include the following (for more details about the diseases themselves, see the individual disease entries later in this section).

Cholera The current injectable vaccine against cholera is poorly protective and has many side effects, so it is not generally recommended for travellers. However, in some situations it may be necessary to have a certificate as travellers are very occasionally asked by immigration officials to present one, even though all countries and the World Health Organization (WHO) have dropped cholera immunisation as a health requirement for entry.

Diphtheria & Tetanus Vaccinations for these two diseases are usually combined and are recommended for everyone. After an initial course of three injections (usually given in childhood), boosters are necessary every 10 years.

Hepatitis A Hepatitis A vaccine provides long-term immunity (possibly more than 10 years) after an initial injection and a booster at six to 12 months. Alternatively, an injection of gamma globulin can provide short-term protection against hepatitis A – two to six months, depending on the dose given. It is not a vaccine, but is ready-made antibody collected from blood donations. It is reasonably effective and, unlike the vaccine, it is protective immediately, but because it is a blood product, there are current concerns about its long-term safety. Hepatitis A vaccine is also available in a combined form with hepatitis B vaccine. Three injections over a six-month period are required, the first two providing substantial protection against hepatitis A.

Hepatitis B Travellers who should consider vaccination against hepatitis B include those on a long trip, as well as those visiting countries where there are high levels of hepatitis B infection, where blood transfusions may not be ad- equately screened or where sexual contact or needle sharing is a possibility. Vaccination involves three injections, with a booster at 12 months. More rapid courses are available if necessary.

Polio Everyone should keep up to date with this vaccination, which is normally given in childhood. A booster every 10 years is necessary to maintain immunity.

Rabies Vaccination should be considered by those who will spend a month or longer in Bahrain, Kuwait or Qatar, especially if they are cycling, handling animals, caving or travelling to remote areas, and for children (who may not report a bite). Pretravel rabies vaccination involves having three injections over 21 to 28 days. If someone who has been vaccinated is bitten or scratched by an animal, they will require two booster injections of vaccine; those not vaccinated require more.

Typhoid Vaccination against typhoid may be required if you are travelling for more than a couple of weeks in Bahrain, Kuwait and Qatar. It is now available either as an injection or as capsules to be taken orally.

Health Insurance Make sure that you have adequate health insurance. See Travel Insurance under Visas & Documents earlier in this chapter for details.

Travel Health Guides *Travellers Health* by Dr Richard Dawood, Oxford University Press, 1995 is comprehensive, easy to read, authoritative and also highly recommended, although it's rather large to lug around.

Travel with Children by Maureen Wheeler, Lonely Planet Publications, 1995, includes basic advice on travel health for younger children.

There are a number of excellent travel health sites on the Internet. From the Lonely Planet home page there are links at www.lonelyplanet.com/weblinks/wlprep.htm#heal to the WHO and the US Centers for Disease Control & Prevention.

Other Preparations Make sure you're healthy before you start travelling. If you are going on a long trip make sure your teeth are OK. If you wear glasses take a spare pair and your prescription.

If you require a particular medication take an adequate supply, as it may not be available locally. Take part of the packaging showing the generic name rather than the brand, which will make getting replacements easier. It's a good idea to have a legible prescription or letter from your doctor to show that you legally use the medication to avoid any problems.

Basic Rules

Care in what you eat and drink is the most important health rule. Although you are unlikely to suffer any stomach upsets in Bahrain, Kuwait or Qatar, you may find some of the following advice useful.

Food In general, the standard of hygiene in restaurants in Bahrain, Kuwait and Qatar, even the smaller ones, is quite good. Take note of the cleanliness of a place when you walk in. If it's clean and flies are few and far between, the kitchen and the food prepared in it is likely to be clean as well. The only food you should consider actively avoiding is shwarma from street stands. The skewered meat that sits on these grills out in the open attracts flies and dirt. You can still get shwarmas from cafes where the meat is cooked indoors. Also, if you are eating at some of the smaller Arab, Indian or Pakistani restaurants, you may want to avoid raw salads. If you are buying food from the market get there early. It's just common sense to buy food which is as fresh as possible. Avoid buying meat from these markets. The risk of disease is too high. It's better to buy packaged meat from supermarkets which has come from Europe, Australia or Saudi Arabia.

Dairy products in the region are manufactured to Western standards, though in more remote places you might want to check the 'use by' date and see whether the products have been stored properly.

Water Although the water in Bahrain, Kuwait and Qatar is safe to drink, it tastes awful as most of it comes from desalination plants. Most people drink bottled water which is readily available from shops and vending machines on just about every street corner in the cities.

In this hot climate make sure you drink enough – don't rely on feeling thirsty to indicate when you should drink. Not needing to urinate or very dark yellow urine is a danger sign. Always carry a water bottle with you on long trips. Excessive sweating can lead to loss of salt and therefore muscle cramping. Salt tablets are not a good idea as a preventative, but in places where salt is not used much adding salt to food can help.

Nutrition Make sure your diet is well balanced. Eggs, beans, lentils (*dhal* in the

Nutrition

If your diet is poor or limited in variety, if you're travelling hard and fast and therefore missing meals or if you simply lose your appetite, you can soon start to lose weight and place your health at risk.

Make sure your diet is well balanced. Cooked eggs, tofu, beans, lentils (*dhal* in India) and nuts are all safe ways to get protein. Fruit you can peel (bananas, oranges or mandarins, for example) is usually safe and a good source of vitamins. Melons can harbour bacteria in their flesh and are best avoided. Try to eat plenty of grains (including rice) and bread. Remember that although food is generally safer if it is cooked well, overcooked food loses much of its nutritional value. If your diet isn't well balanced or if your food intake is insufficient, it's a good idea to take vitamin and iron pills.

In hot climates make sure you drink enough – don't rely on feeling thirsty to indicate when you should drink. Not needing to urinate or voiding small amounts of very dark yellow urine is a danger sign. Always carry a water bottle with you on long trips. Excessive sweating can lead to loss of salt and therefore muscle cramping. Salt tablets are not a good idea as a preventative, but in places where salt is not used much, adding salt to food can help.

region's numerous Indian restaurants) and nuts are all safe ways to get protein. Fruit you can peel (such as bananas, oranges or mandarins) is safe and a very good source of vitamins. Try to eat plenty of grains (including rice) and bread. Remember that although food is generally safer if it is cooked well, overcooked food loses much of its nutritional value. If your diet isn't well balanced or if your food intake is insufficient, you may want to consider taking vitamin and iron supplements.

Medical Problems & Treatment

Self-diagnosis and treatment can be risky, so you should always seek medical help. An embassy, consulate or five-star hotel can usually recommend a local doctor or clinic. Although we do give drug dosages in this section, they are for emergency use only. Correct diagnosis is vital. In this section we have used the generic names for medications – check with a pharmacist for brands available locally.

Note that antibiotics should ideally be administered only under medical supervision. Take only the recommended dose at the prescribed intervals and use the whole course, even if the illness seems to be cured earlier. Stop immediately if there are any serious reactions and do not use the anti-

Everyday Health

Normal body temperature is up to 37°C (98.6°F); more than 2°C (4°F) higher indicates a high fever. The normal adult pulse rate is 60 to 100 per minute (children 80 to 100, babies 100 to 140). As a general rule the pulse increases about 20 beats per minute for each 1°C (2°F) rise in fever.

Respiration (breathing) rate is also an indicator of illness. Count the number of breaths per minute: Between 12 and 20 is normal for adults and older children (up to 30 for younger children, 40 for babies). People with a high fever or serious respiratory illness breathe more quickly than normal. More than 40 shallow breaths a minute may indicate pneumonia.

biotic at all if you are unsure that you have the correct one. Some people are allergic to commonly prescribed antibiotics such as penicillin; carry this information (eg, on a bracelet) when travelling.

Environmental Hazards

Heat Exhaustion Dehydration and salt deficiency can cause heat exhaustion. Take time to acclimatise to high temperatures, drink sufficient liquids and do not do anything too physically demanding.

Salt deficiency is characterised by fatigue, lethargy, headaches, giddiness and muscle cramps; salt tablets may help, but adding extra salt to your food is better.

Anhidrotic heat exhaustion is a rare form of heat exhaustion that is caused by an inability to sweat. It tends to affect people who have been in a hot climate for some time, rather than newcomers. It can progress to heatstroke. Treatment involves removal to a cooler climate.

Heatstroke This serious, occasionally fatal, condition can occur if the body's heat-regulating mechanism breaks down and the body temperature rises to dangerous levels. Long, continuous periods of exposure to high temperatures and insufficient fluids can leave you vulnerable to heatstroke.

The symptoms are feeling unwell, not sweating very much (or at all) and a high body temperature (39° to 41°C or 102° to 106°F). Where sweating has ceased, the skin becomes flushed and red. Severe, throbbing headaches and lack of coordination will also occur, and the sufferer may be confused or aggressive. Eventually the victim will become delirious or convulse. Hospitalisation is essential, but in the interim get victims out of the sun, remove their clothing, cover them with a wet sheet or towel and then fan continually. Give fluids if they are conscious.

Jet Lag Jet lag is experienced when a person travels by air across more than three time zones (each time zone usually represents a one-hour time difference). It occurs because many of the functions of the human body (such as temperature, pulse rate and emptying of the bladder and bowels) are regulated by internal 24-hour cycles. When we travel long distances rapidly, our bodies take time to adjust to the 'new time' of our destination, and we may experience fatigue, disorientation, insomnia, anxiety, impaired concentration and loss of appetite. These effects will usually be gone within three days of arrival, but to minimise the impact of jet lag:

- Rest for a couple of days prior to departure.
- Try to select flight schedules that minimise sleep deprivation; arriving late in the day means you can go to sleep soon after you arrive. For very long flights, try to organise a stopover.
- Avoid excessive eating (which bloats the stomach) and alcohol (which causes dehydration) during the flight. Instead, drink plenty of noncarbonated, nonalcoholic drinks such as fruit juice or water.
- Avoid smoking.
- Make yourself comfortable by wearing loose-fitting clothes and perhaps bringing an eye mask and ear plugs to help you sleep.
- Try to sleep at the appropriate time for the time zone you are travelling to.

Motion Sickness Eating lightly before and during a trip will reduce the chances of motion sickness. If you are prone to motion sickness try to find a place that minimises movement – near the wing on aircraft, close to midships on boats, near the centre on buses. Fresh air usually helps; reading and cigarette smoke don't. Commercial motion-sickness preparations, which can cause drowsiness, have to be taken before the trip commences. Ginger (available in capsule form) and peppermint (including mint-flavoured sweets) are natural preventatives.

Prickly Heat Prickly heat is an itchy rash caused by excessive perspiration trapped under the skin. It usually strikes people who have just arrived in a hot climate. Keeping cool, bathing often, drying the skin and using a mild talcum or prickly heat powder or resorting to air-conditioning may help.

Sunburn In Bahrain, Kuwait and Qatar you can get sunburnt surprisingly quickly, even through cloud. Use a sunscreen, a hat, and a barrier cream for your nose and lips. Calamine lotion or a commercial after-sun preparation are good for mild sunburn. Protect your eyes with good-quality sunglasses, particularly near water and sand.

Infectious Diseases

Diarrhoea Simple things like a change of water, food or climate can all cause a mild bout of diarrhoea, but a few rushed toilet trips with no other symptoms is not indicative of a major problem.

Dehydration is the main danger with any diarrhoea, particularly in children or the elderly as dehydration can occur quite quickly. Under all circumstances *fluid replacement* (at least equal to the volume being lost) is the most important thing to remember. Weak black tea with a little sugar, soda water, or soft drinks allowed to go flat and diluted 50% with clean water are all good. With severe diarrhoea a rehydrating solution is preferable to replace minerals and salts lost. Commercially available oral rehydration salts (ORS) are very useful; add them to boiled or bottled water. In an emergency you can make up a solution of six teaspoons of sugar and a half teaspoon of salt to a litre of boiled or bottled water. You need to drink at least the same volume of fluid that you are losing in bowel movements and vomiting. Urine is the best guide to the adequacy of replacement – if you have small amounts of concentrated urine, you need to drink more. Keep drinking small amounts often. Gut-paralysing drugs such as loperamide or diphenoxylate can be used to bring relief from the symptoms, although they do not actually cure the problem. Only use these drugs if you do not have access to toilets, eg, if you *must* travel. Note that these drugs are not recommended for children under 12 years.

In certain situations antibiotics may be required: diarrhoea with blood or mucus (dysentery), any diarrhoea with fever, profuse watery diarrhoea, persistent diarrhoea not improving after 48 hours and severe diarrhoea. These suggest a more serious cause of diarrhoea and in these situations gut-paralysing drugs should be avoided.

In these situations, a stool test may be necessary to diagnose what bug is causing your diarrhoea, so you should seek medical help urgently. Where this is not possible the recommended drugs for bacterial diarrhoea (the most likely cause of severe diarrhoea in travellers) are norfloxacin 400mg twice daily for three days or ciprofloxacin 500mg twice daily for five days. These are not recommended for children or pregnant women. The drug of choice for children would be co-trimoxazole with dosage dependent on weight. A five-day course is given. Ampicillin or amoxycillin may be given in pregnancy, but medical care is necessary.

Although rare in Bahrain, Kuwait and Qatar, two other causes of persistent diarrhoea in travellers are giardiasis and amoebic dysentery.

Giardiasis is caused by a common parasite, *Giardia lamblia*. Symptoms include stomach cramps, nausea, a bloated stomach, watery, foul-smelling diarrhoea and frequent gas. Giardiasis can appear several weeks after you have been exposed to the parasite. The symptoms may disappear for a few days and then return; this can go on for several weeks.

Amoebic dysentery, caused by the protozoan *Entamoeba histolytica*, is characterised by a gradual onset of low-grade diarrhoea, often with blood and mucus. Cramping abdominal pain and vomiting are less likely than in other types of diarrhoea, and fever may not be present. It will persist until treated and can recur and cause other health problems.

You should seek medical advice if you think you have giardiasis or amoebic dysentery, but where this is not possible, tinidazole or metronidazole are the recommended drugs. Treatment is a 2g single dose of tinidazole or 250mg of metronidazole three times daily for five to 10 days.

Fungal Infections These occur more commonly in hot weather and are usually found on the scalp, between the toes (athlete's foot) or fingers, in the groin and on the body (ringworm). You get ringworm (which is a fungal infection, not a worm) from infected animals or other people. Moisture encourages these infections.

To prevent fungal infections wear loose, comfortable clothes, avoid artificial fibres, wash frequently and dry yourself carefully. If you do get an infection, wash the infected area at least daily with a disinfectant or medicated soap and water, and rinse and dry well. Apply an antifungal cream or powder. Try to expose the infected area to air or sunlight as much as possible and wash all towels and underwear in hot water, change them often and let them dry in the sun.

Hepatitis Hepatitis is a general term for inflammation of the liver. It is a common disease worldwide. There are several viruses that cause hepatitis, and they differ in the way that they are transmitted. The symptoms are similar in all forms of the illness, and include fever, chills, headache, fatigue, feelings of weakness and aches and pains, followed by loss of appetite, nausea, vomiting, abdominal pain, dark urine, light-coloured faeces, jaundiced (yellow) skin and yellowing of the whites of the eyes. People who have had hepatitis should avoid alcohol for some time after the illness, as the liver needs time to recover.

Hepatitis A is transmitted by contaminated food and drinking water. You should seek medical advice, but there is not much you can do apart from resting, drinking lots of fluids, eating lightly and avoiding fatty foods.

Hepatitis E is transmitted in the same way as hepatitis A; it can be particularly serious in pregnant women.

There are almost 300 million chronic carriers of **hepatitis B** in the world. It is spread through contact with infected blood, blood products or body fluids, for example through sexual contact, unsterilised needles and blood transfusions, or contact with blood via small breaks in the skin. Other risk situations include having a shave, tattoo or body piercing with contaminated equipment. The symptoms of hepatitis B may be more severe than type A and the disease can lead to long-term problems such as chronic liver damage, liver cancer or a long-term carrier state. **Hepatitis C and D** are spread in the same way as hepatitis B and can also lead to long-term complications.

There are vaccines against hepatitis A and B, but there are currently no vaccines against the other types of hepatitis. Following the basic rules about food and water (hepatitis A and E) and avoiding risk situations (hepatitis B, C and D) are important preventative measures.

HIV & AIDS

Infection with the human immunodeficiency virus (HIV) may lead to acquired immune deficiency syndrome (AIDS), which is a fatal disease. Any exposure to blood, blood products or body fluids may put the individual at risk. The disease is often transmitted through sexual contact or dirty needles – vaccinations, acupuncture, tattooing and body piercing can be potentially as dangerous as intravenous drug use. HIV/AIDS can also be spread through infected blood transfusions; some developing countries cannot afford to screen blood used for transfusions. In the Gulf countries, blood is said to be screened for AIDS, but there is also a tendency to play down the incidence of AIDS locally. Public information programs tend to present the disease as something dangerous but essentially foreign.

If you do need an injection, ask to see the syringe unwrapped in front of you, or take a needle and syringe pack with you.

Fear of HIV infection, however, should never preclude treatment for very serious medical conditions.

Sexually Transmitted Infections HIV/AIDS and hepatitis B can be transmitted through sexual contact – see the relevant section above. Other STIs include gonorrhoea, herpes and syphilis; sores, blisters or rashes around the genitals and discharges or pain when urinating are common symptoms. In some STIs, such as wart virus or chlamydia, symptoms may be less marked or not observed at all, especially in women. Chlamydia infection can cause infertility

in men and women before any symptoms have been noticed. Syphilis symptoms eventually disappear completely but the disease continues and can cause severe problems in later years. While abstin- ence from sexual contact is the only 100% effective prevention, using condoms is also effective. The treatment of gonorrhoea and syphilis is with antibiotics. The different sexually transmitted diseases each require specific antibiotics.

Cuts, Bites & Stings

See Less Common Diseases for details of rabies, which is passed through animal bites.

Cuts & Scratches Wash well and treat any cut with an antiseptic such as povidone-iodine. Where possible avoid bandages and Band-Aids, which can keep wounds wet. Coral cuts are notoriously slow to heal and if they are not adequately cleaned, small pieces of coral can become embedded in the wound.

Bedbugs & Lice Bedbugs live in various places, but particularly in dirty mattresses and bedding, evidenced by spots of blood on bedclothes or on the wall. Bedbugs leave itchy bites in neat rows. Calamine lotion or a sting relief spray may help.

All lice cause itching and discomfort. They make themselves at home in your hair (head lice, nits), your clothing (body lice), or in your pubic hair (crabs). You catch lice through direct contact with infected people or by sharing combs, clothing and the like. Powder or shampoo treatment will kill the lice, and infected clothing should then be washed in very hot, soapy water and left in the sun to dry. In the case of head lice, make sure that all lice eggs are thoroughly removed from the hair.

Bites & Stings Bee and wasp stings are usually painful rather than dangerous. However, in people who are allergic to them severe breathing difficulties may occur and require urgent medical care. Calamine lotion or a sting relief spray will give relief and ice packs will reduce the pain and swelling. There are some spiders with dangerous bites but antivenoms are usually available. Scorpion stings are notoriously painful and in some parts of Asia, the Middle East and Central America can actually be fatal. Scorpions often shelter in shoes or clothing.

Jellyfish Avoid contact with these sea creatures, which have stinging tentacles – seek local advice. Stings from most jellyfish are simply rather painful. Dousing in vinegar will deactivate any stingers which have not 'fired'. Calamine lotion, antihistamines and analgesics may reduce the reaction and relieve the pain.

Snakes Snakes are something you would only need to worry about if travelling in the desert. To minimise your chances of being bitten always wear boots, socks and long trousers when walking through undergrowth where snakes may be present. Don't put your hands into holes and crevices, and be careful when collecting firewood.

Snake bites do not cause instantaneous death and antivenoms are usually available. Immediately wrap the bitten limb tightly, as you would for a sprained ankle, and then attach a splint to immobilise it. Keep the victim still and seek medical help, if possible with the dead snake for identification. Don't attempt to catch the snake if there is a possibility of being bitten again. Tourniquets and sucking out the poison are now comprehensively discredited.

Less Common Diseases
The following diseases pose a small risk to travellers, and so are only mentioned in passing. Seek medical advice if you think you may have any of these diseases.

Cholera This is the worst of the watery diarrhoeas and medical help should be sought. Outbreaks of cholera are generally widely reported, so you can avoid such problem areas. *Fluid replacement is the most vital treatment* – the risk of dehydration is severe as you may lose up to 20L a day. If there is a delay in getting to hospital, then begin taking tetracycline. The adult dose is 250mg four times daily. It is not rec-ommended for children under nine years nor for pregnant women. Tetracycline may help shorten the illness, but adequate fluids are required to save lives.

Leishmaniasis This is a group of parasitic diseases transmitted by sandflies, which are found in the Middle East as well as other parts of the world. Cutaneous leishmaniasis affects ulceration and disfigurement, and visceral leishmaniasis affects the internal organs. Seek medical advice, as laboratory testing is required for diagnosis and correct treatment. Avoiding sandfly bites is the best precaution. Bites are usually painless, itchy and yet another reason to cover up and apply repellent.

Rabies This fatal viral infection is found in many countries, including Bahrain, Kuwait and Qatar. Many animals can be infected (such as dogs, cats, bats and monkeys) and it is their saliva which is infectious. Any bite, scratch or even lick from an animal should be cleaned immediately and thoroughly. Scrub with soap and running water, and then apply alcohol or iodine solution. Medical help should be sought promptly to receive a course of injections to prevent the onset of symptoms and death.

Tetanus This disease is caused by a germ which lives in soil and in the faeces of horses and other animals. It enters the body via breaks in the skin. The first symptom may be discomfort in swallowing, or stiffening of the jaw and neck; this is followed by painful convulsions of the jaw and whole body. The disease can be fatal. It can be prevented by vaccination.

Tuberculosis (TB) TB is a bacterial infection usually transmitted from person to person by coughing but which may be transmitted through consumption of unpasteurised milk. Milk that has been boiled is safe to drink, and the souring of milk to make yoghurt or cheese also kills the bacilli. Travellers are usually not at great risk as close household contact with the infected person is usually required before the disease is passed on. You may need to have a TB test before you travel as this can help diagnose the disease later if you become ill.

Typhoid Typhoid fever is a dangerous gut infection caused by contaminated water and food. It's very unlikely to affect travellers to Bahrain, Kuwait and Qatar. Medical help must be sought.

In its early stages sufferers may feel they have a bad cold or flu on the way, as early symptoms are a headache, body aches and a fever which rises a little each day until it is around 40°C (104°F) or more. The victim's pulse is often slow relative to the degree of fever present – unlike a normal fever where the pulse increases. There may also be vomiting, abdominal pain, diarrhoea or constipation.

In the second week the high fever and slow pulse continue and a few pink spots may appear on the body; trembling, delirium, weakness, weight loss and dehydration may occur. Complications such as pneumonia, perforated bowel or meningitis may occur.

Women's Health

Gynaecological Problems Poor diet, lowered resistance due to the use of antibiotics for stomach upsets and even contraceptive pills can lead to vaginal infections when travelling in hot climates. Keeping the genital area clean, and wearing skirts or loose-fitting trousers and cotton underwear will help to prevent infections.

Yeast infections, characterised by a rash, itch and discharge, can be treated with a vinegar or lemon-juice douche or with yoghurt. Nystatin suppositories are the usual medical prescription. Trichomonas is a more serious infection; symptoms are a discharge and a burning sensation when urinating. Male sexual partners must also be treated, and if a vinegar-water douche is not effective medical attention should be sought. Metronidazole (Flagyl) is the prescribed drug.

Pregnancy Most miscarriages occur during the first three months of pregnancy, so this is the most risky time to travel as far as your own health is concerned. Miscarriage

is not uncommon, and can occasionally lead to severe bleeding. The last three months should also be spent within reasonable distance of good medical care. A baby born as early as 24 weeks stands a chance of survival, but only in a good modern hospital. Pregnant women should avoid all unnecessary medication, but vaccinations and malarial prophylactics should still be taken where possible. Additional care should be taken to prevent illness and particular attention should be paid to diet and nutrition. Alcohol and nicotine, for example, should be avoided.

Women travellers quite often find that their periods become irregular or even cease while they're on the road. Remember that a missed period in these circumstances does not necessarily indicate pregnancy. There are health posts or family planning clinics, where you can seek advice and have tests to determine whether or not you are pregnant, in the cities of the Gulf countries.

WOMEN TRAVELLERS

Travel in the Gulf poses a special set of problems for women – especially unaccompanied women – but many imagine the situation to be much worse than it actually is. This is partly because the strictest country in the region, Saudi Arabia, is the one which receives the most publicity. Outside of Saudi Arabia women can drive cars, eat in restaurants alone or with men to whom they are not either married or related, shop in stores where men are also present etc.

Sexual harassment is a problem almost everywhere in the world. Some women say it is less of a problem in the Gulf than in other Middle Eastern countries. Certainly the situation in the Gulf is no worse than in, say, Egypt, Tunisia or Morocco. Unaccompanied women will routinely be stared at and will often have lewd comments directed at them. They may be followed and may find strange and unwanted visitors turning up outside their hotel rooms.

Any woman who does not relish being the centre of attention might wish to avoid just about every budget restaurant listed in this book. Some restaurants will have a special area for women (often labelled 'family section'). If the restaurant's owner is personally quite conservative you may be asked to sit there whether you wish to or not. Sitting there by choice is probably your best defence against unwelcome attention from fellow diners.

A few simple rules should be followed whenever possible. Try to stay in the better hotels (possibly a moot point as many budget hotels in the Gulf will not rent rooms to single women), do not flirt or make eye contact with strange men, dress conservatively and do not ride in the front seat of taxi cabs. If a person or a situation is becoming troublesome head for a busy place, preferably where a lot of other foreigners and a few policemen are gathered (a shopping mall or the lobby of a big hotel).

Expat women who have lived for years in the Middle East say the most important thing is to retain both your self-confidence and your sense of humour. Saying that you should not make eye contact with strange men is not the same as saying that you should act timid and vulnerable; there are obviously times when a very cold glare is an effective response to an unwanted suitor.

GAY & LESBIAN TRAVELLERS
Homosexuality is a delicate issue throughout the Gulf. Conventional wisdom has long held that homosexual experimentation is more common among young people in the Gulf than among their counterparts in the West, but that homosexuality as a lifestyle is much rarer. There's a lot of anecdotal evidence to support this theory, but you would have a hard time proving it.

Islam frowns on homosexuality so the region's governments tend to take the attitude that because homosexuality is 'un-Islamic' it does not exist in their societies. Homosexuality's association with the gay lifestyle in the West has only tended to reinforce this.

DISABLED TRAVELLERS
The situation for disabled travellers throughout the Gulf has been getting better in recent years, but that is not saying much. Buildings without ramp access and bathrooms without disabled stalls are still the rule rather than the exception. Special parking spaces are rarer still. Disabled access to public transport is essentially nonexistent.

SENIOR TRAVELLERS
While Arab culture honours the aged, daily life in the region makes few special allowances for them. There are few discounts for seniors available in the Gulf.

TRAVEL WITH CHILDREN
Arab culture is very child-oriented. This can mean that parents let their youngsters run wild in public places. But it also means that the Gulf States are well stocked with amusement parks, coin-operated rides and other things likely to appeal to pre-teens. Many mid-priced hotels have special, large 'family' rooms and family discounts are often available at amusement parks, beach clubs, and on things like dhow drips or desert camping safaris. Pricier eateries will usually have some sort of children's menu, as will the Gulf's ever-growing ranks of US-style fast-food restaurants.

Nappies (diapers), baby food and infant formula are widely available in the region's supermarkets.

DANGERS & ANNOYANCES
Bahrain, Kuwait and Qatar are all pretty safe. Pickpockets and muggers are all but unknown, and as a region the Gulf has largely been spared the political unrest so often associated with other parts of the Middle East.

The main things you are likely to worry about in the Gulf are the appalling driving habits that almost everyone – local and foreigner alike – displays.

BUSINESS HOURS
The end of week holiday throughout the Gulf is Friday. Most embassies and government offices are also closed on Thursday, though private businesses and shops are open on Thursday mornings and many stores will reopen in the evening on Friday. A few companies and embassies have recently gone to a Friday/Saturday weekend, but this remains the exception rather than the rule.

PUBLIC HOLIDAYS & SPECIAL EVENTS

The Gulf States observe the main Islamic holidays of Eid al-Fitr, which marks the end of Ramadan, and Eid al-Adha, which marks the pilgrimage to Mecca. Bahrain, Kuwait and Qatar also observe both the Gregorian new year (1 January) and the Islamic new year (changeable). A list of the dates for Muslim holidays up to the year 2006 appears in the table.

The Hejira Calendar

Islamic religious observances throughout the Arab Gulf States are scheduled according to the Hejira calendar. In English, Hejira dates are usually followed by the letters AH (for *anno hejiri*) to distinguish them from dates computed according to the Gregorian calendar which is used elsewhere.

The Hejira calendar begins in the year AD 622 taking as its starting point the Prophet Mohammed's hejira, or migration from Mecca to Medina. The calendar is based on phases of the moon which makes it about 11 days shorter than the solar-based Gregorian calendar, therefore Islamic holidays move backwards through the Gregorian calendar making a cycle every 33 years or so. Moreover, Hejira months are said to begin only when the new moon is actually sighted – not simply when the calendar says it ought to be sighted – so heavy rain or cloud cover can lead to the start of a new month being postponed a day or two.

For the traveller, the Hejira calendar is important because the construction dates carved over the doorway of many older buildings are given in AH, not AD. That means that a mosque built in 1350 is about 70 – as opposed to 650 – years old. Except for Saudi Arabia, the Hejira calendar is not widely used in everyday life. Sometimes it may appear alongside the Gregorian date at, say, the top of a newspaper.

ACTIVITIES
Cycling

Despite the heat, mountain-biking in the desert is an increasingly popular weekend activity in some Gulf cities. The problem is getting a bike. If you did not bring your own you will find it hard to rent one, and the region's few bike shops carry mostly children's bikes, clunkers used by labourers and the sort of big, heavy mountain bikes that are better suited to teenagers wanting to show off than to serious riding in a hot climate.

Water Sports

Windsurfing, boating and, to a lesser extent, diving are popular pastimes. All tend to be centred around the beach clubs that dot the outskirts of Manama, Kuwait City and Doha though in a few places (such as along Kuwait City's Corniche) boats can be hired by the hour. More upscale boating expeditions – such as dinner on a converted dhow, can also be arranged, especially in Bahrain.

While it is possible to dive in and around the countries covered here, serious divers usually head for Oman, the east coast of the UAE or (provided you can get a visa) Saudi Arabia's Red Sea coast. Most of the waters

Islamic Holidays

Hejira Year	New Year	Prophet's Birthday	Ramadan	Eid al-Fitr	Eid al-Adha
1421	06.04.00	14.06.00	27.11.00	27.12.00	06.03.01
1422	26.03.01	03.06.01	16.11.01	16.12.01	23.02.02
1423	15.03.02	23.05.02	05.11.02	05.12.02	12.02.03
1424	04.03.03	12.05.03	25.10.03	24.11.03	01.02.04
1425	22.02.04	01.05.04	14.10.04	13.11.04	21.01.05
1426	11.02.05	20.04.05	03.10.05	02.11.05	10.01.06

immediately around Bahrain, Kuwait and Qatar are very shallow and do not lend themselves readily to diving.

Off-Road Driving

Off-road driving in Bahrain, Kuwait and Qatar involves use of a 4WD vehicle in the desert. It *can* mean responsible, environmentally sensitive desert camping. It can also mean roaring around the dunes in the ways that are both dangerous and destructive. Both types of excursion are extremely popular with locals, expats and visitors alike.

If you are going to indulge yourself there are some basic, common-sense, rules you should follow. Take a first aid kit. Make sure your vehicle is in good shape – a spare tyre in good condition and some spare petrol are both absolute musts. A cellphone (easy to rent throughout the region) isn't a bad idea. You must also take along adequate food to tide you over in case you get lost. Above all, know where you are going and when you plan to be back and let someone else back in town know as well. Finally, do not just hop in a 4WD and make for the desert if you have no experience with this sort of thing. Desert driving isn't city driving. You'd be surprised how many people forget that.

The bottom line is: off-road driving is a great way to see some spectacular desert scenery and to escape the Gulf's often sterile cities. But it can be dangerous, and should be approached with that in mind. Anyone who is planning an overnight trip in the desert should pick up *Staying Alive in the Desert* by KEM Melville or one of the numerous locally produced books on off-road camping available throughout the Gulf.

COURSES
Language

If you want to learn Arabic, the Gulf is not the place to look. There are a few schools offering Arabic classes, but these tend to be sparsely attended and are offered only irregularly. You should also know that many of these courses are offered by religious institutions and may come with a heavy dose of encouragement to convert to Islam.

WORK

Labour laws throughout the Gulf are extremely strict. Unless you arrive with a contract in hand it's probably a waste of time – as well as being illegal in most places – looking for a job.

ACCOMMODATION
Camping

Though desert camping is popular throughout the Gulf there are no formal camp sites for tourists in Bahrain, Kuwait or Qatar. See 'Off-Road Driving' earlier for more information on desert camping.

Hostels

Bahrain is the only one of the three countries covered here that has a youth hostel. Bahrain is a HI member and hostel cards are required (though sheet sleeping-sacks are not). See the Manama section for more details.

Hotels

There are very few truly horrible hotels in the Gulf. Even in the cheapest places it is rare to find rooms that are not air-conditioned or that lack hot water. Minifridges, satellite TV and other extras are often standard. Even the worst hotels listed in this book may seem quite decent if you have recently arrived from Egypt or India. The flip side of this is that no place in the Gulf is really cheap – outside Bahrain's youth hostel you are going to find few beds for less than US$15 a night. Most places in the Gulf are amply supplied with mid-range (US$25 to US$50) hotels and all of the bigger cities are utterly awash with four- and five-star accommodation.

FOOD

At the turn of the century half the population of Kuwait was said to be living exclusively on dates and camel milk. The Gulf has never been known for its cuisine. Whenever you see Arab or Arabian food advertised you can safely assume that the place is offering a Lebanese menu.

Lebanese meals are built around a wide selection of appetisers, or *mezze*. *Humous*, a paste made from chickpeas, is the standard dish; its quality is the acid test of any

Lebanese restaurant. Fried *kibbe*, balls of spiced finely minced meat filled with pine nuts, is another Lebanese speciality as is *tabouleh*, a parsley salad, often garnished with tomatoes (and apt to be pretty oily unless you specify otherwise). Any decent Lebanese restaurant should also place a selection of vegetables (lettuce, radishes, onions) on the table as a free appetiser. Main dishes consist of grilled chicken, lamb or beef. Be sure to try *shish tawouk*, a skewer of mildly spiced chicken grilled over open coals.

Street food aside, the cheapest meals in the Gulf are almost always found in small Indian/Pakistani restaurants. The menu at these places tends to be very limited: usually *biryani* dishes (chicken, mutton or fish mixed with mildly spiced rice) and chicken and/or mutton *tikka* (dry roasted and spicy) and maybe a curry. And *samosas* (curried vegetables in a pastry triangle). That's it. In some places it is possible to get quite cheap Asian food, Thai and Filipino being the most common.

Street food consists mainly of *shwarma*, which is lamb or chicken carved from a huge rotating spit and served in pita bread, often with lettuce, tomatoes or potatoes. In many places you can also find *fuul* (pronounced 'fool'), a paste made from fava beans, and *ta'amiyya* (or felafel), deep-fried patties made from chickpeas.

For those with more money to spend almost anything from fish and chips to burritos to sushi is available in the main cities.

Ice cream is the most popular dessert throughout the Gulf. You will have no trouble finding both local brands and some well-known foreign ones, such as Wall's from Britain and Baskin-Robbins from the USA. The best known 'Arab' dessert is *baklava*, a pastry made of filo dough and honey. In the Middle East pistachios are often part of the recipe.

DRINKS

Again, there are practically no indigenous or traditional Arabian drinks, though if you want to try camel's milk you can often find it in supermarkets. *Laban*, a heavy, and often salty, buttermilk is a local speciality. Western soft drinks, mineral water and fruit juice are the standard fare. In small Indian/Pakistani restaurants, however, tap water may well be the only liquid available.

For religious reasons there are no local alcoholic drinks, either. Where alcohol is available it has been imported from the West.

ENTERTAINMENT

Outside of Bahrain dining out is the main form of entertainment in the Gulf. Bahrain has a number of pubs and discos catering to almost any musical taste. Qatar's offerings are more limited. Kuwait, despite its ban on alcohol, has some of the region's liveliest restaurants. Traditional Arab coffeehouses in all three countries are a great place to while away an evening over coffee, tea and a *sheesha* (water pipe).

SHOPPING

The Gulf is often hailed as a low-tax shopping paradise. This is only partially true. If you are coming from Egypt or India many consumer goods, particularly electronics, will indeed be a good bit cheaper in the Gulf. If you are coming from Western Europe the prices will be comparable and the selection narrower. If you are coming from the USA you should do your shopping at home.

Compared to anywhere in the West the range available is a problem. Scouting the souq for, say, VCRs you are likely to discover that every shop carries the same two or three models at pretty much the same prices.

In Bahrain and, to a lesser extent, Qatar, gold can often be a good buy. If you are headed to Dubai in the UAE, however, you should know that you'll find a better selection of both gold and electronics at lower prices.

Locally made souvenirs are another story. Some handicrafts are available in most Gulf countries, though the selection is not particularly good. Look for woven items in Kuwait. Bahrain has some local potters and basket weavers. Bahrain is also a good place to shop for Iranian handicrafts, such as boxes with painted miniatures on them and intricately dyed tablecloths from Isfahan.

Getting There & Away

AIR
Airports & Airlines

The vast majority of people who come and go from the Gulf – visitors, expats and locals alike – enter and leave by air.

Bahrain, Kuwait and Qatar's national airlines are, respectively, Gulf Air – based in Bahrain, and co-owned by Bahrain, Qatar, Oman and the United Arab Emirates (UAE) – Kuwait Airways and Qatar Airways. These operate from the airports at Bahrain, Kuwait and Qatar.

You should also be aware of the other national carriers operated by Gulf Cooperation Council member states. These are: Saudi Arabian Airlines, Emirates Airlines – owned by and based in Dubai in the UAE – and Oman Air.

Of these six, Kuwait Airways, Gulf Air and Saudi Arabian Airlines are the oldest, largest and best established. Emirates has an especially good reputation for inflight service, but offers relatively limited routes within the Gulf itself. Oman Air and Qatar Airways, which has been growing very quickly in recent years, are the region's newest carriers.

In addition, all of the major European, Asian and Middle Eastern airlines (with the obvious exception of El Al) serve most of the major cities in the Gulf. There are few direct flights between the Gulf and the USA or Australia, and service to Africa is a bit irregular.

All of the main cities in the Gulf have excellent air links with Europe, India, Pakistan and Asia. The Gulf, however, is still seen by the travel industry primarily as a business destination and, as such, there are very few discount airfares available. Your best bet for cheap plane tickets to or from the Gulf will be to buy them in countries like Egypt, India and Pakistan, which send masses of workers to the region.

Buying Tickets

An air ticket alone can gouge a great slice out of anyone's budget, but you can reduce the cost by finding discounted fares. Stiff competition has resulted in widespread discounting – good news for travellers. The only people likely to be paying full fare these days are travellers flying in 1st or business class. Passengers flying in economy can usually manage some sort of discount. But unless you buy carefully and flexibly, it is still possible to end up paying exorbitant amounts for a journey.

There are plenty of discount tickets which are valid for 12 months, allowing multiple stopovers with open dates. When you're looking for bargain air fares, go to a travel agent rather than directly to the airline. From time to time, airlines do have promotional fares and special offers, but generally they only sell fares at the official listed price.

Many airlines, though, offer some excellent fares to Web surfers. They may sell seats by auction or simply cut prices to reflect the reduced cost of electronic selling.

Many travel agents around the world have Web sites, which can make the Internet a quick and easy way to compare prices, a good start for when you're ready to start negotiating with your favourite travel agency. Online ticket sales work well if you are doing a simple one-way or return trip on specified dates. However, online super fast fare generators are no substitute for a travel agent who knows all about special deals, has strategies for avoiding layovers and can offer advice on everything from which airline has the best vegetarian food to the best travel insurance to bundle with your ticket.

Buying Tickets in the Gulf Every city in the Gulf has far more travel agents than the local market can support and, because of high turnover, their staffs are often of marginal competence. Combine this with the fact that most of the agencies make their money from high-volume corporate clients and have little time for people walking in off the street and you can understand why shopping for plane tickets in the Gulf can be a life-shortening experience.

In any Gulf city your best bet is to check several different places. If you shop around for tickets expect to get similar prices everywhere – they are usually controlled either by the local government or by a cartel organised by the airlines and/or the agents themselves. Shopping around will probably save you some, but not a lot of, money and is mainly a form of insurance. It is almost unheard of to find an agent significantly under- cutting everyone else in town, but it is not at all uncommon to find a few who are quoting markedly higher prices than the norm. Getting quotes in four to six places guarantees that you do not wind up paying too much.

Round-the-World & Stopover Tickets

The cheapest way to visit the Gulf is often to stop over there when travelling between Europe and Asia, or to include it in a round-the-world ticket. Bahrain, because it is a major transport hub, is the most common stop on round-the-world tickets.

If you are flying one of the Gulf-based carriers, it is usually possible to stop over in a Gulf capital at little or no extra cost. Gulf Air offers short-stay packages for people transiting Bahrain en route from Europe to Asia or vice-versa. These packages usually include one or two nights' hotel accommodation, airport transfers and a short tour all for a fairly reasonable flat fee.

Travellers with Special Needs

Most international airlines can cater to people with special needs – travellers with disabilities, people with young children and even children travelling alone.

Travellers with special dietary preferences (vegetarian, kosher etc) can request appropriate meals with advance notice. The meals served on all Gulf airlines, and on most flights to the Gulf by Western carriers, are *halal*, ie, they meet Muslim dietary requirements. If you are in a wheelchair, most international airports can provide an escort from check-in desk to plane where needed, and ramps, lifts, toilets and phones are generally available.

Airlines usually allow babies up to two years of age to fly for 10% of the adult fare, although a few may allow them free of charge. Reputable international airlines usually provide nappies (diapers), tissues, talcum and all the other paraphernalia needed to keep babies clean, dry and half-happy. For children between the ages of two and 12, the fare on international flights is usually 50% of the regular fare or 67% of a discounted fare.

The USA & Canada

Discount travel agents in the USA are known as consolidators (although you won't see a sign on the door saying Consolidator). San Francisco is the ticket consolidator capital of America, although some good deals can be found in Los Angeles, New York and other big cities. Consolidators can be found through the *Yellow Pages* or the major daily newspapers. The *New York Times*, the *Los Angeles Times,* the *Chicago Tribune* and the *San Francisco Examiner* all produce weekly travel sections in which you will find a number of travel agency ads.

Air Travel Glossary

Cancellation Penalties If you have to cancel or change a discounted ticket, there are often heavy penalties involved; insurance can sometimes be taken out against these penalties. Some airlines impose penalties on regular tickets as well, particularly against 'no-show' passengers.

Courier Fares Businesses often need to send urgent documents or freight securely and quickly. Courier companies hire people to accompany the package through customs and, in return, offer a discount ticket which is sometimes a phenomenal bargain. However, you may have to surrender all your baggage allowance and take only carry-on luggage.

Full Fares Airlines traditionally offer 1st class (coded F), business class (coded J) and economy class (coded Y) tickets. These days there are so many promotional and discounted fares available that few passengers pay full economy fare.

Lost Tickets If you lose your airline ticket an airline will usually treat it like a travellers cheque and, after inquiries, issue you with another one. Legally, however, an airline is entitled to treat it like cash and if you lose it then it's gone forever. Take good care of your tickets.

Onward Tickets An entry requirement for many countries is that you have a ticket out of the country. If you're unsure of your next move, the easiest solution is to buy the cheapest onward ticket to a neighbouring country or a ticket from a reliable airline which can later be refunded if you do not use it.

Open-Jaw Tickets These are return tickets where you fly out to one place but return from another. If available, this can save you backtracking to your arrival point.

Overbooking Since every flight has some passengers who fail to show up, airlines often book more passengers than they have seats. Usually excess passengers make up for the no-shows, but occasionally somebody gets 'bumped' onto the next available flight. Guess who it is most likely to be? The passengers who check in late.

Promotional Fares These are officially discounted fares, available from travel agencies or direct from the airline.

Reconfirmation If you don't reconfirm your flight at least 72 hours prior to departure, the airline may delete your name from the passenger list. Ring to find out if your airline requires reconfirmation.

Restrictions Discounted tickets often have various restrictions on them – such as needing to be paid for in advance and incurring a penalty to be altered. Others are restrictions on the minimum and maximum period you must be away.

Round-the-World Tickets RTW tickets give you a limited period (usually a year) in which to circumnavigate the globe. You can go anywhere the carrying airlines go, as long as you don't backtrack. The number of stopovers or total number of separate flights is decided before you set off and they usually cost a bit more than a basic return flight.

Transferred Tickets Airline tickets cannot be transferred from one person to another. Travellers sometimes try to sell the return half of their ticket, but officials can ask you to prove that you are the person named on the ticket. On an international flight tickets are compared with passports.

Travel Periods Ticket prices vary with the time of year. There is a low (off-peak) season and a high (peak) season, and often a low-shoulder season and a high-shoulder season as well. Usually the fare depends on your outward flight – if you depart in the high season and return in the low season, you pay the high-season fare.

Council Travel, America's largest student travel organisation, has around 60 offices in the USA; its head office (☎ 800-226 8624) is at 205 E 42 St, New York, NY 10017. Call it for the office nearest you or visit its Web site at www.ciee.org.

STA Travel (☎ 800-777 0112) has offices in Boston, Chicago, Miami, New York, Philadelphia, San Francisco and other major cities. Call the toll-free 800 number for the office locations or visit its Web site at www.statravel.com.

In Canada, The *Globe & Mail*, the *Toronto Star*, the *Montreal Gazette* and the *Vancouver Sun* carry travel agents' ads and are a good place to look for cheap fares.

Travel CUTS (☎ 800-667 2887) is Canada's national student travel agency and has offices in all major cities. Its Web address is www.travelcuts.com.

The only single-plane services between the USA and the Gulf are Kuwait Airways' four weekly flights (three via London, the fourth via Frankfurt). None of the major American carriers flies to Bahrain, Kuwait or Qatar but most have code sharing agreements with European airlines that can get you to the Gulf quite efficiently. The same goes for Gulf Air, which has a code share agreement with American Airlines covering flights to New York, Chicago and Miami.

With some shopping around you might make it from the Eastern USA to the Gulf for as little as US$1000 return. Gulf Air and Emirates both sell heavily discounted tickets through 'authorised discounters', usually small travel agencies that specialise in travel to the Gulf or Middle East. Kuwait Airways has long been a favourite of New York City's consolidators. The airlines themselves can direct you to such an agency in your area.

If you go this route be sure to ask about add-ons. Emirates, for example, sometimes offers cheap tickets from the USA to Dubai, with onward 'add-on' tickets from Dubai to one of several other Gulf destinations for free or close to it. Usually you can only take one add-on. Such a policy, however, adds greatly to your flexibility in planning a trip. Don't count on an agent to volunteer this sort of in-

formation – be sure to ask. Gulf Air sometimes offers similar add-ons between the cities of the airline's owners (a free stopover in Bahrain on a ticket to Doha, for example).

Australia & New Zealand

Quite a few travel offices specialise in discount air tickets. Some travel agents, particularly smaller ones, advertise cheap air fares in the travel sections of weekend newspapers, such as the *Age* in Melbourne and the *Sydney Morning Herald*. The *New Zealand Herald* has a travel section in which travel agents advertise fares.

Two agents known for cheap fares in Australia and New Zealand are STA Travel and Flight Centre. STA Travel has offices in all major cities and on many university campuses. Call ☎ 131 776 Australia-wide for the location of your nearest branch, or in New Zealand, call ☎ 09-309 0458. STA's Travel Web address is www.statravel.com.au.

Flight Centre (☎ 131 600 Australia-wide, or ☎ 09 309 6171 in New Zealand) has dozens of offices throughout Australia and New Zealand. Its Web address is www.flightcen tre.com.au.

A number of airlines, including Emirates, Gulf Air, Cathay Pacific, Thai International and Egypt Air, operate regular return flights out of Melbourne and Sydney to the Gulf. Emirates and Gulf Air offer the most direct flights from Australia, via Dubai or Singapore, to the Gulf.

Low season return fares to the Gulf start from A$1540 with Thai and Royal Jordanian Airlines, via Bangkok and Amman, to A$1750 with Emirates, via Dubai, and A$1950 with Gulf Air via Singapore.

Return low season fares from New Zealand to the Gulf, via Singapore or Hong Kong, start from around NZ$2199.

The UK & Continental Europe

Airline ticket discounters are known as bucket shops in the UK. Despite the somewhat disreputable name, there is nothing under-the-counter about them. Discount air travel is big business in London. Advertisements for many travel agents appear in the travel pages of the weekend broadsheets, such as the Independent on Saturday and the Sunday Times. Look out for the free magazines, such as TNT, which are widely available in London – start by looking outside the main railway and underground stations.

For students or travellers under 26, popular travel agencies in the UK include STA Travel (☎ 020-7361 6161), which has an office at 86 Old Brompton Rd, London SW7 3LQ, and other offices in London and Manchester. Visit its Web site at www.sta travel.co.uk. Usit Campus (☎ 020-7730 3402), 52 Grosvenor Gardens, London SW1WOAG, has branches throughout the UK. The Web address is www.usitcam pus.com. Other recommended travel agencies include: Trailfinders (☎ 020-7938 3939), 194 Kensington High St, London W8 7RG; Bridge the World (☎ 020-7734 7447), 4 Regent Place, London W1R 5FB; and Flightbookers (☎ 020-7757 2000), 177-178 Tottenham Court Rd, London W1P 9LF.

Across Europe many travel agencies have ties with STA Travel, where cheap tickets can be purchased and STA-issued tickets can be altered (usually for a US$25 fee). Outlets in major cities include: Voyages Wasteels (☎ 08 03 88 70 04 – this number can only be dialled from within France – fax 01 43 25 46 25), 11 rue Dupuytren, 756006 Paris; STA Travel (☎ 030-311 0950, fax 313 0948), Goethestrasse 73, 10625 Berlin; Passaggi (☎ 06-474 0923, fax 482 7436), Stazione Termini FS, Gelleria Di Tesla, Rome; and ISYTS (☎ 01-322 1267, fax 323 3767), 11 Nikis St, Upper Floor, Syntagma Square, Athens.

Most of Europe's major carriers fly to Bahrain or Kuwait, if not both. Service to Doha is a bit harder to come by. The Gulf-based carriers usually offer daily service to London and service several times per week to a handful of other cities (Paris, Frankfurt, Rome and Athens are the most common destinations). Tickets are not especially cheap – getting from London to the Gulf and back often costs UK£ 400 or more.

For now there are no charter flights to speak of to the three countries covered here, though service is sometimes available to Oman and the UAE (usually Sharjah) and it is sometimes possible to pick up cheap tickets to Bahrain, Kuwait or Doha from there. Most charters to the Gulf originate in Britain, Germany or, in a few cases, Switzerland.

Asia
Khao San Rd in Bangkok is the budget travellers headquarters. STA Travel (☎ 02-236 0262), 33 Surawong Rd, is a good and reliable place to start.

In Singapore STA Travel (☎ 737 7188) in the Orchard Parade Hotel, 1 Tanglin Rd, offers competitive discount fares. Singapore, like Bangkok, has hundreds of travel agents, so you can compare prices on flights.

Hong Kong has a number of excellent, reliable travel agencies and some not-so-reliable ones. Many travellers use the Hong Kong Student Travel Bureau (☎ 2730 3269).

In Delhi there are a number of discount travel agencies around Connaught Place. STIC Travels (☎ 011-332 5559), an agent for STA Travel, has an office in Delhi in Room 6 at the Hotel Imperial in Janpath.

In Mumbai, STIC Travels (☎ 022-218 1431) is located at 6 Maker Arcade, Cuffe Parade. Most of the international airline offices in Mumbai are in or around Nariman Point.

All of the big Asian carriers have regular service to the Gulf, near daily service in the case of the airlines based in the Indian subcontinent, and all of the Gulf carriers have frequent service to Bangkok, Singapore, New Delhi, Bombay, Karachi, Lahore, Islamabad, Manila, Hong Kong and Seoul. From the Gulf it is possible to book relatively cheap air/hotel packages to Thailand, Singapore and other popular Asian holiday destinations. Tickets to and from the subcontinent tend to be fairly affordable because of both high volumes on the routes and because the distances are relatively short.

Africa
Nairobi and Johannesburg are probably the best places in East and South Africa to buy tickets. Some major airlines have offices in Nairobi, which is a good place to determine the standard fare before you make the rounds of the travel agencies. Flight Centres

02-210024) in Lakhamshi House, Bishara St, has been in business for many years.

In Johannesburg the South African Student's Travel Services (☎ 011-716 3045) has an office at the University of the Witwatersrand. STA Travel (☎ 011- 447 5551) has an office in Johannesburg on Tyrwhitt Ave in Rosebank.

Few African carriers serve Bahrain, Kuwait or Qatar, though Nairobi, Dar Es-Salaam and Johannesburg are easy enough to reach using the Gulf-based airlines. A number of African carriers serve Jeddah, Saudi Arabia, but transiting through Saudi Arabia can be a difficult and frustrating experience. You are much better off going through Dubai, though the connections from there are less extensive.

Middle East

Cairo, Beirut, Damascus and Amman are all easy to reach from anywhere in the Gulf. Arab North Africa is a bit more difficult. There are only a few flights to Tunis or Casablanca, on either the Gulf carriers or the national carriers of the North African countries. Air service to Yemen is not as good or as frequent as you might expect, considering its position on the Arabian peninsula.

LAND
Border Crossings

Bus It is possible to cross the desert by bus from Turkey, Syria, Jordan and Egypt (via a ferry to Jordan) to Kuwait, Bahrain and, at least in theory, Doha. It is not, however, an easy trip to make. Aside from the sheer length of the journey, you will also need a Saudi Arabian transit visa, not a simple thing to procure (see the boxed text 'Saudi Transit Visas').

There are buses that run directly to Kuwait from Jordan and Egypt via the Trans-Arabian Pipeline road across northern Saudi Arabia. Long distance travel to Bahrain involves taking a bus to Dammam, Saudi Arabia and changing there (though you will need a ticket all the way through to Bahrain before you can get a Saudi transit visa). To go to Qatar from Dammam you'll

---

Saudi Transit Visas

Generally Saudi transit visas are only issued in the capitals of countries bordering Saudi Arabia (Amman for Gulf-bound travellers, Kuwait City, Manama, Doha and Abu Dhabi in the UAE for people headed the other way). You'll have to show the Saudis both a visa for the country you are headed for, and a ticket there.

If you do get a Saudi transit visa, study it carefully. The visa may be for a very limited amount of time (as little as 48 hours) and may restrict you to certain routes. Saudi roads have many police checkpoints and the odds are pretty high that if you deviate from your assigned route you will be caught. If you don't read Arabic have someone translate the Arabic on the visa for you – if there are any mistakes and the Arabic and English text differ it's the Arabic text that counts.

Finally, be aware that Saudi Arabia conducts all official business according to the Islamic Hejira calendar. If a visa says it is valid for use within a month that's a Hejira month and it's several days shorter than a Gregorian one.

---

have to catch a bus to Hofuf and take a private taxi from there to Doha (Saudi bus timetables list a Hofuf-Doha bus, but its existence is doubtful). Realistically, this is only possible for those holding Saudi Arabian residence visas. Without a ticket all the way to Doha, it is highly unlikely that you will be able to get a transit visa.

Car As with bus travel, getting across Saudi Arabia is the main problem. Have a proper carnet, proof that you own the car and a visa for the country at the other end of the road (Jordan if you're headed west, your final Gulf destination if you are headed east) and you ought to be able to get a Saudi transit visa in a day or two.

SEA

There is no scheduled passenger service into the northern Gulf. In the past there has been service between Bahrain and Iran (usually Bandar-é Abbās), but at the time of writing the ferry lines were no longer in service. If you're really interested in travelling by sea from Bahrain to Iran try asking around at Manama's travel agencies. You *can* get to Iran by sea from the UAE. Sharjah is the most common point of entry/departure.

ORGANISED TOURS

Organised tourism in the Gulf usually focuses on the UAE and Oman. Group tours stopping in Bahrain, Kuwait or Qatar are much rarer. In part this is because Bahrain, Kuwait and Qatar have made few efforts to attract package tour operators. Kuwait, officially, remains closed to tourism, though a handful of groups visit each year. Bahrain has traditionally put most of its tourism marketing efforts into attracting stopover traffic transiting the country. Qatar tends to focus on high-profile sporting events, particularly tennis, rally driving and the Asia qualifying rounds of the quadrennial World Cup soccer tournament. While a few agencies (such as Kuoni in the UK) offer group tours visiting the three countries covered here, the field still largely belongs to very expensive upscale tours run by museums and universities in the USA.

The alumni association of Stanford University in Palo Alto, California has run tours to the Gulf a couple of times per year since the mid-'90s. You do not have to be a Stanford alum to go on these. Information can be found on their Web site www.stanfordalumni.org and click on 'travel & vacation'. The American Museum of Natural History in New York City (☎ 212-769 5000) sometimes sponsors similar tours. Check out their Web site on www.amnh.org. Also worth checking out is Lindblad Special Expeditions (☎ 800-397 3348 toll free in the USA, or 212-765 7740), a New York based agency that organises and leads adventure tours around the world.

Getting Around the Region

Although the Gulf is a relatively small area the visa regulations of the region's various countries often make air the only practical way for anyone other than Gulf Cooperation Council nationals to travel. This is mainly because of the problems involved in transiting Saudi Arabia. Buses, for example, link all three of the countries covered by this book via Dammam, Saudi Arabia. The problem is getting a visa which allows you to change buses in Dammam. See the boxed text in the Getting There & Away chapter for more information on Saudi transit visas.

AIR

Bahrain, Kuwait and Qatar have no domestic air services.

Air Passes

Gulf Air's appropriately named, 'Air Pass' allows you to purchase coupons for travel between Bahrain, Qatar, the United Arab Emirates (UAE) and Oman. The coupons cost between US$45 and US$80 per segment, depending on the distance of the journey (Bahrain-Doha is the cheapest and Bahrain-Muscat is the most expensive). This usually works out to between one-third and one-half of the cheapest fare you could purchase in the Gulf. The catch is that you cannot travel between any particular city pair more than once *in the same direction*, not counting transits. In other words, you can make one round trip between, say, Bahrain and Doha but not two. If, however, you have already made that round trip and then want to make a trip to Abu Dhabi it is OK if your return flight involves a change of planes in Doha, provided that you only transit Doha airport.

Some of the city pairs available (prices apply in either direction): Bahrain-Doha US$45, Bahrain-Abu Dhabi US$80, Bahrain -Dubai US$80, Bahrain-Muscat US$80, Dubai-Muscat US$45, Doha-Dubai US$80.

The pass must be purchased outside the GCC and you must also have a return ticket to the Gulf on Gulf Air (though the ticket and

the pass do not have to be purchased together). The ticket must originate outside the GCC (ie, tickets purchased in Saudi Arabia and Kuwait do not make you eligible for the pass), and the pass is not available to anyone who is resident in a GCC country. The pass has a maximum validity of three months. You must have confirmed reservations for all of your intra-Gulf flights before you leave for the region, but those reservations can be changed along the same segments with no penalty. If you want to change your routing there is a US$30 reissue fee, in addition to whatever difference in the cost of the coupons works out to be. Prior to travelling the pass can be refunded with only a US$30 penalty, but once the first coupon has been used the remainder cannot be refunded.

BUS

There is regular bus service from Dammam and Alkhobar, Saudi Arabia to Manama, Bahrain, and from Dammam to Kuwait. Saudi bus timetables also list buses from Dammam and Hofuf to Doha, Qatar, but you'll be hard pressed to find any evidence that these buses actually exist.

The Saudi Arabia to Bahrain route offers five daily departures and, as long as you have organised your Saudi visa in advance, is straightforward. Service to Kuwait is less frequent and, at the time of writing, had been temporarily suspended.

TRAIN

There are no trains in Bahrain, Kuwait or Qatar.

CAR & MOTORCYCLE

Most of the main roads in the Gulf are high-quality two- or four-lane highways. Very few roads are unpaved and 4WDs are only necessary for driving around the desert or other 'off-road' activities. Virtually every site covered by this book can be reached *without* a 4WD (the handful of exceptions are clearly noted). If you are interested in off-road driving pick up one of the numerous locally produced guides on the subject. Also see Off-Road Driving under Activities in the Regional Facts for the Visitor chapter.

Although it doesn't happen often, avoid driving when it rains. Few of the region's city streets have proper drainage with the result that they often turn into rivers.

Rental

Renting a car in any of the Gulf states is quite straightforward. Western driving licences are accepted in all Gulf countries except Bahrain, where an International Driving Permit is required. There are no restrictions on women driving in Bahrain, Kuwait or Qatar.

Rates will usually include unlimited kilometres, but never include petrol (which, in any case, is pretty cheap in this part of the world). It's unlikely that you will find any rental company in the region willing to let you take their cars out of the country.

In Bahrain or Qatar expect to pay about US$25 per day for the smallest car once all the extras are added in. Rates in Kuwait bottom out at around US$35 per day. In Kuwait you will also have to purchase 'insurance' for your licence from home for KD10 (about US$34).

Insurance for the car is also a good idea. In some places rental car insurance is a local monopoly and you will not be given a choice about purchasing it. If you do have a choice you should go ahead and get it anyway. Many of the Gulf's smaller agencies are especially zealous in looking for tiny dings and scratches that allegedly were not there when you took the car out. Western credit card programs that promise insurance coverage for rentals are not likely to be honoured in the Gulf, even if the card company extends coverage there in the first place.

See the Regional Facts for the Visitor chapter or the individual country chapters for more information regarding costs and local regulations.

BICYCLE

While a few daring souls have cycled straight across Arabia this is not a common way of getting around the Gulf. Expat bike clubs exist in a few Gulf cities and mountain biking is growing in popularity. (Check the local English-language press for more information.) But in most of the region the heat, humidity and the dull desert landscape do not lend themselves to cycling.

Most of the bikes you'll see in the Gulf are old clunkers ridden by labourers. The fancy-looking bikes available in the region' few bike shops are often of relatively low quality (extremely heavy, Chinese-made bikes are a common sight). Getting any repairs done on an expensive touring or mountain bike is likely to be difficult, so if you plan a long bike tour take *lots* of spare parts and know how to repair the bike yourself.

HITCHING

Hitching is never entirely safe in any country in the world, and we don't recommend it. Travellers who decide to hitch should understand they are taking a small but potentially serious risk. People who do choose to hitch will be safer if they travel in pairs and let someone know where they are planning to go. Hitching is legal throughout the Gulf, however, if you are white bear in mind that hitching may attract the attentions of the police. This is because hitching throughout the region tends to be the preserve of Gulf Arabs and men from Asia.

The most common way of hitching is to extend your right hand, palm down. Drivers will usually expect you to pay the equivalent bus or service-taxi fare. We don't recommend that women hitch at all in this part of the world.

BOAT

Seaborne passenger services connecting Kuwait, Bahrain and Doha, as well as the UAE and Oman, have been talked about for years but never quite seem to materialise. If and when the boats do start running you can be sure they will be amply advertised around the region.

LOCAL TRANSPORT
Public Transport

Bahrain and Kuwait have very thorough local bus systems. Qatar does not. If you choose not to rent a car in Doha plan on walking long distances or catching taxis.

All three countries covered here also have both good local and (long distance) service-taxi systems.

ORGANISED TOURS

Gulf Air offers Bahrain stopover packages. These must be purchased in conjunction with an airline ticket and usually include one or two nights' hotel accommodation, airport transfers and a half-day city tour.

Officially Kuwait does not issue tourist visas, but a few high-end tours, usually sponsored by universities or museums, stop there each year. See the Organised Tours section of the Getting There & Away chapter for more details.

Should you arrive on your own, full-day, half-day and overnight tours can be booked locally almost anywhere in the Gulf. Some large hotels also run tours and these may be open to people who are not staying at the hotel in question.

As a rule you are going to pay US$20 to US$30 in local currency for a half-day city tour. More elaborate packages, involving 4WD trips into the desert, lunch on a dhow or camping out in a Bedouin tent, run anywhere from around US$90 to US$150. See Organised Tours in the relevant country chapters for details.

The problem for independent travellers is that much of the Gulf's nascent tourist industry remains geared towards groups. If you cannot round up at least four, and possibly as many as 10 or 15, people you may have to pay a supplement. Some companies will not run a tour if enough people do not sign up. Even in busy Bahrain most of the offerings from any given tour company are only available once or twice a week.

Hawar Islands

Almost bumping into Qatar are the 16 islands known collectively as the Hawar Islands. The islands are designated by the Bahraini government as an 'environmental protection area' because Rabad al-Gharbiyah Island has a number of flamingoes and Suwad al-Janubiyah Island has one of the world's largest cormorant colonies. (See the boxed text 'Bird-Watching' in the Qatar chapter for details.)

The islands are claimed by both Bahrain and Qatar and have long been a source of tension between the two countries. Bahrain currently controls them and keeps about 2000 troops stationed there. Therefore, access is only possible on the boats run by the resort. Travel around the islands is restricted and no photos outside the resort area are allowed – but don't let these regulations put you off coming.

Places to Stay & Eat

The modern and impressive *Hawar Resort Hotel* (☎ 849 111, fax 849 100, ✉ hawar@batelco.com.bh) is alongside a beautiful sandy beach. In winter, the resort runs some comparatively cheap overnight packages, including transport, accommodation and three meals, for BD19/32 for singles/doubles, but otherwise rates are high. Children who share a room with their parents cost BD9. Guests and visitors can use the resort's swimming pool, health club and tennis courts for free, but the water sports are an expensive extra.

Getting There & Away

The resort runs a bus-boat service (included in the hotel tariff) to the Hawar Islands from Manama, via the port at Ad-Dur. The resort also offers day trips for BD10 per person, including bus, boat and lunch. A 'tour' of the main island costs another BD1, but is not worth it because so much of the island is off-limits. The evening dhow trip is better, and gives bird enthusiasts a chance to spot some flamingoes and cormorants. All bookings must be made at the resort's office (☎ 290 377, fax 292 659, ✉ hawar@batelco.com.bh) along the Marina Corniche in Manama.

Bahrain

The State of Bahrain

Area: 706 sq km
Population: 620,378
Capital: Manama
Head of State: The Emir, Sheikh Hamad bin Isa al-Khalifa
Official Language: Arabic
Currency: Bahraini dinar (BD)
Time: GMT/UTC +3
Exchange Rate: BD0.377 = US$1

Highlights

- The Bahrain National Museum in Manama is very comprehensive, and worth visiting more than once
- The Beit al-Quran in Manama is absorbing and provides a good general introduction to Islam
- Bahrain has several extensive fields of burial mounds – the best are at A'ali
- Of Bahrain's several forts, the Riffa Fort has the best location and views

The only island-state in the Arab world, Bahrain is about the size of Singapore, but with only a fraction of its population. Although comprising 33 islands, the country is often referred to simply as 'the island'. Bahrain is unique in several ways: Gulf Arabs and foreign expatriates mix more easily here than elsewhere in the region; it's the easiest of the Gulf countries to visit; and, although not cheap, it offers good value for those on a budget. Bahrain is an easy and hassle-free introduction to the Gulf, though anyone making their first trip to an Arab country should still be prepared for a little culture shock.

In Arabic, *bahrain* means 'two seas'. Since the dawn of history Bahrain has been a trading centre and, until about a generation ago, virtually all trade came and went by sea. Occupying a strategic position on

the great trade routes of antiquity, with good harbours and abundant fresh water, the Bahrainis are natural traders.

Facts about Bahrain

HISTORY
Bahrain's island location has proved to be both a blessing and a curse, creating an outward-looking place of open-minded people, whilst attracting the attention of many outsiders. At one time or another Sumerians, Greeks, Persians, Portuguese, Turks, Wahhabis, Omanis and, of course, the British have all taken an interest in Bahrain.

Dilmun
Bahrain's history goes back to the roots of human civilisation. The main island is thought to have broken away from the Arabian mainland some time around 6000 BC, and it has almost certainly been inhabited since prehistoric times.

The Bahrain islands first emerged into world history in the 3rd millennium BC. Known as Dilmun, one of the great trading empires of the ancient world, it continued in some form or other for more than 2000 years. The empire evolved here because of the islands' strategic position along the trade routes linking Mesopotamia with the Indus Valley.

What we now call the Middle East had a much more temperate climate 4500 years ago, although it was becoming increasingly arid. Dilmun, with its lush, spring-fed greenery, became a holy island in the mythology of Sumeria, one of the earliest civilisations that flourished in what is now southern Iraq. The Sumerians grew out of an earlier (4th millennium BC) people who are referred to as the Ubaid culture. Archaeological finds in Bahrain indicate that the islands were in contact with the Ubaids, and the contact continued after the founding of Dilmun some time

BAHRAIN

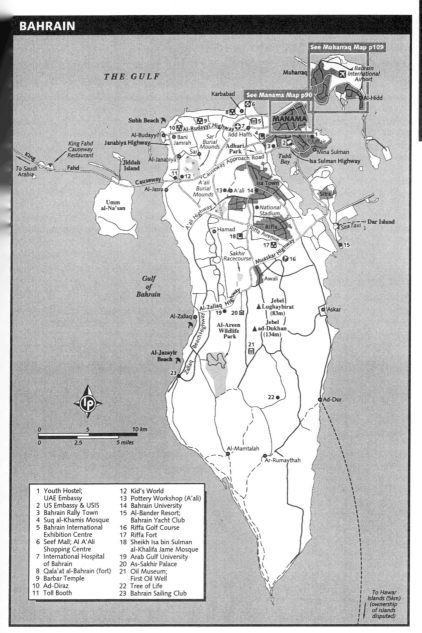

See Muharraq Map p109

See Manama Map p90

THE GULF

King Fahd Causeway Restaurant

To Saudi Arabia

Umm al-Na'san

Gulf of Bahrain

1	Youth Hostel; UAE Embassy
2	US Embassy & USIS
3	Bahrain Rally Town
4	Suq al-Khamis Mosque
5	Bahrain International Exhibition Centre
6	Seef Mall; Al A'Ali Shopping Centre
7	International Hospital of Bahrain
8	Qala'at al-Bahrain (fort)
9	Barbar Temple
10	Ad-Diraz
11	Toll Booth
12	Kid's World
13	Pottery Workshop (A'ali)
14	Bahrain University
15	Al-Bander Resort; Bahrain Yacht Club
16	Riffa Golf Course
17	Riffa Fort
18	Sheikh Isa bin Sulman al-Khalifa Jame Mosque
19	Arab Gulf University
20	As-Sakhir Palace
21	Oil Museum; First Oil Well
22	Tree of Life
23	Bahrain Sailing Club

To Hawar Islands (5km) (ownership of islands disputed)

in the 3rd millennium BC. In its early centuries, Dilmun already had strong trading links with the powerful Sumerian city of Eridu (near Basra, in present-day Iraq).

Dilmun is mentioned in the Babylonian creation myth, and the *Epic of Gilgamesh* describes it as a paradise to which heroes and wise men are transported to enjoy eternal life. In the epic (the world's oldest known poetic saga), Gilgamesh, King of Uruk, spends much of his time seeking out this sacred island. On finding it he meets Ziusudra, the Sumerian equivalent of the biblical Noah. After the flood, Ziusudra had been given the right to live forever in Dilmun, helping Gilgamesh obtain the flower of eternal youth. But a serpent eats the flower while Gilgamesh is on his way home, leaving him wiser but still mortal.

Bahrain's greenery was central to Dilmun's religion. Bahrain's Barbar Temple, the earliest stages of which go back to about 2250 BC, was dedicated to Enki, God of Wisdom and The Sweet Waters Under the Earth. Enki was believed to live in an underground sea of fresh water on which the visible world floated. He was worshipped at an underground shrine built around a sacred well.

Dilmun itself seems to have been founded during the Early Bronze Age, sometime around 3200 BC, and to have come into its own around 2800 BC. Archaeologists divide the civilisation's history into four periods: Formative Dilmun (3200–2200 BC), Early Dilmun (2200–1600 BC), Middle Dilmun (1600–1000 BC) and Late Dilmun (1000–330 BC). Formative and Early Dilmun are the most interesting for the tourist. These periods encompass the construction of many of the island's grave mounds and the Barbar Temple. Middle Dilmun was a period of decline and Late Dilmun saw it absorbed into the Assyrian and Babylonian empires.

From its earliest days Dilmun was a lucrative trading centre. A cuneiform tablet found at Ur (in present-day Iraq) records the receipt of 'a parcel of fish eyes' (probably a reference to pearls) sent from Dilmun around the year 2000 BC.

While we know that Dilmun was powerful, it is much harder to say exactly how powerful it was. There is no question that the Early Dilmun civilisation controlled a large section of the western shore of the Gulf, including Tarut Island (in present-day eastern Saudi Arabia). But there is much dispute over how far north and inland that control extended, and whether Dilmun had any influence on the far side of the Gulf (ie, modern Iran). At times, Dilmun's influence probably extended as far north as modern Kuwait and as far inland as the Al-Hasa Oasis in eastern Saudi Arabia.

There is no doubt, however, that Dilmun fell into decline during the Middle period. This was probably connected with the fall of the Indus Valley civilisation (in Pakistan). Little is known about the culture of this civilisation, but its disappearance in the middle of the 2nd millennium BC would have stripped Dilmun of much of its activity as a trading port on the route from Mesopotamia to the Indus.

The decline of Dilmun continued over the following centuries. Tablets from the 8th century BC mention Dilmun as a tributary state of Assyria and, by about 600 BC, the once great trading empire had been fully absorbed by the Babylonians.

From Alexander to Mohammed

After its absorption by Babylon, Dilmun effectively ceased to exist. At the same time the Gulf and eastern Arabia more or less vanished from recorded history for about 200 years. Little is known about what happened in the Gulf between the fall of Dilmun and the arrival of Nearchus, an admiral in Alexander the Great's army. Nearchus set up a small colony on Failaka Island (now part of Kuwait) in the late 4th century BC and explored the Gulf at least as far south as Bahrain. From the time of Nearchus until the coming of Islam in the 7th century AD, Bahrain was generally known by its Greek name, Tylos.

The period from about 300 BC to AD 300 was reasonably prosperous. Pliny, writing in the 1st century AD, noted that Tylos was famous for its pearls, but few ruins remain from this period. The dominant regional power was the Seleucid Empire, one of the

The Gulf States feature a fascinating juxtaposition of the traditional and the modern ways of life.

Detail of the Sword Arch, Doha, Qatar

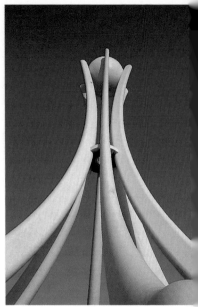

Bahrain's famous Pearl Monument

The Sword Arch spans one of the many roads that have sprung up since the 1950s.

three principal successor states into which Alexander's realm broke up after his death in 323 BC. The Seleucids controlled the swath of land running from present-day Israel and Lebanon through Mesopotamia to Persia. Bahrain lay on the outermost edge of this area, although there is some dispute as to whether it was ever directly controlled by the Seleucids.

The Seleucid Empire, however, was relatively short-lived. Its successor, in what had been the eastern part of the Seleucid lands, was the Parthian Empire. The Parthians were a more explicitly Persian dynasty, though they presented themselves as the protectors of Hellenistic culture and Alexander's legacy. Bahrain was almost certainly directly controlled by the Parthians until the 3rd century AD when it drifted into the empire of the Sassanids, who formally annexed the islands in the 4th century AD.

Around the 3rd or 4th century AD, many of Bahrain's inhabitants adopted the new Christian faith. (Exactly how many, or what percentage of the population they represented, is impossible to determine.) The Sassanian Empire was also a centre for Zoroastrianism and, for a time, Manicheism. Zoroastrianism became the empire's official religion in the late 3rd century AD, and dissenters were persecuted. Although this persecution continued into the late 6th century, Bahrain avoided the worst of it. By the early 5th century, the Nestorian sect of Christianity was firmly established in Bahrain, and along much of the Arabian side of the Gulf. Records show that Muharraq and Manama, then known as Samahij and Tilwun respectively, were the seats of two of the five Nestorian bishoprics which existed on the Arabian side of the Gulf at the time of the coming of Islam. Muharraq also housed a Nestorian monastery. The two Bahraini bishoprics survived until at least AD 835.

There is also some evidence that during this period the Bahrain islands controlled at least part of the adjacent coast. Sassanian chronicles state that the king settled some members of a conquered tribe in Bahrain, namely in Darin. (Darin is the main town of Tarut Island, which lies north of Bahrain and is now part of Saudi Arabia.) Around this time, Bahrain Island also came to be known as 'Awal', a name which Bahrainis used for the main island until the early years of the 20th century.

The Coming of Islam

Bahrainis pride themselves on having been one of the first territories outside the Arabian mainland to embrace Islam. Around AD 640, the Prophet Mohammed sent a letter to the ruler of Bahrain (possibly a Christian Arab who served as governor on behalf of the Sassanian Persians) inviting him to adopt Islam. The ruler did so, though Christians and Muslims continued to live peacefully together in Bahrain for another two centuries. Even today Bahrain has a tiny community of indigenous Christians.

From the 9th to the 11th century Bahrain was part of the Umayyad and, later, Abbasid empires. Although Bahrain in this period had neither the wealth nor the importance it had enjoyed some 2000 years earlier, it was reasonably prosperous, well run and, once again, on the trade routes between Mesopotamia and the Indian subcontinent.

In the middle of the 12th century, the great Arab/Spanish geographer Al-Idrisi described the people of Bahrain as satisfied with their ruler, an independent king owing nominal allegiance to the Abbasid caliph in Baghdad. Al-Idrisi referred to the Bahrainis as the people of 'the two banks', a reference either to Bahrain and Muharraq islands, or an indication that Bahrain's ruler still controlled a portion of the mainland coast.

During the Middle Ages, Bahrain changed hands fairly frequently, which is hardly surprising considering its position as a trading centre, often on the geographical fringe of two or more competing empires. Also, the entire Gulf during this period was run by various petty sheikhs who were constantly at war with each other.

The Omanis were the next major power to take an interest in Bahrain. They conquered Bahrain and Muharraq islands around 1487, and built Arad fort in Muharraq. This fort was to supplement the older fortifications (the ruins known as the Islamic Fort at the

Qala'at al-Bahrain site) they had taken over on the north coast of Bahrain Island.

The Portuguese & the Persians

Around 1485, a Portuguese explorer named Duarte Barbosa became the first European to visit the islands and, noting both the number and quality of Bahrain's pearls, called the islands 'Barem'.

About 36 years later, the Portuguese navy conquered the islands as part of their procession up the Gulf from Muscat (Oman) and Hormuz. As one of the main pearling ports in the Gulf, the Bahrain islands clearly had economic value. Bahrain's ample supply of fresh water. Its position about halfway between the Strait of Hormuz and the head of the Gulf, also afforded it military value in the struggle for control of the area. In the first half of the 16th century, Bahrain was on the front line as Portugal and the Ottoman Turks battled for control of the Gulf. The second half of the century was somewhat quieter, with the Portuguese by then firmly in control.

In the end it was the Bahrainis themselves, not the Turks or the Omanis, who drove the Portuguese from the islands. In 1602, the Portuguese governor made the critical mistake of executing the brother of one of the island's richer traders, Rukn el-Din, who then led an uprising and drove the Europeans out. Rukn quickly appealed to Persia for protection. This was a shrewd political move: aside from the need for help in case the Portuguese returned to punish the Bahrainis, appealing to Persia seemed less provocative than appealing to the Turks, with whom the Portuguese were competing for influence in the Gulf. On the other hand, Bahrain became, once again, part of a Persian empire, and so it remained for the rest of the 17th century.

The Arrival of the Al-Khalifa Family

The Al-Khalifa, Bahrain's ruling family, first arrived in the archipelago in the mid-18th century. They came to Bahrain from Kuwait where they helped their distant relatives, the Al-Sabah family, establish power. The Al-Khalifa settled in Al-Zubara, on the north-western edge of the Qatar peninsula,

apparently hoping to become involved in the region's lucrative pearling trade.

In 1782 or 1783, Sheikh Ahmed al-Fatih a member of the Al-Khalifa family, drove out the Persian garrison and occupied the main islands of the Bahrain group, apparently with some help from his Al-Sabah cousins in Kuwait. Bahrain and Muharraq islands were particularly important prizes because their position off the Arabian mainland made them relatively immune to Wahhabi raids. These raids, led by the ancestors of the present Saudi royal family, were a regular feature of life in Al-Zubara from the late-18th century until the Ottoman suppression of the Wahhabis in 1818. Ahmed ruled until his death in 1796 when his two sons, Abdullah and Sulman, took over as joint rulers. Three years later, however, the Omanis returned in force to the Bahrain islands, from which the Portuguese had driven them over 275 years earlier. Sulman was forced to retreat to Al-Zubara and Abdullah went into exile on the Arabian mainland.

In 1820, the brothers managed to reconquer the islands, and a few years of relative tranquillity ensued. Shortly thereafter a treaty was signed with the British, who had been present in the region for over 200 years in the form of the ubiquitous East India Company. This treaty, in which the Bahrainis agreed to abstain from what the British defined as 'piracy' (ie, any threat to British shipping), became the model for similar treaties signed – or imposed – by the British throughout the Gulf over the next 20 years or so. Sulman died in 1825, and his son Khalifa continued to rule jointly with Abdullah until Khalifa's death in 1834.

Abdullah ruled alone for a few years. It was during this period that the British began to formalise their presence in the Gulf. India was becoming an increasingly important part of the British Empire, and Britain saw security in the Gulf as vital to its trade and supply routes to the Indian subcontinent. In 1835, the rulers of Bahrain and the other sheikhdoms of the Gulf had a peace treaty more or less dictated to them by Britain's Royal Navy. Like the earlier treaty signed with Bahrain, the purpose of this agreement was to end 'piracy' in the region. The British also pressured the sheikhs into outlawing slavery.

Despite the best efforts of the Royal Navy, however, things did not stay quiet. Around 1840, a string of events began which led to three turbulent decades in Bahrain. A few years after Khalifa's death, his son, Mohammed bin Khalifa, began to challenge Abdullah's authority. Eventually he set himself up in Muharraq as a co-ruler and rival. In 1843, he conquered Al-Zubara (in Qatar) and deposed Abdullah, who died in exile five years later. Mohammed ruled unopposed for a few years and, in 1861, signed a 'Treaty of Perpetual Peace and Friendship' with the British. This treaty was the first of the so-called 'Exclusive Agreements', under which Mohammed (and other Gulf rulers who later signed similar documents) ceded to Britain control of their foreign affairs, in exchange for protection from attack. Other agreements with the British were signed in 1881 and 1891.

Mohammed bin Khalifa was soon challenged by his cousin, Mohammed bin Abdullah (Sheikh Abdullah's son). Seeking revenge for his father's deposition, Mohammed bin Abdullah began raiding Bahrain from a base on the Arabian mainland. In the midst of this already turbulent situation a war broke out between Bahrain and Qatar, which ended in 1868 when Mohammed bin Khalifa fled to Qatar while his brother Ali proclaimed himself ruler of Bahrain.

In Qatar, Mohammed bin Khalifa built a new fleet, invaded Bahrain again and killed Ali in 1869. But Mohammed bin Khalifa made one crucial mistake: he buried the hatchet with his cousin, Mohammed bin Abdullah, and gave him a post in the reconquering force. Once they controlled Bahrain, Mohammed bin Abdullah, who apparently had not forgotten who deposed his father, promptly overthrew and imprisoned Mohammed bin Khalifa.

From their base in Būshehr (on the Persian coast), the British probably watched all this with a combination of annoyance and alarm. The topsy-turvy Bahraini politics of

1869 was the last straw. Not long after Mohammed bin Abdullah's coup, the Royal Navy sailed down from Būshehr, deported both of the Mohammeds to Bombay (present-day Mumbai, India) and installed Ali's 21-year-old son, Sheikh Isa bin Ali, as emir. The British also leaned on Isa to appoint a crown prince to remove any doubts about the succession, and Sheikh Isa's line has ruled Bahrain ever since. (The current emir of Bahrain, Sheikh Hamad bin Isa al-Khalifa, is his great-great-grandson.)

After installing Isa as emir, the British largely stayed out of local politics for the remainder of the 19th century. Their main concern was to keep the Turks, who then controlled eastern Arabia, out of the region. (This was also a concern for the sheikhs, and one of the reasons why they signed the agreements with the British in the first place.) Both Turkey and Persia continued to claim Bahrain as part of their respective empires well into the 20th century, but neither was willing to challenge the British for control of the islands.

Threats to Bahrain's sovereignty from its larger neighbours continued up until 1970. For decades Persia (as Iran was known prior to 1934) refused to recognise Bahrain's existence as anything other than a renegade province. Tehrān threatened military action several times in the 1950s and '60s, and refused entry to Iran to travellers whose passports showed evidence of travel to Bahrain. The claim was finally dropped in 1970 after Britain talked the Shah of Iran into accepting the results of a United Nations mission to the island to determine whether or not the inhabitants wanted to be part of Iran. In the wake of Iran's 1979 Islamic Revolution, one of Tehrān's senior clerics briefly revived the issue, but Iran's spiritual leader, Āyatollāh Khomeinī, disapproved and the Islamic Republic let the matter drop.

The 20th Century

Sheikh Isa bin Ali, whom the British installed in 1869, reigned until his death in 1932. Isa was notoriously conservative, opposing even modest reform or modernisation: in 1923, the British forced him to hand over the day-to-day running of the country to his son, Hamad, who ruled until 1942.

Almost immediately upon Hamad's taking power in 1923, modernisation in Bahrain began. A decade later, when the oil money started coming in, the pace quickened. Schools, hospitals and new mosques were built, much of the country received electricity and an airport was constructed to serve as a stop on Imperial Airways' London to India route.

In addition to the discovery of oil (see the boxed text opposite), the years after WWI also saw another event with long-term significance for Bahrain – the arrival, in 1926, of a new British adviser to the emir, Charles Belgrave. Described in later years by the archaeologist Geoffrey Bibby as 'tall, cool, cheroot-smoking, very, very efficient', Belgrave (who got the job, believe it or not, by answering an ad in a London newspaper) remained in Bahrain for over 30 years. He was instrumental in setting up the island's education system and supervised much of Bahrain's early infrastructural development. (Because he was so powerful, Bahraini officialdom now tends to treat Belgrave as something of a nonentity.)

Bahrain declared war on the Axis powers one day after Britain did in 1939. The Bahrain oil refinery was then one of only three in the Middle East, and its continued operation was crucial to the war effort, particularly as both Japan and Germany had been trying to gain footholds in the Gulf during the 1930s. However, the war years in Bahrain were generally quiet.

When Sheikh Hamad died in 1942, he was succeeded as emir by his son, Sulman. Sulman's 19 years on the throne saw a vast increase in the country's standard of living as oil production boomed in Saudi Arabia, Kuwait and Qatar. At that time, none of these other areas could match Bahrain's level of development, health or education. Although the country's oil output was tiny compared to its neighbours, Bahrain was well positioned to serve as the Gulf's main entrepot.

The 1950s were unsettling years throughout the Arab world. The rise of the Egyptian Pan-Arabist leader Gamal Abdel Nasser, and his fiery rhetoric and assaults on the colonial privileges enjoyed by Britain and other Western countries in the Arab world (including most areas which were at least nominally independent), galvanised people throughout the Middle East. In the years immediately after WWII, wealthy Bahrainis had begun sending their sons (not, usually, their daughters) abroad to further their education. They studied in Cairo, Beirut or, for the very rich and/or well connected, London. This new class of well-educated technocrats proved to be particularly resentful of British domination.

In 1952, reform-minded members of the country's Sunni and Shi'ite communities formed an eight-person Higher Executive Committee. They demanded Western-style trade unions, a parliament and, more to the point, the sacking of Belgrave. Their demands for a more open political system even received some tacit support from the British government (though not, presumably, from Belgrave). Belgrave stayed, but the emir agreed to some of the Committee's demands – a victory which seems to have encouraged them to ask for more.

Matters came to a head in 1956, when stones were thrown at the British Foreign Secretary, Selwyn Lloyd, while he visited Bahrain. In retaliation, several members of the Committee of National Union (the Higher Executive Committee's successor) were deported. During November of that year, several people were killed in anti-British riots in Bahrain during the Suez Crisis. The British landed troops to protect the oilfields, but at about the same time the Saudis, regarding Bahrain as too closely under Britain's thumb, cut off the supply of oil to the refinery (which even then refined significantly more Saudi oil than Bahraini oil). Not long afterwards Belgrave 'retired'. Though the emir appointed another Brit to replace him, the crisis had passed, calm prevailed and Bahrainis went back to their first love – making money.

Sheikh Sulman died in 1961, and was succeeded by his son Sheikh Isa bin Sulman al-Khalifa, who ruled until his death in March 1999. He was succeeded by his son, Sheikh Hamad bin Isa al-Khalifa.

The Discovery of Oil

Ancient texts contain the occasional reference to oil being found in natural pools, or seepages, in Bahrain. It was traditionally used to fuel lamps and to help make boats waterproof. Seepages, however, do not necessarily imply the presence of crude oil in exploitable quantities.

In 1902, a British official wrote to his superiors that he had heard stories about oil spouting from the sea bed at a point close to Bahrain's shoreline. An engineer was sent to investigate, but his report was not promising. Interest among British officials revived in 1908 after oil was found in large quantities in Persia (now Iran). Still, the Anglo-Persian Oil Company, which then dominated the Middle East's nascent oil industry, seemed more interested in litigation than exploration. They sought to guarantee that no-one else had the opportunity to prospect for oil in Bahrain, but at the same time made no attempt to look for it themselves.

The man who spurred the search for oil, not only in Bahrain but also in eastern Saudi Arabia, was Frank Holmes, a New Zealander who had recently retired from the British Army (hence the habit of referring to him as Major Holmes). Virtually every book ever written on oil and the Gulf describes Holmes as eccentric, though few make it clear what was so eccentric about him except for his firm conviction that oil was to be found underneath Arabia. After a great deal of convoluted toing and froing, Holmes' tiny Eastern & General Syndicate was granted a concession to drill for oil in Bahrain in late 1925. The only problem was that neither Holmes nor the syndicate had the money required to launch such an operation.

Holmes spent the next five years trying to round up the necessary funds. When he found a backer in Standard Oil of California (SOCAL, the precursor of today's Chevron) he was then forced to embark on another series of legal contortions. The terms of the concession agreement stipulated that it could not be assigned to any 'foreign' (meaning non-British) company. Eventually SOCAL set up a subsidiary in Canada, which was apparently British enough to get the foreign office in London to agree, and exploration went ahead. Oil in commercial quantities was found in June 1932, the first such strike on the Arab side of the Gulf. Exports began soon afterward and a refinery opened in 1936.

The discovery of oil could not have come at a better time for Bahrain, as it roughly coincided with the collapse of the world pearl market which had been the mainstay of the Bahraini economy.

Equally important was the fact that oil was discovered in Bahrain before it was discovered elsewhere in the Gulf. The Bahrainis were the first to enjoy the benefits that came from the oil revenues – notably a dramatic improvement in the quality of education and health care. This led to the island assuming a larger role in Britain's operations in the Gulf. The main British naval base in the region was moved to Bahrain in 1935. In 1946, the Political Residency, the office of the senior British official in the region, was moved from Būshehr (Iran) to Bahrain.

The island's oil reserves are quite small, and its revenues from oil sales have never approached those of Kuwait, Saudi Arabia or the United Arab Emirates on a per capita basis. Today, Bahrain produces only a token quantity of oil, and in one sense, this has been a boon. Lacking the resources for extravagance, Bahrain has proceeded into the 21st century in a reasonable, measured way. The Bahrainis were forced to think about diversifying their economy far earlier than any of the other Gulf States and this, combined with their long history as a trading nation and lengthy contact with the outside world, has proved an advantageous blend of circumstances.

Independence

After Britain announced its intention to withdraw from the Gulf by the end of 1971, Bahrain participated in attempts to form a federation with Qatar and the seven Trucial States (now known as the United Arab Emirates). As the most populous and advanced of the nine emirates, Bahrain demanded greater representation on the council which was to govern the proposed federation.

When the other rulers refused, Bahrain decided to go it alone and declared its independence on 14 August 1971 (a decision which also prompted Qatar to pull out of the federation).

A constituent assembly charged with drafting a constitution was elected at the end of 1972. The emir issued the constitution in May 1973, and another election was held later that year for a National Assembly which convened in December. But the assembly was dissolved only 20 months later when the emir decided that radical assembly members were making it impossible for the executive branch to function. The country is now ruled by emiri decree, exercised through a cabinet. In 1975, all trade unions were disbanded and strikes were outlawed.

During the 1970s and '80s, Bahrain experienced huge growth, partly from the sky-rocketing price of oil, but also because its infrastructure was well ahead of much of the rest of the Gulf. In recent years, Bahrain's status as an entrepot has declined somewhat, but its economy has also become more diversified and less dependent on oil. Bahrain has established itself as one of the region's main banking and finance centres, a business that used to be centred almost entirely in Beirut. There were a few violent pro-Iranian demonstrations in late 1979 and early 1980, but the unrest soon died out.

Despite the economic downturn felt throughout the Gulf in the late '80s, Bahrain remained both calm and prosperous. The country's main shipyard did a roaring trade during the mid-'80s, patching up tankers hit by one side or the other in the Iran-Iraq war. The opening of the King Fahd Causeway between Bahrain and Saudi Arabia in 1986 gave a boost to business and tourism.

The early '90s saw a vast improvement in Bahrain's relations with Iran, marked by the resumption of air service between Manama and Tehrān. Relations with Iraq, on the other hand, went sharply downhill – Bahrainis will not forget that Saddam Hussein ordered a Scud missile attack on their country during the Gulf War (the missile landed harmlessly in the sea). After the war Bahrain became the base for UN weapons inspectors working in Iraq, though in mid-1999 the Bahraini government asked the UN to close down its Bahrain-based operations.

In recent years the quiet world of Bahraini life has been rocked by sporadic waves of unrest. The trouble began in 1994 when the emir refused to accept a petition, reportedly signed by some 25,000 Bahrainis, calling for greater democracy. Anger at this incident boiled over into rioting in November with protests centred in the predominantly Shi'ite villages west of Manama. The main demands of the demonstrators were a restoration of the long-suspended parliament and a broader distribution of the country's wealth (unemployment in the Shi'ite community was estimated at about 30% at the time). In all, 16 people died in the unrest, and hundreds were jailed.

There was more unrest in 1995, and in February 1996 the upmarket Diplomat and Meridien hotel lobbies were bombed. Throughout spring and into early summer, several other bombs either exploded, or were discovered and diffused, around the country. The government, through the state-controlled media, accused Iran of inciting the violence.

In 1997, unemployed Bahraini youths staged a number of arson attacks to protest the number of jobs occupied by Asian workers, alleged discrimination against the majority Shi'ite (the ruling Al-Khalifa family is Sunni), and the general lack of democratic reform. The Bahraini government again accused Iran of training and funding the troublemakers and launched a severe crackdown on dissidents. Since then the country has quietened down considerably, and violence is now rare.

GEOGRAPHY

Bahrain is a low-lying archipelago of 33 islands, including the disputed Hawar Islands (see the 'Hawar Islands' boxed text in the Getting Around chapter for further information).

Bahrain Island is the largest at about 50km long and 16km wide. Other than Muharraq Island and Sitra Island, which have been largely given over to industry, most other islands are little more than specks of sand or rocks, some of which disappear at high tide. Several islands have been linked to Bahrain or Muharraq by roads and causeways in such a way that they are now extensions of the two main islands rather than separate entities.

The total area of Bahrain Island is 590 sq km. Jebel ad-Dukhan, the highest point in the country at 134m above sea level, is in the centre of Bahrain Island. The country's population is heavily concentrated in the northern third of Bahrain Island, and on the southern edge of Muharraq Island.

The centre of Bahrain Island is mostly limestone, which supports little or no vegetation (only about one-third of the island is fertile), so animal and plant life is limited in quantity and variety.

CLIMATE

Bahrain can get extremely hot and humid from May to September, with temperatures averaging 36°C during the day; there are normally about 12 days per year over 40°C. November to March tends to be quite pleasant with warm days and cool (though not really cold) nights, and with a minimum temperature of 14°C and maximum of 24°C.

The average temperature and humidity in winter (December to February) is 18°C and 77%; and in summer (June to August), 35°C and 59%.

In summer, dust storms and hot winds may make matters worse. Rain normally falls between December and late April, but is unlikely to bother visitors: Bahrain averages only about 70mm of rain a year.

ECOLOGY & ENVIRONMENT

The main threats to the Bahraini environment are obvious and sadly common among other Gulf countries: unrestrained development; perpetual land reclamation; rampant industrialisation; an inordinate number of cars (about 200 per sq km); and pollution of the Gulf from oil leakages.

Some of the endangered species in Bahrain include rheem gazelle, terrapin,

sooty falcon, Arabian oryx and dugong. Also under threat are the mangroves, the destruction of which can harm the fragile marine ecosystem, kill birds and exacerbate erosion. Nearly 500,000 sq metres of mangroves around Tubli Bay have been set aside by the government as a protected area.

The Bahraini government is slowly beginning to understand the importance of conservation. For example, it has insisted that the new golf course at Riffa (see Spectator Sports in the Facts for the Visitor section later in this chapter) use recycled water for irrigation. The government has also established a Wildlife Protection Day (4 February) to raise awareness among the populace, especially children, about the importance of the environment. Two government agencies which are responsible for the environment are the Environmental Protection Committee (☎ 293 693) and the National Committee for Wildlife Protection (☎ 714 828), both under the auspices of the Sub-Department of Environmental Affairs. One private agency involved in environmental issues is the Bahrain Natural History Society (☎ 685 882).

GOVERNMENT & POLITICS

Bahrain is an absolute monarchy, and the only Gulf country with a strict rule of primogeniture, where power is always inherited by the eldest son. The emir is Sheikh Hamad bin Isa al-Khalifa, who assumed power on the death of his father, the long-ruling Sheikh Isa bin Sulman al-Khalifa, in March 1999. The emir's uncle, Sheikh Khalifa bin Sulman al-Khalifa, has served as prime minister for many years. The emir appoints and dismisses members of the cabinet, though turnover at the upper echelons of government is relatively rare.

Many of the potential laws, and the day-to-day running of the government, are discussed in consultation with the 40 members of the Shura council, which meets once a week. Members of the council are appointed by the emir for a period of four years. They reflect a reasonable cross section of society and have a vast range of skills and experience, but no women are represented.

ECONOMY
Oil

Pearling was the primary industry (see boxed text 'Pearls & Pearling') in Bahrain until oil was discovered in 1932. Since then the oil industry and its offshoots were, until recent times, the linchpin of Bahrain's economy.

In 1998, Bahrain produced only about 37,200 barrels of oil per day – in contrast, the UAE pumps over two million barrels a day. However, it also refines a large quantity of oil from Saudi Arabia which arrives via an undersea pipeline. Income from oil production and refining was about BD393 million (over US$1 billion) in 1998, accounting for about 60% of government revenue. This figure, though, has declined in the past few years, and now only represents

Pearls & Pearling

A report filed in 1900 by a British official in Bahrain stated that half of the island's male population was employed in the pearling industry. This is hardly surprising: pearling had been a part of the local economy since the 3rd millennium BC, and by the early 1800s, when most of the trade routes that had straddled the Gulf were ancient history, pearls and dates were virtually the only things the region had to offer the rest of the world.

Today, pearling is viewed rather nostalgically, but the fact is that diving for pearls was a truly terrible way to make a living. The pearl trade made a few 19th-century Arab families spectacularly rich, but for just about everyone else involved it was physically and economically brutal. It probably survived as long as it did largely by default – there simply was no other way for most people in the Gulf to earn a living.

The pearling season began each year in late May when the boats would leave Bahrain and the other settlements around the Gulf for the offshore pearl banks. They remained constantly at sea until mid-October. Supplies were ferried out by dhow.

The workers were divided into divers and pullers. A diver's equipment often consisted only of a nose-clip and a bag. More fortunate divers might also have some sort of thin cotton garment to provide (limited) protection against jellyfish. Rocks were tied to the divers' feet as weights. They would leap into the water with a rope tied around their waists and usually stayed under for about a minute at depths of up to 15m. A tug on the rope meant it was time for the pullers to return the diver to the surface.

Neither the divers nor the pullers were paid wages. Instead, they would receive shares of the total profits for the season: a puller's share was half to two-thirds of a diver's. Boat owners would advance money to their workers at the beginning of the season. The divers were often unable to pay back these loans, got further into debt with each year and, as a result, were often bound to a particular boat owner for life. If a diver died his sons were obliged to work off his debts. It was not unusual to see quite elderly men still working as divers. British attempts in the 1920s to regulate and improve the lot of the divers were resisted by the divers themselves; riots and strikes became a regular feature of the pearling seasons in the late '20s and early '30s.

In addition to its own long-established pearl trade, Bahrain by the 19th century was also serving as the main trans-shipment point for almost all the pearls produced in the Gulf. From Bahrain, pearls were shipped to Bombay (now Mumbai) in India where they were sorted, polished and drilled. Most were then exported to Europe.

Around 1930, the Japanese invented a method of culturing pearls and this, combined with the Great Depression, caused the bottom to fall out of the international pearl market. Bahrain has never quite forgiven the Japanese, and Bahrain still bans the importation of cultured pearls.

The pearl merchants could all instantly tell the difference between natural and cultured pearls but most other people could not, and didn't care anyway. Today, pearls are more common – and far less valuable – than they were 75 years ago.

about 13% of the Bahrain's gross domestic product (GDP). Because of its relatively limited oil reserves, Bahrain has developed a somewhat more diversified economy than many other Gulf countries.

Other Industries

When Lebanon imploded in the late 1970s, the Bahraini government made a conscious effort to lure the region's bankers (until then mostly based in Beirut) to Manama, and met with a great deal of success. In the late 1980s, Bahrain's large financial services sector branched out into offshore banking.

Economically, the Gulf War proved to be a mixed blessing. Manama's hotels and bars were filled for many months, first by soldiers and sailors on leave and journalists at work, and later by a string of entrepreneurs hoping to cash in on the post-war reconstruction work in Kuwait. But in the longer term, the war damaged the country's financial services industry.

Besides oil, banking and tourism, Bahrain's other important industries include a large aluminium smelter, fishing, natural gas production and a paper mill. The Bahraini government continues to seek foreign investment by not collecting any income tax, allowing 100% foreign ownership and not imposing any controls on the movement of capital. The main disincentives for foreign investment, however, are the lack of available fresh water, which could run out by about 2010, according to Bahraini government studies (and can't be supplemented by the current number of desalination plants), and the civil unrest which haunted the country in the mid-1990s.

Tourism

Tourism is an obvious alternative to oil as a method of earning vital foreign exchange. The 1980s saw the beginning of a calculated drive to attract tourists to the country, and now over two million foreigners visit Bahrain every year. The government hopes to broaden Bahrain's tourist base beyond the long-standing flow of people coming down from Kuwait or across from Saudi Arabia on weekends. Tourism now constitutes 9.2% of Bahrain's GDP and employs about 17% of the workforce.

POPULATION & PEOPLE

At the last count (July 1997), Bahrain had a population of 620,378, with a density of about 877 per sq km. About 50% of the population is under 25 years of age and the annual growth rate is a comparatively high 3.8%. Bahrainis are Arabs, though many are at least partially of Persian ancestry.

Nearly 40% of Bahrain's residents are labelled 'non-Bahraini' or 'expatriate', and foreigners make up over 60% of the workforce. Manama is one of the Gulf's most cosmopolitan cities with more Western, Indian, Pakistani and Filipino businesspeople and shop owners than Bahrainis.

EDUCATION

Bahrain provides completely free education for all of its citizens. School is compulsory from age six to 15. Literacy is an impressive 84%, and education is the third largest expenditure, after security and defence, for the Bahraini government.

Many children of wealthier Bahrainis still travel abroad to further their primary and tertiary education, particularly to the UK and USA. There are two universities: Bahrain University, with about 9000 students, and the far smaller Arabian Gulf University with some 700 students.

ARTS
Pottery & Handicrafts

Pottery and ceramics are made in the village of A'ali, and can be bought in the various handicraft centres around the country, such as the Craft Centre in Manama.

Traditional weaving of carpets, wall hangings and cushions is still carried out in the villages of Ad-Diraz and Bani Jamrah, but the quality is not always high and materials are often imported. Bahraini weaving usually features unusual styles and brightly dyed wool.

Other traditional crafts include dhow building on Muharraq Island; gold and silver jewellery in the Manama *souq* (market), although a lot of the work is now done abroad, particularly in the Indian subcontinent; hand-woven cloth from Bani Jamrah; and textiles from Al-Jasra. Refer to the Around Muharraq Island and Around Bahrain Island sections for further information. The Bahrain National Museum (see the Manama section later in this chapter) also has handicrafts on display.

Palm Leaves & Paper
Before the oil – and subsequent construction – boom, houses were often made from palm leaves (palm trees were also used in the construction of dhows). Today, villagers in Karbabad weave baskets with palm leaves from the plethora of date palms surrounding the village. The Craft Centre in Manama also has an innovative workshop where women make paper products from palm leaves.

Embroidery
The art of traditional embroidery or *tatrees* has been passed from one generation of Bahraini women to another. Particularly popular are *al-nagde*, intricately embroidered ceremonial gowns decorated with gold and silver threads, worn by women. Some tiny villages on Muharraq Island are renowned by Bahrainis for tatrees, but only recently has the tradition been revived under the auspices of the Craft Centre in Manama.

Modern Art
Modern art exhibitions are often held in the Bahrain National Museum and various upmarket hotels. The magazines, booklets and English-language daily newspapers mentioned under Newspapers & Magazines in the Facts for the Visitor section later in this chapter list upcoming exhibitions. Exhibitions of Bahraini art are often shown abroad, notably in Europe.

Private galleries in Bahrain include the Rashid al-Oraifi Museum in Muharraq, the Arts Centre in Manama, and the Muharraqi Gallery in A'ali, which features the surreal works of Abdullah al-Muharraqi. There is also a selection of modern art in the Art Gallery inside the Bahrain National Museum.

SOCIETY & CONDUCT
As flashy and modern as central Manama seems, the basic rhythms of life in the island's many villages, and in parts of Manama itself, remain remarkably conservative. Use your common sense: for women, no miniskirts, short shorts, bikini tops etc. Men should not walk around bare-chested or in overly tight clothing. Women should stick to one-piece bathing suits at the beach, though bikinis are OK at swimming pools at upmarket hotels. Conservative dress is particularly in order in rural areas.

Most mosques are open to visitors, but in practice only the Al-Fatih, Suq al-Khamis and Friday mosques are visited by non-Muslims with any regularity. Visitors should restrict their mosque-viewing to these three.

RELIGION
Islam is the state religion. About 85% of Bahrainis are Muslims, of which about 70% are Shi'ite. The Sunni minority includes the royal family and most of the leading merchant families.

Facts for the Visitor

SUGGESTED ITINERARIES
One Day
This gives you just enough time to rush around the Bahrain National Museum and Beit al-Quran, go shopping at the Craft Centre and walk around the souq in Manama.

Two Days
Linger longer at the places mentioned above, plus take a day trip to places close to Manama, such as Karbabad village for handicrafts, the ruins at Qala'at al-Bahrain and Barbar Temple, the fascinating burial mounds at A'ali, the majestic Riffa Fort and the Suq al-Khamis Mosque.

One Week
In addition to the places mentioned above: take further day trips to go shopping for handicrafts at Al-Jasra, Bani Jamrah and A'ali; admire a sunset (or two) from Al-Budayyi'; drive across the King Fahd Cause-

way to the Saudi border and enjoy the superb views from the top of the tower; explore the Al-Areen Wildlife Park, hang around some beaches or a hotel swimming pool; enjoy some racing, diving or golf; walk around Muharraq and visit the weekly bazaar at the Qala'at Arad fort and take a boat trip to Dar Island.

PLANNING
When to Go
The best time to visit is between November and March, when it's not too hot. You may also want to stay away during Ramadan and other Muslim festivals (see Public Holidays & Special Events in the Regional Facts for the Visitor chapter earlier in this book). At these times Bahrain is swamped with visitors from Saudi Arabia and Kuwait, and hotel rooms become difficult to find and are overpriced.

Maps
If you're staying in Manama, and exploring Bahrain by public transport or on an organised tour, the maps in this guidebook will be sufficient. If you're driving around you should pick up a detailed map – but be careful, because most maps of Bahrain and Manama are out of date.

The best is the 3rd edition of *Bahrain – with City Map of Al Manama*, published by Geo Projects (BD3). Ignore the obsolete earlier editions. *Bahrain Map* (BD1), published by the Ministry of Information, is the most useful if you're driving a car. *Bahrain*, available free from one or more of the tourist offices, is colourful, and surprisingly detailed. Most of these maps are available at the souvenir shop at Bab al-Bahrain in Manama.

TOURIST OFFICES
Local Tourist Offices
The 'official' tourist office is in the centre at Bab al-Bahrain. The Tourist Department (☎ 231 375) (upstairs) is not interested in providing general information to tourists, though you can often find some useful brochures in the souvenir shop downstairs. The Directorate of Tourism & Archaeology (☎ 211 199, fax 210 969) is directed mainly

at businesspeople though staff claim to want to help tourists. The best is the tourist information desk at Bahrain International Airport, but it isn't always staffed. Get more information at the government-run Web site: www.bahrain.tourism.com.

Businesspeople should contact Bahrain Promotions & Marketing Board (☎ 533 886, fax 531 117, ✆ bahrain7@batelco.com.bh).

Tourist Offices Abroad
Bahrain does not have any tourist offices abroad, and Bahraini embassies and consulates are not generally interested in becoming quasi-tourist offices. Bahrain is represented at many international travel fairs, but is more concerned with promoting trade and encouraging business in Bahrain. The overseas offices of Gulf Air may have some information, but don't count on it. The best sources of tourist information are the Internet sites mentioned under Internet Resources later in this section.

VISAS & DOCUMENTS
Visas
Most visitors to Bahrain can obtain visas on the King Fahd Causeway or on arrival at Bahrain International Airport. Visas are generally valid for up to two weeks (which is enough for most visitors), but extensions are possible. A two-week visa on arrival costs BD5 for UK citizens, Australians, New Zealanders, Europeans and Canadians. US citizens are charged BD10/15 for a visa for three days/one week. The fee must be paid in Bahraini dinars. There are foreign exchange offices next to the immigration counter at the airport, and at the border post on the causeway to Saudi Arabia.

Americans and Canadians can obtain a five-year, multiple-entry visa at a Bahraini embassy/consulate for about US$40. Most other nationalities can get an (extendable) visa from a Bahraini embassy/consulate for about US$25/40 for three/seven days, but visas on arrival in Bahrain are often cheaper, and certainly easier to get. If you're transiting Bahrain, and travelling on to Saudi Arabia by land (and can prove it), the visa fee on arrival for all nationalities is BD2.

Visa Extensions Foreigners overstaying their visas are fined about BD30 per week. Visa extensions are available at the chaotic General Directorate of Immigration & Passports (☎ 535 111) in Manama. You must first find a sponsor, which can be any Bahraini resident – a friend, or your hotel will oblige. Then fill out a detailed form, and provide the directorate with your passport and one passport-size photo. Extensions cost BD15 for one week, and BD25 for one week to one month, and will take up to one week to process.

To avoid this hassle, your hotel (but only if you're staying at a mid-range or top-end place) can sponsor your visa extension, and deal with the chaos at the directorate, for a negotiable fee of about BD5 (plus extension fee). This is definitely worth considering, but make sure that the hotel doesn't inflate the total cost of the extension – insist that it obtain a receipt from the directorate for the extension fee, or ring the directorate to find out what it charges.

Work Visas Many foreign workers come to Bahrain from the Indian subcontinent and North Africa. Regulations regarding foreigners coming to work in Bahrain are still extremely strict. All foreign workers must obtain a work permit (BD100), valid for two years, from the Ministry of Labour & Social Affairs. Permits can be renewed every two years for BD150. But once you're accepted by the ministry as a foreign worker, you cannot change employers without their approval. Your employer must organise all the necessary paperwork before you arrive.

Other Documents

No special documents are needed to enter or travel in Bahrain. Health certificates are not required, unless you're coming from an area of endemic yellow fever, cholera etc. If you plan to rent a car, an International Driving Permit might be helpful. (See Car & Motorcycle in the Getting Around section later in this chapter for more details.) An International Student Card is next to worthless.

EMBASSIES & CONSULATES
Bahraini Embassies & Consulates

Bahraini embassies/consulates overseas are of little use to the traveller. They usually only handle residence and work visas, which are only issued after approval has been received from Manama, and most nationalities receive tourist visas on arrival anyway.

Addresses of the more important Bahraini embassies and consulates around the world are listed below. (There is no Bahrain embassy in Qatar.)

Canada
  Consulate: (☎ 450-931 7444, fax 931 5988) Rene, Levesque West Montreal, Quebec H3H IR4
France
  Embassy: (☎ 01 47 23 48 68, fax 01 47 20 55 75) Bis, Place Des Stats UNIS 75116 Paris
Germany
  Embassy: (☎ 228-957 6100, fax 957 6190) Plittersdorfet Str 91 53173 Bonn
Kuwait
  Embassy: (☎ 531 8530) Surra District, Street 1, Block 1, Building 24, Kuwait City
Oman
  Embassy: (☎ 605074 or 605133, fax 605072) Al-Kharjiyah St, just off Way 3015, Shatti al-Qurm
UAE
  Embassy: (☎ 02-312 200, fax 311 202) Al-Najda St, behind Abu Dhabi Islamic Bank
UK
  Embassy: (☎ 020-7370 5132, fax 7370 7773) 98 Gloucester Rd, London SW74 AU
USA
  Embassy: (☎ 202-342 0741, fax 362 2192) 3502 International Drive, NW Washington DC 20008

Embassies & Consulates in Bahrain

The nearest embassies representing Australia, Canada and Ireland are in Riyadh, Saudi Arabia. Most of the embassies in Bahrain are in the 'diplomatic area' in Manama, between King Faisal Hwy and Sheikh Hamad Causeway. Opening hours are from around 8 or 8.30 am to between noon and 2 pm. The Saudi embassy is only open from 9 to 11 am. All embassies and consulates are closed on Thursday and Friday.

France
Embassy: (☎ 291 734, fax 293 655) Al-Fatih Hwy
Germany
Embassy: (☎ 530 210, fax 536 282) Al-Hassaa Bldg, Sheikh Hamad Causeway
Kuwait
Embassy: (☎ 534 040, fax 536 475) King Faisal Hwy
Netherlands (handles all Benelux countries)
Consulate: (☎ 713 162, fax 212 295) ABN Bldg
Oman
Embassy: (☎ 293 663, fax 293 540) Al-Fatih Hwy
Saudi Arabia
Embassy: (☎ 537 722, fax 533 261) King Faisal Hwy
UAE
Embassy: (☎ 723 737, fax 727 343) Juffair
UK
Embassy: (☎ 534 404, fax 536 109) Government Ave
USA
Embassy: (☎ 273 300, fax 272 594) Just off Sheikh Isa bin Sulman Hwy, Al-Zinj

CUSTOMS

Non-Muslims are allowed to import 1L of wine or spirits, or six cans of beer; 200 cigarettes or 50 cigars; 250g of loose tobacco; and eight ounces (227 mL) of perfume.

Visitors must fill out a Disembarkation Card on arrival, which you should keep and return to immigration authorities on departure. You may be asked if you're carrying a video camera and, if so, this fact may be recorded in your passport to guarantee that you take it out again. Beyond that, the items on the forbidden list include pornography, guns and ammunition, and cultured pearls.

Customs procedures at the Bahrain International Airport can be intense, but foreigners are often waved through. Customs and immigration procedures both sides of the Bahrain–Saudi Arabia border are fairly quick and painless.

MONEY
Currency

The Bahraini dinar (BD) is divided into 1000 fils. Notes come in denominations of BD½, 1, 5, 10 and 20. Coins are 5, 10, 25, 50 and 100 fils. The Bahraini dinar is a convertible currency and there are no restrictions on its import or export. Saudi riyals (SR) are used almost interchangeably with Bahraini dinars for small transactions at a standard rate of BD1 = SR10, so don't be surprised if you get a few SR1 notes as change.

Exchange Rates

The Bahraini dinar is pegged to the US dollar at the official rate of US$1 = BD0.377, and rarely fluctuates. The other exchange rates are:

country	unit		dinar
Australia	A$1	=	BD0.241
Canada	C$1	=	BD0.253
euro	€1	=	BD0.431
France	10FF	=	BD0.670
Germany	DM1	=	BD0.221
Japan	¥100	=	BD0.333
New Zealand	NZ$1	=	BD0.208
UK	UK£1	=	BD0.627
USA	US$1	=	BD0.377

Exchanging Money

The exchange rate offered by banks is generally slightly less than that offered by moneychangers. Hotels, particularly the top-end places, generally offer much poorer rates and you should avoid them if possible.

Banking hours are Saturday to Wednesday from 7.30 am to midday, and most banks close at 11 am on Thursday. Many moneychangers keep longer hours and usually reopen later in the afternoon. Changing money on a Friday will be difficult anywhere, except at a big hotel.

Most banks, moneychangers and hotels do not charge a commission, but remember to check first. If carrying US dollars in cash, you'll find it easier to change the new variety of US$20, US$50 and US$100 notes. Currencies from Qatar, Saudi Arabia and the UAE are easy to buy and sell at banks and moneychangers.

Credit Cards It's also very easy to obtain money from automated teller machines (ATMs) located in most residential areas around Bahrain. Visa is the most useful for ATMs around Bahrain. Most branches of the British Bank of the Middle East have an ATM accepting Visa and MasterCard (as long as the clearing system used by the bank matches the one used by your card – refer to ATMs under Money in the Regional Facts for the Visitor chapter earlier in this book for more information). The Bank of Bahrain & Kuwait (BBK) accepts Visa, MasterCard and American Express. Refer to Money in the Manama section later in this chapter for more information about banks and ATMs in the capital.

The American Express office (☎ 228 822, fax 224 040) is on the 2nd floor of the ABN building in central Manama. It will hold mail for clients, but does not change AmEx travellers cheques or give cash advances on AmEx cards (but the BBK bank does).

Costs

If you stay in a budget hotel, walk a lot, use public transport, don't drink alcohol and eat in the cheapest restaurants, it's possible to get by on BD10/8 per person per day travelling as a single/double. However, BD12/10 is more realistic for a budget hotel, an occasional splurge on a good meal, short trips in taxis once or twice a day and entrance fees to tourist sites.

Tipping & Bargaining

A service charge is added to some bills in Bahrain, but it generally goes to the shop, not the waiter. In a restaurant, an appropriate tip for good service is about 10%. While tips are not expected they will be much appreciated.

Almost all prices in Bahrain are negotiable up to a point. You might be able to talk the price of souvenirs for sale in the souq down by 10% or 20%, but Bahrainis, and Indian/Pakistani shop owners, are hard bargainers. The bargaining range on items like electronic goods varies a lot depending on the market at the time, from almost nothing to about 15%. Hotel rates are almost always negotiable, but prices for meals, food, organised tours and all transport (except unmetered taxis) are not.

POST & COMMUNICATIONS
Postal Rates

Sending a postcard costs 155 fils to the UK and Europe, and 205 fils to the USA, Canada, Australia and New Zealand. Letters per 10g cost 205 fils to the UK and Europe, and 255 fils to the USA, Canada, Australia and New Zealand. Parcels cost a standard minimum to all of these countries – BD3 for the first 500g then BD1 to UK and Europe, and BD1.500 to the USA, Canada, Australia and New Zealand for each additional 500g.

Sending Mail

Mail to and from Europe and North America takes about a week; allow 10 days to/from Australia. The General Post Office (GPO) is near Bab al-Bahrain in Manama, and there are smaller post offices in all major residential areas, as well as in the Central Market in Manama and at the airport. Most major international express mail and package companies have offices in Manama.

Receiving Mail

The GPO does have poste restante facilities. Address your letters to: Your Name, c/o Poste Restante, Manama Post Office (Counter Section), Government Ave, Manama, Bahrain.

Telephone

The excellent telecommunications system is run by the government monopoly, Bahrain Telecommunications Company (Batelco). It has headquarters in Manama, offices in major residential centres around the country, and a branch at the airport. Virtually every country in the world can be dialled directly, and without problems. The country code for Bahrain is 973, followed by the local number; there are no area or city codes within Bahrain.

International calls from Bahrain cost BD0.510 per minute to most Western countries, eg, the UK, Europe, Australia, New Zealand and North America. Rates are reduced to BD0.390 from 7 pm to 7 am every day, and all day Friday and public holidays.

Useful Phone Numbers Several help lines have English-speaking operators:

Local directory assistance	☎ 181
International directory assistance	☎ 191
International calls by an operator	☎ 151
Special inquiries number	☎ 100

Bahrain is linked to over 100 countries through the Home Country Direct Dial. Refer to the front of the English-language Bahrain telephone book for details.

Local calls anywhere within Bahrain cost 100 fils for six minutes. The blue payphones take coins: insert a minimum of one 100 fils coin, and a maximum of nine. The red payphones take phonecards, widely available around Bahrain, in denominations of BD1, 2, 3.500, 6.500 and 15. International calls can be made at most payphones, and some specially marked booths also accept Visa and MasterCard for international calls.

Fax
Fax services are available at most mid-range and top-end hotels, and at the Batelco building in Manama. The cost is normally based on the time it takes to send the fax, and is about the same as a telephone call.

Email & Internet Access
The only Internet Service Provider is Batelco. There is an Internet Centre in Manama – refer to the Manama section later in this chapter for details.

INTERNET RESOURCES
If you have the following Web sites are worth checking out:

Arab Net Very useful, with good links.
  www.arab.net/bahrain
Bahrain Promotions & Marketing Board
  Mainly for business.
  www.bpmb.com
Gulf Daily News Local current affairs.
  www.gulf-daily-news.com

BOOKS
Guidebooks
The best all-round guide to the country's architecture, archaeology and curiosities is *Bahrain: A Heritage Explored* by Angela Clark. Her driving instructions to the archaeological sites around Bahrain are sometimes a bit out of date, but one can usually manage to follow them.

Anyone living and working in Bahrain should pick up one of these three detailed, colourful and up-to-date guidebooks: *Bahrain – A MEED Practical Guide* (BD10); *Bahrain Island Heritage* by Shirley Kay (BD8); or *Resident in Bahrain* (BD6.500), by Parween Abdul Rahman & Charles Walsham, which has a particularly good history section, and is ideal for anyone doing business in Bahrain.

History & Archaeology
Possibly the best book on Bahrain is *Looking for Dilmun* by Geoffrey Bibby, an Anglo-Danish archaeologist who supervised the early professional archaeological work in Bahrain. This is essentially an account of Bibby's digs in Bahrain and the slow discovery and reconstruction of the history of the ancient Dilmun civilisation, but it also provides a fascinating picture of life in Bahrain and the rest of the Gulf in the 1950s and 1960s.

Archaeology buffs might also want to pick up *Bahrain Through the Ages: The Archaeology* by Sheikha Haya Ali al-Khalifa & Michael Rice. Rice also collaborated with Sheikh Abdullah bin Khalid al-Khalifa on the comprehensive, but bulky, *Bahrain Through the Ages: The History*. Both are available in Bahrain, but are heavy and expensive: about BD22.

NEWSPAPERS & MAGAZINES
Two English-language newspapers are printed every day, except Friday, in Manama. They both have good coverage of local and international news and sports, and cost 200 fils. *Gulf Daily News* is a newsy tabloid, with a detailed classifieds section and a useful *What's On* column. The *Bahrain Tribune* is a less interesting broadsheet. English dailies from elsewhere in the Gulf, such as the *Kuwait Times* and *Khaleej Times* (from Dubai), are also widely available on the day of publication.

Local Arabic-language newspapers include *Al-Ayam* and *Akhbar al-Khaleej*.

International magazines, such as *Time* (BD1.400), and major newspapers from the USA and UK (about BD1), are available in some bookshops and the lobbies of upmarket hotels one or two days after publication.

All visitors should buy the monthly *Bahrain This Month* (BD1), a treasure of entertainment ideas and other useful information. If you plan to stay a while, also pick up the *Visitor's Complete Guide to Bahrain* (BD1.500), published by the Ministry of Cabinet Affairs & Information. It's updated annually and is very comprehensive, colourful and helpful. Also useful is the pocket-sized (and free) bimonthly *What's On in Bahrain*, available at the souvenir shop at Bab al-Bahrain, or possibly from your hotel. *Bahrain Gateway*, available free at Bahrain International Airport, has a few interesting articles and some helpful information, but is mostly full of ads for duty-free perfumes.

RADIO & TV

Radio Bahrain broadcasts in English 24 hours a day on several FM and MW frequencies. The main station is 96.5FM, and country music is on Studio 1 (91.4FM), rock music on 106.2FM and jazz and classical music on 101.4FM. FM radio stations broadcasting for US forces based in the Gulf are also easy to pick up. BBC World Service, Voice of America and other European short-wave services are easy to find.

Bahrain Television broadcasts in English on Channel 55 from late afternoon. Bahrain Television's Arabic broadcasts are on Channel 4. Other stations available over the airwaves include Channel 44, from Egypt, in Arabic; Channel 46, the Middle East Broadcasting Channel relayed from London, in Arabic; and the BBC World Service in English on Channel 57. Most satellite programs, such as CNN and MTV, are available in top-end hotels. You can also usually pick up several other regional broadcasts, notably Channel 33 from Dubai in the UAE, and the English and Arabic-language channels from both Saudi Arabia and Qatar.

All local radio and television programs are listed in the two English-language daily newspapers, and in *Bahrain This Month* magazine.

PHOTOGRAPHY & VIDEO

Popular brands of print and slide film, and video cassettes, are widely available. A roll of 24/36 colour print film costs about BD1/1.200. Colour prints can be developed often in less than 30 minutes; the standard cost is 500 fils for developing, plus 100 fils per print. A roll of 36 exposure slide film costs BD3.500 including processing (without mounting). Developing slides is more expensive (BD4 for a roll of 36), and takes about two days. Many photo shops around central Manama also offer passport photos for about BD2 (for four).

LAUNDRY

If you don't feel like doing your washing in the hotel room, ask your hotel about its laundry service, or go to one of the numerous tiny Indian/Pakistani-run laundries around central Manama. They charge a very reasonable 200 fils or so for a shirt, skirt or trousers.

TOILETS

Most toilets in mid-range and top-end hotels are the European sit-down variety. Public toilets are available at most tourist attractions, but vary in standard and cleanliness, and are often the hole-in-the-ground type. Toilet paper is usually available in mid-range and top-end hotels, and can be bought at most grocery shops and supermarkets.

HEALTH

Bahrain has a highly developed health-care system and while treatment is not free, it is, by Western standards, moderately priced. The quality of medical care in Bahrain is very high and there is normally no need to evacuate a patient abroad for anything other than serious, specialised procedures. If you're staying in a medium-sized or larger hotel there will almost certainly be a doctor on call to deal with minor ailments. Otherwise – and for more serious care – contact your embassy, which may refer you to its own doctor or provide you with a list of doctors who speak English. (Almost every doctor in Bahrain speaks good English anyway.)

Hygiene standards for food preparation are quite high except in a few of the darker corners of the souq. The tap water in Bahrain is not really suitable for drinking; it won't kill you, but you won't feel so great after drinking it, either. Bottles of mineral water and cans of soft drinks are widely available.

There are plenty of well-stocked pharmacists (chemists) in Manama and major residential areas. The two English-language daily newspapers list the stores which are open 24 hours.

Refer to the Health section in the Regional Facts for the Visitor chapter earlier in this book for more general information; and to the Manama section later in this chapter for a list of hospitals in and near the capital.

TRAVEL WITH CHILDREN

Bahrain is a reasonably modern country with a wide range of activities that children will enjoy. These activities are created for the residents of Bahrain, however, and are often only accessible by private car – though tourists are always welcome. Most upmarket hotels cater well for children. The best source of information about sports, activities, events and clubs for children is the 'Kids Options' column in the *Bahrain This Month* magazine.

One of the more accessible parks is Manama's **Water Garden** (also known as **Qasari Garden**), which boasts some welcome greenery, and has paddle boats for rent. **Andalus Garden** in Manama is dry and dreary; **Al-Sulmaniya Garden,** nearby, is slightly better. The best in the country is **Adhari Park**, but it's less accessible – see the separate heading in the Around Bahrain Island section later in this chapter for details.

The most pleasurable spots to take the kids are probably the two corniches in Manama. Along King Faisal Corniche you'll find the small, and fairly tacky, **Kids Kingdom** amusement park, with a few rides. Along the nicer Marina Corniche is the **Funland Centre** (☎ 292 313) with ten-pin bowling and ice skating; **Dolphin Park,**

which is nothing special and costs BD2/4 for children/adults; and **horse and camel rides** on a small piece of ground between the Dolphin Park and Al-Fatih Mosque. Another good place is the **Qala'at Arad** in Muharraq, where there are children's rides, and music, on Thursday and/or Friday afternoons – see the separate heading in the Around Muharraq Island later in this chapter for details.

More modern fun includes **video games** at the Arcadia video arcade in the GOSI Shopping Complex in Manama and at the Seef Mall, just outside the city. Recent Western films can be seen at the capital's **cinemas** (see Entertainment in the Manama section).

If you have access to a car, there are other great places to go on Bahrain Island. **Bahrain Rally Town** (☎ 612 992) has minigolf, go-karts and fast-food outlets. It's open daily from 10 am to 10 pm, and is located on Sheikh Isa bin Sulman Hwy. Entrance prices vary, and are cheaper from 9 am to 3 pm on weekdays (ie, Saturday to Wednesday). **Kid's World** (☎ 611 614), on Janabiya Hwy, has all sorts of loud but popular games.

Fun & Games in Bahrain

Although many Bahraini children enjoy going to video arcades and amusement parks these days, many still like playing traditional games. Girls like to play *al-shaqhah* by lining up and jumping over the hands or feet of their friends; *al-kerdiyah*, which is story telling based around rag dolls, made by the children from bits and pieces of available fabric; and *al-khabash*, where the girls try to guess where others have buried some beads, which they can keep if they find them.

Boys like to play *al-lomsabaq*, ie, racing tiny hand-made boats created from bits of rubbish; and more commonly known games such as *al-lityal* (marbles) and *al-bilbool*, involving a traditional spinning top. Bahraini boys and girls always enjoy a game of hide and seek, or *al-khaishaisheh*.

DANGERS & ANNOYANCES

Bahrain is a very safe place. Violent crime is quite rare, and visitors can walk around the centre of Manama late at night without fear. Despite the number of cars, traffic is not too bad, though drivers love to speed when they get a chance.

Several bombings and arson attacks in 1996 and 1997 led to heightened security throughout the country, and a severe government crackdown on dissent. Antigovernment violence, particularly in Bani Jamrah, Suq al-Khamis and other villages south-west of Manama, remains an occasional problem, but there is no evidence that foreigners were, or will be, targeted. The safest course is to contact your country's foreign ministry, or access the Web sites listed under Internet Resources earlier in this section, for an update on the situation before travelling.

LEGAL MATTERS

If you get arrested, contact your embassy immediately, but you will receive little or no sympathy if you have blatantly broken an obvious law, such as drug smuggling. The police in Bahrain are making a concerted effort to reduce the alarming number of deaths from car accidents, and fines are heavy for speeding, not wearing seat belts and, especially, drunk driving. For the latter, fines of BD500 are common.

BUSINESS HOURS

Shops and offices of private businesses are generally open from around 7 am until 2 pm, Saturday to Wednesday, and close earlier (or they may not open at all) on Thursday. Many shops, particularly those in the souqs, reopen in the late afternoon from about 4 pm until 7 pm, and 'cold stores' (small grocery shops) are open all day, often until very late into the evening. Banks usually open from 7.30 am to midday, Saturday to Thursday, but close at about 11 am on Thursday. Most Western embassies, and virtually all government offices, are closed all day Thursday (though many Arab embassies will be open on Thursday mornings) and Friday.

PUBLIC HOLIDAYS & SPECIAL EVENTS

In addition to the main Islamic holidays described in Public Holidays & Special Events in the Regional Facts for the Visitor chapter, Bahrain observes National Day (16 December) and Ashura, 10th day of Muharram (changeable), which marks the death of Hussein, the grandson of the Prophet Mohammed, at the battle of Karbala in AD 680. Processions led by men flagellating themselves, take place in many of the country's predominantly Shi'ite areas.

ACTIVITIES

An excellent source of information about local activities is the 'Sports' section of *Bahrain This Month* magazine.

Swimming

Although Bahrain is surrounded by water, the public beaches are generally poor. The sand, and parks nearby, are pleasant enough for a picnic, but the water is usually no good for swimming, mainly because the Gulf is so shallow (you can wade as far as 500m out and the water is often still only up to your knees). The best beaches are almost all man-made and are the property of upmarket hotels and private clubs.

Al-Jazayir Beach, Bahrain's best beach, is one of the hardest to reach. It has some welcome shade, plenty of clean sand, swimmable water, and small huts for rent for the day – ask around for costs. It's accessible only by private transport; a taxi ride there will be expensive.

Water Sports

Jet skis can be rented from next to the Funland Centre, along the Marina Corniche in Manama. Other water sports, such as windsurfing, fishing and sailing, are only available at private clubs. The main clubs for water sports are the Al-Bander Resort (☎ 701 201) and Bahrain Yacht Club (☎ 700 677), both on Sitra Island; the Bahrain Sailing Club (☎ 580 000) at Al-Jazayir; and the Marina Club (☎ 291 527) in Manama – but you'll have to join, or be invited as a guest, before you can rent any equipment.

Diving in the Gulf

Pearl diving has been a tradition, and lucrative business, for centuries in Bahrain, but only recently has scuba diving become popular. The advantages of diving in the Gulf around Bahrain are its shallow (sometimes *very* shallow) and warm water (wet suits are often not needed in summer); good visibility; 200 or so species of fish, including rays, barracuda and dugongs; 30 types of coral; and many wrecks of ships, tugboats and planes.

Diving is possible all year around, but is best from September to November. Snorkelling is also possible most of the year in shallow, sheltered waters around coral reefs closer to Bahrain. Some of the best scuba diving sites are about 70km from Bahrain, often in international waters, so a good boat, and experienced boatmen, are essential.

There are a few members-only diving clubs, such as the British Club (☎ 728 245) and Dilmun Club (☎ 692 986), and one reputable diving agency: Aquatique (☎ 271 780, fax 251 408, ✉ talamruk@batelco.com.bh) in Manama. The agency rents diving and snorkelling equipment, and can arrange diving and snorkelling trips and courses, but nothing is cheap. Aquatique has an informative Web site: www.pearldive.com.

Clubs

Social and sporting clubs dominate the social life of most Western expatriates. They are often members of one or more private clubs, such as the British Club (☎ 728 245) in the Al-Mahuz district of southern Manama, and the Bahrain Yacht Club (☎ 700 677) on Sitra Island, or private resorts like the Al-Bander Resort (☎ 701 201) on Sitra. These clubs have pools, sports facilities, tennis courts, gyms and expensive bars and restaurants, but are not open to the public. Membership is often exclusive, and always expensive (about BD200 per person per year). Tourists can normally only visit a club as a registered guest of a member, so if you're keen, ring one of the clubs and ask a member to invite you, or ask for temporary tourist membership. Most clubs have dress codes.

Horse Riding

A small area along the Marina Corniche has horse and camel rides. More serious horse riding – and riding lessons – are available at the Awali Riding Club (☎ 756 525), out in the countryside, and the Bahrain Riding School (☎ 690 448) near Riffa.

Other Activities

The Bahrain Hash House Harriers meet every week, and organise several serious races throughout the year: check the local papers for contact numbers. There is tenpin bowling, and even ice skating, at the Funland Centre (☎ 292 313), in Manama. Other sports, eg, tennis and golf, are mentioned under Spectator Sports later in this section.

COURSES

Most courses cater to Western expatriate residents. Tourists are welcome to attend, but most courses are held once or twice a week for a few months, which is obviously no good for anyone with a two-week visa.

Some general courses are run by the British Council, Alliance Française de Bahrein and USIS (see Cultural Centres in the Manama section later in this chapter), and others are run by private schools, such as the International School (☎ 290 209). Courses in traditional Bahraini and Arabic art and music are sometimes offered by the Bahrain Arts Society (☎ 590 551), and occasionally Arabic language courses are run by private teachers and the Ministry of Education (☎ 714 795) PO Box 43, Manama.

WORK

Bahrain is not the sort of place where a traveller can expect to pick up casual, short-term work, either legally or illegally. Plenty of Westerners work in Bahrain, but they are sponsored, and the government is making an effort to trim the overall number of foreign workers in the country.

As more Bahrainis obtain better skills and qualifications, the chances of any foreigner, including the spouse of a foreign worker, finding work are diminishing. Most Bahrainis are taught English at school, so there is no demand for English tutors, but there is a possible demand for tutors/teachers of other European languages. Experienced and qualified nurses, school teachers and computer experts are currently in demand.

The best places to look around for casual or permanent work are the classifieds sections of the two English-language daily newspapers. It's best to contact the Ministry of Cabinet Affairs & Information or the Bahrain Promotions & Marketing Board (see under Tourist Offices earlier in this section) before you leave home if you want to work in Bahrain.

ACCOMMODATION

Bahrain's only youth hostel is in the suburb of Juffair, south-east of central Manama – see Places to Stay in the Manama section for details. Good, cheap hotel rooms with air-conditioning, a private bathroom with hot water, and TV (but not satellite), cost from BD7/10 for singles/doubles. Bahrain has a glut of four- and five-star hotels, which can mean some bargains if you look out for ads in the English-language daily newspapers, and ask at the hotel reception desks. Refer to Places to Stay in the Manama section later for information about rental accommodation.

FOOD

Anyone staying a while should pick up the *Bahrain Restaurant Guide* (BD1). This marvellous pocket-sized booklet highlights the best of the 2000 or so restaurants throughout the country, and is updated every year. However, it's written for the Western expat, so the listings are normally upmarket establishments.

There is no such thing as 'Bahraini cuisine' and restaurants serving quality Arabic food are surprisingly scarce. Most cheap restaurants are run by, and cater to, Asian workers. Many of these tiny Indian and Pakistani places have an extremely limited menu, often consisting of biryanis and samosas and little else, but the food is al-

ways cheap and filling. Chinese and Filipino food is a bit more expensive, and tends to be better. A few traditional coffeehouses remain, but there are far more places offering cappuccino and cakes than sweet tea and *sheesha* (water pipes) these days.

There are plenty of Western fast-food joints in the major shopping centres, and around the main streets of Manama. The service may be quick, but the food isn't cheap; the same thing at a local restaurant will cost about half as much.

DRINKS

Pepsi, Coke and 7Up are all popular, as are delicious fruit juices and milkshakes. Alcohol is expensive: a can of beer starts at 900 fils; hard liquor from BD1.200.

SPECTATOR SPORTS

Soccer (football) is the major sport. Games are held at the National Stadium near A'ali, and at smaller stadiums in the residential areas of Muharraq, Riffa and Isa Town.

Between October and March the Equestrian & Horse Racing Club (☎ 440 330) holds about six races every Friday beginning at 2 pm, at the Sakhir Race Course, near Awali. It's an impressive grassed arena in the middle of the desert, and the large grandstand is often full on race day. The highlight of the season is the Bahrain Silver Cup, held at the end of February. Entrance to the race course is free for all events.

A new, lush golf course has been recently carved out of the desert in the Riffa Valley. The 18-hole Riffa Golf Course was built at a staggering cost of BD7 million, and features five man-made lakes, 600 trees (mainly palms) and 60 bunkers. Details about costs and memberships were not available at the time of research.

Other popular sports include motor racing and go-karts under the auspices of the Bahrain Motor Club (☎ 536 895). Volleyball, badminton, basketball, cricket and handball are also popular among locals. Upcoming events, and the results of competitions, are published in the two local English-language daily newspapers.

SHOPPING

Bahrain's specialities – pearls and gold – are good value, but shoppers should know something about quality and price before spending too much money. The best place to look around is the souq in Manama. Other local items which make great souvenirs include pottery and ceramics from A'ali, woven baskets from Karbabad, hand-woven cloth from Bani Jamrah and textiles from Al-Jasra – refer to the relevant headings in the Around Bahrain Island section later in this chapter for details.

One of the best places to watch handicrafts being made, and to buy something nice, is the Craft Centre in Manama. If you're not heading to Iran, Bahrain is one of the better places in the Gulf to look around for carpets, rugs and tablecloths. Prices are not too bad, and shops in the souq in Manama have a wide range of carpets/rugs made of wool or silk from Iran, Turkey and the Central Asian republics.

Getting There & Away

AIR

Bahrain is a part-owner of Gulf Air, which regularly flies between Bahrain and London, Frankfurt, Amsterdam, Rome and Paris, major cities on the Indian subcontinent, Melbourne/Sydney in Australia, and all over the Middle East. Other regional airlines, such as Saudi Arabian Airlines and Royal Jordanian, also fly to/from Bahrain, and have connections to Europe and North America.

Bahrain International Airport is on Muharraq Island, about 10 minutes' drive from central Manama. It is one of the busiest in the Gulf. The departure area has an array of duty-free shops, a restaurant, coffee shop, bar, post office and ATM for American Express cards. Flight information is available on a special number (☎ 325 555).

Always remember to reconfirm flights 72 hours in advance, particularly if you're travelling with Gulf Air, Saudi Arabian Airlines or Kuwait Airways. Most airline offices are open Saturday to Wednesday, from about 8 am to 12.30 pm and 3 to about 5 pm; and Thursday morning. Many offices and agencies are located along Al-Khalifa Ave near Bab al-Bahrain, and in the Chamber of Commerce & Industry building and Manama Centre.

Airlines rarely offer any special deals to Bahrain. However, from Bahrain, special deals to Europe, and more often to the Middle East, eg, the UAE and Oman, are regularly available. Check the windows of the travel agents in the souq in Manama for the latest offers.

Departure Tax

The airport 'Passenger Service Fee' (ie, the departure tax) at the Bahrain International Airport is BD3. You can pay this at the airport, or sometimes at the travel agency or airline office if you buy your ticket in Bahrain. A few large hotels sell vouchers that allow their guests to pre-pay the fee, avoiding lines at the airport.

The USA & Canada

There are no direct flights between Bahrain and North America. Gulf Air offers competitive fares to/from Bahrain via London, with code share connections to North America on American Airlines. The best idea is to get a cheap flight via Europe, or find out what other Middle Eastern airlines, eg, Royal Jordanian, Saudi Arabian Airlines or Kuwait Airways, can offer directly between the USA/Canada and Amman, Riyadh or Kuwait, and then get an onward connection to Bahrain.

Australia & New Zealand

Gulf Air flies between Bahrain and Melbourne and Sydney three times a week, with a stopover in Singapore. New Zealand-bound travellers will have to get a connecting flight.

The UK & Continental Europe

Bahrain is well connected to the major hubs in Europe. British Airways flies nonstop every day between London and Bahrain, and Gulf Air flies to/from London nonstop at least once a day, and several times a week via Abu Dhabi (UAE). From Frankfurt, Lufthansa flies to Dubai (UAE) and Kuwait most days, and has connections on Gulf Air to Bahrain. Gulf Air offers a more convenient nonstop service between Bahrain and Frankfurt several times a week.

KLM flies nonstop between Amsterdam and Bahrain nearly every day and Gulf Air goes to Amsterdam daily. Gulf Air has nonstop flights between Bahrain and Paris three times a week, and more flights each week via Abu Dhabi and Doha (Qatar). Gulf Air also flies nonstop between Bahrain and Rome.

Africa

One of the more interesting, but more expensive, options is the daily flight between Dubai (UAE) and Addis Ababa (Ethiopia) on Ethiopian Airlines, with connections to/from Bahrain on Gulf Air.

Asia

The best deals are on the airlines which serve the thousands of workers from the Indian subcontinent living in Bahrain. PIA flies between Karachi and Bahrain three times a week; and Gulf Air has regular flights to/from Karachi, Islamabad and Lahore. Gulf Air flies to Chennai (Madras) every day, usually via Muscat (Oman); to Delhi, three times a week; and to Mumbai (Bombay), several times a week. Air India has a similar schedule between major Indian cities and Bahrain.

Gulf Air offers regular flights between Bahrain and Bangkok, Singapore and Hong Kong, and Singapore Airlines flies between Bahrain and Singapore most days.

Middle East

Normal fares for flights from Bahrain to some other Middle Eastern cities are:

destination	one way/return (BD)
Abu Dhabi (UAE)	– /53
Amman (Jordan)	140/193
Cairo (Egypt)	168/188
Damascus (Syria)	140/130
Doha (Qatar)	34/27
Dubai (UAE)	77/62
Jeddah (Saudi Arabia)	88/116
Kuwait City	52/69
Muscat (Oman)	120/95
Riyadh (Saudi Arabia)	36/49
Sharjah (UAE)	77/62
Shīrāz (Iran)	69/88
Tehrān (Iran)	108/140

One-way tickets to most places in the Middle East from Bahrain tend to be significantly more expensive than the cheapest available returns. Obviously, if you need to go only one way, buy a return ticket and simply throw away the second coupon.

Special fares from Bahrain to the UAE and Oman are sometimes available. These usually take the form of 'weekend' fares that allow travel only on Wednesday, Thursday and Friday, or 'weekend' packages including airfare and a couple of nights in a hotel in Dubai (UAE) or Muscat (Oman). Check the windows of the travel agents in Manama for the latest offers.

LAND
Border Crossings

The only land border is with Saudi Arabia, across the incredible King Fahd Causeway (see the Around Bahrain Island section later in this chapter for details). Bahrain is, therefore, often used as a transit point for international travel to/from eastern Saudi Arabia.

Most tourists won't have a car, or be allowed to drive between Saudi and Bahrain in a rental car, so this border is normally only crossed by foreigners using the Saudi-Bahrain bus service. From Bahrain, it is possible to charter a taxi to the border, cross the border independently on foot, and then hitch a ride into Saudi Arabia. All provided, of course, that you can get a Saudi visa (see the boxed text 'Saudi Transit Visas' in the Getting There & Away chapter).

Bus

Saudi Bahraini Transport Co (SABTCO; ☎ 263 244, fax 244 297) runs a bus service between Manama and Dammam, in Saudi Arabia. All buses also stop in the Saudi town of Alkhobar. Buses leave six times daily, between 8 am and 8.30 pm, and cost

BD4 one way. From Dammam, there are regular connections to Riyadh and Jeddah (Saudi Arabia).

From Dammam, the Saudi Arabian bus company, SAPTCO, also runs long-distance international buses. You can buy tickets from Manama all the way to Amman (Jordan) for BD25; Damascus (Syria), BD25; Abu Dhabi, Dubai and Sharjah (UAE), all for about BD17; and Kuwait, BD14. In all cases you'll take the SABTCO bus across the causeway to Dammam, and change to a SAPTCO bus for the remainder of the trip (some of these may also involve a change of buses in the Saudi capital, Riyadh). All departures are from the International Bus Terminal in Manama, where the SABTCO office is located.

Private Vehicle

To get on the causeway to Saudi Arabia, all drivers (and passengers in taxis) must pay a toll of BD2, regardless of whether they're travelling to Saudi Arabia or just as far as the border. The toll booth is on the western side of the intersection between the appropriately named Causeway Approach Rd and the Janabiya Hwy.

Anyone crossing the border from Bahrain to Saudi Arabia will be given a customs form to complete, and drivers entering Bahrain from Saudi Arabia must purchase temporary Bahraini insurance for their vehicle and sign a personal guarantee (essentially a promise that you will take the car back out of the country).

The SABTCO bus company also offers a chauffeur-driven limousine service from the Bahrain International Airport, or central Manama, to Alkhobar or Dammam (Saudi Arabia) for BD35/60 one way/return. For BD100/180 they will take you all the way to Riyadh. Service to Doha (Qatar) costs BD140 (one way). The Europcar (☎ 692 999) rental company, which has an agency at the airport, can also provide chauffeur-driven vehicles to Dammam for BD40/70.

SEA

There is currently no passenger ferry or boat service to or from Bahrain. The service of-

fered by the Iranian shipping company, Valfajre-8, between Bahrain and Bandar Abbas, has been abandoned. Though a service between Bahrain and Qatar has long been discussed it has never actually materialised.

ORGANISED TOURS

Bahrain's tourist industry is still largely aimed at stopover and transit passengers, and weekend visitors from Saudi Arabia, and to a lesser degree, the UAE and Kuwait. A number of regional airlines, notably Gulf Air, offer short-stay stopover packages in Bahrain for passengers travelling between Europe and Asia or Australia. Very few foreign travel agencies offer packages or organised tours to, or around, Bahrain. For a list of agencies in Bahrain which organise tours around the country, see Organised Tours in the Getting Around section below.

Getting Around

BUS

Bahrain has a fairly straightforward public bus system which links most of its major towns to the bus terminals in Manama and Muharraq. Buses run every 40 to 60 minutes from about 6 am until about 8 pm, depending on the route. The Manama Bus Terminal is on Government Ave, and there are terminals in Isa Town, Muharraq and Riffa. The fare is a flat 50 fils per trip.

Some of the more useful buses (which travel in both directions) are:

Bus No 1 Manama to Muharraq, via the airport
Bus No 2 Isa Town to Muharraq, via Al-Khamis and Manama
Bus No 3 Manama to Juffair, and then heads south and west
Bus No 5 Al-Budayyi' to Manama, via Ad-Diraz
Bus No 7 Riffa to Muharraq, via Isa Town, Al-Khamis and Manama
Bus No 9 Al-Zallaq to Isa Town, via Hamad and A'ali
Bus No 11 Hamad to Ad-Dur, via Riffa
Bus No 12 Sar to Hamad, via Al-Budayyi'
Bus No 15 Hamad to Isa Town, via A'ali

A few private buses and minibuses ply these same routes, and cost about 100 fils per trip.

CAR & MOTORCYCLE

Before driving a private or rented vehicle around Bahrain, there are a few matters to be aware of:

- Many attractions have different opening hours, so plan your trip accordingly. The best days to find most things open are Wednesday and Thursday.
- Although most attractions are signposted, buy a detailed driving map of Manama and/or Bahrain. But remember that many maps are out of date (see Planning in the Facts for the Visitor section earlier in this chapter for more information), and car rental companies do not usually provide maps for customers.
- Most foreigners will find the names of some roads and highways sound and look similar, and the transliterations from Arabic to English vary. In some cases, the name of the road/highway is ignored completely by locals and the thoroughfare is informally referred to as, for example, the 'Riffa Rd' (ie, the road through Riffa), or a roundabout is named after a fast-food restaurant on the corner.
- Some roads south of the Tree of Life are off limits – but there's no need to go any further south than this anyway.

Road Rules

Bahraini law requires people driving cars and riding in the front seat to use seat belts. Speed limits are rigorously enforced, and drunk-driving laws are also quite strict. Driving is on the right-hand side. Parking meters in most suburbs operate from 7 am to 1 pm and 3 to 7 pm, Saturday to Wednesday, and 7 am to 1 pm on Friday; and cost 100 fils for 30 minutes. Fines for illegal parking range from BD5 to BD10.

Petrol

Petrol comes in two grades. The lower grade, known as *jayyid*, costs 80 fils per litre; premium, or *mumtaz* (literally 'special'), costs 100 fils. Petrol stations are fairly common, especially along the highways, and stations are well signed.

Rental

Everything in Manama can be seen on foot but, outside of the capital, getting around can be a problem without a car. The major international car rental companies are all represented at the airport; many also have offices elsewhere, although they can be hard to find.

Avis	☎ 531 144
Budget	☎ 534 100
Europcar	☎ 692 999
Hertz	☎ 321 287

A few local companies, such as Oscar Rent a Car (☎ 291 591), charge a dinar or so less per day, but these companies may not be as reliable. There is nowhere to rent motorbikes.

The major firms charge from about BD10/60 per day/week for the smallest four-door sedan, but rates do vary, so shop around. This rate includes unlimited kilometres but not petrol. They may or may not include insurance; if not, it's worth paying the extra fee of about BD2 per day to avoid an excess of BD20 to BD300 in case of an accident.

A UK, US or Australian driving licence, or a licence issued by either Bahrain or another GCC country, should enable you to rent a car. However, an International Driving Permit may still be helpful, and all car rental agencies require a credit card for a deposit. All rates are for 24 hours. Agencies usually only accept drivers over 21, and over 25 for more expensive cars.

LOCAL TRANSPORT
Taxi

Most of Bahrain's taxis are metered, and while you can hire them by the hour to see sights outside Manama, you should only do this if you really need the cab to wait for a long time at some remote spot (like Qala'at al-Bahrain or the Al-Areen Wildlife Park), where you're unlikely to find another taxi to take you to your next destination. If you intend to see a few sights in one day, it's probably cheaper to rent a car.

If you are intent on hiring a taxi and driver by the hour, bargain hard. Since few places in Bahrain are much more than 30 minutes' drive from anywhere else in the country, a fare of BD6 to BD7 per hour is reasonable, particularly if the taxi is going to wait while you walk around the site.

Taxis in Bahrain have meters, but foreigners often have to be very persistent before drivers use them. Taxi drivers are particularly reluctant to use the meter when going to or from the airport, and when you pick up the taxi outside a top-end hotel or upmarket shopping centre. Any quoted (unmetered) fare by the driver will be at least double the metered fare, so if the driver is still reluctant to use the meter get another taxi, press the 'For Hire' button on the meter yourself, or threaten to ring the Taxi Complaint Line (☎ 683 500). You can prebook a taxi through Speedy Motor Service (☎ 682 999), although it's more expensive than hailing one on the street.

The flag fall of 800 fils will take passengers 1.5km. Thereafter, the meter ticks over in 100 fils increments every 1km. For all trips from – but not to – the airport there is a BD1 surcharge, and official taxi fares increase by 50% between 10 pm and about 6 am.

Small trucks and other vehicles with a yellow circle painted on the door are unmetered service-taxis: save yourself grief by sticking to the metered kind. If you insist on an unmetered ride in a service-taxi negotiate the fare in advance to avoid problems at the end of the trip.

Service-Taxis

Any pick-up truck, car or other vehicle with a yellow circle on the driver's side door is a service-taxi. They often, but not always, follow the same routes as the buses, but are not bound to these routes. Drivers are free to go wherever they wish and this can lead to confusion since the route and destination of any given vehicle can change from minute to minute as passengers are picked up and set down. Service-taxis do not use meters, and passengers normally pay about 200 fils per trip, depending on the distance travelled.

Service-taxis can be found, and chartered, at, or very close to, the main bus terminal, central market and Sulmaniya Hospital in Manama; and the bus terminals in Isa Town, Riffa and Muharraq. They can also be hailed anywhere. Like normal taxis, service-taxis often toot at foreigners on foot, assuming that anyone walking must want a lift.

Service-taxis are certainly cheaper than chartering a taxi, but are invariably less comfortable and less regular. Few Westerners in Bahrain ever travel this way and you may find that the service-taxi you've picked becomes a 'special' taxi – with appropriately 'special' fares – as soon as you get in.

ORGANISED TOURS

There are an inordinate number of travel agencies in Manama, but most only sell airline tickets and only a few offer organised tours. If you're travelling in a group of two or more, it's cheaper to hire a car for the day, though an organised tour should be less hassle and more informative.

One of the best, most interesting and reliable agencies is the government-run Gulf Tours (☎ 294 446, fax 291 947), previously known as Tourism Projects Company, and based at Bab al-Bahrain. Gulf Tours offers one-hour/full-day dhow cruises for BD3/6 per person; trips to Dar Island for BD12; and several different half-day tours, concentrating on mosques, archaeology, crafts, Manama, the desert and wildlife, from BD7.

Other agencies which run interesting organised tours are:

Al-Reem (☎ 710 868, fax 640 814, ✉ saeed@al reem.com) Specialises in 'ecotourism and wildlife packages' around the desert and remote islands.
Arab World Tours (☎ 963 737, fax 254 297) Similar offerings to Gulf Tours (above), plus other trips with emphasis on photography, outdoor activities, fishing and camel riding.
Orient Travel & Tours (☎ 531 000, fax 533 172) Offers all sorts of tours in major European languages.

Manama

Manama is the very new capital of a very old place – many of the hotels and official buildings along Government Ave sit on reclaimed land, offering an idea of how small the island used to be – or just how much reclamation has taken place. But don't be fooled: only a few blocks inland from the shiny new hotels are sections of the city which have changed little in the last 50 years.

BAHRAIN

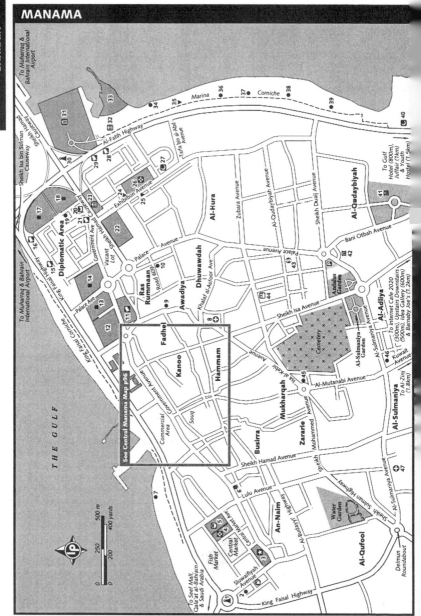

MANAMA

To Muharraq &
Bahrain International Airport

Sheikh Isa bin Sulman Causeway

Al-Fatih Highway

31

33

32

34   35   Marina   36   37   Comiche   38   39   40

30

28   29

27

26   24   23   Exhibition Avenue   25

Al-Hura   Zubara Avenue   Al-Qudaybiyah Avenue   Sheikh Duaij Avenue   Al-Qadaybiyah

17   18   19   21   22

Diplomatic Area   Government Ave   Sheikh Hamad Ave

16   15   14   13   12   11

King Faisal Highway

Palace Avenue   Ras Rummaan   Awadhiya   Dhuwawdah   Road 609   10   9

Khalat al-Asfoor Ave

Palace Avenue   Bani Otbah Avenue   42   43   44   Andalus Garden   41   Al-Adliya

8   Sheikh Isa Avenue   45   46   Al-Sulmaniya Garden   Al-Sulmaniya Avenue   To Internet Cafe 2020 (300m), Upstairs Downstairs (500m), Idea Gallery (600m) & Barnaby Joe's (1.2km)

Kuwait Avenue

Al-Mutanabi Avenue   Al-Sulmaniya

Cemetery

To Al-Zini (1.8km)

To Gulf Hotel (800m), Juffair (1km) & Youth Hostel (1.5km)

Fadhel   Kanoo   Hammam   Isa al-Kebir Avenue

See Central Manama Map p96

Commercial Area   Souq   Commercial Avenue   Mukharqah   Zararie   Busirra   Mohammed Avenue   Sheikh

THE GULF

7

Sheikh Hamad Avenue

Lulu Avenue   6

An-Naim   Al-Budayyi' Highway   Sheikh Sulman Highway   Al-Sulmaniya Avenue   47   Al-Fool

5   4   Central Market Avenue   Water Garden

Fish Market   Central Market   3   2   1   Suwaifiyah Avenue

Delmun Roundabout

To Seef Mall, Qala'at al-Bahrain & Saudi Arabia   King Faisal Highway

To Al-Zini

500 m
400 yards
0   250   200

N

PLACES TO STAY
6 Tylos Hotel; The Saddle
   Restaurant & Bar
13 Sheraton Bahrain
14 Bahrain Hilton
17 Holiday Inn
18 The Diplomat

PLACES TO EAT
24 Isfahani Restaurant
25 French Corner Cafe
35 Laialy Zaman

OTHER
1 Pearl Monument
2 Al-Osra Supermarket
3 Police Station
4 Lulu Shopping Centre
5 International Bus Terminal;
   SABTCO Office

7 Kid's Kingdom
8 American Mission Hospital
9 Family Bookshop
10 Wind Tower
11 UK Embassy
12 Bahrain Commercial Complex
15 Saudi Embassy
16 Kuwaiti Embassy
19 Avis
20 Post Office
21 German Embassy
22 General Directorate of
   Immigration & Passports
23 Beit al-Quran
26 GOSI Shopping Complex;
   Arcadia (Video Arcade)
27 Abu Bakr al-Sadiq Mosque
28 French Embassy
29 Omani Embassy
30 Sail Monument

31 Bahrain National Museum
32 Arts Centre
33 Marina Club
34 Funland Centre;
   Jet Ski Hire
36 Gulf Tours Dock
37 Hawar Resort Hotel Booking
   Office
38 Dolphin Park
39 Horse & Camel Rides
40 Al-Fatih Mosque
41 Al-Qudaybiyah Palace
42 Old Palace
43 Bank of Bahrain & Kuwait
   (ATM)
44 Awal Cinema
45 Craft Centre
46 Directorate of Tourism &
   Archaeology
47 Sulmaniya Hospital

Orientation

Manama's main street is Government Ave, which runs roughly east-west through the city. Al-Khalifa Ave, which runs more or less parallel to, and one block south of, Government Ave, is where many of Manama's cheaper hotels and numerous small restaurants are located. The area between Government Ave and the King Faisal Hwy contains a collection of government offices, banks and hotels. Many embassies are in the Diplomatic Area between the King Faisal Hwy and the start of the Sheikh Hamad Causeway. The area south of Government Ave is the souq, or marketplace. Bab al-Bahrain (the Bahrain Gate) is the main entrance to the souq, and the small roundabout in front of it is Manama's centre of activity.

The King Faisal Hwy runs along the city's northern coast and turns south around the Holiday Inn, changing its name to the Al-Fatih Hwy. The western limit of the city centre is the Pearl Monument roundabout (named after the pearl, which rests above six curved legs, each representing the Gulf Cooperation Council States founded in 1981), while the Bahrain National Museum and the Sheikh Hamad Causeway to Muharraq mark the centre's eastern boundary.

Exhibition Ave, which runs south from the Sheikh Hamad Causeway to Sheikh Duaij Ave, has a number of smaller hotels, notable mostly for containing a few of Bahrain's night spots. A few airline offices, car rental agencies and fast-food joints are in the same neighbourhood.

Information

Tourist Offices Refer to Tourist Offices in the Facts for the Visitor section earlier in this chapter for a rundown of Manama's tourist offices.

Money Several banks are located along the side street between the General Post Office (GPO) and the parking lots in front of the Regency Inter-Continental hotel. There are also a number of banks and moneychangers on Government Ave between the GPO and the Delmon International Hotel – one of the best moneychangers is Zenj Exchange on Al-Khalifa Ave in the souq. A few more moneychangers are dotted along northern Municipality Ave.

There are ATMs at most branches of the British Bank of the Middle East and the Bank of Bahrain & Kuwait (BBK). An ATM for American Express cards is in the departure lounge of the airport.

For more information refer to Money in the Facts for the Visitor section earlier in this chapter.

Post The GPO is open daily, except Friday, from 7 am to 7.30 pm. Poste restante facilities are available. There is another handy post office in the Diplomatic Area.

Telephone There are telephone booths and payphones for local and international calls all over the city. International calls can also be made at the Batelco building in Manama. See Post & Communications in Facts for the Visitor earlier in this chapter for information about the price of calls.

Email & Internet Access There are surprisingly few Internet centres in Manama. The Idea Gallery (☎ 714 828) charges BD2 per hour, and is open every day from about 10 am to midnight. It's located in the Al-Adliya district, south of the Gulf Hotel and near the Titus Arch Restaurant. A new outfit, Internet Cafe 2020, has opened nearby on Asama bin Zaid Ave (near the Ramada Hotel) and offers five minutes of free email use. Charges are very reasonable: 600 fils for half an house and BD1.2 per hour. There are half-a-dozen terminals and soft drinks are available.

Travel Agencies Dozens of travel agencies are located on either Government Ave or Al-Khalifa Ave, but most only sell airline tickets. (For information about local tours, see Organised Tours in the Getting Around section earlier in this chapter). These agencies sometimes offer cheap fares (London, Bangkok, Turkey, India and Pakistan are common destinations for discounted fares) and package tours in the Middle East, especially to Dubai (UAE) and Muscat (Oman).

Bookshops Al-Hilal bookshops are found all over Manama – in many top-end hotels, such as the Sheraton Bahrain and Regency Inter-Continental; shopping centres, eg, the Yateem Centre; and in the souq. One well-stocked bookshop, which has some Lonely Planet titles (but few about other Middle East destinations), is Books Plus in the Seef Mall. The Family Bookshop, down the road from the American Mission hospital, also has a selection of books in English.

Cultural Centres The main Western cultural centres in Bahrain are:

Alliance Française de Bahrein (☎ 683 295) In Isa Town, behind Bahrain University's Polytechnic College, off 16th December Hwy. I shows films (usually in French) on Wednesday evening – all are welcome. The centre is open from 9 am to 1 pm, and 3 to 7 pm, Saturday to Wednesday; and 10 to 12 pm and 4 to 6 pm on Thursday.
British Council (☎ 261 555) In the Ahmed Mansour al-Ali Building (opposite the BMW showroom) on Sheikh Sulman Hwy. The library, on the ground floor, is open Saturday to Wednesday from 9 am to midday, and 3 to 6 pm.
USIS (☎ 273 300) Has a library (open to all) with American newspapers and magazines. The centre, at the US embassy, is open Saturday to Wednesday from 2 to 4 pm.

Laundry Numerous tiny Indian/Pakistani-run laundries are dotted around the souq and central Manama, and charge 200 fils or so to wash a shirt, skirt or trousers. A few very cheap and reliable places are located just off Al-Khalifa Ave, behind the Shadow Restaurant.

Medical Services Medical treatment is relatively easy to obtain, and there are several public and private hospitals in Manama (and in other residential areas around Bahrain):

American Mission Hospital (☎ 253 447) Oldest and smallest, but well equipped, and offers walk-in consultations.
International Hospital of Bahrain (☎ 591 666) The largest private medical facility in the country.
Sulmaniya Hospital (☎ 255 555) The largest public hospital, and well equipped.

Emergency The main police station is near the markets, but the station opposite Bab al-Bahrain is more convenient.

Fire, police & ambulance   ☎ 999 (free call)
Traffic & Accident   ☎ 688 888

Bahrain National Museum

This museum (☎ 292 977) is by far the most popular tourist attraction in the country. The collection is exceptionally well labelled, and the museum is easy to get around if you follow the signs to each gallery in order. The museum also has a small **auditorium**, which shows free films; it often features **exhibitions** of art and sculpture in the foyer; there's a **museum shop** with an excellent range of expensive books about Bahrain and the museum; and there's a small cafeteria with a limited range of drinks and snacks.

Adjacent to the parking lot is an area with reconstructions of a number of **traditional buildings**. These include a small mock village complete with mosque, house with wind tower, souq and several dhows.

The museum is open Saturday, Sunday and Tuesday from 7 am to 2 pm; Wednesday and Thursday, 8 am to 2 pm, and 4 to 8 pm; and Friday 3 to 8 pm. Admission is 500 fils. Photography is permitted except in the Documents & Manuscripts and Dilmun galleries. The museum is easy to enter from Al-Fatih Hwy, and there's plenty of parking.

Hall of Graves There are some 85,000 burial mounds – Bahrain's best-known tourist attraction – covering about 5% of Bahrain's total area. (Mound burials in various forms took place from 2800 BC until the coming of Islam in the 7th century AD.) The centrepiece of the room is a cross section of a large 'late type' burial mound. There are also several smaller reconstructed burial sites of other types. Printed displays explain the various types of burial mounds and the differences between them. Grave contents are also on display with captions detailing their functions.

Dilmun The Dilmun gallery has more displays about archaeological techniques. It also includes exhibits on Dilmun seals, as well as engraving, metal casting, pottery and a thorough outline of temples and temple building. There is a display on the different stages of construction of the Barbar Temple (see the Around Bahrain Island section for more information), which is worth examining if you plan to visit the site.

Costumes & Traditions The displays in this gallery cover birth, childhood, marriage, traditional ceremonies, timekeeping, medicine, toys and games. The education display highlights the differences between traditional Quranic schools and 20th century government schools (founded in 1919).

Traditional Trades & Crafts Largely an extension of the Costumes & Traditions gallery on the lower floor, this section houses displays on pearling and fishing, weaving and pottery. There's also a charming reconstruction of an old street in a souq.

Tylos & Islam This gallery is a bit sparse: most of the material is from Islamic times, reflecting a dearth of finds from Bahrain's Tylos (Greek) period. A lot of space is devoted to grave architecture. There's also a large display on the country's various forts.

Documents & Manuscripts Displays in this gallery include historical records, manuscripts and old Qurans. There are also exhibits of Arabic writing, bookbinding and calligraphy, a short history of pearl diving, and informative explanations about the history of Bahrain.

Hall of Natural History When you have visited the six galleries mentioned above, go to the Hall of Natural History on the ground floor (the entrance is flanked by a stuffed eagle and oryx). This section contains several impressive displays and dioramas about wildlife in the main geographical regions of Bahrain, namely the desert, plantations and coastline.

Art Gallery Stairs from the Hall of Natural History lead to the Art Gallery. This gallery features a small collection of modern art by Bahraini artists, all with traditional Middle Eastern themes such as the teahouse, souq, family life and desert.

Heritage Centre

The Heritage Centre occupies a villa which was built in 1937 to house the Ministry of Justice and Islamic Affairs. The centre was closed at the time of research, but promises to be bigger and better soon.

In the parking lot by the main door an old-style canoe and scale model of an ocean-going dhow are displayed. The courtyard features a reconstruction of a traditional *diwan* (meeting room) under the staircase. The rooms surrounding the courtyard contain photographs of state occasions and the comings and goings of numerous Arab and foreign dignitaries who visited Bahrain during the 20th century.

Currently, there are also displays on pearl diving, seafaring, musical instruments and the various uses of the date palm, and a reconstruction of the High Court. The upper level of the centre houses a series of one-room displays of antique weapons, games, medicine, traditional costumes and scenes from everyday life.

The main entrance is on Government Ave, but there's an old carved door at the back of the building, facing Al-Khalifa Ave. This was the main entrance when the building served as Bahrain's High Court, and the door has been beautifully preserved.

The Heritage Centre is open Saturday to Wednesday from 8 am to 2 pm, and Thursday from 10 am to 5 pm. Admission is free, but photography is prohibited.

Wind Towers

Bahrain's pre-electricity form of air-con can be seen in several places in the older parts of town. The towers are designed to catch the slightest breeze and funnel the air down inside the house (see Traditional Architecture under Arts in the Facts about the Region chapter). The easiest one to find is along Road 609. Walk south of the roundabout between the Hilton and Sheraton hotels along Palace Ave for about 10 minutes,

and turn right at the corner where the Al Baraka Car Centre is located.

Friday Mosque

This mosque was built with Bahrain's firs oil revenues in 1938, and is easily identifi able by its colourful mosaic minaret. The minaret is, in fact, the mosque's most inter esting architectural feature, and you're no missing much if you just look at the mosque from the outside. The juxtaposition of the mosque with the tall, modern Bahrain Tower provides a perfect 'reflection' (literally) of old and new Manama.

Bab al-Bahrain

The 'Gateway to Bahrain' was built by the British in 1945 to house government offices and serve as a formal entry to the old city. The gateway was designed by Sir Charles Belgrave, the long-time British adviser to the rulers of Bahrain. It was restored in 1986 and given a more Islamic look. The small square in front of the Bab was once the terminus of the customs pier – which provides some idea of the extent of land reclamation in the area. The building now houses the Tourist Department, the Gulf Tours office and a souvenir shop.

Beit al-Quran

A striking bit of architecture at the eastern end of Government Ave, Beit al-Quran or Koran House (☎ 290 101) was opened in 1990 as a museum and research centre. It houses a unique collection of Islamic manuscripts and artefacts. Everything is well labelled in English: it's a particularly good introduction to Islam in general, and to the art of Islamic calligraphy in particular.

The museum's centrepiece is a large collection of Qurans, manuscripts and wood carvings. On the left as you pass through the outer lobby is the small Al Rahman Mosque with an extremely elaborate *mihrab* (prayer niche indicating the wall facing Mecca). Above it is an incredible dome made of stained glass windows, kaleidoscopic in colour and bound by Arabic script.

The first hall is a general introduction to Islamic art, and includes a fine collection of are astrolabes (tools used by medieval astronomers). Also on display are glass and namelware, manuscripts, tile work and a variety of miniature paintings from Iran, India and Turkey.

From this hall a series of open galleries, built around a single long staircase, leads through the development of the Islamic world's highest form of art: calligraphy. In a cabinet on the left wall of the first hall is a rare Quran from the 7th century. It probably originated in either Iraq or the Hejaz, and is written in an early form of Kufic script (without the dots that are an integral part of modern written Arabic). Another rare Quran from 8th century Hejaz dominates the centre of this hall in a display case.

The next level concentrates on illumination, the art of decorating the margins of religious manuscripts. Samples from 13th century Syria through to 18th century Persia and 19th century Turkey are on display. The final part of the museum – on the upper level – includes examples of ornately bound Qurans exchanged by Muslim leaders on important occasions, and copies of translations of the Holy Book into a wide variety of foreign languages.

Admission to the Beit al-Quran is free, but a donation is requested – and visitors should dress conservatively. The main entrance is on the southern side of the building. The museum can be reached from the Manama Bus Terminal on bus Nos 1, 2 and 5, or a 25-minute walk from the souq. It's open Saturday to Wednesday, from 9 am to midday, and 4 to 6 pm; and Thursday, 9 am to midday. An excellent, but pricey, **craft & book shop** is located in the foyer.

Al-Fatih Mosque

The Al-Fatih Mosque, also known as the Great Mosque, dominates the Al-Fatih Hwy at the far southern end of the Marina Corniche. It's the largest building in the country (about 6300 sq m), and is capable of holding up to 7000 worshippers. The complex also houses the Religious Institute of Islamic Affairs, a library and conference facilities.

Non-Muslims are welcome to visit the mosque between Saturday and Wednesday, 8 am to 2 pm. (It is not open to visitors on Thursday, Friday, national holidays and during prayer time.) Visitors should check in at the library immediately to the right inside the main door. Women will be given, and are expected to wear, a hooded black cloak while inside the prayer hall. Neither men nor women will be admitted if they're wearing shorts. The mosque is not on a bus route, so the only way to get there is on foot or by taxi.

Places to Stay

For general information about places to stay in Bahrain, see Accommodation in the Facts for the Visitor section earlier this chapter.

Places to Stay – Budget

Hostels The spartan but clean *Youth Hostel (☎ 727 170, No 1105 Road 4225)* has toilets and showers in a separate building. Kitchen facilities are available. Beds cost BD2 per person for HI members; BD4 for nonmembers. The hostel is in the suburb of Juffair, opposite the Bahrain School and just beyond the UNDP and UNICEF offices. It is signposted in English from the Al-Fatih Hwy, and easy enough to reach by taxi or bus No 3 from Manama.

Hotels Most of the hotels listed below have air-con, TV (not satellite) and an attached bathroom with hot water. All rates listed are initial quotes and are mostly negotiable, especially during the week. Most of Manama's budget hotels raise their rates over the weekend, which usually means on Wednesday and Thursday nights. If you check in before the weekend and stay through it, you should only be charged the weekday rate, but check first with the management to avoid any misunderstandings.

Bahrain Hotel (☎ 227 478, fax 213 509, Al-Khalifa Ave) is one of the best in this range. Large, comfortable rooms with a fridge cost a reasonable BD7/10 for singles/doubles, but some rooms can be a little dirty, and most have no outside windows. The hotel is in a quiet part of town, but it's also a little inconvenient.

Al-Kuwait Guest House (☎ 210 781, fax 210 764), just south of Al-Khalifa Ave and

BAHRAIN

CENTRAL MANAMA

PLACES TO EAT
2 Kwality Restaurant
6 Al-Osra Restaurant
15 Dairy Queen
20 Food Fantasy
29 Joyous Restaurant
32 Honey Restaurant
35 Woody's Corner
38 Charcoal Grill
52 Pizza Hut
54 Shadow Restaurant

OTHER
1 Government House
3 BBK Bank (ATM)
4 Friday Mosque
5 Aquatique Diving Centre
7 Ministry of Foreign Affairs
8 Gulf Air; KLM; Lufthansa
9 Manama Centre
10 Kuwait Airways
11 British Bank of the
     Middle East (ATM)
12 Heritage Centre
13 Batelco; McDonald's
14 ABN Building; ABN-AMRO
     Bank; American Express;
     Dutch Consular Agency
16 Chamber of Commerce &
     Industry
17 General Post Office
18 Citibank
21 Standard &
     Chartered Bank
23 Municipality Building
26 Manama Bus Terminal
27 Ahmed Abdul Rahim's
     Coffeehouse
34 Bank of Bahrain &
     Kuwait (ATM)
37 Zenj Exchange
39 Tourist Department;
     Gulf Tours; Souvenir Shop
40 Police Station
42 British Airways
43 Yateem Centre; Al-Hilal
     Bookshop
46 Al-Hilal Bookshop
47 Al-Zeinah Shopping Centre
53 Money Exchange Offices
55 Laundries
56 National Bank of Bahrain

PLACES TO STAY
19 Regency Inter-
     Continental
22 Seef Hotel
24 Delmon International
     Hotel
25 Gulf Gate Hotel
28 Bah'ain Hotel
30 City Centre Hotel;
     Saudi Arabian Airlines
31 Al-Burge Hotel;
     Money Exchange
     Offices
33 Bahrain International
     Hotel; Al Pasha Grill
36 Gulf Pearl Hotel
41 Bab al-Bahrain
     Hotel; KFC
44 Oriental Palace Hotel
45 Capital Hotel
48 Aradous Hotel
49 Al-Jazira Hotel
50 Al-Kuwait Guest
     House
51 Awal Hotel
57 Adhari Hotel
58 Sahara Hotel
59 Al-Dewania Hotel

The Al-Fatih Mosque, Bahrain, is the country's largest building.

Reflections of Bahrain

The Portuguese fortress at Qala'at al-Bahrain is slowly being restored to its original form.

Beit Seyadi and mosque, Bahrain

Doha Fort housed Qatar's Turkish garrison in the 19th century.

TONY WHEELER

CHRIS MELLOR

CHRISTINE OSBORNE

CHRISTINE OSBORNE

The waters of the Gulf were traditionally used for pearling and fishing, usually in hand-stitched dhows. Today, however, the waters are as often used for relaxation and water sports (middle left).

The 20th century saw oil take over from pearling, trading and fishing as the main economic activity of the Gulf States. Oil was first found in commercial quantities in Bahrain in 1932.

Intricately carved or decorated doors adorn some of Bahrain's grand homes and imposing buildings, including Manama's old High Court, now the Heritage Centre (top left & bottom right).

ehind the Al-Jazira Hotel, has small, spartan and uncarpeted rooms, some with hole-in-the-floor toilets. Many rooms badly need some renovation, so check out a few before you decide to stay. It is in an interesting part of town, however, and comparatively good value at BD7/10.

Awal Hotel (☎ *211 321, fax 211 391*) is signposted off Al-Khalifa Ave, but the entrance is along an alley off the main road. It is quiet and clean, but overpriced at BD15/20, and the management know it so they will negotiate.

Al-Dewania Hotel (☎ *263 300, fax 259 709*) is down a tiny lane off Sheikh Abdullah Ave. It is reasonably quiet, central and the staff are affable. The rooms are tiny but clean and well furnished, and cost BD10/15.

Seef Hotel (☎ *224 557, fax 593 363*), near the Municipality Building just north of Government Ave, is relatively quiet but the rooms are small and poorly furnished – choose one with a view and sea breezes. The tariff is BD8/12, and usually negotiable.

Capital Hotel (☎ *255 955, fax 211 675, Tujjaar Ave*) charges BD10/13/19 for singles/doubles/triples, including breakfast, but is only good value if you can convince the manager to discount down to BD8/10/15 (not that difficult). The hotel is in the *souq* (market), which you can admire from the tiny balconies attached to most rooms.

These two places are last resorts: *Oriental Palace Hotel* (☎ *223 331, fax 214 141, Tujjaar Ave*) is OK, but overpriced, for BD16/20; *Al-Burge Hotel* (☎ *213 163, fax 213 512, Municipality Ave*), formerly known as the Abu Nawas Hotel, has small, grubby and spartan cubicles for BD8/10 with a bathroom; BD6/8 without.

Places to Stay – Mid-Range

Manama's mid-priced hotels are a varied lot: a good room in a decent budget hotel is often better than something ordinary in an unexciting mid-range hotel. Amenities in hotels in this range include a fridge, TV (usually satellite) and telephone. A 15% service charge and 5% 'government levy' are invariably added to hotel bills (and included in the listed rates). The rapid growth of mid-range hotels in the capital over the last few years has led to a general lowering of prices. Moreover, during slow periods negotiations of a dinar or two off the rates quoted below are possible, but don't count on it.

Bab al-Bahrain Hotel (☎ *211 622, fax 213 661*), opposite Bab al-Bahrain, is an old favourite, but it's really a budget-style place with a mid-range price. It is central (and therefore noisy), but ask for a discount from the official rate of BD18/30/36 for singles/doubles/triples.

Gulf Pearl Hotel (☎ *213 877, fax 213 943, Government Ave*) is cheaper at BD16/20 for singles/doubles, but discounts to BD13/18 can be easily negotiated. It is central and well furnished, but undergoing some extensive renovations.

Delmon International Hotel (☎ *224 000, fax 224 107, Government Ave*) is central, quiet and very comfortable. The rooms are good value at BD25/30.

Al-Jazira Hotel (☎ *211 810, fax 210 726, Al-Khalifa Ave*) is good value, and offers better rooms and service than other places in the immediate area. The bright and well-furnished rooms cost a reasonable BD12/15, and the staff are friendly.

Bahrain International Hotel (☎ *211 313, fax 211 947,* @ *bihhotel@batelco.com.bh, Government Ave*) is also central and modern, and boasts large, well-appointed rooms and a health club. For BD25/30, it's as good as some top-end places charging double or more.

Sahara Hotel (☎ *225 580, fax 210 580, Municipality Ave*) is one of several decent mid-range places in the area. The rooms at the Sahara are comfortable, have balconies with good views, and cost BD10/18.

Adhari Hotel (☎ *224 242, fax 214 707, Municipality Ave*) nearby has small, but comfortable rooms with balconies for BD18/24, and is in an enchanting, central location.

Aradous Hotel (☎ *224 343, fax 210 535, Wali al-Ahed Ave*) is under the same management as the Adhari and is about the same standard, but discounts from the official tariff of BD15/20 are often happily offered. It boasts an excellent location in the middle of the souq, and the rooftop pool is definitely an added attraction.

City Centre Hotel *(☎ 229 979, fax 224 421, Government Ave)* is central, modern and comfortable, so it's often full. Rooms cost BD16.800/23. Check out their Web site: www.city-centre-hotel.com.

Tylos Hotel *(☎ 252 600, fax 252 611, Government Ave)* is luxurious, with small, airy and clean rooms for BD24/30. Discounts of 20% are often possible.

Places to Stay – Top End

Manama has the usual array of luxurious top-end hotels. The rates listed below are the main rack rates. Corporate discounts of up to 30% are available, but the hotel's generosity depends on the occupancy rate at the time. Some of these places offer weekend discount packages, which you have to book in advance.

Bahrain Hilton *(☎ 523 523, fax 532 071, Palace Ave)* charges from BD84/96 for singles/doubles. This was the first five-star hotel in Bahrain, and is now looking a bit faded.

The Diplomat *(☎ 531 666, fax 530 843, King Faisal Hwy)*, across from the Bahrain National Museum, charges from BD78 to BD90 for doubles. It boasts one of the nicer locations, and many rooms have great views, but it's inconvenient to downtown Manama.

Holiday Inn *(☎ 531 122, fax 530 154, King Faisal Hwy)* charges from BD66/78 for very luxurious rooms.

Regency Inter-Continental *(☎ 227 777, fax 229 929, ✆ bahrain@interconti.com, King Faisal Hwy)* is more convenient than the other places, and popular with businesspeople from around the Gulf. Rooms cost from BD72/82.

Sheraton Bahrain *(☎ 533 533, fax 534 069)* is at the intersection of Palace and Government Aves. It's an old favourite and well situated with plenty of shops nearby and as luxurious as one would hope for at BD72/82.

Places to Stay – Rentals

Western expats normally rent a house or apartment (flat) through their employers. The classifieds in both English-language daily newspapers list rental properties, but demand for good places often exceeds supply because foreigners cannot own property in Bahrain.

Along the western side of the very busy Al-Fatih Hwy, and overlooking the Marina Corniche, are a number of hotels and housing blocks that offer apartments for short-term rental. These mainly cater for families on holiday from other Gulf countries, but foreigners are still welcome. Renting an apartment can be cheaper for a family or small group than staying in a top-end hotel, especially if you are staying longer than one week.

Places to Eat

Anyone staying a while should pick up the *Bahrain Restaurant Guide* – see Food in the Facts for the Visitor section earlier in this chapter.

Restaurants There are loads of good and cheap places to eat in central Manama, especially along (or just off) Government and Al-Khalifa Aves, and around Bab al-Bahrain.

Al-Osra Restaurant *(☎ 240 098, Government Ave)* offers well over 100 Chinese, Indian, Western and Arabic dishes. It's open from 7 am to 1 am, and is great for breakfast. Spicy curries start at 800 fils, and the sandwiches and burgers (about 400 fils) are excellent.

Charcoal Grill, opposite Bab al-Bahrain, has tasty kebabs with salad from BD1.200, and curries for about BD1.600, but is a little pricey because of the excellent location.

Honey Restaurant *(☎ 274 392, Municipality Ave)* has appealing decor, and a vast menu specialising in Chinese and Filipino food. It's slightly more expensive than other places: burgers cost up to 800 fils; fried rice, BD1; and seafood, BD1.500 to BD2.

Kwality Restaurant *(Government Ave)* has a similar menu to the Al-Osra. The surroundings are more pleasing, but the food isn't as good and the prices are slightly higher.

Laialy Zaman *(☎ 293 097, Marina Corniche)* is one of the surprisingly few places to take advantage of the welcome sea views and breezes. Prices are very reasonable: Western-style snacks cost less than BD1, ain meals about BD1.500, and patrons can uff on the sheesha. It's not signposted, but close to the obvious Funland Centre.

Manama also boasts an impressive array f international restaurants. *Isfahani 'estaurant (☎ 290 027, Exhibition Ave)* offers a number of excellent Iranian dishes rom BD1.600 to BD2. *French Corner 'afe (☎ 531 232)*, almost opposite the Isfaani, is not cheap, but is quaint and reasonbly authentic.

Many of the better restaurants are inside, r attached to, mid-range and top-end hotels. *'he Saddle Restaurant & Bar (☎ 252 600, 'ylos Hotel)* is a popular Tex-Mex restauant serving tasty enchiladas and nachos and xcellent margaritas. On weekend nights ou might want to make a reservation.

Al Pasha Grill, on the ground floor of the 3ahrain International Hotel, is good value, g, about BD1 for chicken meals. *Pearl 3rills (☎ 217 333)* at the Gulf Pearl Hotel las delicious burgers for about 500 fils. *Food Fantasy (☎ 215 799)* at the Seef Hotel is a bit seedy, but the vast selection of Filipino, Chinese, Mexican, Italian and Arabic dishes should please most patrons.

In Al-Adliya, *Upstairs Downstairs*, has been recommended as offering outstanding European fare in an atmospheric, two-storey house with a courtyard. Meals range from BD3 to BD10.

Fast Food Small Indian/Pakistani-run eateries catering to Asian workers are dotted around the souq. They have unimaginative names like 'Bombay Cafeteria', and serve acceptable biryanis for about 500 fils, as well as tasty curries and cheap samosas. Two of the better places are *Shadow Restaurant* and *Joyous Restaurant*, both along Al-Khalifa Ave.

Fruit juice stands and *sandwich shops* around the souq offer small but tasty sandwiches or burgers for about 500 fils, and delicious fruit juices and milkshakes cost from 200 fils. *Woody's Corner* on Al-Khalifa Ave is a great place for tasty and cheap hamburgers and milkshakes.

Western *fast food* outlets such as Pizza Hut, McDonald's, KFC and Dairy Queen

are dotted around Manama, and located in the main shopping complexes, such as Seef Mall. Some are open 24 hours a day.

Self-Catering Dozens of small grocery stores (called 'cold stores') are dotted around the residential areas, and are open from about 7 am to 10 pm. These stores sell cold drinks, some fruit and vegetables and a few canned goods. There are large, well-stocked supermarkets at the major shopping centres, such as Seef Mall, but the Al-Osra Supermarket, near the Pearl Monument, is more convenient for anyone without private transport. The Central Market is the best place for fruit, spices, vegetables and meat; and fish is, naturally, the speciality at the adjoining Fish Market. However, the area covering both markets is slated for redevelopment and/or relocation soon.

Entertainment

To find out what is going on, check out the 'What's On' column of the *Gulf Daily News*, *Bahrain This Month* magazine and the *What's On in Bahrain* booklet – see Newspapers & Magazines in the Facts for the Visitor section earlier in this chapter. Radio Bahrain is also a good source of information.

Cinemas Two cinema complexes regularly show recent Western films in their original language (almost always English): Delmon Cinemas (☎ 296 090) in the GOSI Shopping Complex; and the Seef Cineplex (☎ 582 220) in the Seef Mall. Awal Cinema (☎ 274 121) also sometimes shows Western films, but mainly features films from India. Details about programs are advertised in both English-language daily newspapers or on a flyer available in some of Manama's hotels and shops, and are also available by ringing the Hot Line (☎ 864 666), or the cinema direct. Tickets cost BD2, and all cinemas are air-conditioned.

Special films are also shown at the Bahrain National Museum on Sunday evening; Alliance Française de Bahrein (see Cultural Centres earlier in this chapter), usually on Wednesday evening; and the Bahrain Cinema Club (☎ 725 959) in Juffair on Wednesday evening. Ring these places directly for details, or check out the *Bahrain This Month* magazine.

Concerts & Theatre Western rock stars occasionally drop in for one-off performances, the five-star hotels regularly bring theatre companies out from the UK (and occasionally France) for three or four-night runs, and the cultural centres often sponsor plays from England, France and the Indian subcontinent. Tickets for foreign plays are often expensive – up to BD18 – and are heavily promoted in the English-language dailies.

In addition, the Bahrain International Exhibition Centre (☎ 229 046) often has recitals of Bahraini music, usually featuring the Bahrain Orchestra for Arabic Music; and Beit al-Quran has occasional Quran recitals. Bands playing traditional music appear at the Qala'at Arad fort in Muharraq on Thursday and Friday afternoon.

Bars & Discos All serious drinkers and nightclubbers should pick up the detailed *Bahrain Restaurant Guide*, which also lists recommended bars and nightclubs. Live shows are often listed in the 'Showtime' section of *Bahrain This Month* magazine, and in the daily English-language newspapers. The best source of information about the trendiest places to go are the (younger) crowd of Western expats.

Hotel bars include the comfortable-but-generic *Clipper Room* at the Regency Inter-Continental hotel, with live music most nights; the bizarrely thematic *Sherlock Holmes Bar* at the Gulf Hotel, with live music every night; and the *Hunter's Lodge Bar* at the Adhari Hotel, one of the nicer, inner-city bars.

Currently trendy are: *The Saddle Restaurant & Bar* at the Tylos Hotel (for country music); *U2opia* at the Delmon International Hotel; and *Barnaby Joes* (BJs) – but *only* after midnight!

Many of the cheaper hotels offer live music from Filipino bands, and sometimes visiting Russian or Sri Lankan quartets, but most are fairly tacky and include scantily

clad female singers to delight the mostl male audience. If you want to see some de cent live music, stick with bands playing a the upmarket hotels and restaurants.

Bahrain's most interesting bars tend to b attached to otherwise unremarkable hotels and are often entered through a separat door. (Hotels have an easier time gettin liquor licences than freestanding restau rants, which explains this rather odd state o affairs.) Bahrain's liquor licensing law have set some of these places up as 'mem bers only' clubs (the BD1 or BD2 cove charge represents a 'day membership'), bu many places seem to ignore this.

Arabic Teahouses There are very few tra ditional tea/coffee houses left in centra Manama; most of the more accessible an welcoming (for foreigners) are located in o around Municipality Square. One authentic hangout is *Ahmed Abdul Rahim's Coffee-house* on Government Ave. The sign is only in Arabic, but it's hard to miss with all those old men sitting on blue benches puffing or the sheesha and sipping piping hot drinks from tiny glasses. *Laialy Zaman* (see Restaurants) is an excellent place for views, breezes, tea/coffee and a puff on the sheesha.

Shopping
The Souq Bab al-Bahrain serves as the main entrance to the souq, which covers roughly the area between Al-Khalifa and Sheikh Abdullah Aves, and between Municipality Square and an area a few hundred metres east of the Bab. Electronic items and women's clothing seem to be the souq's main stock in trade – as well as pearls and gold – but in the great tradition of Middle Eastern bazaars almost anything can be found. Most shops are open from about 8 am to 12.30 pm, and 3.30 to 8 pm, Saturday to Thursday, and usually on Friday morning only.

Shopping Centres A lot of wealthier locals, Western expats and tourists do their shopping at modern, Western-style shopping centres. They all sell beautiful jewellery, exquisite souvenirs and fashionable clothes and many have shops selling Western brand name goods, fast-food outlets and video arcades. Naturally, prices in the shopping centres are higher than anything in the souq, but many shops have sales in October or November. One attraction, however, is that these shopping centres are air-conditioned and open every day, often from about 9 am to 9 pm, though some shops within each centre occasionally close for several hours in the early afternoon each day.

In central Manama, you'll find the modern Yateem Centre, the GOSI Shopping Complex, and the smaller Lulu and Al-Zeinah shopping centres. The Bahrain Commercial Complex (also known as the Sheraton Complex, because it's close to that hotel) is popular. In the suburbs, Seef Mall is the newest and brightest with several stores familiar to Western expats and tourists including JC Penny and Marks & Spencers. Also worth a look is the nearby Al A'Ali shopping centre. Both are only accessible by private vehicle or taxi.

Souvenirs A wide selection of local crafts are on sale at the souvenir shop at Bab al-Bahrain, and at stalls all over the souq. The Arts Centre, which is an impressive building just south of the Bahrain National Museum, has a collection of very expensive, modern paintings. Music cassettes are authentic, quite cheap (about BD2) and available at several places along Al-Khalifa Ave. Tailored shirts, trousers and dresses are comparatively good value if you shop around. Refer to Shopping in the Facts for the Visitor section earlier in this chapter for further information.

The Craft Centre With a number of workshops in a central location, the Craft Centre (☎ 254 688) is the best place to go if you want to watch handicrafts being made, and buy something authentic. Thirteen different types of handicrafts, mostly with products from Bahrain and all made by Bahrainis, are on sale: stained glass windows and lamps; paper made from the leaves of date palms; pottery; carvings, often made from recycled driftwood; ironware; and calligraphy. Other souvenirs include dolls, paintings and embroidered clothes. The centre is very relaxed, with little or no hard selling, and is open Saturday to Wednesday, 8.30 am to 1.30 pm; and Thursday, 9 am to midday.

Carpets If you don't manage to get to Iran, or Afghanistan, Bahrain is flooded with Persian carpets, from small prayer mats to enormous pure silk double-stitched rugs costing up to BD2000.

Getting There & Away

Air For flights into Bahrain International Airport, see the Getting There & Away section earlier in this chapter.

The addresses and phone numbers of the larger carriers serving Bahrain are:

British Airways (☎ 801 359) Al-Khalifa Ave
Cathay Pacific Airways (☎ 226 226) Government Ave, just west of Bab al-Bahrain
Gulf Air (☎ 335 777; ☎ 338 844 at the airport) Manama Centre, Government Ave. Open from 7 am to 7 pm, Saturday to Thursday; and Friday, 8 am to midday.
KLM-Royal Dutch Airlines (☎ 224 234) Manama Centre
Kuwait Airways (☎ 223 300) Manama Centre
Lufthansa Airlines (☎ 210 026) Manama Centre
Saudi Arabian Airlines (☎ 211 550) City Centre Hotel complex, Government Ave

Getting Around

To/From the Airport Bahrain International Airport is on Muharraq Island, about 6km from central Manama. Bus No 1 runs between the airport and the Manama Bus Terminal every 40 minutes, every day between about 6 am and 8.45 pm. A metered taxi from central Manama to the airport should cost about BD2. For trips *from* the airport there is a BD1 surcharge, and taxi drivers are very reluctant to use the meter.

Taxi Taxis are easy to find, and there are taxi stands outside Bab al-Bahrain, many upmarket hotels and the shopping centres. Refer to the Getting Around section earlier in this chapter for information about hiring taxis.

Around Bahrain Island

The main island is about 82% of the land mass of the country. Technically it is known as Awal Island, but most people just call it Bahrain Island or Al-Bahrain.

KARBABAD

This village is best known for **basket weaving**. Village folk sit outside their homes making baskets, place mats and chicken coops from the fronds of the plentiful date palms which surround the village. Things are for sale, but it's not really set up for tourism in the same way as the handicrafts centre at Al-Jasra.

Karbabad is a short walk from Qala'at al-Bahrain, and accessible from Manama along Sheikh Khalifa bin Sulman Hwy (the western extension of King Faisal Hwy). It's best to charter a taxi; there are no public buses.

QALA'AT AL-BAHRAIN

Bahrain's main archaeological site, also known as Bahrain Fort and the Portuguese Fort, is a complex containing four separate excavations. The site has been undergoing extensive work (and will be for many years to come), apparently with the goal of restoring to its original form the ruined Portuguese fortress long familiar to visitors to Bahrain. Despite the construction, and an ongoing archaeological dig near the main fort, the site remains open during daylight hours every day. Admission is free.

This was the site of the earliest professional archaeological digs in Bahrain, the ones described so wonderfully in Geoffrey Bibby's *Looking for Dilmun*. When Bibby began digging here in the winter of 1953–54, the Portuguese Fort was the only thing visible. It was obvious, however, that the Portuguese structure was sitting on a *tell*, a hill formed from the rubble of previous cities. The digging went on well into the 1980s and what emerged was a much broader and more complex pattern of settlement than had been expected. In all, seven layers of occupation were discovered. Bear in mind when looking at the fort and excavated areas that in ancient times the coastline was closer to the ruins than it is today.

Things to See

The site appears to have been occupied from about 2800 BC, the time when Dilmun was coming into its own as a commercial power. The settlement was then fairly small. The oldest excavated part of the site is the portion of a defensive wall from the City II period (circa 2000 BC). This was the Early Dilmun period during which the Dilmun civilisation was at the height of its power. The ruins of this wall are all that survive from this era of the site's history. They indicate, however, that this spot on the northern coast of the island was regarded as important. (Why else would the previously undefended site have been surrounded with a wall?) The largest visible section of the wall lies just east of the Portuguese ruins.

The excavated remains of Cities III and IV are referred to as the Kassite and Assyrian Buildings. These date from 1500 to 500 BC and lie just south of the Portuguese fortress. The main thing to see in this area is the ruin of a house with a 3m high entryway (in the monumental style familiar to anyone who has spent a few minutes in the Assyrian gallery of the British Museum in London). The house probably dates from the latter part of the City IV period.

City V was a Hellenistic settlement of which no excavated remains are visible. The area toward the sea contains City VI, the Islamic Fort, of which little remains. This is generally thought to have been built in the 11th century AD though some archaeologists believe it shows characteristics of much earlier construction, indicating that it may have been built on top of (or by making significant alterations to) an earlier structure.

Then there is City VII, the mid-16th century Portuguese fort surrounded by a dry moat. Two of the bastions are in sturdy shape and restoration work still continues.

Getting There & Away

Qala'at al-Bahrain is about 5km west of Manama, and easy to reach by car. Drive along the King Faisal Hwy, and its extension, the Sheikh Khalifa bin Sulman Hwy, and follow the signs. At the end of the paved road, drive along a dirt track over a low hill to the site.

From Manama, bus No 5 goes along the Al-Budayyi' Hwy, from where it's a 3.5km walk to the ruins. If you hire a taxi, tell him to wait for you at the site. If you pay him and he promises to 'pick you up later', he probably won't and you'll be stranded.

BARBAR TEMPLE

Barbar is a complex of three 2nd and 3rd millennium BC temples. These were probably dedicated to Enki, the God of Wisdom and The Sweet Waters Under the Earth. In a country as blessed with natural springs as Bahrain this god of fresh waters was, understandably, an important one.

There is officially no admission fee, but a guide pressures visitors to sign a guest book and make a donation (BD1 is enough). The site is open every day during daylight hours.

Things to See

Temples I and II are both from the 3rd millennium BC. In general, the oldest portions of the complex are those closer to the centre. Though the entire site was enclosed by a wall during the Temple II period, the thick-wall areas, including the one with a rounded corner, are from Temple III (early 2nd millennium BC).

The excavated complex can be seen from a series of walkways, which provide a great overview, but it's hard to understand without a detailed map (eg, in *Bahrain: A Heritage Explored* by Angela Clark), or whatever guidebook or map is available at the site.

Getting There & Away

From Manama, take the Al-Budayyi' Hwy and turn right (north) at the sign to Barbar. Follow this road; the temple is on the right. The closest bus stop is in 6 village, about 30 minutes' away from Barbar Temple on foot.

AD-DIRAZ

The village of Ad-Diraz has two attractions: the small ruins of a temple, and a workshop showcasing some traditional arts and crafts.

Ad-Diraz Temple

Ad-Diraz is the other Dilmun-era temple to the west of Qala'at al-Bahrain. Ad-Diraz was excavated in the mid-'70s, but less is known about it than some of the other Dilmun temples. It dates from the 2nd millennium BC, and is several centuries younger than the Barbar Temple, from which it differs significantly.

The centrepiece is a stone base, which was probably surrounded by columns; the column bases are still intact. The stone base originally supported either an altar or a statue of the god to whom the temple was dedicated. In the centre of the temple is another stone which was an altar of some sort. The drain hole in the floor was probably used to channel offerings away from the altar.

The temple is open during daylight hours, and admission is free.

Craft Workshop

Ad-Diraz also boasts a workshop where nearly 50 women weave locally produced wool to make wall hangings, cushions and carpets – all under the auspices of the Craft Centre in Manama (see Shopping in the Manama section earlier in this chapter). Ask directions to the workshop from Ad-Diraz village or temple, or arrange a special visit through the Craft Centre.

Getting There & Away

The turn-off to the village is clearly signposted along the Al-Budayyi' Hwy from Manama (but not if you're driving in the other direction). Bus No 5 between Manama and Al-Budayyi' normally stops in Ad-Diraz village, and within walking distance of the temple and craft workshop.

BANI JAMRAH

Bani Jamrah village, just south of the Al-Budayyi' Hwy, is known for its **cloth weavers**, but only a few workshops remain. The looms themselves are very complex.

BAHRAIN

The weaver sits in a small hollowed-out concrete area inside a shack. Yarn is drawn into the loom from a skein placed in a bag secured to a wooden post eight to 10m away. The resulting cloth is available for sale at negotiable prices. All sorts of different patterns are available.

Bani Jamrah is well signed from Al-Budayyi' Hwy, but is not accessible by public bus directly from Manama.

AL-BUDAYYI'

This small village marks the western edge of Bahrain Island. There are stunning **views** of the beach at sunset, and of the King Fahd Causeway. The mammoth building overlooking the sea is **Sheikh Hamad's Fort House**, a private residence not open to the public. Al-Budayyi' is at the far western end of Al-Budayyi' Hwy, and accessible by bus No 5 from Manama.

SUQ AL-KHAMIS MOSQUE

The original mosque is believed to have been built in the early 8th century by Omar bin Aziz, one of the first caliphs, but an inscription dates the construction of most of the remains to the second half of the 11th century. The mosque was originally built without minarets; these were added in the 11th and 12th centuries (and restored recently). The mosque was the first built in Bahrain, and is one of the oldest in the region. Reconstruction work has been continuing for several years.

The mosque is open to visitors Saturday to Wednesday, from 7 am to 2 pm; and Thursday and Friday, 8 am to midday. Admission is free. It's about 2.5km south-west of central Manama. Take the Sheikh Sulman Hwy to Al-Khamis village; the mosque is on the right side of the road. The mosque is also accessible from Manama on bus Nos 2 and 7.

ADHARI PARK

Adhari Park (☎ 273 616) is a garden and amusement area. The natural spring and a pool containing fish and tortoises are a welcome respite from Manama's noise. The park is free to enter, but rides cost 300 to

400 fils each. It's open every day from 8 am to midday, and 3.30 to 9 pm, but is empty most weekdays (Saturday to Wednesday), when you could have the place to yourself. The park is poorly signed, and only accessible when heading west from Manama along Sheikh Isa bin Sulman Hwy – turn right just after the Dairy Queen fast food restaurant.

A'ALI
Burial Mounds

There are thousands of burial mounds all over Bahrain. Many are concentrated in about half-a-dozen major mound fields. The most impressive mounds are the so-called 'Royal Tombs' near the village of Λ'ali. These are the largest burial mounds in Bahrain. While the mounds may have been the tombs of kings, they were originally pronounced 'royal' simply because of their size: the largest are 12 to 15m high and up to 45m in diameter.

The area where the mounds are located is unsigned, and has no entrance or explanations, but it's a great place to wander around. The Bahrain National Museum in Manama has more information about the mounds.

Arts & Crafts

A'ali is the site of Bahrain's best-known **pottery workshop**. A'ali pottery is on sale at several stalls around the village, and in the souvenir shop at Bab al-Bahrain in Manama. A'ali is also home to the Muharraqi Gallery (☎ 642 200), which features modern Bahraini art.

Getting There & Away

From Manama, take the Sheikh Sulman Hwy south past Isa Town. Then turn west along A'ali Hwy and follow the signs to the village, pottery workshop or burial mounds. Buses are problematic: Bus Nos 2 and 7 go from Manama to Isa Town, from where bus No 9 goes to A'ali village – but it's still a 20-minute walk to the burial mounds from the village.

SAR

Sar was the site of another Dilmun settlement. Some of the **burial mounds** there are

BAHRAIN

now being excavated, and archaeologists are excited about their other finds too: a small commercial village with a main street, a temple and dozens of homes dating back about 4000 years. When excavations are finished, there are plans to turn the site into a major tourist attraction, with a museum. Like the mounds at A'ali, the area has no entrance or explanations.

Although the site seems close, there is no access from the Causeway Approach Rd. First, go to Sar village, from the signposted road heading south from Al-Budayyi' Hwy or from Janabiya Hwy, and then follow the signs to the burial mounds.

There is no direct bus from Manama: the only bus to Sar village is bus No 12 from Hamad. From Sar village, it's a 15-minute walk to the burial mounds.

KING FAHD CAUSEWAY
The causeway connecting Bahrain and Saudi Arabia is an impressive piece of engineering. Customs and immigration formalities are carried out on an artificial island halfway across the narrow strait separating the two countries. Two needle-like towers dominate the island – one in Saudi Arabia, and the other in Bahrain.

The *King Fahd Causeway Restaurant* in the tower on the Bahraini side has ordinary food, but the views from the restaurant (and elsewhere in the tower) are superb. A ride

in the glass elevator to the top of the tower costs 500 fils (which is refunded if you buy anything at the restaurant). The tower is open every day from 9 am to 11 pm. The best time to drive across the bridge and go up the tower is at dusk, when the sun sets over the ocean.

All drivers (and passengers in taxis) must pay a BD2 toll per vehicle at a booth along the Causeway Approach Rd, whether going to Saudi Arabia or not. No local public bus goes along the causeway. Refer to Land in the Getting There & Away section earlier in this chapter for information about crossing the border by bus and private vehicle.

JANABIYA CAMEL FARM
The unexciting village of Al-Janabiya has a camel farm with over 200 of the beasts. The farm is a private concern, and not really a tourist attraction, but foreigners are normally welcome. The best time to see the camels is at daybreak or late in the afternoon, when they're being led out to pasture. Al-Janabiya village and the camel farm are easy to reach from along Janabiya Hwy. There is no direct bus from Manama.

AL-JASRA
The pleasant village of Al-Jasra has two worthwhile attractions: an historic house, and a handicrafts centre nearby.

Al-Jasra House
This is one of several historic homes around Bahrain that have been restored to their original condition. The present emir's father, Sheikh Isa bin Sulman al-Khalifa, was born here on 3 June 1933. The house was built in 1907 mainly of coral and gypsum, with palm tree trunks used to strengthen the walls.

The house is low set, and there has been a lot of landscaping work around the outside of the compound and in the large courtyard that separates the main gate from the house itself. The house is open Sunday to Tuesday, from 8 am to 2 pm; Wednesday and Thursday, from 9 am to 6 pm; and Friday from 3 to 6 pm. Admission costs 200 fils.

King Fahd Causeway

This incredible causeway, named after the current king of Saudia Arabia, was conceived during the oil boom of the late 1970s. It took four years to build, and was finished in 1986 at a cost of approximately SR3000 million (about US$718 million). The causeway is 25km long, and made up of over 500 huge concrete columns, five separate bridges (the longest is about 5.2km), and seven embankments. The concrete is carefully made to withstand the severe tides, though the water surrounding the bridge is never more than 13m deep.

BAHRAIN

Al-Jasra Handicraft Centre

The government-run Al-Jasra Handicraft Centre (☎ 611 900) is a modern and well-designed collection of workshops which specialise in numerous handicrafts, such as textiles, basket-weaving and mirrors. Open from about 9 am to 4 pm everyday, the centre is adjacent to a bus stop in Al-Jasra village, and a few hundred metres before Al-Jasra house.

To reach Al-Jasra House (which is not particularly well signed) from Manama, go along the Causeway Approach Rd, look for the exit to Al-Jasra (before the toll booth for Saudi Arabia), go past two roundabouts, through a residential area and past the Handicraft Centre. There is no direct bus from Manama to Al-Jasra, but bus No 12 between Sar and Hamad stops outside the handicrafts centre, from where it's about 10 minutes on foot to Al-Jasra House.

RIFFA

The main town in the centre of Bahrain Island, Riffa is subdivided into the modern, and green, West Riffa, where the emir and members of his family live, and the older East Riffa. The **Sheikh Isa bin Sulman al-Khalifa Jame Mosque** in West Riffa is modern and impressive, and worth a look. Riffa is well connected to Manama by bus No 7.

RIFFA FORT

The well-renovated Riffa Fort (☎ 779 394) stands majestically overlooking the Riffa Valley, and was originally built in the 17th century by Sheikh Fraer bin Rahal to observe the valley and the villages in the Riffa region. It was rebuilt between 1795 and 1812 and became a private residence (with 35 rooms) for Sheikh Sulman bin Ahmed al-Fateh. It was restored to its present state in 1983.

The fort is made entirely from local products, such as clay, lime and mangroves. It has three square-shaped towers and one round one in the north-west corner. Not much is known about the history of the **mosque** next door (which you can also visit if it's open); it was probably built at the same time as the fort. It is now used for worship by the villagers.

The limited displays in the fort are captioned in Arabic. It's still worth visiting for the enchanting **views** over the valley. The fort is open Sunday to Tuesday, 8 am to 2 pm; Wednesday and Thursday, 9 am to 6 pm; and Friday, 3 to 6 pm. Admission is 200 fils.

Riffa Fort is easy to spot from several main roads, but is surprisingly hard to reach and poorly signed. Access is only possible along Sheikh Hamood bin Sebah Ave, which runs south off Riffa Ave. Bus Nos 7 (from Manama) and No 11 (from Hamad) travel along Riffa Ave, and stop near the turn-off to the fort.

AL-AREEN WILDLIFE PARK

This reasonably interesting 10 sq km reserve (☎ 836 116) in the south-west of Bahrain Island is a conservation area for species indigenous to Arabia, such as the Arabian oryx, and others native to the Middle East and North Africa, such as the zebra. After a short introductory film (in Arabic), a small bus leaves about every hour for a 20-minute jaunt (with commentary in Arabic and English) past some of the 240 species of birds and animals (mostly oryx and gazelle). The main building has a *cafeteria* and gift shop.

Admission is BD1; 500 fils for children under 13. The park has strange opening times: 8 to 11 am every day, and from 3 to 5 pm (February to July) and 2 to 4 pm (September to January) – but is closed during Ramadan and August. It's best to call the park office, or check out the 'What's On' column in the *Gulf Daily News*, before heading out.

From Manama, follow the signs to Riffa and then to Awali along Sheikh Sulman Hwy, and then continue towards to Al-Zallaq along the Al-Zallaq Hwy. The turn-off to the park is along the Zallaq Beach Hwy. There is no public transport anywhere near the park.

AL-JAZAYIR BEACH

Bahrain's best beach is also its most inconvenient. Al-Jazayir has a sandy beach, shade, clean water for swimming and huts for overnight camping – but these are only available to Bahrainis with special permission. Al-Jazayir can only be reached by private transport. From Manama, follow the signs along the highways towards Riffa, Awali and Al-Zallaq, and then continue along the Zallaq Beach Hwy. There is no public bus in the area.

AS-SAKHIR PALACE
The remains of this old palace, the former residence of Sheikh Hamad bin Isa al-Khalifa, are not currently open to the public, but they may open some time in the future.

Check with the Tourist Department in Manama. To reach the palace, turn south from Al-Zallaq Hwy, not far west of Awali. The palace is not accessible by bus.

OIL MUSEUM
In the shadow of Jebel ad-Dukhan (Mountain of Smoke) – Bahrain's highest point at a very modest 134m – is the Oil Museum (☎ 753 475). This museum has exhibits, photographs and explanations about the oil industry in Bahrain (the first country on the Arab side of the Gulf to strike 'black gold'). It was built in 1992 to commemorate the

The Garden of Eden?

And the Lord God planted a garden eastward in Eden; and there He put the man whom He had formed. And out of the ground made the Lord God to grow every tree that is pleasant to the sight, and good for food; the tree of life also in the midst of the garden, and the tree of knowledge of good and evil.

Genesis 2:8-9

Bahrain's greenery, and its depiction in Sumerian mythology as an enchanted place where people lived a life free of death and disease, has led some archaeologists and scholars to conclude that it may have been the geographical location of the biblical Garden of Eden. This idea is reinforced by the Tree of Life, the traditional name given by Bahrainis to the lone tree, fed by an underground spring, which stands in the southern desert of Bahrain Island.

On one level, the identification of Bahrain with Eden may not be as implausible as it seems. Most scholars believe that the Old Testament is a product of the mingling of centuries of traditions from throughout the Middle East. Trade routes and conquering kings brought the religious traditions of many societies into contact with one another. In the *Epic of Gilgamesh*, Dilmun (Bahrain) is portrayed as an Eden-like paradise. When he arrives in Bahrain, Gilgamesh is met by the Sumerian equivalent of Noah. It is not unreasonable to suppose that, in the centuries before the Book of Genesis was written down, the Hebrew and Sumerian traditions of paradise and the creation became, to some extent, intermingled. Genesis itself actually combines two separate creation stories and includes (chapter 2, verses 10–14) an account of Eden's location which most modern scholars believe to be a later addition, probably by an ancient scholar who was trying to clarify the text.

According to those verses, 'a river went out of Eden ... and from thence it was parted and became into four heads' (2:10). It then names the four rivers. One is the Euphrates and another is obviously the Tigris, but the identification of the other two is much less clear. Some scholars have identified the other two rivers, named Pison and Gihon, with the Indus and the Nile respectively. Although the Nile flows north and the other three rivers flow south, the idea of all four having a common source would not have seemed as strange then as it does today. The era's geography, such as it was, could envisage the Nile looping up to originate on the northern side of the Mediterranean. This would give the four rivers a common source, probably either somewhere in what is now southern Turkey or in north-central Iraq. So, even with an ancient map, it's hard to see those (or any other) four rivers having a common source at Bahrain.

As the *Encyclopaedia Britannica*'s entry on Eden notes, dryly: 'The attempt to locate a mythological garden is bound to be attended by considerable difficulty'.

60th anniversary of the discovery of oil. (The boxed text 'Discovery of Oil' in the Facts about Bahrain section earlier in this chapter has more details.) A few metres way, you can see the country's **First Oil Well**, which was constructed in 1932.

The museum is open only on Thursday and Friday from 9 am to 6 pm, but ring ahead to find out its current opening hours. The museum is along an unnamed road south of Awali, and well signposted from that town. There is no bus service in the region.

TREE OF LIFE

The Shajarat al-Hiya (Tree of Life) is a lone tree, belonging to the *acacia* family, but is most famous because it somehow survives in the barren desert, presumably fed by an underground spring. The tree is also the centrepiece of the 'Bahrain-was-the-Garden-of-Eden' theory (see the boxed text on the previous page) advanced by some archaeologists, scholars and, enthusiastically, by the tourist office. (For the record: no angel, flaming sword in hand, has recently been seen guarding the tree though the military does occasionally use the area for manoeuvres.) Recent digs have found indications of ancient houses and lookouts nearby.

Although touted as a major tourist attraction, there's nothing else to see or do, and it's a fair way from Manama. The best time to visit is around dusk – but leave before it's too dark, and don't park any vehicle in a sandy area. The site is not easy to find. From Manama, follow the Sheikh Sulman Hwy and Riffa Ave to Riffa, head towards Awali along the Muaskar Hwy, and then look for the signposted turn-off. If possible, go with a knowledgeable local, or on an organised tour (see Organised Tours in the Getting Around section earlier in this chapter for details). There is no bus service within about 15km.

Muharraq Island

Muharraq Island (about 21 sq km) is home to the Bahrain International Airport and the eponymous town, which was once the capi-

tal of Bahrain. Muharraq is easy to get around on foot, though you might want to hop in a taxi for the trip to Qala'at Arad. Bus Nos 1, 2 and 7 travel between the bus terminals in Muharraq and Manama every 30 minutes.

BEIT SHEIKH ISA BIN ALI & BEIT SEYADI

These two traditional houses are well worth visiting for a look at pre-oil life in Bahrain.

Beit Sheikh Isa bin Ali was being renovated at the time of research, and should be more impressive when it re-opens. The house was built in around 1800, presumably by one of Muharraq's wealthier citizens. Later in the 19th century, the then-emir, Sheikh Isa bin Ali, acquired the house for use as his residence and seat of government. Although the rooms are currently bare, the uses of the different sections of the house are well marked in English. The carved doors and restored plasterwork throughout the house are very interesting.

By the main door, there's a large map of the house. The courtyard has a well, and the large room on the right side of the courtyard contains a number of photographs of Ali and his family. It also contains a working **wind tower** – offering tourists one of Bahrain's few opportunities to marvel at these structures' ability to catch even the tiniest breeze. Beyond this room, a passageway leads to the family's living quarters, with its carefully restored reed-and-wood ceilings. More living areas are to be found upstairs.

Beit Seyadi is a smaller house of similar age, with less restoration work, but it's still worth visiting. An old mosque is attached to the house.

Beit Sheikh Isa bin Ali is open Saturday to Wednesday, from 9 am to 2 pm; and Thursday, from 9.30 am to 5 pm. Beit Seyadi is open Saturday to Thursday, from 2 to 6 pm. Admission to both is free, though Beit Sheikh Isa bin Ali may charge a modest entrance fee when restoration work is completed.

Getting There & Away

If driving from Manama, use the Sheikh Hamad Causeway, and look for the signs to both houses at the roundabout on the corner

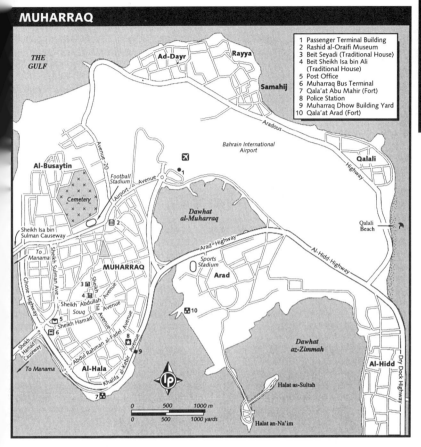

MUHARRAQ

1 Passenger Terminal Building
2 Rashid al-Oraifi Museum
3 Beit Seyadi (Traditional House)
4 Beit Sheikh Isa bin Ali
  (Traditional House)
5 Post Office
6 Muharraq Bus Terminal
7 Qala'at Abu Mahir (Fort)
8 Police Station
9 Muharraq Dhow Building Yard
10 Qala'at Arad (Fort)

of Sheikh Sulman and Sheikh Abdullah Aves. Walking to either house from the Muharraq bus terminal shouldn't take more than 15 minutes.

To reach Beit Seyadi from Beit Sheikh Isa bin Ali on foot – you can't drive there – go straight ahead, and then a bit to the right, as you come out the door of the house and cross a patch of waste ground keeping the mosque to your right and the electrical transformer to your left. This will take you into a narrow alley for about 50m. When you emerge from the alley, the minaret of the mosque attached to Beit Seyadi will be easy to see.

QALA'AT ABU MAHIR

This small fort now occupies the south-western tip of Muharraq Island, but was originally on an island a few hundred metres off Muharraq's southern shore. It is now part of Muharraq because of the huge land reclamation program of the last 40 years. Along with Qala'at Arad it once guarded the approaches to Muharraq Bay. Parts of Qala'at Abu Mahir dates from the 16th century, though parts of it have been rebuilt several times since.

The fort is not particularly impressive: it consists of a single watchtower with a very

BAHRAIN

narrow building attached to its landward side, and only the parts facing across the bay to Manama have been restored. The watchtower, however, does afford excellent **views** of Manama's skyline.

Qala'at Abu Mahir lies within the grounds of the Muharraq coastguard station, so access is usually limited. However, if you present yourself at the gate on a weekday (Saturday to Wednesday), between 7 am and 2 pm, and ask politely, they may let you in. Be especially careful to ask permission before taking any pictures – it is, after all, a military base.

If driving from Manama, use the Sheikh Hamad Causeway, and turn right along Khalifa al-Kabeer Ave.

MUHARRAQ DHOW BUILDING YARD

Muharraq's small dhow yard, on the coast between Qala'at Abu Mahir and the turn-off for the airport, is where fishing dhows are built and repaired. It's an interesting place to wander around. There's no admission charge, but remember to ask permission before taking pictures.

Dhow building is an ancient craft.

QALA'AT ARAD

The Arad fort (☎ 672 278) was built in the early 15th century by the Portuguese. However, much of what is visible today was built and used as the headquarters of the Omani military during the brief Omani occupation of Bahrain in the early 1800s.

Parts of the fort have been beautifully restored, but the fort does look better from a distance. It is not quite as thoroughly re-

stored overall as visitors may initially believe. Inside, there is not really a lot to see except an old well, but the location overlooking the bay is superb.

The fort is open Sunday to Tuesday, from 8 am to 2 pm; Wednesday and Thursday, from 9 am to 6 pm; and Friday, from 3 to 6 pm. The tower by the entrance gate has a display on the fort's history. Admission is free.

From about 4 to 7 pm on Thursday and/or Friday, the forecourt of the fort hosts the popular bazaar, with craft stalls, children's rides and sometimes an entertaining band playing traditional music. Check the listing in the 'Regular Attractions' column in *Bahrain This Month* magazine for current details.

If driving from Manama, take the Sheikh Hamad Causeway, and follow the signs along Khalifa al-Kabeer Ave and then Arad Hwy.

RASHID AL-ORAIFI MUSEUM

Bahrain's newest museum (☎ 335 616) is really a private art gallery dedicated to the work of its artist-owner. It is built around a collection of Al-Oraifi's paintings, most of which are on Dilmun-related themes. A **shop** in the museum sell postcards, silverwork and prints.

The museum is open Saturday to Thursday, from 8 am to midday, and 4 to 8 pm; and Friday, 8 am to midday. Admission costs BD1.

If driving from Manama, take the Sheikh Isa bin Sulman Causeway, turn left along Ghose Hwy, then right along Airport Ave, and look for the signs. Bus Nos 6 and 10 regularly travel between the Muharraq Bus Terminal and the junction of Airport Ave and Sheikh Isa Ave, from where the museum is a few minutes' walk.

MUHARRAQ SOUQ

The Muharraq souq is a lot less modern than the Manama souq and, for that reason, is rather more interesting, but it is considerably smaller. The heart of the souq is the area between Sheikh Abdullah and Sheikh Hamad Aves.

Dar Island

The main attractions are the sandy **beach** and **water sports**, and expensive *restaurant* and *bar*. There is nowhere to stay.

Getting to Dar is a bit haphazard. Go to the special sea taxi terminal on Sitra Island and ask around about a sea taxi to Dar. If there isn't one there already, ring the special telephone number listed in the telephone box indicated in the terminal as 'Sea Taxis Pick Up Point'. Sea taxis leave the terminal when required anytime between 9 am and sunset, every day, and the 20-minute trip to the island costs BD2.500. Sea taxis are easier to organise on Friday and public holidays, but the island is far busier then.

Kuwait

The State of Kuwait

Area: 17,818 sq km
Population: 2.2 million
Capital: Kuwait City
Head of State: The Emir, Sheikh Jaber al-Ahmed al-Sabah
Official Language: Arabic
Currency: Kuwaiti dinar (KD)
Time: GMT/UTC +3
Exchange Rate: KD0.303 = US$1

Highlights

- Take a day trip to Failaka Island.

- If anyone invites you to a *diwaniya* ... go. These informal gatherings, usually at someone's home, are the place where Kuwaitis (well, Kuwaiti men) chat about everything from soccer scores to the day's debates in parliament.

- The National Museum and its small gallery of works by Kuwaiti artists are essential viewing during any visit to Kuwait.

- The National Assembly building is one of the city's architectural landmarks – take in an assembly session (English translation available).

- In the suburbs the Tareq Rajab Museum has a small but excellent collection of Islamic art and artefacts.

Kuwait has always been something of an acquired taste. There are some who rank it as one of the world's great backwaters. And then there are others – the ones who know that Kuwait is different and, for that reason, interesting.

In the 1950s Kuwait was the prototype of what we now call an oil sheikhdom. Today, it is the only place in the Gulf where you can watch that usually exalted species, the cabinet minister, get grilled in a very pub-

lic way by members of parliament. Whatever you may think of politics per se, it is Kuwait's parliament, the only one in the Gulf, that makes it special.

Having some semblance of democratic government has long given the Kuwaitis a sense of themselves as a people different from their neighbours. And more than once it has made the neighbours nervous – and suspicious of Kuwait. In many ways this is the most open place in the Gulf: the press is more-or-less uncensored, visitors can watch the parliament, or hang out on the floor of the stock exchange. Not that these are tourist draws, but they do all help to explain why Kuwait does not have the very tightly controlled feel of much of the rest of the Middle East.

Walking around Kuwait City – a place no-one has ever labelled beautiful – it is difficult to imagine the destruction visited on this small country a decade ago. The Iraqis arrived in August 1990, and were driven out at the end of February 1991. A few years later reconstruction was complete and the city looked almost *exactly* as it had before the invasion.

Beneath the surface, however, very much had changed. Liberation brought a new degree of openness to Kuwaiti life and made the city easier to visit. If Dubai has long been the place in Arabia that *feels* different, Kuwait is the place where things really *are* different. It isn't your run-of-the-mill tourist destination – but that's what makes it so fascinating.

Facts about Kuwait

HISTORY
A Greek Colony in the Gulf
Compared to Bahrain, Kuwait is a newcomer to the world scene. The headland now occupied by Kuwait City was settled only some 300 years ago. Prior to that, the most important part of what is now the

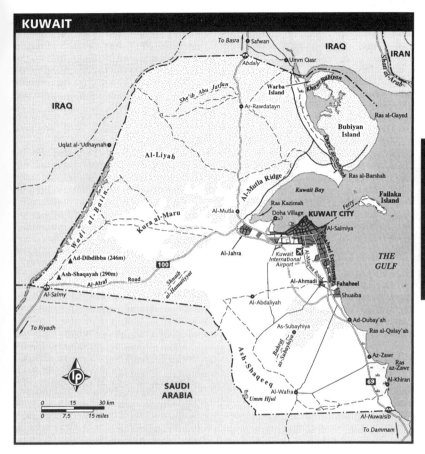

KUWAIT

To Basra • Safwan
Abdaly
Umm Qasr
IRAQ
IRAN
She'ib Abu Jarfan
Warba
Island
Ar-Rawdatayn
Khawr 'Abdullah
IRAQ
Ras al-Gayed
Uqlat al-'Udhaynah
Al-Liyah
Bubiyan
Island
Khawr as-Sabiyah
Al-Mutla Ridge
Ras al-Barshah
Kuwait Bay
Failaka
Island
Ras Kazimah
Al-Mutla
Doha Village
KUWAIT CITY
Ferry
Al-Salmiya
Al-Jahra
Kuwait
International
Airport
Jabal Expressway
THE
GULF
Ad-Dibdibba (246m)
100
Shuaib
al-Humaliyyat
Al-Ahmadi
Fahaheel
Ash-Shaqayah (290m)
Al-Atraf   Road
Shuaiba
Al-Salmy
Al-Abdaliyah
As-Subayhiya
Ad-Dubay'ah
Ras al-Qulay'ah
To Riyadh
Bahrat
as-Subayhiya
Az-Zawr
Ras
az-Zawr
Al-Khiran
Ash-Shaqeeq
SAUDI
ARABIA
Al-Wafra
Umm Hjul
69
0   15   30 km
0   7.5   15 miles
Al-Nuwaisib
To Dammam

State of Kuwait was the small island of Failaka, which lies just outside the mouth of Kuwait Bay and controls the sea lanes approaching it (a point which, many centuries later, was not lost on the Iraqis, who heavily garrisoned the island). The island also served as a convenient stopover for travellers en route from Mesopotamia to the Indian Ocean and beyond.

Failaka was inhabited during the Bronze Age, though it is not entirely clear whether it then belonged to the Bahrain-based Dilmun Empire or was a southern outpost of Sumeria. It was the Greeks, however, who put Failaka, which they called Ikaros, on the map.

By 325 BC, Alexander the Great had crossed the Indus River and conquered parts of what is now India. As he prepared to return to Babylon, Alexander ordered a Cretan commander in his army, Nearchus, to build a fleet and return to Mesopotamia by sea, reconnoitring the coast of Persia while Alexander went by land. The fleet was built near present-day Karachi, and Nearchus eventually rejoined Alexander in Babylon. By then the young king was considering a campaign to conquer Arabia, probably with

KUWAIT

an eye towards the wealth of the frankincense-producing regions in southern Arabia. Nearchus was sent back to the Gulf, this time with the task of scouting the Gulf's Arabian coastline. He launched several different survey vessels, and his troops are known to have travelled at least as far as Hormuz. But the Arabian campaign was never to be. Alexander died at Babylon only days before he planned to depart for Arabia.

By the time Alexander's empire collapsed, a Greek colony had been established on Failaka. Alexander himself is said to have christened the island Ikaros. Though the island was inhabited when Nearchus arrived, its earlier character was rapidly Hellenised. Ikaros became a centre for trade, fishing and pearling. It was no great metropolis, but it seems to have been reasonably prosperous.

The Beginnings of Kuwait

Failaka may have been prosperous but throughout most of the Christian era it was not a place of importance. The adjacent areas of the mainland had even less to recommend them and it was not until the 17th century that anything much happened there.

It is unclear both when Kuwait was founded and when the Al-Sabah, Kuwait's ruling family, first arrived. Official tradition says the family arrived in the area in 1716, though other sources give 1722 or even 'sometime in the 1670s' as the date. What is known is that the Al-Sabah were members of the Utbi tribal confederation and that they, and many others, migrated to the Gulf from the Najd region in central Arabia following a period of drought and famine. The Utbis initially went to Basra (in present-day Iraq) where they appealed for help to the Ottoman authorities. From Basra they are thought to have wandered south to the headland where Kuwait City now stands.

The word *kuwait* is an Arabic diminutive meaning 'small fort'. The term is thought to refer to a fort or storehouse where the local sheikh kept arms and/or food and livestock; at the time of the Utbis' arrival, Kuwait was nothing more than a few tents and the storehouse-cum-fort. The land was arid and any agriculture or grazing was negligible. The site did, however, have one clear asset: the bay is one of the best natural harbours on the Arabian side of the Gulf.

The Utbis placed themselves under the protection of the Bani Khalid, then the most powerful tribal confederation in eastern Arabia and the Gulf. They divided among themselves the responsibilities attached to the new settlement: the ancestors of the Al-Sabah family were appointed to handle local law and order and relations with the Bani Khalid. Another family, the Al-Khalifa, was put in charge of the pearl trade, though within a generation it had departed for the better pearling banks of the central Gulf, and by the end of the 18th century had conquered Bahrain where they still rule.

In 1752 the Utbis confirmed the right of the Al-Sabah family to rule Kuwait. Today's ruling family takes its name from an ancestor who was confirmed as ruler in that year and reigned until 1756. He spent this brief period taking the first steps to establish Kuwait as a major trading centre.

Turks, Persians & Britons

The small settlement grew quickly. A Dutch trader who visited Kuwait in 1756 wrote that it had a fleet of some 300, mostly small, boats. The town could also muster 4000 armed men in times of crisis. The mainstay of the economy was pearling. By 1760, when the town's first wall was built, Kuwait's dhow fleet was said to number 800 and camel caravans based there travelled regularly to Baghdad, Riyadh and Damascus.

The great Danish explorer Carsten Neibuhr visited Kuwait, which he called Graine, in 1765 and described it as a town of some 10,000 people, though during the summer 70% of its inhabitants would disappear to work the pearl banks or travel with the caravans. According to Neibuhr, in spite of (or maybe because of) the town's prosperity the Utbi and the Bani Khalid still periodically fought over it. Failaka, he said, served as a retreat for noncombatants.

By the early 19th century Kuwait was a busy and thriving trading port. The British traveller WG Palgrave, who visited in 1865, attributed this prosperity to the town's good government.

But trouble was always, quite literally, just over the horizon. It was often unclear whether Kuwait was part of the Ottoman Empire or not. Certainly the Ottomans maintained a claim to the emirate, even after it formally became a British protectorate at the end of the 19th century. Official Kuwaiti history is adamant that the Al-Sabah domains were always independent of the Ottomans. In any event, Constantinople's control of the fringes of its empire had always been pretty nominal and never more so than during the 19th century.

International politics in 18th- and 19th-century Kuwait meant playing the Ottomans against the Persians. It was a game at which the Al-Sabah became remarkably adept. As the years went by, the British became involved as well. The East India Company temporarily moved its Basra office to Kuwait twice in the late 18th century (in 1776 and again in 1793–95) to escape the wars between the Ottomans and Persia. In return, the British drove back the Ottomans when they threatened Kuwait in 1795.

During the second half of the 19th century the Kuwaitis generally got on well with the Ottomans. They skilfully managed to avoid being absorbed into their empire as the Turks sought (not entirely successfully) to solidify their control over eastern Arabia, then known as Al-Hasa. The Al-Sabah did, however, agree to take the title of provincial governors of Al-Hasa.

It was that decision which led to the rise of Sheikh Mubarak al-Sabah al-Sabah, commonly known as Mubarak the Great (reigned 1896–1915), the pivotal figure in the history of modern Kuwait. Mubarak was vehemently opposed to accommodating Turkey. Deeply suspicious of the Ottomans and convinced (probably correctly) that Constantinople planned to annex Kuwait, he overthrew and murdered his brother, Sheikh Mohammed, did away with another brother (Jarrah) and installed himself as ruler.

After the palace coup Mubarak's reign was both prosperous and quiet. The population more than tripled (to 35,000 in 1910) and the

first schools were opened. Two of Mubarak's four sons went on to become rulers. It is only from these two branches of the royal family that the country's emirs are now chosen.

In 1899 Mubarak signed an agreement with Britain modelled on the exclusive agreements Britain had signed with the other Gulf rulers over the previous four decades. In exchange for the Royal Navy's protection, he promised not to give away territory to, take support from or negotiate with any other foreign power without British consent.

The Ottomans continued to claim sovereignty over Kuwait, but they were now in no position to enforce it. Britain's motive for signing the treaty of 1899 was a desire to keep Germany, then the main ally and financial backer of Turkey, out of the Gulf. The Germans had already built a railway line from Constantinople to Baghdad, and an extension to Basra and Kuwait was planned. The treaty was London's guarantee that there would never be a railway link from Europe, via Turkey, all the way to the Gulf.

In 1913 the British confirmed Kuwait's independence from the Ottomans by defining the emirate's border with the Ottoman province of Basra. (When Iraq became independent in 1932, it reluctantly accepted this border but renounced it after Iraq's monarchy was overthrown in 1958.) The Turkish threat faded when Britain occupied Mesopotamia during WWI.

The 1920s, however, saw a new threat. Around the turn of the century Mubarak had played host for several years to the Al-Saud family, who had been driven from their base in Riyadh and had ended up in Kuwait after wandering along the edge of the Empty Quarter desert for a time. It was from Kuwait that the young Abdul Aziz bin Abdul Rahman al-Saud set out, first to reclaim Riyadh, and then to restore the kingdom stretching from the Gulf to the Red Sea which his family had ruled in the late 18th and early 19th centuries.

As he became master of more and more of Arabia, Abdul Aziz never made much secret of his belief that the entire peninsula was, by rights, part of the Saudi kingdom. His years in Kuwait notwithstanding, he eventually turned his attention to the city and unleashed the *ikhwan*, or brotherhood, his much feared army of Bedouin warriors. Though Abdul Aziz himself was unusually broad-minded the same could not be said of many of his followers, and they took a dark view of what they saw as the loose-living ways of the Kuwaitis.

At the time, Kuwait had no defensive wall so one was hurriedly erected. The (re-constructed) gates along Al-Soor St in modern Kuwait City are all that remain of it today. Hoping to put an end to the Saudi threat, the British, in 1922–23, negotiated a formal treaty under which Abdul Aziz recognised Kuwait's independence. His price, however, was two-thirds of what the ruler, Sheikh Ahmed, had always understood to be his land. The British told Sheikh Ahmed that it was a small price to pay to guarantee the country's independence. The attacks, however, did not stop until some years later (the last one took place in 1930), when Abdul Aziz was forced to crush the ikhwan, who had by then become a threat to his own throne.

The First Oil State

In 1911 the Anglo-Persian Oil Company (the forerunner of today's British Petroleum, or BP) requested permission from the British government to negotiate a concession agreement with the ruler of Kuwait. The British refused, but did go to the trouble of sending an official of their own to inspect the seepages which had attracted Anglo-Persian's attention in the first place.

With much political manoeuvring, in which the British tried in vain to keep US companies out of the region, it was not until 1934 that an oil concession was granted. The contract went to a joint venture owned fifty-fifty by Anglo-Persian and the US-based Gulf Oil Company. Together, the two companies set up the Kuwait Oil Company (KOC) through which they ran their operations in the emirate.

The first wells were sunk in 1936, and by 1938 it was obvious that the sheikhdom was virtually floating on oil. The outbreak of WWII forced KOC to suspend its activities

for several years, but when export operations took off after the war so did the country's economy. Though Kuwait's royalties were slightly lower than those received by Saudi Arabia, Iraq and Iran, the emirate's relatively small population made the revenues huge when calculated on a per capita basis.

The first great rush of oil money came in 1951. In that year Iran's prime minister, Mohammed Mossadiq, nationalised the assets of the Anglo-Iranian Oil Company (as Anglo-Persian was renamed after Persia became Iran in 1935), effectively cutting off the flow of Iranian oil to the company's operations outside the country. Both Anglo-Iranian and its competition rapidly stepped up production elsewhere, including Kuwait, to take up the slack. Between 1946 and 1956 Kuwait's output rose from 800,000 to a staggering 54 million long tons per year.

Emir Abdullah al-Salem al-Sabah (reigned 1950–65) became the first 'oil sheikh'. His reign was not, however, marked by the kind of profligacy with which that term later came to be associated. Kuwait's trading wealth had, up to that point, given it a very high standard of living in local terms and had brought with it some degree of development.

As a trading city, particularly one with a long history of contact with both the British and the Turks, Kuwait had also developed an open-minded society rather than a xenophobic one. Moreover, when foreign workers began to flood into the country, the Kuwaiti government went out of its way to ease potential tensions by seeing to it that as many of those workers as possible were Arabs.

As the country became dramatically wealthy, health care, education and the general standard of living improved. In 1949 Kuwait had only four doctors. By 1967 it had 400. The city wall was torn down in 1957 to make way for the rapid, oil-driven growth.

With this flood of money Kuwait was quickly transformed almost beyond recognition. This, however, was meagre compared to what happened in the '70s. In 1973

Kuwait's oil revenues totalled US$1.7 billion. In 1978 they totalled US$9.2 billion.

Though the fourfold jump in the price of oil between 1973 and 1975 accounted for much of this increase in revenue, another significant factor was the nationalisation of KOC. In 1974 the government bought 60% of the company. In March 1975, with tension between the Arab world and the West still high in the wake of the 1973–74 oil embargo, Kuwait announced that it was taking over the remaining 40% of the company, though this action was not implemented until December of that year.

Independence

On 19 June 1961 the treaty with Britain was terminated by mutual consent and Kuwait became an independent state.

In the years leading up to independence, the Al-Sabah family's position in society had been reinforced by the fact that the early oil revenues were paid directly to the ruler. Many, however, including the emirate's large population of Egyptian and Palestinian workers, still saw Kuwait as little more than a British colony.

Abdullah was succeeded by Sheikh Sabah al-Salem al-Sabah (reigned 1965–77). The current emir, Sheikh Jaber al-Ahmed al-Sabah, served as finance minister under Abdullah before becoming crown prince and prime minister under Sabah.

Wealth alone could not guarantee stability. The country's labour unions struck in 1967, accusing the government of not giving sufficient support to the Arab and Palestinian cause during that year's Arab-Israeli war. The government sought to placate them, first by briefly cutting off the flow of oil to the West during the war, and later by taking a prominent role in the Arab summit that took place in Khartoum several months after the war. At Khartoum, Kuwait promised huge sums of money to the 'frontline' states confronting Israel and to various Palestinian organisations. When war broke out again in 1973, the government sent Kuwaiti troops to fight along the Suez Canal, partly to blunt the criticism it expected in the National Assembly, or parliament.

The 1980s: From Boom to Slump

During the late 1970s Kuwait's economy seemed to be roaring ahead. The country's stock exchange (the first in the Gulf) was among the top 10 in the world and bankers were lining up to buy securities denominated in Kuwaiti dinars.

By the mid-'80s everything was different. In the winter of 1985–86, the price of oil collapsed and the economies of all the Gulf States were severely affected. But in Kuwait there were other problems as well. In addition to its regular stock market the country had developed a parallel financial market which, while not strictly legal, was allowed to operate openly and with virtually no regulation. The market, known as the Souq al-Manakh, operated on a system of postdated cheques which made it virtually impossible for investors to lose money. In 1982, however, panic ensued when some investors got jittery, tried to reclaim their money and found that the dealers were unable to honour the cheques. Within days the entire system collapsed and hundreds of people became bankrupt. The scandal left behind US$90 billion in worthless postdated cheques and a mess which the Kuwaiti government has been trying to sort out ever since.

Just as the government began to deal with the fallout from the Souq al-Manakh fiasco, another problem arose. As the Iran-Iraq war, which had begun in 1980, dragged on into its third year, the emirate's location only a few miles from the frontlines made investors nervous. Though some Kuwaiti companies made a lot of money shipping embargoed goods to Iraq the war was, on the whole, a disaster for the country's economy. It did not help matters much that from 1983 Iran sought to punish (officially neutral) Kuwait for its thinly veiled support for Iraq. From 1983 to 1985 the country suffered a string of Iranian-inspired terror-bombings, including highly publicised attacks on the US and French embassies. These attacks scared off foreigners, exacerbated the Sunni-Shi'ite division in the population and made the government fanatically security conscious.

KUWAIT

As the 1980s drew to a close, things began to change. The Iran-Iraq war ended, bringing with it a marked lessening of the regional tensions. That, in turn, brought strong demands from quite a few Kuwaitis for a restoration of parliament, which had been suspended during the Iran-Iraq conflict. This had happened because the emir believed that debates in the parliament at the time were creating internal discord at a moment when the greatest need was for the country to pull together. In late 1989 and early 1990 thousands of Kuwaitis turned out to call for democracy. As a percentage of the population these demonstrations were, in fact, larger than anything seen in Eastern Europe around the same time. The government, however, rejected the democracy movement and launched a clampdown on dissent.

The Gulf War – A Chronology

1990

16 July	Iraq sends letter to the Arab League complaining that Kuwait is exceeding its OPEC oil quota and stealing oil from an oilfield straddling the Iraq-Kuwait border.
17 July	Iraqi President Saddam Hussein repeats the charges in a speech marking Iraq's Revolution Day.
26–27 July	Egyptian President Hosni Mubarak and Saudi Arabian Foreign Minister Saud Al-Faisal travel to Baghdad and Kuwait City in separate attempts to diffuse the growing crisis. Iraq agrees to meet Kuwait for reconciliation talks in the Saudi city of Taif on 31 July.
1 August	Iraq walks out of Taif talks.
2 August	2 am – Iraqi forces invade Kuwait. By the end of the day the country is occupied. Kuwait's emir and his cabinet flee to Saudi Arabia. In New York, the UN Security Council condemns the invasion and imposes an embargo on Iraqi oil exports.
6 August	Iraq annexes Kuwait.
9 August	King Fahd of Saudi Arabia accepts US offer of troops to defend the kingdom against a possible Iraqi invasion. The troops begin arriving the following day and number 10,000 by 14 August. Iraq refuses to allow Western residents and travellers to leave the country and begins efforts to round up Western residents of Kuwait.
10 August	Emergency Arab League summit convenes in Cairo but Saddam refuses to attend. The summit passes a resolution criticising Iraq, but the league is deeply split by Saudi Arabia's decision to allow US troops onto its soil.
18 August	US President George Bush mobilises reserve units of the US military. Iraq announces that it will hold Westerners as hostages at military and civilian facilities to guard against a US attack, and threatens to respond to any such attack with chemical and biological weapons.
23 August	Iraq releases some French hostages. Over the next four months all of the hostages are released, usually in small groups of particular nationalities after personal appeals to Saddam by various celebrities and politicians.
10 September	Bush and Soviet President Mikhail Gorbachev, meeting in Helsinki, condemn Iraq's occupation of Kuwait and call for a full withdrawal of Iraqi forces.
Mid-September	Iraqi troop strength in Kuwait reaches 360,000.
Oct-Nov	Amnesty International issues a report condemning Iraq for torture and other atrocities in Kuwait as the two sides in the conflict continue to build up their troop strength and dig in.

Iraq & Kuwait

Iraq has never really accepted the idea of Kuwait as an independent state: the 1990 invasion was only the latest attempt by Iraq to challenge Kuwait's existence. Minor skirmishes and the occasional major incident have been regular features of Iraqi-Kuwaiti relations since the 1950s. Within hours of Kuwait gaining independence from Britain in 1961, Iraq reasserted its long-standing claim to the emirate. The emir called in the British who sent a small force to Kuwait. This proved to be enough to deter the Iraqis in the short term, and the force was replaced three months later by a joint Arab League force.

The most serious of the two countries' many border clashes took place in March 1973 when the Iraqis moved an estimated 3000 troops onto Kuwaiti territory, occupied

The Gulf War – A Chronology

8 November	The USA announces that it is sending an additional 200,000 troops to the Gulf. The anti-Iraq coalition eventually numbers 425,000 US troops and 265,000 troops from 27 other countries. The coalition commands more than 150 ships and 2000 aircraft.
29 November	The UN Security Council authorises the use of force to drive Iraq out of Kuwait if Baghdad fails to withdraw from the emirate by 15 January 1991.
6 December	Iraq releases the last of its foreign hostages.

1991

9 January	US Secretary of State James Baker and Iraqi Foreign Minister Tariq Aziz hold more than six hours of talks in Geneva in a fruitless attempt to resolve the crisis.
12 January	A joint resolution by the US Congress gives President Bush the authority to use force against Iraq.
17 January	3 am – Coalition forces begin bombing Iraq.
18 January	Iraq launches the first of more than a dozen missile attacks on Israel, with strikes against Tel Aviv and Haifa. The USA sends antimissile systems, and crews to operate them, to Israel in exchange for an Israeli promise not to retaliate against Iraq.
20 January	Iraq begins pumping oil into the Gulf in an apparent attempt to poison Saudi Arabia's drinking water supply. Within a week the slick is 16km wide and 56km long. Eventually it grows to be 64km wide and 160km long.
29 January	Iraq attacks, and briefly occupies, the Saudi Arabian border town of Khafji.
12 February	The US military announces that satellite evidence indicates that Iraqi forces are deliberately setting fire to Kuwait's oil wells.
13 February	A US bomb destroys an Iraqi air raid shelter filled with civilians, including many women and children.
24 February	Ground offensive begins.
27 February	Iraqi troops begin withdrawing from Kuwait, setting remaining oil wells on fire as they go. Coalition aircraft trap and massacre a retreating column of Iraqi forces near Kuwait's Al-Mutla ridge. Coalition forces enter Kuwait City.
28 February	Bush orders suspension of hostilities bringing ground offensive to an end after only 100 hours.
March	Kuwait's crown prince and emir return from exile and rebuilding begins. Martial law is declared.
November	Press censorship lifted in Kuwait. Last oil well fire extinguished.

KUWAIT

one Kuwaiti border post and shelled another. After a short time, Iraq withdrew under pressure from the Arab League (led by Egypt, which was then preparing for war with Israel and regarded the Iraq-Kuwait border dispute as an unnecessary distraction). Even then, however, Iraq's foreign minister went out of his way to assert a claim to Warba and Bubiyan islands.

On the other hand, Iraq had never, not even in 1961, attempted to launch an all-out invasion of Kuwait, and by 1990 the Kuwaitis could reasonably claim that Baghdad was in their debt: throughout the eight-year-long Iran-Iraq war, Kuwait had been a vital lifeline for goods flowing into Iraq and exports flowing out. Even after the 1983–85 Iranian-sponsored terrorist bombings and a later Iranian decision to shell Kuwaiti territory, the emirate stood by Iraq politically and contributed enormous sums of money to the Iraqi war effort (partly because Kuwait was concerned that an Iranian victory would spill the Islamic revolution into its territory). At the end of May 1990, the emir of Kuwait travelled to Baghdad for an Arab summit where, in the traditional Arab manner, he was embraced and kissed by President Saddam Hussein.

Nobody knows exactly when, or why, Saddam decided to invade Kuwait. It is easy to note, in retrospect, that there were signs of trouble. Months before the invasion, for example, the Iraqis signed a treaty defining once and for all their border with Saudi Arabia. Kuwaiti officials sought a similar treaty and were rebuffed in Baghdad. Some have seen this as the first sign that Saddam was planning to swallow his smaller neighbour. Saddam has never, however, been overly fastidious about international law.

Saddam is known to have badgered the Kuwaitis about money during a closed session of the Baghdad summit. He accused them of waging 'economic warfare' against Iraq by exceeding their OPEC oil production quota which, he claimed, they were doing in an attempt to hold down the price of oil artificially. Both then and after the invasion, the Iraqis also claimed that Kuwait was demanding repayment of the loans it had ex-

tended to Baghdad during the war with Iran, a claim that the Kuwaitis have consistently denied. It had been generally understood at the time that the loans were, in fact, gifts.

The first clear public sign of trouble came on 16 July 1990 when Iraq sent a letter to the Secretary-General of the Arab League accusing Kuwait of exceeding its OPEC quota and of stealing oil from the Iraqi portion of an oil field straddling the border. Iraq's foreign minister told an Arab League meeting in Tunisia that 'we are sure some Arab states are involved in a conspiracy against us'. The charge of quota violations was true: Kuwait had long been one of OPEC's most notorious overproducers; but there was nothing new in this and Iraq itself was hardly blameless on that score. Iraq's accusations over the oil field were harder to pin down but ultimately lacked substance: the Kuwaiti portion of the disputed Rumailah oil field produced a paltry 25,000 barrels per day.

The day after the Arab League meeting, Saddam repeated his accusations in a speech marking Iraq's Revolution Day and vaguely threatened military action against Kuwait and the United Arab Emirates (UAE). Over the next two weeks the Secretary-General of the Arab League, the Saudi Arabian foreign minister and President Hosni Mubarak of Egypt all travelled between Kuwait City and Baghdad seeking to diffuse the growing crisis Iraq had manufactured.

At the end of July 1990, the Kuwaitis were rapidly discovering that all the money they had lavished on development projects around the region over the previous 30 years had not bought them many allies. In addition, Saddam increasingly appeared determined to pick a fight. In the two weeks leading up to the invasion, the various mediators bent over backwards to offer Iraq a graceful way out of the dispute on five or six occasions. Each time Iraq replied by launching another verbal salvo in the direction of Kuwait. The Iraqis agreed to attend reconciliation talks with the Kuwaitis in Saudi Arabia in late July but then stalled over the ground rules for the talks, and continued to amass troops just north of the border.

When the tanks came crashing over the border at 2 am on 2 August the Kuwaitis never had a chance. The Iraqis were in Kuwait City before dawn and by noon they had reached the Saudi border. The emir and his cabinet fled to Saudi Arabia.

The United Nations quickly passed a series of resolutions calling on Iraq to withdraw from Kuwait. The Iraqis replied that they had been invited in by a group of Kuwaiti rebels who had overthrown the emir. The absurdity of this claim was shown up by the failure of the Iraqis to find even one Kuwaiti willing to serve in a quisling government. On 6 August Iraq annexed the emirate.

An emergency summit of the Arab League was held in Cairo on 10 August but Saddam refused to attend. The Iraqis contended that Saudi Arabia's decision a few days earlier to ask the USA for troops to defend the Kingdom was at least as significant a threat to the region's security as Iraq's annexation of Kuwait, and a number of the league's members agreed. The league passed a resolution condemning the invasion but was deeply split.

Western countries, led by the USA, began to enforce a UN embargo on trade with Iraq by stopping and searching ships bound for Iraq and Jordan. In the months that followed, US and other forces flooded into Saudi Arabia as the diplomatic standoff over Kuwait deepened. Tens of thousands of refugees, many of them Arabs and Asians who had been working in Kuwait, fled the emirate only to find themselves sweltering in makeshift transit camps on the Iraqi-Jordanian border in mid-summer.

The anti-Iraq coalition's forces eventually numbered 425,000 US troops and 265,000 from 27 other countries. They were backed up by an increasingly long list of UN Security Council resolutions calling on Iraq to withdraw from Kuwait. Harrowing tales of appalling atrocities were publicised around the world by Amnesty International, Middle East Watch and Kuwait exiles. At the end of November, the USA and the UK secured a UN resolution authorising the use of force to drive Iraq out of Kuwait if Baghdad did not pull out voluntarily before 15 January 1991.

With less than a week to go before the expiration of the 15 January deadline, US Secretary of State James Baker met with Iraqi Foreign Minister Tariq Aziz in Geneva. The talks lasted for nearly six hours but came to nothing. In the final hours before the deadline a number of national leaders, including Mubarak of Egypt and French President François Mitterrand, televised appeals to Saddam to withdraw from Kuwait before it was too late. Yasser Arafat of the PLO rushed to Baghdad to try to broker a deal.

The deadline passed, the Iraqis did not budge, and within hours waves of allied (mostly US) aircraft began a five-week bombing campaign over Iraq and Kuwait.

The ground offensive, when it finally came, lasted only 100 hours and was something of an anticlimax. Iraq's army, which had been touted in the west for the previous six months as one of the world's most fearsome military machines, simply disintegrated. While there were relatively few casualties on the allied side, controversy has persisted over the number of civilian and military deaths in Iraq and Kuwait. Numbers from 10,000 to 100,000 or more have been offered.

Liberation & Beyond

When allied forces arrived in Kuwait City on 27 February 1991 they were greeted by jubilant crowds. The city's infrastructure had been almost completely destroyed during the war, though many buildings had survived relatively intact (the same could not be said of their contents which had, in many cases, been looted by the Iraqis).

For the first few days anarchy reigned in the liberated city. Some Kuwaitis turned their fury on what was left of the emirate's large Palestinian population. Yasser Arafat had been widely regarded as a supporter of the invasion, and many Palestinians had remained in the emirate throughout the occupation (in some cases because they had nowhere else to go). Many Kuwaitis thus assumed that all Palestinians had collaborated with the Iraqis and dealt with them

KUWAIT

accordingly. After liberation a number of people, most of them Palestinians, were convicted by special martial law courts on charges of collaboration.

Kuwaiti society seemed split between those who had stayed throughout the occupation and those who had fled. The government declared martial law but the crown prince, who also served as martial law administrator, did not return from exile in Saudi Arabia until six days after liberation, and it was another 10 days before the emir himself returned. The royal family was slightly embarrassed by the fact that both the UK and US embassies in Kuwait City were reopened several days before the crown prince returned. By the time the emir returned, both British prime minister John Major and US secretary of state James Baker had come and gone.

Amid criticisms that it was moving too slowly, the government set about rebuilding the country, concentrating first on roads and utilities and afterwards on repairing homes and businesses and clearing the country of land mines. As they withdrew from Kuwait, the Iraqis had systematically blown up most of the country's oil wells and set them on fire. For many months thereafter the country was covered in a dense cloud of black smoke from the burning wells, the last of which was extinguished in November 1991, 8½ months after the end of the war.

Even before press censorship was lifted at the end of 1991, a heated debate had begun over the country's political future. In keeping with a promise the opposition had extracted from the emir during the occupation, the 1962 constitution was restored and elections for a new National Assembly took place in October 1992. The opposition shocked the government by winning over 30 of the new parliament's 50 seats. In keeping with Kuwaiti tradition, the crown prince was reappointed as prime minister. Opposition MPs secured six of the 16 seats in the cabinet, though the Al-Sabah family retained control of the key defence, foreign affairs and interior ministries. As with past elections the 1992 vote was restricted to the

70,000 or so adult Kuwaiti males holding 'first-class' citizenship (those whose ancestors had been resident in Kuwait prior to the 1920s).

By the second anniversary of the invasion, Kuwait's government had done an admirable job of erasing many of the physical scars of war and occupation. Healing the psychological and personal scars is clearly going to take much longer.

Hundreds of Kuwaitis disappeared during the occupation and many remain unaccounted for, a fact which visitors to the country are reminded of almost daily. Iraq remains a threat. Several times in the years since liberation Iraqi troop movements have prompted Kuwait, the USA or both to mobilise their forces. In 1994 Kuwait convicted several Iraqis on charges of attempting to assassinate former US president George Bush when he visited the emirate in 1993. The plot, according to the Kuwaitis, was uncovered and foiled at the last minute.

As the tumultous '90s drew to a close life in Kuwait had returned to normal. In Kuwait, the most obvious legacy of the Gulf War was political – the restoration of Kuwait's parliament at home, and an unashamed pro-Western tilt in the country's foreign policy. The end of the decade saw the beginnings of reconciliation between the Kuwaiti government and some of the Arab countries it felt had not backed it during the occupation, most notably Jordan and Yasser Arafat's Palestinian Authority. Relations with Iran, where the strains go back to the early '80s, were also improving.

GEOGRAPHY

Kuwait's 17,818 sq km of land are mainly flat and arid with little ground water (much of which is brackish, anyway). The desert is generally gravelly. The country is about 185km from north to south and 208km from east to west. Its coastline is unexciting and the desert inland is uninteresting. The only significant geographic feature is the now infamous Al-Mutla ridge where allied aircraft massacred a column of retreating Iraqi forces in the closing hours of the Gulf War.

The Water Trade

Kuwait has long been known for its fine natural harbour, but like so many places in the Middle East it is chronically short of water. Today Kuwait has an abundant supply of fresh water and even bottles its own mineral water, but during the first half of this century the rapidly growing town actually imported drinking water from Iraq.

From 1907 until 1950 traders drew fresh water from the Shatt al-Arab waterway at the head of the Gulf, loaded it onto dhows and shipped it down to Kuwait. The trade peaked in 1947 when it was estimated that 303,200L of water per day were arriving in Kuwait by boat. It was a far cry from the 19th century when Kuwait was small enough that, despite its famously arid landscape, it could still meet its needs from rainwater and the area's few wells.

Not surprisingly, Kuwait invested some of its early oil revenues in a mostly unsuccessful search for ground water.

Kuwait's first desalination plant was built in 1950, bringing to an end the sea trade in fresh water. But although the desalination capacity now far exceeds the country's demand for fresh water, the government still devotes significant sums of money to research new desalination techniques. Desalination is just about the most expensive way imaginable to acquire fresh water and the technology has not improved much over the last 50 years. Kuwait's own consumption has risen radically over that period, from 6822L per capita in the '50s to 83,380L per capita in the mid-80s, according to the government's own figures.

Natural resources are precious and, as any Bedouin can tell you, in the desert water is far more valuable than oil.

KUWAIT

CLIMATE

In the summer (April to September) Kuwait is hellishly hot and temperatures can reach the high 40s°C. Its saving grace is that it is nowhere near as humid as Bahrain. The winter months are often pleasant but can get fairly cold, with daytime temperatures hovering around 18°C and nights being genuinely chilly. A good medium-weight jacket and a jumper are essential travelling items for a winter visit to the emirate. Sandstorms occur throughout the year but are particularly common in spring.

GOVERNMENT & POLITICS

Kuwait's government is something of a hybrid: not exactly an absolute monarchy, but not really a democracy either. Under Kuwait's 1962 constitution the emir is the head of state. By tradition the crown prince serves as prime minister, making him head of government. The emir 'appoints' the prime minister who appoints the cabinet (usually reserving key portfolios such as defence, interior and foreign affairs for other members of the ruling family). The constitution allows the emir not only to reign but also to rule, although in practice the current emir leaves day-to-day governance to the crown prince/prime minister.

The ruling Al-Sabah family itself picks the emir from one of two specific branches of the family. These are known as the Jaber and the Salem branches and refer to two of the four sons of Mubarak the Great who ruled Kuwait from 1896 to 1915. The choice of the emir alternates between these two branches (though this pattern has been broken once since Mubarak's death). The current emir, Sheikh Jaber al-Ahmed al-Sabah, is from the Jaber branch of the family while the crown prince (who is two years younger than the emir), Sheikh Saad al-Abdullah al-Salem al-Sabah, is from the Salem branch.

The powers of the emir, crown prince and cabinet are tempered by the 50-member National Assembly. The emir has the power to dissolve the assembly whenever he pleases, but is required by the constitution to hold new elections within 90 days of any such dissolution – a requirement that, historically, has not always been honoured.

The National Assembly

The Kuwaiti parliament, or National Assembly, has had quite a history. In 1921 the British first talked the then-ruler, Sheikh Ahmed, into appointing an advisory council, though he soon dissolved it and returned to ruling alone. A Constituent Assembly, charged with drafting a constitution for the new state, was elected a few months after independence in 1961. The constitution itself was officially promulgated in 1962. Elections for Kuwait's first National Assembly were held later that year and the assembly first convened in 1963. Though representatives of the country's leading merchant families occupied the bulk of the seats, radicals had a toehold in the body from its inception. The first years of constitutional government were turbulent: leftists in the National Assembly almost immediately began pressing for faster social change and the country had three cabinets between 1963 and 1965.

In August 1976 the cabinet resigned, claiming that the assembly had made day-to-day governance impossible. The emir suspended the constitution, dissolved the National Assembly and asked the crown prince/prime minister of the outgoing government to form a new cabinet, which he did the following day. When new elections were held in 1981, it was only after the electoral laws had been revised in a way which, the government hoped, would guarantee that the radicals won no seats in the new parliament. While this succeeded after a fashion, the assembly's new conservative majority proved just as troublesome as the radicals had been. Parliament was dissolved again in 1986. The emir said then that public arguments over policy were dividing Kuwaitis at a time when the country was coming under threat from Iran during the Iran-Iraq War. Some Opposition figures have long contended that the assembly's real sin was to question the degree to which the Al-Sabah family continued to dominate Kuwait's government.

In December 1989 and January 1990, an extraordinary series of demonstrations took place calling for the restoration of the 1962 constitution and the reconvening of the suspended parliament. The demonstrators challenged the emir's right to rule without the National Assembly and were met by riot police, tear gas and water cannon. In June of that year, elections were held for a Consultative Council which was supposed to spend four years advising the government on possible constitutional changes prior to the election of a new assembly. Pro-democracy activists demanded the reconvening of the old assembly and denounced the Consultative Council as unconstitutional.

During the Iraqi occupation of Kuwait, Opposition leaders and the government, meeting in exile in Saudi Arabia, agreed to return to parliamentary rule and the 1962 constitution after the country's liberation. Elections were held in late 1992 and the government and legislature returned to their, by now, traditional roles of bickering over both the details of legislation and the division of power.

The assembly was suspended by emiri decree in 1986. It was reinstated in 1992, as part of a deal struck in the fall of 1990 between the emir and crown prince on the one hand and leading opposition members on the other. Under that agreement the opposition gave its wholehearted support to the government, then in exile in Saudi Arabia, in exchange for a return to constitutional rule following liberation.

Voting for the assembly was long restricted to adult, male, 'first-class' Kuwaiti citizens. Naturalised citizens are not permitted to vote, though their children are. In May 1999 the cabinet voted to extend the franchise to Kuwaiti women holding first-class citizenship. The move came too late to apply to the 1999 elections and, because parliament was dissolved at the time, required confirmation by the new assembly. But the new assembly twice refused to confirm the decree in the months following the election, leaving the issue in limbo for the time being.

The emir's move to extend suffrage to women came shortly after he had dissolved the assembly and called a snap election. The election, held that July, was a response to atempts by the assembly to censure the min-ster for Islamic affairs. There are no politi-cal parties in Kuwait, so numbers can only be approximate, but the 1999 vote (in which women's suffrage predictably emerged as the main issue) represented a mild setback for the government and a modest gain for both Liberals and Islamists. Alliances among Kuwait's 50 elected MPs shift from issue to issue but, broadly, the government can count on a core of about 20 votes on most issues. Islamists make up the next largest bloc with about 15 seats, though these are split among Sunnis, Shi'ites and supporters of the Muslim Brotherhood – factions which rarely agree on very much. Liberals hold between 10 and 12 seats.

Prior to the Iraqi invasion, Kuwait was known for maintaining a markedly inde-

pendent foreign policy. For many years it was the only Gulf State to have diplomatic relations with the former Soviet Union and its allies. It was a particularly vocal sup-porter of the Palestinians and was active in the nonaligned movement. In the wake of the invasion it has drawn decidedly closer to the West. Since liberation, defence agree-ments have been signed with the USA, the UK and France, and a somewhat softer line has been taken on Arab-Israeli relations. The government quietly supported the 1993 Israel-PLO peace agreement (though some individual members of the National Assem-bly vigorously condemned it) and was rep-resented by its foreign minister at the March 1996 anti-terrorism summit in Egypt, an event that was also attended by Israel's prime minister.

Post-War Politics

Those who remember the Kuwait of the late 1980s know that the emirate today is a vastly different place. After years marked by terror-ism and the constant rumble of the Iran-Iraq war just over the horizon, Kuwait (circa 1988) was a tense place.

In the wake of the Iraqi occupation a very different country rose from the ashes. Today's Kuwait boasts some of the more liberal news-papers in the region and a parliament that is unique on the Arab side of the Gulf. Kuwaitis are very open and willing to discuss the poli-tics of the day (itself a change from many other Gulf countries), and if you are in the country for any length of time it is easy to keep up on local politics through Kuwait's two English-language newspapers.

Some issues to watch for: in the wake of the emir's move to give women the vote – and the National Assembly's subsequent reje-tion of that decree – you can expect voting rights issues to dominate public debate for the next few years. As you might expect in a country where foreigners outnumber citizens, immigration issues are often discussed in par-liament. Relations with both Iran and the USA are other perennial hot topics.

ECONOMY

Among the Gulf States, Kuwait's oil re-serves are second only to those of Saudi Arabia. Kuwait produces about 1.8 million barrels of oil per day and also has a large petrochemical industry. This was built up from the late '60s onward as a way for the country to keep control of more of the rev-enues generated by its oil.

Attempts to diversify the economy have met with mixed success. The government sank a lot of money into agriculture in the '70s, particularly into growing alfalfa and into dairy and poultry farming, but most of the country's food has always been im-ported and there is no sign of that changing in the short term.

The country has little in the way of a non-oil related economy and much of the coun-try's non-oil industry remains state controlled. As is the case in many Gulf States, the government has long paid lip service to privatisation, but to little practical effect.

Apart from oil, the country is best known for its investment policies. These sometimes bring unwelcome publicity, as when the London-based Kuwait Investment Office (KIO) began buying large blocks of stock in BP. A British court later forced the KIO to sell some of the stock, though there was a certain delicious irony in the government of

Kuwait making even a veiled bid for control of one of the oil companies that had originally made it rich. The government has also sought to diversify the country's role in the oil industry to make it a player on all levels, rather than simply being a producer/refiner of crude oil. It has purchased distribution networks and petrol stations (such as the Q8 chain in the UK) in other parts of the world.

The Fund for Future Generations was established in 1976 as a hedge against the day when oil ran out. For many years 10% of all oil revenues were paid into the fund, the balance of which could not be touched for a minimum of 25 years. At the time of the Iraqi invasion the fund was thought to hold about US$100 billion. It provided an invaluable source of cash during the occupation, when the government used it to support Kuwaitis living in exile and to pay some of the costs of the allied coalition. These expenses plus reconstruction costs used up a large portion of the fund. In early 1999 the fund was thought to have about US$50 billion in assets.

In 1961 the government set up the Kuwait Fund for Arab Economic Development, the first such development fund in the Gulf. In the '70s and '80s, Kuwait gave away as much as 10% of its GNP in aid (as against the figure of 0.7% which the UN recommends and which very few industrialised countries meet).

POPULATION & PEOPLE

While no exact figures are available, Kuwait's population is thought to be around 2.2 million. Of these about 750,000 (around 34%) are Kuwaitis. The percentage of Kuwaitis has been increasing slowly over the last 10 years (in the late '80s Kuwaitis may have numbered as little as 25% of the overall population), but it is still a far cry from what the government would like it to be. Nationalisation of the work force has been a major topic of discussion for years, but with only limited results.

Immediately after liberation, the government announced that it would never again allow Kuwaitis to become a minority in their own country. This implied a target population of about 1.2 million, but

within months there were indications that the occupation had not blunted Kuwaitis' desire for servants and drivers or made them any more willing than before to do manual labour. As a result, by early 1992 the foreign population of the emirate was thought to have crept back ahead of the native population and within a couple of years it had more or less returned to pre-invasion proportions.

What has changed significantly since liberation is the cast of Kuwait's large expatriate population. Prior to August 1990 the country's professional classes were dom- inated by Arabs in general and Palestinians in particular. Manual labour was largely done by Egyptians. While there were certainly a large number of Indians, Pakistanis and Sri Lankans in the country, pre-invasion Kuwait never took on the decidedly subcontinental air that cities in Saudi Arabia or the UAE often evince. This was the result of a concerted government policy to keep Kuwait as 'Arab' as possible. If the country did not have a Kuwaiti majority in August 1990, it certainly had an Arab one.

In the wake of the war, the Kuwaiti government began to encourage the recruiting of non-Arabs, South-East Asians in particular, fearing that large populations of expatri- ate Arabs could pose a security threat during any future crisis. Palestinians were the most visible sector of society affected but even the number of Egyptians in the country was drastically reduced, despite Cairo's enthusiastic participation in the anti-Iraq coalition. Asians were thought to be more docile politically, less likely to become attached to Kuwait's Arab culture over a number of years and, ultimately, easier to deport if there were ever trouble.

Today, Kuwait's population presents much the same mix one finds in the rest of the Arabian Gulf: labourers from South and South-East Asia, mid-professionals from India, Pakistan, Egypt and Lebanon, and a handful (relative to other foreign communities) of Westerners occupying upper-level professional jobs.

EDUCATION

Kuwait has long provided free education to all Kuwaitis and, before the invasion, to many of the foreigners living in the country. As early as the 1950s Sheikh Abdullah was stressing the importance of education, including women's education (an unusual attitude in the Gulf in those days). The University of Kuwait was founded in 1964; since 1980 more than half its students have been women. The government has been trying to channel more young Kuwaitis into the country's eight technical colleges as part of its long-term goal of getting more Kuwaitis into the work force.

ARTS

The arts scene in Kuwait is fairly limited. One gallery of the National Museum displays the works of local painters and a few small galleries (notably Dar al-Fanoon) sometimes organise exhibits. Sadu House (see the Kuwait City section later in this chapter) is a cultural foundation dedicated to preserving Bedouin art traditions, especially weaving.

SOCIETY & CONDUCT

There's not a lot of traditional culture left. Even before the Iraqis arrived, the Kuwaitis had managed to eliminate most vestiges of life-before-oil in Kuwait City. Weekend picnics in the desert, which were part of the traditional lifestyle, are clearly out of the question because of the lingering danger of mines throughout the country (see Dangers & Annoyances later in this chapter).

Kuwait is a lot more relaxed about matters of public conduct than other Gulf countries. Women should dress modestly (no skirts above the knee, halter tops etc), but there is never any need for a woman to wear an *abayya* (a long, cloak-like black garment), veil or headscarf. Non-Muslims may enter mosques, even during prayer time, as long as proper dress is observed.

Refer to the Society & Conduct section of the Facts about the Region chapter earlier in this book for a rundown of the general dos and don'ts when travelling in an Islamic country.

RELIGION

Islam is the state religion and *Sharia'a* (Islamic law) is identified in the constitution as 'a main source of legislation'. Kuwait's brand of Islam is not as strict as that practised in Saudi Arabia, but the country is not as liberal as Bahrain. Most Kuwaitis are Sunni Muslims, though there is a substantial Shi'ite minority.

Facts for the Visitor

SUGGESTED ITINERARIES
One Day

If you've only got one day in Kuwait begin with a drive along Arabian Gulf St. This gives you a quick look at a number of interesting buildings, including the National Assembly, Sief Palace, the Great Mosque, the former Political Agency and the Kuwait Towers. Make time for visits to the National Museum and Sadu House. Then, in the afternoon, travel further down Arabian Gulf St to one of the traditional houses five or six kilometres south of the centre. If you get an early start you can visit the Tareq Rajab Museum with its fine collection of Islamic art and antiquities in the morning and do all of the above in the afternoon.

Two Days

An extra day allows you to add a side trip to either Failaka Island or to Al-Jahra and the Exhibition of Sailing Ships. If you've got kids, this also gives you the option of a half-day at Entertainment City amusement park.

One Week

Given a week it would be pretty easy to cover everything listed in this chapter and still have plenty of time to lie by the pool. These extra few days allow you plenty of time to spend a morning taking in the debates at the National Assembly and some time hanging out at the stock exchange.

PLANNING
When to Go

The best time to visit is from mid-October to mid-March, although if you come in summer it is a relief to know that Kuwait is somewhat less humid than the Gulf's other cities (but no less hot).

Maps

The *GeoProjects Map of Kuwait*, identifiable by the photo of the Kuwait Towers on the cover, is the best of the locally available maps. Most hotel bookshops have it for KD3 to KD4. A better map, easy to recognise because of its yellow cover, is published by the Ministry of Information and distributed free at Kuwaiti embassies abroad but is impossible to find in Kuwait itself.

What to Bring

Aside from the usual Gulf necessities of sunglasses, a hat and long-sleeved, loose clothing, people visiting in the winter months might want to bring at least a medium-weight jacket and a jumper. These are often necessary at night and could prove useful during the day as well.

TOURIST OFFICES

There are no tourist offices in Kuwait and not much in the way of tourist infrastructure. For information on what is happening around town the two English-language newspapers, *Arab Times* and *Kuwait Times*, are your best sources of information.

VISAS & DOCUMENTS
Visas

Everyone except nationals of the other Gulf States needs a visa to enter Kuwait, and everyone entering the country is required to have a sponsor.

Kuwait does not issue tourist visas per se, but most of the country's hotels can sponsor visas for travellers holding a Western passport.

Getting a visa through a hotel is a fairly straightforward process: you send a fax to the hotel with your passport data (date and place of issue, date of expiry, date of birth, etc), arrival and departure dates, flight numbers and reason for visit (generally 'business' though 'tourism' is increasingly OK too). Most people will receive a single-entry visa valid for one month and for a one-month

stay, though business travellers from Western countries that played a large role in the anti-Iraq coalition (eg, the USA, UK, France and Canada) are often given multiple-entry visas valid for anywhere between one and 10 years. These allow the holder to come and go at will, though you can still stay in the country for only one month at a time.

The visa processing fee that the hotel has to pay to the immigration department is KD3.500 and this will certainly be passed on to you. The hotel may also charge you a fee for carrying out this service. This is usually KD5, but could go as high as KD12. Be sure to ask about the costs when you are making your visa arrangements. Hotels also usually require that you stay with them for three nights and some may charge you for whatever the agreed minimum number of nights was if you check out early. It usually takes three to four working days for a hotel to process a visa; at the cheapest places it may take a bit longer.

Business travellers visiting a company in Kuwait are sponsored by that company, which files various papers with the Ministry of Interior in Kuwait City before the visa can be issued.

Visas are usually picked up at a Kuwaiti embassy (though in some Western countries, such as the USA, it is possible to mail your passport in). While visas, once approved, can be picked up at any Kuwaiti diplomatic mission, the pick-up point has to be specified at the time the papers are filed. If a company in Kuwait has sponsored your visa you may be asked to show either a letter from the sponsoring company confirming this fact, a letter of accreditation from your own company or both. It is often a good idea to call ahead to see exactly what sort of documentation the people at the embassy want you to supply.

In a few cases large hotels may leave the visa at the airport for pick-up. If they do this, be sure that the hotel provides you with a fax *that includes the visa number*, otherwise the airline may not let you fly.

The embassies themselves are of little use to the casual traveller as they only issue visas against instructions from Kuwait. In

In the 4th century BC, the Gulf's only Greek colony was established on Kuwait's Failaka Island.

Kuwait possesses a long coastline with many picturesque beaches.

Gathering Station 14, a stark reminder of the Gulf War in Kuwait

The stock exchange building is an example of Kuwait's heavy investment in modern architecture.

other words, you cannot simply walk in and apply for a visa.

If your passport contains an Israeli stamp you will be refused entry to Kuwait.

Visa Extensions It is rather difficult to stay in Kuwait for more than one month on a business visa. Even the one-year multiple-entry visas only allow you to remain in the country for a month at a time. People with multiple-entry visas needing to remain in Kuwait for longer than a month have to fly out every 30 days and then come back in (Bahrain is the most common destination). Thus, for business travellers there really is no such thing as an exit/re-entry visa.

Entry Permits When you receive a Kuwaiti visa it will come with two slips of paper. This is your entry permit. One copy will be retained by the immigration people at your port of entry, the other must be kept with your passport and turned in when you leave the country. If you have a multiple-entry visa and are using it for the second (third, fourth, etc) time you will be issued a new entry permit at the border or airport each time you enter the country.

Other Documents

Health certificates are only necessary if you are arriving from a part of the world with a disease problem. An International Driving Permit is not usually necessary but it is valid in Kuwait, as are most national driving licences.

EMBASSIES
Kuwaiti Embassies

Addresses of some Kuwaiti embassies are:

Bahrain (☎ 534 040, fax 533 579) King Faisal Hwy, Manama
Canada (☎ 613-780 9999, fax 780 9905) 80 Elgin St, Ottawa ON, K1P IC6
Egypt (☎ 02-360 2661, fax 360 2657) 12 Nabil al-Wakad St, Dokki, Giza
France (☎ 01-47 23 54 25, fax 01-47 20 33 59) 2 Rue de Lubeck, 75016 Paris
Germany (☎ 228-378 081, fax 378 936) Godesberger Allee 77-79, 53175 Bonn

India (☎ 11-600 791, fax 687 3516) 5A Shantipath-Chanakyapuri, New Delhi 110021
Iran (☎ 21-878 5997, fax 878 6003) 39 Babec Brahimi St, Tehrān
Jordan (☎ 06-605 135, fax 681 971) Jabal Amman, 4th Circle, Amman
Oman (☎ 699626 or 699627, fax 699628) Jameat ad-Duwal al-Arabiyya St, Al-Khuwair
Qatar (☎ 832 111, fax 832 042) Diplomatic Area, beyond the Doha Sheraton Hotel, Doha
Saudi Arabia (☎ 01-488 3500, fax 488 3682) Diplomatic Quarter, Riyadh
UAE (☎ 02-446 888, fax 444 990) Diplomatic Area, Airport Rd (behind the Pepsi Cola plant), about 10km south of the centre.
UK (☎ 020-7590 3400, fax 7823 1712) 2 Albert Gate, Knightsbridge, London SW1X 7JU
USA (☎ 202-966 0702, fax 364 2868) 2940 Tilden St NW, Washington DC 20008

Embassies in Kuwait

Bahrain (☎ 531 8530, fax 533 0882) Surra district, St 1, Block 1, Building 24
Canada (☎ 256 3025, fax 256 4167) Da'iya district, El-Mutawakil St, Area 4, House 24, adjacent to the Third Ring Rd
Egypt (☎ 251 9955, fax 256 3877) Da'iya district, Istiglal St, Block 4
France (☎ 257 1061, fax 257 1058) Mansouria district, St 13, Block 1, Villa 24
Germany (☎ 252 0857, fax 252 0763) Bahiya district, St 14, Block 1, Villa 13, off Abdullah al-Salem St
India (☎ 253 0600, fax 252 5811) Diplomatic Area, off Arabian Gulf St south of the centre; look for a very large red building
Iran (☎ 256 1084, fax 252 9868) Bneid al-Gar district, Istiglal St
Italy (☎ 481 7400, fax 481 7244) Shuwaikh district, Jamal Abdul Nasser St
Lebanon (☎ 256 2103, fax 257 1682) Da'iya District
Netherlands (☎ 531 2650, fax 532 6334) Jabriah district, St 1, Block 9, House 76, near the Fifth Ring Rd and opposite Bayan Palace
Oman (☎ 256 1962, fax 256 1963) Udailia district, St 3, Block 3, House 25, by the Fourth Ring Rd
Qatar (☎ 251 3606, fax 251 3604) Diplomatic Area, Istiglal St, south of the centre off Arabian Gulf St
Saudi Arabia (☎ 240 0250, fax 242 0654) Sharq district, Arabian Gulf St
Sweden (☎ 252 3588, fax 257 2157) Faiha district, Shahba' St, Block 7, Villa 3

KUWAIT

Switzerland (☎ 534 0175, fax 534 0176) Cordoba district, St 1

UAE (☎ 252 1427, fax 252 6382) Istiglal St, Diplomatic Area, Qaseema 7, Al-Assaffa, PO Box 1828, Kuwait 13019

UK (☎ 240 3334, fax 240 7395) Arabian Gulf St, near the Kuwait Towers and Dasman Palace

USA (☎ 539 5307, fax 538 0282) Al-Masjid al-Aqsa St, Plot 14, Block 14, Bayan about 17km south of the centre

CUSTOMS

Alcohol is banned in Kuwait and before you get it into your head to smuggle in a bottle or two you should be aware that it is rare for anyone to get past customs without their baggage being thoroughly searched. The duty-free allowance for tobacco is 500 cigarettes or 50 cigars or half a kilogram of loose tobacco.

Bans on pornographic material, guns and ammunition apply.

MONEY
Currency

The Kuwaiti dinar (KD) is divided into 1000 fils. Notes come in denominations of KD¼, ½, 1, 5, 10 and 20. Coins are worth 5, 10, 20, 50 or 100 fils.

Exchange Rates

The Kuwaiti dinar is a hard currency and there are no restrictions on taking it into or out of the country (nor are there restrictions on the import or export of foreign currencies). Exchange rates are as follows:

country	unit		dinar
Australia	A$1	=	KD0.242
Canada	C$	=	KD0.211
euro	€1	=	KD0.332
France	10FF	=	KD0.510
Germany	DM1	=	KD0.170
Japan	¥100	=	KD0.280
New Zealand	NZ$1	=	KD0.149
UK	UK£1	=	KD0.494
USA	US$1	=	KD0.303

Exchanging Money

For a country with a sophisticated financial system, Kuwait can be a remarkably frustrating place to change money. Banks tend to charge excessive commissions (and we will not even discuss hotels) but moneychangers, the option of choice elsewhere in the Gulf, often refuse to change travellers cheques.

Wherever you change money be sure to check the rate at a couple of other places and remember to ask about the commissions being charged. Some advice on this subject is offered in the Kuwait City section, but the rule is to get whatever you figure you'll need, and as much cash as you are comfortable carrying, in large transactions. The only bright spot in this picture is that even Kuwait's cheap (if you can call them that) hotels take plastic, and this can help reduce the wad of money you have to carry around.

Automatic teller machines (ATMs) are also a good option. Gulf Bank's machines are linked to the Cirrus, Plus and Maestro systems. Commercial Bank of Kuwait's ATMs are on the Plus system.

Costs

Kuwait is very expensive. Rooms at the cheapest hotel in Kuwait City start at KD10, which is about US$45. Bus and taxi fares are reasonable, and it is possible to feed yourself for around KD1. A rock-bottom budget would be KD17.500 per day.

Tipping & Bargaining

Generally a tip is not expected except in fancier restaurants. As in the rest of the Gulf the service charge added to your bill in such places goes into the till, not to the waiters.

Bargaining is not as common as you might think. If you ask for a discount at, say, a hotel it is likely to be offered but that initial discount probably represents the bottom line. The main exception to this rule is consumer electronics, but since Kuwait is probably the most expensive place in Arabia to buy such things you would be well advised to look elsewhere.

POST & COMMUNICATIONS
Postal Rates

Postal rates for letters or postcards weighing up to 20g are 25 fils within Kuwait, 50 fils to Arab countries and 150 fils to the rest of the world. For cards or letters weighing 20g to 50g postage costs 40 fils domestic, 80 fils in the Arab world and 280 fils everywhere else. Aerograms cost 50 fils for delivery in the Arab world and 150 fils to everywhere else. The rate for postcards is 100 fils, no matter where they are going. Mumtaz Post (express service) and registration are available for an additional 200 fils each.

Mumtaz Post rates for small parcels (up to ½ kg) are KD5 to Arab countries and KD6 to everywhere else. After that add KD2 per ½ kg.

Sending Mail
Post boxes are a rare sight around Kuwait City, so you will have to brave the lines at the post office if you need to send anything and do not already have stamps. If you are in even a medium-sized hotel it might be a good idea to see whether the front desk sells stamps, or can even mail the letters for you.

Receiving Mail
There is no poste restante service so a friend's office or your hotel is your best bet.

Telephone
Kuwait has an excellent telephone system and calling pretty much anywhere in the world is quick and easy.

When calling Kuwait the country code is 965, followed by the local seven-digit number. There are no area or city codes.

The USA Direct access code from Kuwait is ☎ 800-288. For MCI Worldphone, dial ☎ 800-624. These services connect you directly to an operator in the USA. You may then make a collect (reverse charges) call or bill the call to a phone company credit card. Unfortunately the service is not yet available to other countries.

Payphones take 50 and 100 fils coins, though they are increasingly giving way to cardphones. Phonecards come in KD1, KD3, KD5 and KD10 denominations.

Basic rates for direct-dial or cardphone calls are 550 fils per minute to the USA, 500 per minute to most European countries and 700 fils to Australia. From 7 pm to 7 am

and all day on Friday and holidays the rates are about 25% lower.

Fax, Telex & Telegraph
These services are available from the government communications centres. It's probably easier, but more expensive, to go to a big hotel and send a fax or telex from there.

Email & Internet Access
There are several cybercafes in Kuwait City, but most are far from the centre. The exception is Cafe Olé in the Salhiya Commercial Centre (see Places to Eat under Kuwait City later in this chapter). Your only other options for Internet access in the city centre are the business centres at the large hotels (notably the Meredien and the Safir International). These are, as one might expect, efficient but pricey.

INTERNET RESOURCES
Because tourism is relatively new to Kuwait there is not a lot of information online. Feeding the word 'Kuwait' into a major search engine usually yields lots of banks, five-star hotels and trading companies.

Kuwait Online (www.kuwaitonline.com) is a decent general site with background on the country's history and culture, though there is little practical travel information to be found there. KuwaitBook (www.kuwait book.com) is an online yellow pages service with fairly similar offerings.

The Kuwait pages within the Web's main Arab-oriented umbrella sites are an equally good place to start. These include Arab View (www.arabview.net; alternatively try www.kuwaitview.com which takes you directly to the Kuwait pages within the Arab-View site), ArabSites (arabsites.com), and Arab Net (www.arab.net).

BOOKS
History
There are few good books on Kuwait. *The Merchants* by Michael Field has a chapter on the Alghanims, arguably Kuwait's most important merchant family. Geoffrey Bibby's *Looking for Dilmun* includes several chapters

KUWAIT

on the archaeological excavations on Failaka Island. It also paints an interesting picture of life in Kuwait in the '50s and '60s.

The New Arabians by Peter Mansfield has a summary of Kuwait's history and *Kuwait: Vanguard of the Gulf* (1990), by the same author, is a more general history of Kuwait, though, as the title implies, it has a very official feel about it. *The Modern History of Kuwait 1750–1965* by Ahmad Mustafa abu-Hakima is a detailed historical account written by a Kuwaiti scholar. It is widely available in Kuwait and is worth a look especially for the old photographs documenting life in Kuwait in the early 20th century.

General

The hotel bookshops around Kuwait City stock the usual collection of glossy coffee-table books, and the Ministry of Information publishes several books of facts and figures on the country as well as a number of books on the invasion and war. Among these, *The Mother of Crimes Against Kuwait in Pictures* is a gruesome collection of photographs of Iraqi atrocities in occupied Kuwait. *Tides of War – Eco-Disaster in the Gulf*, by Michael McKinnon and Peter Vine, looks at the ecological consequences of the oil slicks intentionally released and oil fires intentionally lit by the retreating Iraqis.

See the Facts about the Region chapter earlier in this book for a list of more general books on the Gulf and the Middle East.

There are practically no guidebooks to Kuwait. Most of the 'guides' you will see on sale in the emirate are little more than advertising circulars. In terms of local phone numbers the *Kuwait Pocket Guide* (available in most bookshops for around KD3.500) can be useful, if only because it is updated every year.

NEWSPAPERS & MAGAZINES

The *Arab Times* and the *Kuwait Times* are Kuwait's two English-language newspapers. If you are interested in Kuwait's political scene, which is freewheeling by Gulf standards, the *Arab Times* is definitely the superior newspaper. However, both provide adequate foreign coverage, largely reprinted

from the British newspapers and the international wire services.

Newsstands in the big hotels and some of the larger shopping malls (eg, Sharq Market and the Sultan Centre) are the best places to look for foreign newspapers and magazines. These tend to appear a day late. The *International Herald Tribune*, the main British papers and *Le Monde* are usually available, as are magazines like *Time* and *Newsweek*. Foreign publications are subject to government censorship, so it is a good idea to check that all, or at least most, of the pages are there before you put out a couple of dinars.

RADIO & TV

Radio Kuwait – aka the 'Super Station' – broadcasts on 99.7 FM, playing mostly rock and roll with a bit of local news and features mixed in. The US military's Armed Forces Radio & Television Service (AFRTS), on 107.9 FM, broadcasts a mixture of music, news and chat shows. A similar programing mix can be found on the Voice of America at 95.7 FM.

If you are looking for news and do not have a short-wave radio to tune in to the BBC, AFRTS is the place to turn. AFRTS carries 'Morning Edition' and 'All Things Considered', the high-quality news programs produced by the USA's National Public Radio. Because of the time difference the morning program comes on in the late afternoon and All Things Considered in the dead of night. Neither AFRTS nor VOA can be heard outside Kuwait City.

Channel 2 of Kuwait TV broadcasts programs in English each day from around 5 pm until midnight. Many hotels, even the smaller ones, have satellite TV.

PHOTOGRAPHY & VIDEO

In theory a photography permit is necessary to take pictures of anything in Kuwait. The problem is that the permits must be approved personally by the Minister of Information, which makes them effectively unobtainable for anyone but a working journalist.

In practice this is not something you need to worry about provided you exercise a modicum of common sense. Photographing what are obviously 'tourist' sites (ie, the Kuwait Towers, the courtyard of the National Museum or the Red Fort in Al-Jahra) is never a problem and over the years the list of 'sensitive' places has shortened quite a bit. Taking a picture of the Great Mosque, for example, is not a problem today whereas it would have been 10 or 15 years ago.

If you are discreet and do not photograph anything sensitive you should be OK. Also remember that in addition to military areas, the palaces and the airport, all embassies and government buildings are strictly off limits for shutterbugs and that people – especially women – should never be photographed without their permission.

LAUNDRY
Laundrettes are unknown in Kuwait. If you don't feel like washing your clothes in the sink in your hotel room, your only option is the hotel laundry or one of the many small laundry shops offering 24-hour service to wash and iron clothes.

HEALTH
Health care in Kuwait is on a level with what is available in most Western countries. See the Kuwait City section later in this chapter for more information on how to get medical treatment in Kuwait, and the Regional Facts for the Visitor chapter earlier in this book for a more general discussion of health in the Gulf.

The drinking water in much of the country is not good and you would be well advised to stick to bottled water. The tap water will not kill you, but it might not leave you feeling very good, either.

WOMEN TRAVELLERS
Harassment of women is a recurrent problem in Kuwait. The best advice is to dress conservatively, not to respond to approaches in the street and to avoid eye contact with men. Women should not travel alone at night in unfamiliar neighbourhoods. If you are followed go to a public place, such as the lobby of a big hotel.

A number of embassies keep records of harassment of their female nationals and if

you have any problems you might want to report it to your embassy's consular section. They may not be able to do anything on the spot, but the collective numbers will, at least, be brought to the government's attention that way.

TRAVEL WITH CHILDREN
Kuwait offers a wide variety of diversions for families with small children. Entertainment City, a large, Western-style amusement park west of Kuwait City is probably the most obvious, but there are a number of smaller fun parks closer to the centre. Some of these look rickety, to put it gently, so parents would be well advised to look a place over before spending any money. There's a decent-sized amusement park at the base of the Kuwait Towers, and the strip of beach between the towers and the Al-Sharq Centre is being developed into a long, narrow park with lots of playground equipment.

Shopping aside there is less to keep teenagers entertained, though the recent growth in Kuwait's small stock of movie theatres might help.

DANGERS & ANNOYANCES
Street crime has never been a significant problem in Kuwait, and the post-war danger of mines and other unexploded ordnance has largely receded (largely, but not entirely).

Kuwait City and the residential sections of other urban centres like Al-Jahra and Al-Ahmadi are clear of mines. The desert is another story. Desert mine clearance is, at best, an inexact science. Sand dunes can shift, covering mines for months, or even years, only to shift again, leaving unexploded mines exposed in what are, theoretically, safe areas. This problem is hardly unique to Kuwait – Egypt, Israel, Libya and a host of other Middle Eastern countries are still dealing with unexploded ordnance left over from the various Arab-Israeli wars and even WWII. Seaborne mines are no longer a significant problem. It has been a long time since a mine washed up on the beach near the

KUWAIT

Kuwait Towers, which is not to say that it could not happen again.

Off-road driving is still very dangerous in Kuwait and you ought to think long and hard before indulging yourself. Desert camping in well-trod camping areas is a better bet. Most of these are south of Kuwait City. They are usually fairly close to the main roads and are often signposted. The wisest course is to camp with someone who knows the area in question and has been there before.

Above all, whenever you are in the desert, or on Failaka Island: *don't pick up any unfamiliar object*. It is difficult to stress this point too much. Kuwait is no longer the frighteningly unsafe place it once was – but people who keep track of these things emphasise that stuff still blows up every month. When in doubt, play it safe.

If you are going north, the Iraqi border is now pretty hard to miss. A trench, fence, earth wall and various other fortifications have replaced the open desert across which the Iraqis rolled in August 1990. That said, the unsettled situation between Iraq and Kuwait means that you really should *not* be anywhere north of the Kuwaiti army checkpoint on the Al-Mutla ridge without a very good reason. If you do run into trouble with the Iraqis (who have been known to cross into Kuwaiti territory and snatch the odd foreigner) you should know that the UN troops who patrol the border zone have no authority to help you.

BUSINESS HOURS

Shops are open Saturday to Wednesday from 8 or 9 am until about 1 pm and from about 4 pm until 6 or 7 pm. Shops in large shopping centres usually stay open until 9 pm. On Thursday most businesses will only be open in the morning. Government offices work Saturday to Wednesday from 7 am to 1.30 pm but may close at 11.30 or noon on Thursdays. Friday is the weekly holiday and almost nothing is open during the day, though some shops in the centre and in the *souq* (market) may open in the late afternoon and early evening.

PUBLIC HOLIDAYS & SPECIAL EVENTS

Secular holidays are New Year's Day (1 January) and National Day (25 February). Liberation Day (26 February) is not an official holiday but everyone seems to treat it as one. In deference to the families of those still missing after the war and occupation, National Day and Liberation Day tend to be rather muted affairs.

Religious holidays are tied to the Islamic Hejira calendar. Eid al-Fitr (the end of Ramadan), Eid al-Adha (the end of pilgrimage season), Lailat al-Mi'raj (the Ascension of the Prophet), the Prophet's Birthday and the Islamic New Year are all observed (for dates see the Public Holidays & Special Events section in the Regional Facts for the Visitor chapter earlier in this book).

ACTIVITIES

The problem of land and, to a lesser extent, seaborne mines has pretty well put what used to be a bustling water-sports culture in Kuwait into the deep freeze. Mines have also put an end to organised desert safaris and off-road driving.

WORK

With very few exceptions it is not legal to work in Kuwait on a business visa. A business visa cannot be changed to a residence permit in Kuwait. You have to go back to your country of origin and get a residence visa there. Coming to Kuwait to look for a job is illegal and a waste of time.

ACCOMMODATION

Getting a bed for the night in Kuwait has never been cheap but the situation has improved a bit over the last few years. There was a time, shortly after the Gulf War, when it was nearly impossible to find a hotel room for much under US$100 per night. That is no longer the case, but there are still very few rooms for less than US$50. At the bottom end, expect to pay at least KD15/20 for a single/double. At the top end, prices continue to rise with around US$200 a night being the benchmark at the time of writing.

Flat Rental

If you are going to live and work in Kuwait, your employer will most likely be providing you with housing. If not, you will have to consider renting. Small one or two-bedroom flats in the parts of the city where most foreigners live start at around KD400 per month. Flats are a lot cheaper in other parts of the city, notably the mid-to-outer suburbs such as Hawalli.

FOOD

Your choices for cheap food in Kuwait are numerous. Most of Kuwait's cheapest restaurants are either Indian places that serve *biryanis* (chicken, mutton or fish mixed with mildly spiced rice), or small stalls that serve those Middle Eastern staples, *fuul* (stewed fava beans) and *ta'amiyya* (deep fried balls of crushed chickpeas in flat bread). Eating at any of these places should cost you KD1 or less. Western fast food, burgers, pizza etc, are also widely available, though they tend to cost a bit more.

Cafes, mostly located either in hotels or shopping centres, offer Western-style snacks and sandwiches at reasonable prices and the city is well stocked with good, up-market eateries.

DRINKS

All drinks are nonalcoholic (alcohol is illegal in Kuwait). The usual selection includes soft drinks, mineral water, fruit juice, coffee and tea.

SHOPPING

Kuwait is not exactly a shopper's paradise. You can buy traditional Bedouin weavings in Kuwait City at Sadu House, a cultural foundation dedicated to preserving Bedouin art, but there is little else in the way of locally produced souvenirs. Interesting upscale art and handicrafts can be purchased at Dar al-Fanoon, a gallery in a restored coral house on the edge of the centre. Many of their offerings come from the Arab world (Moroccan pottery, for example), though little or none of it comes from Kuwait itself.

As is the case elsewhere in the Gulf, most of the 'Arabian'-looking items you will see for sale around the country are produced elsewhere.

Getting There & Away

AIR

Kuwait International Airport is 16km south of Kuwait City centre. There are currency exchange facilities and ATMs on both the upper (departure) and lower (arrival) levels. Check-in time is officially two hours prior to flight time, but some carriers insist on three hours, so you should call the airline to double-check. Kuwait has always been pretty serious about enforcing the 'only one carry-on bag' rule so this is not the place to try to get three or four pieces of hand baggage through security (unless you are flying in business or 1st class).

If you need to make a call, note that the pay phones in both the arrival and departures areas marked 'local calls only' are free.

Kuwait has never made a serious effort to compete with the massive duty-free shopping complexes run by Abu Dhabi, Dubai and Bahrain. Like much of the rest of the country the airport is functional without being unnecessarily elaborate. The departure lounge has a cafe, snack bar, some phones and a very modest duty-free operation, but not much else.

For general information, including flight arrivals and departures, call ☎ 433 5599 or 433 4499.

Departure Tax

There is an airport departure tax of KD2. If this was not added into the price of your ticket at the time of purchase you can expect it to be collected in cash at the airport. Tickets sold outside Kuwait often have not had the tax added in. Look for 'KWD 2.000' or something similar in the 'tax' box just below the part of the ticket that shows the cities between which you are travelling.

Be sure to be at the airport two hours before departure time. Check-in times are sometimes even longer for long-haul flights to Europe, Asia and North America, but for any flight it would be a good idea to double-check the rules in advance. Before you actually get inside the terminal your car may be searched at a checkpoint on the Airport Rd and all baggage is X-rayed at the entrance to the airport. This can sometimes be a cumbersome process, so allow some extra time for it.

The USA
Fares to New York start around KD360 one way and KD460 for a two-month return (10-day minimum stay). Individual airlines, especially those from what used to be the Eastern Bloc, sometimes have special fares on offer.

Australia
There is no direct air service from Kuwait to Australia. You should figure KD300 in the low season (early September to mid-December and mid-January to May) as a starting point.

The UK & Continental Europe
The 10-day minimum/three-month maximum stay return tickets to London start at KD339 and one-way fares from KD285. Return tickets during the high season (May to August and a couple of weeks either side of Christmas) will cost KD15 to KD20 more. Making a tour of airline offices to check for special offers could save you KD100 or more.

The cheapest published one-way/return fares to Rome are KD231/268, again with a 10-day/three-month limit on your stay. High season tickets are about KD10 more.

Asia
Fares to the Indian subcontinent are no longer the (relative) bargains they once were out of Kuwait. The cheapest regular fare to New Delhi is KD129 for a return ticket allowing a four-month stay (seven-day minimum). The one-way fare to New Delhi is KD150.

Bangkok, often a good deal from other Gulf countries, is fairly pricey at KD288 for a return ticket (seven-day minimum/one-month maximum), KD240 one way.

Middle East
A one-way fare to Cairo is KD96, the cheapest return costs KD125. No minimum stay is required and the maximum stay allowed on this fare is one month. To Amman, expect to pay KD69 one way and KD99 return (no minimum/one-month maximum). One-way fares to Beirut are about the same, but returns cost about KD10 more. You can often find discounted packages to Beirut offering flights and a few nights in a hotel for around KD100.

Sample one-way and return fares to other cities in the Gulf in Kuwaiti dinars include (all returns require a two-day minimum/14-day maximum stay):

destination	one way/return (KD)
Abu Dhabi	55/76
Bahrain	31/43
Dhahran	31/43
Doha	40/54
Dubai	55/76
Jeddah	76/99
Muscat	77/106
Riyadh	44/59

LAND
Bus
Buses operate between Kuwait and Cairo via Aqaba in Jordan and Nuweiba in Egypt. Agents specialising in these tickets (the trip takes about two days) are in the area around the main bus station. In Cairo there are a number of agents on Talaat Harb St and Tahrir Square advertising bus transport to Kuwait.

Getting Around

BUS & TAXI
Very cheap intercity bus service is available to Al-Jahra, Al-Ahmadi, Fahaheel and a handful of other destinations outside Kuwait City. Most intercity bus fares are 250 fils. Most of the coaches used by the bus company are reasonably comfortable and well maintained, and local regulations prohibit drivers from picking up extra pas-

sengers when the bus is full (ie, the bus will never be packed beyond bursting point as sometimes happens in India or Egypt). Note, however, that only the handful of services with route numbers above 500 use air-conditioned vehicles. Tickets are purchased from the driver.

The main bus station is in the centre at the intersection of Al-Hilali and Abdullah al-Mubarak Sts. There are also secondary stations at the Orthopaedic Hospital to the west of the centre and in Sharq to the east, as well as several smaller lay-bys. See Kuwait City's Getting Around section later in this chapter for more details.

There are no service-taxis in Kuwait. There is a taxi stand next to the main bus station, but these are simply local taxis whose drivers hang out here when not cruising around looking for fares. While they are not intercity taxis per se, you could probably negotiate a fare to pretty much anywhere in the country, though the drivers are likely to demand so much money that you might as well rent a car instead. Expect to pay at least KD10 for a trip to either Al-Jahra or Al-Ahmadi.

CAR

Driving in Kuwait is on the right, and right turns are allowed at red lights. Roads throughout the country are in excellent condition, and the local driving style could best be described as fast and aggressive. If you hold a driving licence and residence permit from another Gulf country you can drive in Kuwait without any further paperwork. Holders of driving licences from other countries can also drive on their home licences, or on an International Driving Permit, but will also be required to purchase 'insurance' for their licence for KD10 per month (KD15 for three months if you hold a three-month visit visa). The cost of the insurance is simply added on to your bill from the rental car company and 'applying' involves nothing more than filling in an extra form when you are doing the paperwork to rent the car. This is mandatory so you really have no choice except to grin and bear it.

Rental

Kuwait is the most expensive place in the Gulf to rent a car. The major agencies (Avis, Europcar, Budget) all charge around KD10 per day for their smallest cars. There are local agencies, such as Al-Mulla, which charge (slightly) cheaper rates. For more details see Kuwait City's Getting There & Away section later in this chapter.

LOCAL TRANSPORT
Bus

Kuwait has an extensive system of local buses. Though since none of them run down Arabian Gulf St in the city centre a number of the main tourist sights are not directly accessible by bus. Still, if you're willing to walk a few blocks, and know where you're going, the bus can be an affordable alternative to cabs. Buses run from 6 am until about 10.30 pm. Fares are 100 to 250 fils. Route maps are available at the main bus station for 150 fils.

Taxi

Most Kuwaiti taxis have no meters. Bargaining the fare in advance may save you some grief at the end of the trip but it may also cost you money. Around town, taxis are orange-coloured and can be found in ranks near the main bus station and at all the big hotels as well as cruising around the centre. Simply wave your arm at taxis on the street to get them to stop. Few of the drivers speak any English. See Taxi in Kuwait City's Getting Around section later in this chapter for details of the proper fares and more information on the city's taxi system.

Kuwait City

This is a lovely place to be in: the weather delicious, hot at noon, but too cold to sit in the shade without a *very* warm coat.

So wrote Freya Stark on her arrival in Kuwait in March 1937 (reproduced in a letter in her book *The Coast of Incense).* Things change. In the decades since oil was discovered 'lovely' is a word few have used

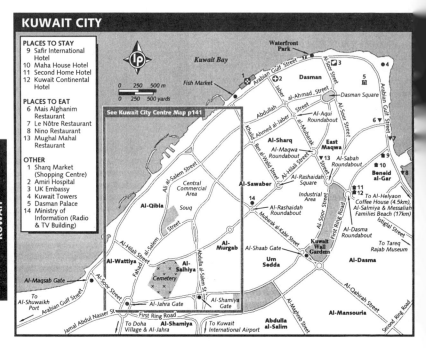

KUWAIT CITY

PLACES TO STAY
9 Safir International Hotel
10 Maha House Hotel
11 Second Home Hotel
12 Kuwait Continental Hotel

PLACES TO EAT
6 Mais Alghanim Restaurant
7 Le Nôtre Restaurant
8 Nino Restaurant
13 Mughal Mahal Restaurant

OTHER
1 Sharq Market (Shopping Centre)
2 Amiri Hospital
3 UK Embassy
4 Kuwait Towers
5 Dasman Palace
14 Ministry of Information (Radio & TV Building)

to describe Kuwait City. That said, the years since the liberation have turned Kuwait City into a remarkably easy-going place, at least by Arabian standards. Inspiring? Rarely. Interesting? Always.

Orientation

Kuwait City could still do with a few more street signs although there are more now than there were a few years ago. It is not very difficult to find your way around. The commercial centre is the area from Kuwait Bay inland to Al-Soor St, between the Al-Jahra gate and Mubarak al-Kabeer St. The coastal road is commonly called Arabian Gulf St and appears that way on some maps. The few signs on the ground, however, say 'Al-Khalij al-Arabi St' (same thing, only transliterated, instead of translated, from the Arabic). The National Assembly building, the National Museum, Sief Palace and the Great Mosque all lie along Arabian Gulf St.

The main shopping and commercial area of Kuwait City is Fahad al-Salem St, which becomes Ahmad al-Jaber St north of Al-Safat Square, where the commercial centre begins to taper off. The souq is the area between the Municipal Park and Mubarak al-Kabeer St. Upmarket shopping has largely left the centre, migrating out to fancy malls, most notably the Sharq Market on Arabian Gulf St, next to the fish souq.

From the centre the city spreads inland, becoming ever broader. The main arteries are a series of numbered ring roads and Arabian Gulf St, which continues far down the coast to Al-Salmiya and beyond.

Information

Tourist Office As there is officially no tourism in Kuwait, there is no tourist office. The local English-language papers are your best source of information on a day-to-day basis. Both publish extensive 'what's on' sections.

Money You will find banks pretty evenly distributed throughout the city. There are a few around Fahad al-Salem St, a couple near the Science & Natural History Museum on Abdullah al-Mubarak St and one in the Salhiya Commercial Centre on Mohammed Thunayyan St. People staying in or near the Safir International Hotel (formerly the Kuwait International Hotel and, before that, the Hilton) should use the National Bank of Kuwait branch in the hotel's upper lobby.

Moneychangers can offer slightly better rates than banks (and, usually, lower commissions), but finding one in the centre which will change travellers cheques can be a problem. Try the Al-Jawhara Exchange Centre which is in the Souq al-Watya shopping centre, next to the Sheraton Hotel. It changes travellers cheques at decent rates with no commission.

American Express (☎ 241 3000) is represented in Kuwait by Al-Ghanim Travel, on the 2nd mezzanine level of the Salhiya Commercial Centre. It is open Saturday to Thursday from 8 am to 1 pm and 4 to 7 pm, but is closed on Friday. AmEx card holders can cash personal cheques but the office will not hold mail for clients.

Post & Communications The GPO is on Fahad al-Salem St near the intersection with Al-Wattiya St. It is open Saturday to Wednesday from 7.30 am to 7.30 pm, Thursday from 7.30 am to 3.30 pm and Friday from 9 to 11 am and from 3.30 to 7.30 pm. The GPO has a cardphone booth from which international calls can be made and phonecards are on sale at a nearby window. Poste restante facilities are not available. The Safat Post Office, at the intersection of Abdullah al-Mubarak and Al-Hilali Sts, is mainly for post office box holders but counter services are offered as well. It is open the same hours as the GPO.

The main telephone office is at the intersection of Abdullah al-Salem and Al-Hilali Sts at the base of the communications tower. It is open 24 hours a day. Cardphones (for which cards are on sale) are available for international calls. You can also book international calls and prepay the cost, but this is much more expensive than using the cardphones. Telex and fax services are also available.

Travel Agencies Travel agencies in Kuwait operate a comfortable, if strict, cartel. A few years ago virtually every airline office and travel agency in the city was displaying a poster from the Kuwait Travel & Tourism Agencies Association announcing that, in the interest of 'improved customer service', all travel agents were 'agreeing' (in other words, being ordered) to adhere to KTTAA's unified pricing policy. 'That means no discounts', one clerk said when asked about the signs. He was less candid when asked how a price-fixing agreement was supposed to provide 'improved customer service'.

Still, as is the case just about everywhere else in the Gulf, there are far too many travel agencies in Kuwait and in their desperation for business most are willing to bargain down the price of tickets, but don't expect a large discount. Since they are cutting into their already slim commissions you can't expect to knock more than 5% off a ticket price and the trade-off for that will be locking yourself into the dates and times on the ticket. Shop around. The farther you are travelling (ie, Los Angeles as opposed to Bahrain), the better your chances are of getting some sort of discount.

Fahad al-Salem St and Al-Soor St (between the Al-Jahra gate and the Radio & TV building) both have lots of small travel agencies; ask hotel staff or expat acquaintances for advice on finding a competent one.

Bookshops In the centre, the best place to look for English-language books is the large Kuwait Bookshops Co. Ltd, on the basement level of the Al-Muthanna Centre shopping complex on Fahad al-Salem St. They have a decent selection of titles, though the prices are quite high. They also have a large selection of magazines in English, French and German. Otherwise there are very few bookshops which stock English-language books other than textbooks and technical works on subjects like civil engineering.

Cultural Centres According to Kuwaiti law, cultural centres are obligated to charge a membership fee. This has managed to cramp the style of even the French. (Kuwait is the only place in the Gulf where the French run their cultural centre directly out of the embassy.)

Circle Francophone (☎ 257 4803) In the French embassy, Mansouria district, St 13, Block 1, Villa 24. The KD40 annual membership fee covers use of its library and invitations to films, exhibitions and the occasional play or lecture.

British Council (☎ 253 3204) On Al-Arabi St in the Mansouria district, next to the Nadi al-Arabi stadium. The library is open Saturday to Wednesday from 4 to 8 pm and Thursday from 9 am to 1 pm. Anyone can use the library for free, but an annual membership (KD15) is required before you can borrow books.

German Cultural Association (☎ 253 0000) On the 2nd floor of the Safir International Hotel. The association is not a formal 'cultural centre' as defined by Kuwaiti law, so there is no membership fee. On the other hand, apart from a small library of German-language books and magazines, it doesn't have a lot to offer. The association is open only on Sunday from 5 to 7 pm.

Laundry Al-Shurouq Laundry, on the corner of Abu Bakr al-Siddiq and Al-Wattiya Sts in the city centre, offers 24-hour service. Cleaning and pressing costs 600 fils for a pair of trousers, 750 fils for a skirt, from KD1.250 for dresses, 300 fils for a shirt, 500 fils for a blouse, 250 fils for a pair of socks and 200 fils for each piece of underwear. One-hour service is available for double these rates. They are open Saturday to Thursday from 8 am to 1 pm and from 3 to 9 pm and Friday from 8 am to noon.

Another option in the centre is Fajr Kuwait Laundry on Al-Soor St. Depending on the item, it is generally a little bit cheaper (100 fils here or there) than Al-Shurouq and offers the same 24-hour turnaround time. It is open daily from 9 am to noon and from 5 to 9 pm.

Medical Services From March 2000 medical care for foreigners in Kuwait ceased to be free. The good news is that it remains quite affordable. Visitors in need of medical care should make their way to the nearest hospital or polyclinic. The hospitals provide long-term and emergency care. Polyclinics handle everyday patient matters and referrals. They are open from 8 am to 1 pm and 4 to 7 pm. Walk-ins will be charged a token KD1 per visit, though you can expect huge lines and long waits in most places. Wherever you go, be sure to have your passport or residence card with you. If your ailment is not severe most large hotels have a doctor on staff (if you are visiting friends or family, ask if you can see your host's company doctor). In addition, foreigners living in Kuwait must pay KD60 per year for medical insurance.

There are also private doctors, and two private clinics, for whose services you will be expected to pay. Note that private medical practice is quite strictly regulated and the private doctors cannot, among other things, administer vaccinations, though they can prescribe continuing medication (which was not the case a few years ago).

If you need quick medical attention and are willing to pay for it, the Kuwait Clinic (☎ 573 9277, 24-hour emergency service ☎ 573 9251) in Al-Salmiya, just north of the entrance to the Ras Salmiya ferry terminal, is a good bet. Their formal address is Salem al-Mubarak St, Area 2, Block 12, Building 56. The clinic is open daily except Friday from 9 am to 1 pm and from 4 to 8.30 pm (4 to 7 pm on Thursday).

National Museum
What remains of the National Museum is open Saturday to Wednesday from 8.30 am to 12.30 pm and 4 to 7 pm, and Thursday and Friday from 8.30 to 11 am and 4 to 7 pm. Admission is free but you must bring a passport or *iqama* (residence permit). The museum compound fronts on Arabian Gulf St but is entered through the gate around the corner from Sadu House (look for a short road leading to a parking lot).

KUWAIT CITY CENTRE

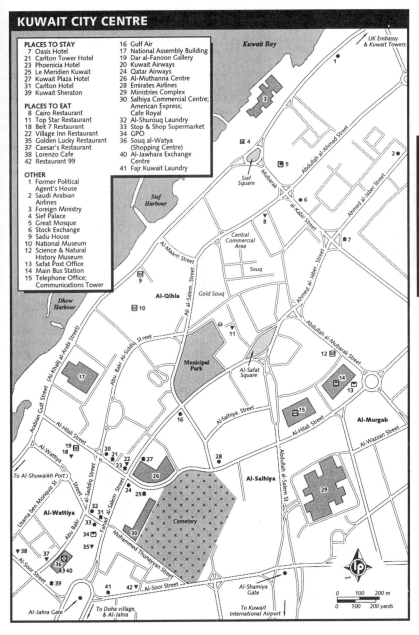

PLACES TO STAY
7   Oasis Hotel
21 Carlton Tower Hotel
23 Phoenicia Hotel
25 Le Meridien Kuwait
27 Kuwait Plaza Hotel
31 Carlton Hotel
39 Kuwait Sheraton

PLACES TO EAT
8   Cairo Restaurant
11 Top Star Restaurant
18 Beit 7 Restaurant
22 Village Inn Restaurant
35 Golden Lucky Restaurant
37 Caesar's Restaurant
38 Lorenzo Cafe
42 Restaurant 99

OTHER
1   Former Political
    Agent's House
2   Saudi Arabian
    Airlines
3   Foreign Ministry
4   Sief Palace
5   Great Mosque
6   Stock Exchange
9   Sadu House
10 National Museum
12 Science & Natural
    History Museum
13 Safat Post Office
14 Main Bus Station
15 Telephone Office;
    Communications Tower

16 Gulf Air
17 National Assembly Building
19 Dar al-Fanoon Gallery
20 Kuwait Airways
24 Qatar Airways
26 Al-Muthanna Centre
28 Emirates Airlines
29 Ministries Complex
30 Salhiya Commercial Centre;
    American Express;
    Cafe Royal
32 Al-Shurouq Laundry
33 Stop & Shop Supermarket
34 GPO
36 Souq al-Watya
    (Shopping Centre)
40 Al-Jawhara Exchange
    Centre
41 Fajr Kuwait Laundry

KUWAIT

The Legacy of the Gulf War

A coalition of 28 nations fought to drive Iraq's military out of Kuwait in January and February of 1991. In the months that followed, an equally impressive international effort was required to clean up the mess left behind.

The environmental damage caused by the Iraqis – much of which can only be described as spiteful – was on a truly massive scale. On 20 January 1991, the third day of the war, Iraqi forces opened the valves at Kuwait's Mina al-Ahmadi and Sea Island oil terminals, intentionally releasing millions of litres of oil into the waters of the Gulf.

The result was an oil slick 64km wide and 160km long. Between six and eight million barrels of oil are thought to have been released (though some estimates go much higher) – at least twice as much as in any previous oil spill. At least 460km of coastline, most of it in Saudi Arabia and Bahrain, was affected.

Releasing the oil appears to have been an attempt by the Iraqis to poison Riyadh's drinking water supply (much of which comes from two desalination plants near Jubail); shut down the kingdom's offshore oil industry, which was providing fuel to the anti-Iraq coalition; and block an amphibious attack on occupied Kuwait. Some of the smaller releases appear to have been the inadvertent result of coalition bombing raids against targets in Kuwait.

The slick was fought by experts from nine nations, the European Community and the Gulf States themselves. Aramco and other oil companies eventually managed to recover, and reuse, around a million barrels of crude oil from the slick.

Despite a massive rescue effort, the slick devastated marine life along much of the coast. While the war was still being fought, stories began circulating about the affect of the slick on the Gulf's large population of cormorants, migratory birds that typically spend the winter months in the Gulf. Dolphins, fish, several endangered species of sea turtles and many other animals died in large numbers as a result of the slick, as did hundreds of hectares of mangroves along the coast.

Though some of Kuwait's famous oil fires may well have been set off by allied bombing, the Iraqis began the systematic torching of the emirate's oil wells (of which there were just under 1000 at the time of the invasion) in mid-February. By the time the war ended, two weeks later, nearly every well was burning, including many that had not even been in production at the time of the invasion. The conservative estimate was that at least two million barrels of oil per day were being lost. The resulting cloud literally turned day into night across the country.

Like the slick, the fires devastated wildlife throughout the region, but they also had a direct impact on public health in Kuwait and the northern Gulf. Black rain and snow caused by the fires were reported as far away as India.

Once the fire on each well was out, the flow of oil itself still had to be controlled. Cleaning up the oil lakes left behind after the fires – in some places up to 2m deep and saturating the sand to a depth of 35 or 40cm – took much longer than putting out the actual blazes.

Initial reports predicted that it might take as long as five years to put out all the fires, but that proved pessimistic. Another massive international effort, combined with a fair dose of innovation on the part of the firefighters, led to the extinguishing of the last fire after only eight months. The crews did the job so quickly that one well had to be reignited so that the emir of Kuwait could pull a lever to 'put out the final fire' before a large group of reporters flown in for the occasion in November 1991.

The museum was once the pride of Kuwait and its centrepiece, the Al-Sabah collection, was one of the most important collections of Islamic art in the world. During the occupation, however, the Iraqis systematically looted the exhibit halls. Having cleaned out the building they smashed everything and set what was left on fire. It does not look too bad from the street, but the scene inside is far from pretty. The interior of the building has been shored up to prevent its collapse but has otherwise been left as the Kuwaitis found it after liberation. It is the only major building in Kuwait City that has not been restored to its pre-war state, and the government has declared that the ruined museum will be maintained forever as a monument to the memory of the Iraqi occupation.

Most of the museum's collection was eventually returned by the Iraqis but many pieces had been damaged during their transit to Iraq or had been poorly stored while they were there.

From the entry gate head straight in towards the courtyard, go up the ramp and then turn right. This is where the Al-Sabah collection used to be. Another destroyed section of the building is open on the ground level to the left of the entry gate. This is where the archaeological and ethnographic exhibits were. This hall is particularly poignant due to an exhibition of photographs of some of the things you used to be able to see in the hall. The Planetarium, which was also torched, is open for inspection at the back of the compound. The ship on the side of the building facing Arabian Gulf St is a replica of the original one that used to sit there (the Iraqis burned that, too).

A series of galleries at the far end of the courtyard houses the museum's current exhibits: small displays on traditional life among the Bedouins and in the city in the pre-oil era, a few artefacts depicting seafaring and pearl diving, a dozen or so Islamic manuscripts (most from the 17th century or later) and a few artefacts from the Hellenistic archaeological site on Failaka Island. The upper level displays paintings and a few works of sculpture by Kuwaiti artists.

Buses 12 and 16 will get you to within a couple of blocks of the museum.

Sadu House

Sadu House (☎ 243 2395) is a small building near the National Museum on Arabian Gulf St. The house is supposed to be a museum and cultural foundation dedicated to

preserving Bedouin arts and crafts, particularly weaving (*sadu* is the Arabic word for 'weaving'). While you can still occasionally see weavers at work (the house is the site of periodic weaving demonstrations or clinics), it is now mostly a sales outlet.

If Sadu House is a bit of a disappointment as a museum it remains the best place in the country to buy Bedouin goods. Large pieces suitable for use as carpets or wall hangings cost KD100 to KD150, pillows around KD15 and small bags from KD7 to KD15.

The house itself is also worth a close look. Though a bit worse for wear (not, by the way, because of the war – it looked this way before the Iraqis showed up) it is built of gypsum and coral. Note the carved decorative work along the roof-level of the courtyard.

The building is open every day except Friday from 8 am to 1 pm and from 4 to 8 pm. Admission is free.

National Assembly Building

This is the distinctive white building with the sloping roofs on Arabian Gulf St south of the National Museum. The building was designed by Jorn Utzøn, the Danish architect who also designed the Sydney Opera House. The two sweeping roofs are supposed to evoke Bedouin tents. One shades a parking area on the side of the building facing the sea. The other is over the legislative chamber itself.

Kuwait has long been the only country in the Gulf with a parliament and, for that reason alone, this building occupies an especially important place in the national consciousness. In the late '80s, when the first rumblings of what became Kuwait's 1989–90 democracy movement were heard, the government drove home the message that the old parliament was not returning by changing the building's name to the Permanent Chamber of the Council of Ministers. The Iraqis badly damaged the interior and its restoration became a government priority after liberation. When the National Assembly was reinstated in 1992, the building once again became the home of Kuwait's parliament.

The complex also houses a restaurant and the offices of Kuwait's 50 MPs. Parliament is usually in session throughout the year, except for Muslim and national holidays and a summer recess in August, September and October. Regular sessions are held on Tuesday and, sometimes, Saturday. They are open to the public. Go to the gate at the rear left of the building (the inland side). You will need to bring your passport or iqama. Sessions usually begin at 9 am and wrap up in the early afternoon. These mostly consist of questioning of cabinet ministers by the assembly's members. The ministers sit in the front row.

Once inside you will probably be directed to the upper gallery. The lower level – the rows of seats immediately behind the MPs' desks – is generally reserved for diplomats, working journalists, parliamentary staff and visiting VIPs. If they will let you sit down below, however, you should do so as the view is much better.

As amazing as it may sound, simultaneous translation of parliamentary debates into English is available. Ask for a set of earphones as you enter the chamber. If no-one offers you a headset go to the lower level of the gallery and try to get the attention of one of the people in the translation booths (on the right side of the lower gallery as you face the Speaker's Chair). If you need a headset but the guards will not let you into the chamber on the lower level ask one of the guards to get one from the translation people for you.

Buses 12, 21 and 29 stop a few hundred meters from the Assembly at the intersection of Fahad al-Salem and Al-Hilali Sts.

Sief Palace

Sief Palace, at the intersection of Mubarak al-Kabeer and Arabian Gulf Sts north-east of the National Museum, is the official seat of the emir's court. The oldest parts of the building date from the turn of the century. The Iraqis practically demolished the place and it required extensive reconstruction after the war. The huge annexe at the western end of the palace complex is a post-war addition. The interior of the palace is not open to the public. The main thing you can see from the street is the beautiful clock tower.

Photographing the palace is generally OK these days. But note that photographing the Foreign Ministry (the low-set, modern building next door with lots of soldiers around it) is not.

The closest you can get to the palace by bus is the intersection of Mubarak al-Kabeer and Ahmed al-Jaber Sts. Buses 11, 12, 14, 15, 16, 18, 20 and 22 all stop there.

Great Mosque

This huge, modern mosque opposite the Sief Palace was opened in 1986. It cost KD13 million to build and the government says that it can accommodate over 5500 worshippers. The central dome is 26m in diameter and 43m high.

Kuwait Stock Exchange

The stock exchange is the modernistic brown building on Mubarak al-Kabeer St, a block or so inland from the Great Mosque, and is the Gulf's largest. Trading takes place Saturday to Wednesday from 9.30 am to 12 pm. The exchange is an electronic market, so the 'trading floor', which occupies most of the ground level of the building, looks rather like the waiting area of an airport. You'll see lots of people sitting around tracking their investments on the tally boards hanging from the roof, but none of the running about and shouting usually associated with Western financial markets. Brokers have offices around the floor's edge.

Former Political Agency (Beit Dixon)

About 750m along Arabian Gulf St from Sief Palace (towards the Kuwait Towers) you will find a modest white house with blue trim. From 1904 until the late '30s this was the Political Agency, the British headquarters in Kuwait. Freya Stark spent most of March 1937 here. She adored Kuwait and lavished praise on her host, Gerald de Gaury, but was less impressed by the building, which she referred to as a 'big ugly box'.

Viewed straight on it seems quite small, but from the side its true dimensions are clearer.

The house is also known as 'Beit Dixon' after the last British Political agent (whose widow continued to live here for many years, usually spending her winters in the emirate well into the 1980s). At this writing the building (which has not been open to the public in the past) was being restored.

There is no bus service to the house.

Kuwait Towers

On Arabian Gulf St beyond the UK embassy, the towers are rather hard to miss. Designed by a Swedish architectural firm and opened in 1979, they have long been the country's main landmark. The largest of the three towers rises to a height of 187m.

The upper globe houses a two-level observation deck. The upper level, at 123m, revolves, taking 30 minutes to make a circle. The largest tower's lower globe (at 82m) has a restaurant, a coffee shop and a private banquet room. The lower globe on the largest tower and the single globe on the middle tower are used to store water. The small tower with no globes is used to light up the other two.

The observation deck is open daily from 9 am to 11 pm. In the lower globe the restaurant (which is very expensive) is open from 12.30 to 3.30 pm and from 7.30 to 11.30 pm. The (cheaper) cafe is open from 10 am straight through until 11 pm. Admission to the observation deck costs 500 fils. You can go to the restaurants for free. Because the towers overlook the Dasman Palace, cameras with zoom lenses are not permitted and you will have to leave these at the ticket booth.

The towers are not on any main bus route, but they are close enough to the city centre that you can walk if the heat is not too bad. A cab should cost around KD1 from anywhere in the centre, though be warned: the towers can be a difficult place to find a taxi when you want to get back into town.

Tareq Rajab Museum

This museum is at House 16, St 5, Block 12, in the Jabriya district. Look for a house on a corner two blocks north and one block west of the New English School, near the intersection of the Fifth Ring Rd and the Fahaheel Expressway. It is open Saturday to Thursday from 9 am to noon and 4 to 7 pm, and Friday from 4 to 7 pm. Admission is free. There is no sign on the building but it is easily identified by its entrance – a carved wooden doorway flanked by two smaller doors on each side. All four of the door panels are worked in gilt metal.

The museum, which is housed in the basement of a large villa, is a private collection that was assembled by Kuwait's first minister of antiquities. The focus is on Islamic art. Amazingly, it appears to have survived the occupation and war entirely intact, a fact that makes the collection all the more important considering the fate that befell the National Museum's treasures.

Turn left at the entrance to the galleries and the first thing you will see is a small display of daggers from Oman and Yemen. Immediately beyond this, and sharply left, is a narrow hall with a display of early Islamic manuscripts. The main gallery on this side of the museum is straight ahead as you pass through the daggers. This includes an excellent display of Arabic manuscripts and calligraphy. Be sure to see the talismanic shirts, worn as undergarments in India in the 17th and 18th centuries, printed with prayers and verses from the Quran. The same hall also has a wide selection of ceramics and pottery from various parts of the Islamic world. A small hall between this gallery and the main entrance contains antique clothes and jewellery.

Traditional costumes and jewellery are displayed in the hall to the right of the entrance. The exhibit is particularly interesting because it covers not only Islam's Arab/Middle Eastern heartland but also much farther flung areas such as Kazakhstan and Uzbekistan.

Buses 25 and 32 serve Jabriya, though neither stops within easy walking distance of the museum. A taxi from the centre should cost around KD2.500, but you'll probably have to call a cab to get back into town, as there are few cruising taxis this far out.

KUWAIT

Science & Natural History Museum

On Abdullah al-Mubarak St, the museum is open Saturday to Thursday from 8.30 am to noon, but is closed on Friday and holidays. Admission is free. Though the collection seems to consist largely of stuffed animals, there is some variety. The ground floor also contains animal skeletons, including a few dinosaurs. The 1st floor has a display on space exploration and many more stuffed critters.

The museum is a short distance from the main bus station at the intersection of Abdullah al-Mubarak and Al-Hilali Sts.

Communications Tower

The communications tower at the intersection of Al-Hilali and Abdullah al-Salem Sts is unmistakable – it is the tallest structure in Kuwait, dominating the city's skyline from almost any angle. There is an observation deck about two-thirds of the way up the tower, though at this writing it was not yet open to the public on a regular basis.

Old City Gates

Four of Kuwait City's five gates – Al-Shaab, Al-Shamiya, Al-Jahra and Al-Maqsab – lie along Al-Soor St, the street which follows the line of the old city wall (*soor* is the Arabic word for 'wall'). The Al-Maqsab gate, occupying a small green site between the Sheraton Hotel and Arabian Gulf St, is a relatively recent reconstruction. At the end of the war only its foundations remained intact. The fifth gate (Dasman gate) was near the Dasman Palace by the Kuwait Towers. The wall, which the gates were part of, was only constructed around 1920. It was built in a hurry as part of the effort to defend the city against the ikhwan, the group of Islamist warriors loyal to Abdul Aziz bin Abdul Rahman al-Saud, later the first King of Saudi Arabia. The wall was torn down in 1957.

Covered Souq

The souq, broadly defined, lies between the Municipal Park and Mubarak al-Kabeer St, from Ahmad al-Jaber St to Ali al-Salem St.

Moneychangers, gold sellers, electronics merchants, etc, tend to group into specific areas. The meat and vegetable market, which opens quite early in the morning and is arguably the most interesting part of the souq, is in the very centre of the souq area. The gold souq is just off Ali al-Salem St. At the time of writing large sections of the old souq were walled off due to renovations.

The fish souq is away from the rest in a massive new complex on Arabian Gulf St next to the Sharq Market shopping centre.

Waterfront Park

Along Arabian Gulf St between the Sharq Market shopping centre and the Kuwait Towers you'll find a large complex of gardens, walkways, volleyball courts, playgrounds and public toilets.

Exhibition of Sailing Ships

This small, largely unknown and utterly fascinating tourist site lies far out beyond the edge of the city on the road to Doha Village. It consists of about half a dozen different dhows and other traditional sailing vessels ranging in size from small fishing boats to a large ocean-going dhow. Several of the boats fly the red flag that Kuwait used prior to independence from Britain in 1961. All of the boats have been carefully restored and ramps provide access for curious visitors. A very small seafaring museum rounds out the site. It's a long drive out from the city but absolutely worth the trip.

The exhibition is open every day from 8 am to 8 pm. Admission is free.

To reach the site take the Al-Jahra Rd west out of Kuwait City. Follow the signs for Entertainment City and turn onto the Doha Spur Rd. Make a U-turn just *before* you reach the roundabout at the entrance to Entertainment City, then turn immediately right onto a small road. The exhibition will be on your left after 3.5km. There are no buses to this area of Kuwait. Unless you have a car, a taxi will be your only option. This should cost KD3 to KD5 one way, depending on your negotiating skills. Since you don't have a hope of getting a ride from here, a round-trip costing around KD8 is robably your best bet. For that price you might be able to get the driver to include a stop in Doha Village.

There is no way to get anywhere near the exhibition using public transport.

Beach & Health Clubs

Most of the health clubs at the big hotels are available only to hotel guests and people holding long-term memberships. At the time of writing a new health club was under construction on Arabian Gulf St between the Sharq Market shopping mall and the Kuwait Towers.

Some 20km south of the centre along Arabian Gulf St the Messaliah Families Beach is a good place to go if you have kids or if you're an unaccompanied woman seeking to swim without too many prying eyes following you. Admission to the club is 500 fils (250 fils for children under six) and is limited to women and families (ie, no unaccompanied men). In addition to a beach and a swimming pool there is a lot of play space for children. There are several fast-food restaurants at the club. If you are travelling without kids be warned that this place can get pretty noisy on Friday afternoons.

Boating

If you feel like renting a boat, head for the Sultan Centre Restaurants complex about 6km south of the city centre on the sea side of Arabian Gulf St. Note that the Sultan Centre Restaurants complex is several kilometres closer to the centre than the main Sultan Centre shopping complex. In the parking lot you will find a small kiosk. For KD2 per person (minimum five people) you can take a short cruise to the Kuwait Towers and back. Parasailing is also available for KD5 per person (KD7 with a larger, more powerful boat). The office is open from 9 am to 11 pm daily.

Organised Tours

Kuwait has no formal tour industry. The Safir International Hotel offers a free three-hour tour of Kuwait City on Fridays from 10 am to 1 pm but this is open to hotel guests only.

Shopping

This is, arguably, Kuwait's favourite leisure activity. For a shopping tour that charts the city's growth, wealth and Americanisation do this: start in the old souqs (state of the art shopping in Kuwait, circa 1950), move on to the dowdy, downmarket Al-Watiyah Centre (state of the art shopping, circa 1970). Next, move a few blocks north to the Salhiya Commercial Centre (the swishest Kuwaiti mall of the mid-to-late '80s). If you've got a car take a detour down Arabian Gulf St to the Sultan Centre (*the* place to be in the post-war years) and finish up at the vintage turn-of-the-millennium Sharq Market, a massive complex on Arabian Gulf St which boasts movie theatres, big department stores, a US-style food court and even its own marina.

Places to Stay

All of Kuwait's hotels are able to arrange visas for travellers visiting Kuwait. See Visas & Documents in the Facts for the Visitor section earlier in this chapter for further details.

For general information about Accommodation in Kuwait, see Accommodation in the Facts for the Visitor section earlier this chapter.

Places to Stay – Budget & Mid-Range

Kuwait has lost a few of its budget-priced hotels in recent years. The good news is that some of the cheaper hotels, including a few of the seriously overpriced places (such as the Continental) have dropped their rates a bit. The bad news is that it is still nearly impossible to find a bed in Kuwait for under US$50 a night.

Every hotel room in Kuwait has air-conditioning, a private bath and a TV set (usually one that receives several satellite channels) and most also offer minifridges. Some of the cheaper places do not have heating in the rooms and you will certainly notice this in December or January. Though you are unlikely to bargain more than KD1 or KD2 off any given price, most of the country's hotels also hit you with a 15% service charge which you may be able to negotiate this away as a 'discount'. The rates listed here are initial quotes and do not include the service charge, if there is any.

Maha House (☎ *252 3211, fax 257 1220)*, located on an unmarked street behind the Safir International Hotel in Beneid al-Gar is, at KD10/20 for singles/doubles, the country's cheapest hotel. It's not as bad as it once was, but that is not saying much. You should also be aware that both the heating and the air-con are dodgy at best. From the centre, the hotel can be reached by bus No 15. Get off at the Al-Dasma roundabout where you see the Kuwait Continental Hotel. Walk behind the hotel. The Maha House is on a back street behind it.

Second Home Hotel (☎ *253 2100, fax 253 2381)* is just behind the much larger Kuwait Continental Hotel off the Al-Dasma roundabout in Beneid al-Gar. All things considered, this is Kuwait's best value hotel. For KD15/20 you get small but exceedingly tidy rooms. There's a decent little coffee bar in the lobby. *Kuwait Continental Hotel* (☎ *252 7300, fax 252 9373)* is one of the handful of places where prices have fallen a bit in recent years. Rooms now go for KD25/30.

Phoenicia Hotel (☎ *242 1051, fax 242 4402)*, on the corner of Fahad al-Salem and Al-Hilali Sts, is slightly musty but generally reliable and by far your best bet if you want to be in the centre. Rooms cost KD17/23, including breakfast.

Carlton Hotel (☎ *242 3171, fax 242 5848)* further down Fahad al-Salem street is another Kuwait stand-by offering rooms that are decent, if a bit ragged around the edges, for KD15/20.

Carlton Tower Hotel (☎ *245 2740, fax 240 1624)* is on Al-Hilali St just off al-Salem St. A bit more upscale, this represents what passes for the middle-range in Kuwait. It offers very spacious rooms for KD30/40.

Oasis Hotel (☎ *246 5489, fax 246 5490)*, at the intersection of Ahmad al-Jaber and Mubarak al-Kabeer Sts, is very clean and orderly. This hotel is closer to Kuwait's bank headquarters and office towers than most. It has long been popular with budget-minded business travellers and rooms cost KD30/35, including breakfast.

Places to Stay – Top End

Five-star hotels offer the fastest and most reliable service for visa seekers but, boy, do you pay for the privilege. Unlike Manama or Doha, Kuwait is not awash in top-end hotel space: the result is a cosy cartel among the top hotels and room rates that routinely top US$200 per night. Prices quoted here are rack rates and do not include the near-universal 15% service charge. Unless you're eligible for some sort of corporate or frequent-traveller discount you should not count on knocking more than KD5 or so off these prices.

Kuwait Plaza Hotel (☎ *243 6686)* is on Fahad al-Salem St near Al-Muthanna Centre in the city centre. Singles/doubles cost KD48/57.

Kuwait Sheraton (☎ *242 2055, fax 244 8032)* is at the intersection of Fahad al-Salem and Al-Soor Sts, in the city centre, near the Al-Jahra gate. Rooms cost KD60/70.

Le Meridien Kuwait (☎ *245 5550, fax 243 8391, Al-Hilali St)* has rooms for KD67/78 – probably the best value for money in this price category.

Messilah Beach Hotel (☎ *562 4111, fax 562 9402)* is at Messilah Beach, south of the centre on the road to Al-Ahmadi. Rooms cost KD52/56.

Radisson SAS Hotel Kuwait (☎ *575 6000, fax 575 2788, Arabian Gulf St)* has rooms for KD66.700/77.800.

Safir International Hotel (☎ *253 0000, fax 256 3797, Arabian Gulf St)*, in Beneid al-Gar district, is the favoured haunt of visiting VIPs and Western journalists. It's overpriced at KD68/75.

Places to Eat

Restaurants just off Fahad al-Salem St behind the Phoenicia Hotel is the *Village Inn Restaurant*, a pretty good bet if you are looking for a cheap meal in the city. Though the menu features both Chinese and Indian food the clientele is mostly middle-class Indian expatriates, so you would be well advised to stick to the Indian food (which, anyway, is cheaper). Indian main dishes cost KD1 to KD2.

Caesar's (Abu Bakr al-Saddiq St), offers the best affordable Chinese food in the city (it's not far from the Sheraton Hotel; another Caesar's, a few blocks up the street towards the Kuwait Airlines building, serves only Indian food). The restaurant is very popular with both Kuwaitis and expats and you may have to wait for a table, especially on weekends. Main dishes cost KD1.200 to KD3.

Nino (☎ 254 1900, Arabian Gulf St) a South African-run Italian restaurant just south of the Safir International Hotel, offers excellent food in a fun atmosphere. Appetisers cost KD1.250 to KD2.500, pizza and pasta dishes go for around KD3.

Mais Alghanim on Arabian Gulf St, between the Kuwait Towers and the intersection with Al-Soor St, is the place to go if you only eat out once during your stay in Kuwait. A white prefab building, which also contains the local DHL office, hides a terrific Lebanese restaurant. The restaurant is at the end of the building closer to Al-Soor St (the large sign is in Arabic only but there's a smaller one in English by the door). Founded in 1953 it is one of the country's older establishments and has long been something of a local institution. Meals cost about KD3 to KD4. It is worth going out of your way for. Expect queues for the garden tables in the winter and the indoor (air-conditioned) ones in the summer. They do not take dinner reservations on Wednesday, Thursday, Friday or holidays – which are the only days you would want to make reservations in the first place.

Mughal Mahal on Jaber al-Mubarak St, near the intersection with Al-Hilali St in the Al-Sharq district, offers what, in a city with many Indian restaurants, has long been regarded as the best value-for-money around. Great meals cost KD4 to KD6.

Shirinbanu, the Persian restaurant at the Safir International Hotel, has excellent service but the food isn't quite as good. Main courses cost KD5 to KD6, and full meals around KD10.

Beit 7 (pronounced *bayt sab'a*) is probably the best restaurant in the country. It is in an old Kuwaiti coral house, near Kuwait's churches. The house was built in 1949 (ancient, by local standards) and is on the government's list of historic sites. Main dishes cost KD5 to KD7, and isers mostly start at KD2.500. For late risers they also serve breakfast and morning coffee beginning at 10 am.

Cafes On the ground floor of the Salhiya Commercial Centre is the *Cafe Royal* which offers mostly Western food (omelettes, burgers etc) starting from about KD2. It also has quite good hot and cold sandwiches for KD1.500 to KD1.800 and salads for KD1.500 to KD2. Local papers are available for customers to read and the cafe is popular with Kuwaitis and expats alike. The cafe's position, next to a fountain, evokes a sidewalk cafe atmosphere: it's not exactly Paris but come July you'll value the fact that it is indoors. It is, by the way, vastly better in terms of both price and atmosphere than the ground-floor mall's other coffeehouse, the overpriced *Ritz Cafe*.

Cafe Olé on the second mezzanine level of the Salhiya Commercial Centre is the centre's best Internet cafe. Snacks and good Turkish coffee are on the menu and Internet access is KD2 per hour (you only pay for the portion of the hour you use) on Compaq PCs with Pentium II processors.

Lorenzo Cafe (Al-Soor Street) is probably Kuwait's most upmarket Western-style cafe. The coffee (and reportedly most of what goes into the pastries) is imported from Italy. It has excellent cappuccino, espresso and cakes as well as chocolates made on the premises. It is very expensive – and on weekend evenings it is also very crowded – but definitely worth a visit. A cappuccino costs KD1.100 and cakes start at KD1.500 a slice.

Le Nôtre, a French cafe and restaurant in a two-storey glass building overlooking the ocean near the Safir International Hotel, wins the prize as Kuwait's most painfully toney Western-style eatery. Cappuccino is fairly steep at KD1.250 a cup. An excellent choice if you are in the mood for a pricey, upmarket breakfast.

Fast Food Cheap food is pretty easy to find in the city centre and, mercifully, it no longer consists only of biryanis. If you're spending more than KD1 on a meal you are not really trying to eat cheaply.

Among the biryani places a couple of the city's old stand-bys still merit mention: *Top Star Restaurant* in the souq remains one of the best. Enter the souq from the south-west end of Al-Safat Square by the big Citizen sign, take the third alley on the left after the sign and head up the stairs. Another is the *Golden Lucky Restaurant* on Fahad al-Salem St at the small plaza just by the GPO. Both of these places offer menus consisting only of biryanis, fried chicken or fish and snacks. The biryanis cost about KD1 and samosas are 150 fils apiece.

Cheap Arab food is also fairly easy to find. For some of the best fuul this side of Egypt try the (appropriately named) *Cairo Restaurant* on a small-steet corner just west of both the Great Mosque and the stock exchange. Fuul and ta'amiyya sandwiches cost 100 fils apiece. The sign is only in Arabic, but the Cairo is the place one in from the corner, next door to the Al-Muzaini Exchange Co's office tower.

Kabablek is a small but noteworthy kebab stall on Arabian Gulf St south of the Safir International Hotel, near the Shabb Leisure Park. They have a couple of small tables, and will also bring the food out to your car. The offer pretty decent Lebanese mezze, shwarma and kebabs.

Restaurant 99 on Al-Soor St, near the al-Jahra Gate, is a relatively new arrival and has rapidly become one of the city's best bets for cheap eats. It's basically an upscale Arab takeaway with a few tables. *Humous* (cooked chickpeas ground into a paste), *shwarma* (grilled meat sliced from a spit and served in pita bread with salad) and a wide variety of things stuffed into Lebanese-style bread are on offer for a few hundred fils apiece.

Self-Catering The Stop & Shop Supermarket on Al-Wattiya St in the centre is a good bet for do-it-yourself meals. If you are in search of Western products you will have to make your way to the Sharq Market or take a car or taxi far down Arabian Gulf St to the Sultan Centre.

Entertainment
Coffeehouses *Beit Lothan* is on Arabian Gulf St just north of the intersection with Qatar St, several kilometres south of the centre. This is probably Kuwait's best-known traditional coffeehouse. It offers coffee, tea and *sheesha* (water pipes) in a quiet, open garden. The main building also houses an art gallery. There is no bus service down this part of Arabian Gulf St; a taxi from the centre should cost KD1.500 to KD1.750.

Al-Helmiyaon is another good traditional coffeehouse on Arabian Gulf St, about 5km south of the Safir International Hotel. It is a cleaner, more modern version of a traditional Egyptian coffeehouse offering kebabs and ta'amiyya sandwiches for 250 to 500 fils, shish tawouk for KD1 and sheesha pipes for 500 fils. The sign is only in Arabic, but the seaside complex is fairly large.

Cinemas Kuwait's newest, fanciest cinema is the three screen complex at the Sharq Market. First-run American movies can be seen here only a few months after they are released in the USA. Check the *Arab Times* for show times. Admission is KD2.500, but on weekends the theatre can be very crowded and it would be a good idea to drop by the box office early in the day to buy tickets for afternoon or evening shows.

Amusement Park Entertainment City, on the western outskirts of Kuwait City, near Doha Village, is Kuwait's only real amusement park. It is not very large by Western standards but it is a far cry from the small (and rather rickety looking) rides that dot the beachfront restaurants at the southern end of Arabian Gulf St in Kuwait City.

In the winter the park is open Sunday to Wednesday from 3 to 11 pm. On Thursday and Friday the hours are 10 am to 10 pm. In the summer the park is open only from 4 pm to 11 pm, Sunday through Friday. It is closed Saturday. Tickets are KD3.500 for both adults and children (children who can pass below the ticket window – up to 4 or 5 years old – get in free). To reach the park take the main road west out of Kuwait City towards Al-Jahra and follow the signs. The park is not accessible by public transport. Getting there by taxi will cost around KD4, but you may not find it all that easy to get a taxi back into the city.

Shopping

There are very little antiques to buy in Kuwait. Al-Badia Antique Est. (☎ 242 1136) on the ground floor of the Al-Muthanna Centre has a small selection of silver jewellery, a good stock of Iranian miniature paintings and some more general expensive gift items (small wooden dhows etc). Sadu House is a good place to shop for souvenirs. See the entry on Sadu House earlier in this chapter for an idea of its prices.

Consumer electronics are widely available but the prices are pretty high.

If you are looking for that old but expensive Gulf stand-by – gold jewellery – the gold souq is your best bet.

Getting There & Away

Air Some of the airlines that fly to/from Kuwait International Airport are:

Air France (☎ 243 0224) Hussain Makki al-Juma Travels, Al-Hilali St, near the Meridien Hotel
Air India (☎ 243 8185) Ali al-Salem St, near the intersection with Fahad al-Salem St
Air Lanka (☎ 242 4444) Fahad al-Salem St, between Ali al-Salem St and the Al-Muthanna Centre
British Airways (☎ 240 7912) Corner of Fahad al-Salem and Ali al-Salem Sts
Balkan (☎ 241 6474) Just off Al-Hilali St, next to the Al-Muthanna Centre
EgyptAir (☎ 242 1603) Al-Soor St, between Mohammed Thunayyan St and the Sheraton roundabout
Emirates Airlines (☎ 242 5566) Corner of Al-Hilali and Ali al-Salem Sts
Gulf Air (☎ 244 6804) Ali al-Salem St, near the intersection with Fahad al-Salem St
Indian Airlines (☎ 245 6700) Al-Soor St, near the Al-Jahra gate
KLM (☎ 242 5747) Mezzanine level of the building on the corner of Al-Safat Square and Abdullah al-Salem St

Kuwait Airways (☎ 171 – This is a special number that works from any phone in Kuwait) Kuwait Airways tower, Al-Hilali St
Lufthansa Airlines (☎ 242 2493) Al-Soor St, between Mohammed Thunayyan St and the Al-Jahra gate
Middle East Airlines (MEA) (☎ 242 3070) Intersection of Fahad al-Salem and Ali al-Salem Sts
Olympic Airways (☎ 242 0002) Fahad al-Salem St, between Ali al-Salem St and the Al-Muthanna Centre
Pakistan International Airlines (PIA) (☎ 242 1043) Intersection of Fahad al-Salem and Ali al-Salem Sts
Qatar Airways (☎ 245 8888) Intersection of Fahad al-Salem and Al-Hilali Sts
Saudi Arabian Airlines (☎ 242 6310) Al-Sharq district, Ahmad al-Jaber St
Turkish Airlines (☎ 245 3820) Off Fahad al-Salem St, near the Village Inn Restaurant

Bus Kuwait has only a handful of intercity bus routes. All long-haul trips cost 250 fils and, like buses inside Kuwait City, run every six minutes from approximately 6 am to 10.30 pm (at least in theory; in practice every 15 minutes is probably a better guess). Some of the buses originate at substations in either the Sharq district, east of the centre near the Dasman Palace, or in Al-Jleeb, south-west of the centre, near the airport. Intercity routes are:

Route 40 Sharq bus station, Airport Rd, Shuwaikh, Kheitan, Subhan, Al-Daher, Fintas, Fahaheel
Route 101 Main bus station, Airport Rd, Sixth Ring Rd, Sabah al-Salem district, Al-Qurin, Al-Ahmadi
Route 102 Main bus station, Istiglal St, Third Ring Rd, Cairo St, Fahaheel
Route 103 Main bus station, Fahad al-Salem St, Al-Jahra Rd, Al-Jahra
Route 502 Main bus station, Istiglal St, Khartoum St, Fahaheel Rd, Fahaheel (incl. air-con)

International bus service to Cairo and Dammam (Saudi Arabia) can be booked through any of the small travel agencies at the intersection of Abdullah al-Mubarak and Al-Hilali Sts.

Taxi While there is a taxi rank across the street from the main bus station, there is no

KUWAIT

formal service-taxi system operating in Kuwait. You could strike a deal with one of the drivers to go to another city but it would be hit-or-miss.

Car The international car-rental agencies all charge around KD10 per day for their smallest cars. Al-Mulla is the cheapest of the larger local agencies with cars from KD7.500 per day. These rates usually include unlimited kilometres, but full insurance will cost an extra KD2 to KD4 per day. Discounts on these rates can usually be negotiated, and with some shopping around you should be able to get a car for around KD8 to KD9 per day net.

Al-Mulla has offices in the Kuwait Plaza (☎ 243 6686) and Safir International (☎ 256 3869) hotels.

Getting Around

To/From the Airport Taxis charge a flat KD4 between the airport and the city. Bus 501 (which has air-con) runs between the main bus station and the airport every 30 minutes from 5.30 am to 9 pm. The fare is 250 fils.

Bus Kuwait's municipal buses are of only limited use for the traveller. Many of the country's better known sights (such as the Kuwait Towers) cannot be reached by bus, and others (such as the National Museum) are a long walk from the nearest bus stop.

Mircab, the central station for Kuwait's municipal buses, is near the intersection of Al-Hilali and Abdullah al-Mubarak Sts. Large secondary stations are located at the Orthopaedic Hospital (also known as Al-Azam Hospital) on the western edge of Kuwait City and in Al-Sharq, at the northeastern edge of the centre. Smaller stations can be found at the Al-Jahra gate and in the districts of Sulaibiya, Al-Jleeb, Kheitan, Jabriya, Messila and Al-Salmiya.

An office on the ground floor of the Kuwait Public Transport Company building at the main station sells a route map for 150 fils.

Buses start running around 5 am and continue until around 10 pm. Officially every route has buses at six-minute intervals, but every 12 to 20 minutes is a more realistic estimate. Fares are 100, 150 or 200 fils depending on how far you travel. Route numbers are displayed on the front of buses but destinations are not. Only the buses numbered 500 and above are operated using airconditioned coaches, though the rest of the bus fleet is reasonably well maintained.

Taxi Unfortunately, Kuwait has developed one of those taxi systems where there are no meters and the trick is to know before you get in what you ought to be paying. Bargaining in advance may save you some grief at the end of the trip but it will most likely end up costing you more money.

The only difference between the older, orange-coloured, taxis (which are always driven by Kuwaitis) and the more modern taxis (usually driven by foreigners) is that the air-conditioning is likely to work better in the latter. You'll wind up paying the same amount of money whichever type you choose.

In general, any ride within the city centre is about KD1. Longer trips just outside the centre (eg, from the Sheraton to the Safir International Hotel) cost about KD1.500. If you bargain, or take the taxi from a rank in front of a five-star hotel, expect to pay double this. You might also try calling Ibrahim Taxi (☎ 244 6720). Its service gets good reviews locally and it costs about the same as hailing a cab on the street.

Around Kuwait

FAILAKA ISLAND

The home of Kuwait's main archaeological site, Failaka Island is definitely worth the trip, though it requires a bit of caution: you do not need to be a military genius to figure out Failaka's strategic value during a war – control the island and you control seaborne access to Kuwait City. Not surprisingly the Iraqis turned Failaka Island into a heavily fortified base. After liberation it was found to be filled with mines and for many years was closed.

Officially, the island has now been rendered safe, but it's worth noting that the government has evacuated the entire civilian population to the mainland and visitors are still routinely urged to stay on paved roads everywhere outside the archaeologic- al site and to stay on obvious vehicle tracks inside the site). Failaka is definitely worth the trip, but be careful.

History

Failaka, which the Greeks called Ikaros, is the best known, and probably the earliest, Hellenistic settlement in the Gulf. It was also the first part of Kuwait to attract the attention of professional archaeologists, who began digging here in early 1958, as documented in Geoffrey Bibby's book, *Looking for Dilmun*.

Though it is best known as a Hellenistic site, Failaka's history goes back to the Bronze Age Dilmun civilisation which was centred in Bahrain. The Greeks arrived in the 4th century BC in the form of a garrison placed here by Nearchus, one of Alexander the Great's admirals. A very small settlement existed on the island prior to this, but it was as the Greek town of Ikaros that the settlement became a proper city or at least a large town.

As you enter the site, the road swings around to the left and ends in front of a group of prefabricated buildings. These are the archaeological museum and the on-site administrative offices.

Visiting the Island

Exactly whether you need a permit to visit Failaka Island remains unclear. The museum staff insist that the island is still a closed military zone, which is obviously not the case, although foreign diplomats and large groups *do* need permission from the Kuwaiti military to visit the island.

As for the site itself, the two guards on duty the day we visited were undecided about the necessity of permits. Be prepared to use a bit of diplomacy.

In any event, you must bring a passport or iqama with you as this will certainly be checked as you get off the ferry at the island, and may have to be shown to enter the archaeological site.

Visiting the Site

The **mud house** on a small rise between the sea and the road is the first thing you will see as you approach the site coming from the ferry. Before the war it contained a display of island life prior to the discovery of oil. The interior, however, was gutted during the occupation and has not been restored.

Tel Sa'ad, the most ancient of Failaka's three excavated sites, is the excavation next to the mud house. This was a Bronze Age settlement. Its centrepiece is the **Temple of Anzak**, the large open area in the centre of the excavation. Anzak was the chief god of Dilmun. The easiest way to locate the temple is to look for the column base that marks one of its corners. Beyond the temple, the area towards the sea may have been a fortification of some sort. The area behind the temple (away from the sea) probably also contained houses.

The **inn** is a bit farther up the coast (away from the site entrance) and is easy to spot – just look for the small metal lookout tower nearby. Little of the building remains, but the floor plan is clearly visible.

The **temple** is the centrepiece of Failaka. It, too, is easy to spot from a distance, look for a small sun shelter erected over part of the excavation. It is about 100m inland from the inn. This was the heart of the Hellenistic settlement. The temple, which was probably dedicated to Artemis, lay at the centre of a square fortress that extended 200m on each side. Two re-erected columns mark the entrance to the temple, which is of the standard Greek two-chamber type. The remains of the altar are also clearly identifiable in front of the temple. Kuwait's most famous archaeological find, the **Ikaros Stele**, was found here. It would have stood to the left of the temple entrance, as one faces the temple from the altar. Prior to the Iraqi invasion, the stele was on display at the Kuwait National Museum. It went missing during the occupation and was not among the antiquities the Iraqis returned to Kuwait after the Gulf War. Surrounding the temple is a large excavated area of houses and fortifications. The entire complex dates from 330 to 150 BC.

To reach the site from the ferry, turn right as you exit the terminal building. Almost immediately you will see the mud house on a low hill to the right beyond a wall. The entrance is a gate in this wall with seals on either side marked Kuwait National Museum.

Elsewhere on Failaka

Before you leave, take some time to wander around the ruins of the residential area near the archaeological site. The ruins of Failaka's Post and Telecoms building are about a 15-minute walk past the archaeological site along the same street. Across the street from the Post and Telecoms building, the traffic department headquarters also shows war damage. If you turn left out of the ferry terminal and follow the road on foot for about 15 minutes you will come to what was the Failaka branch of the Science and Natural History Museum (it's on the left, there is a sign in English).

Getting There & Away

Ferries to Failaka depart from Ras Salmiya (also known as Ras al-Ard), on Arabian Gulf St south of the centre in Al-Salmiya. The terminal area can be reached via buses Nos 14, 15, 24, 34 and 200.

Ferries only make the trip from Ras Salmiya to the island once per day. The trip takes 90 minutes. The ferry stays at the island for three hours before making the return trip. This is enough time for a quick look at the archaeological site and a look around what's left of the nearby residential area but not much else. If you miss the ferry back you will be stuck on the island until the following day. Since there are no hotels and the danger of landmines makes camping inadvisable, don't miss the ferry!

The fare is KD2.500 return. If you want to drive onto and off the ferry you must buy a return ticket for KD40. This covers the car and driver, but any passengers will need to buy regular tickets. Call the ferry company on ☎ 574 2664 for information on sailing times and to see whether frequency has increased from one per day.

The ferry keeps an erratic schedule that is updated every month. The outbound run to the island usually leaves at 8 am, but may depart at 8.15, 8.45, 9, 9.15, 9.45 or even 10 am depending, mainly, on the tides. Passengers are expected to be on board 15 minutes before the ferry sails. A printed schedule with exact departure times is available at the ferry terminal and is updated every two weeks.

AL-AHMADI

Built to house Kuwait's oil industry in the 1940s and '50s, Al-Ahmadi was named after the then-emir, Sheikh Ahmad. It remains, to a great extent, the private preserve of the Kuwait Oil Company (KOC). As with Dhahran in Saudi Arabia and Awali in Bahrain, the visitor driving through Al-Ahmadi's streets has the vague feeling of being in a suburb somewhere in the southwestern USA. Unlike Dhahran (but like Awali), the gates have long since come down and one need not have a reason to be allowed to drive into 'Little America'.

Al-Ahmadi has shops, supermarkets, banks, travel agents, parks, recreational facilities and a stadium. What it does not have is a hotel. There is a guest house for people having business with KOC but it does not accept non-KOC guests. The town's two sites of note are the Oil Display Centre on Mid 5th St and the public gardens.

The **Oil Display Centre** (☎ 398 2747) exhibits are a brief introduction to oil from its formation underground through the prospecting process to extraction, refining, sales and distribution. The display is small but well organised and rather self-congratulatory. There are also the requisite exhibits on the occupation, war, liberation, POWs and cleaning up the mess the Iraqis left behind. When you enter the building turn right and follow the exhibits in a counter-clockwise circle. The centre is open Saturday to Wednesday from 7 am to 3 pm. Admission is free.

Al-Ahmadi also has a small, pleasant **pubic garden** that is worth a visit.

Getting There & Away

To reach the town, take the Al-Safr Motorway south out of Kuwait City until you each the Al-Ahmadi exit. Follow, first, the blue signs for North Al-Ahmadi, and then the smaller white signs for the display centre. After the turn for North Al-Ahmadi go left on Mid 5th St (the first roundabout). To reach the public gardens from here, continue along Mid 5th St and turn left on 7th Ave (the first left past the display centre). Take the first right turn (onto Mid 7th St) and follow the road until it ends at the entrance to the public gardens. Bus No 101 runs from the main bus station in Kuwait City to Al-Ahmadi (passing by the Oil Display Centre as it enters town) several times an hour. The town, however, really is not worth going out of your way for.

AL-JAHRA

Al-Jahra, an industrial and agricultural town approximately 32km west of Kuwait City, has a name that lives in Kuwait's history as a battle site, though those with memories of the Gulf War will remember it for a much more recent battle.

History

In 1920 Kuwait's ruler, Sheikh Salem bin Mubarak, learned that Abdul Aziz bin Abdul Rahman al-Saud, the future founder and King of Saudi Arabia, planned to turn his much-feared warriors, the ikhwan, loose on Kuwait. Salem decided to make his stand at Al-Jahra. After being routed by the ikhwan in a battle near the city, the Kuwaiti forces retired to Al-Jahra's Red Fort from where they sought to wear down the more numerous Saudis in a war of attrition. In the meantime, a messenger was sent to the British to invoke the 1899 Anglo-Kuwaiti treaty. A relatively minor British show of force in the waters off Al-Jahra was enough to turn the tide of the siege in the Kuwaitis' favour. The victory also established the Al-Sabah more firmly in Kuwait itself. Two years after the battle of Al-Jahra, Abdul Aziz was prevailed upon to open talks with the Al-Sabah which ended in his recognising Kuwait's independence in exchange for a large chunk of its territory.

Al-Jahra's role in the most recent war over Kuwait is somewhat less romantic. In the final hours of the Gulf War, as Iraqi troops began to withdraw from Kuwait City, a huge traffic jam developed just outside Al-Jahra, where the main road from Kuwait City turns north towards the Iraqi border. The convoy stalled on the approach to the Al-Mutla ridge, just west of Al-Jahra, where it was caught by a coalition air attack. The convoy was demolished by the allies and the debris pushed off to the side of the road to rust. For several years a gruesome collection of the mangled remains of cars, trucks and a few tanks was visible along the road but time and scavengers have now picked the area clean.

Orientation

Al-Jahra's main street is Marzouk al-Mat'aab St, starting from the point beyond the Red Fort where the road loops around to the right at an intersection (marked on maps as a traffic circle, though it's not really that big) to its intersection with Da'abal al-Khazaai St, which runs back to the expressway. The stretch of road in question has a number of small restaurants though most have signs only in Arabic.

Red Fort

The town's only site is the Red Fort (also known as the Red Palace), famous in Kuwaiti history for its role in the 1920 siege. It is a low rectangular mud fort near the highway. The name is thought to derive from the colour of the walls. The fort is built around a large open courtyard with several annexes on its west side. Small signs (in Arabic and English) scattered around the complex identify the functions of the various parts of the complex, though after a while one empty mud-walled room starts to look pretty much like another. The low towers at the fort's corners can be climbed to get a better view.

The annexe in the fort's south-west corner (through the large wooden door with a number 4 above it) was the harem, the emir's private enclosure. Moving north, the next annexe includes a small mosque. Note

KUWAIT

the simple, unadorned *mihrib* (prayer niche) in the south wall.

The fort is on Marzouk al-Mat'aab St next to a park. In the winter it is open daily from 7.30 am to 1.30 pm and 3.30 to 6.30 pm. In summer the hours are 7 am to 1 pm and 4 to 7 pm. The fort is closed throughout the year on Saturday afternoons. At all times the closing hours are flexible. Admission is free. Photography is permitted but videos are not. Call ☎ 477 2559 for more information.

Getting There & Away

Coming from Kuwait City, take the second of the three Al-Jahra exits from the expressway onto Marzouk al-Mat'aab St. The Red Fort is on the right, about 200m south of (ie, inland from) the highway, though you can't see it until you are right in front of it. Al-Jahra can be reached via bus No 103, which passes directly in front of the Red Fort.

DOHA VILLAGE

On an arm of land jutting out into Kuwait Bay, Doha Village is the site of some small dhow-building yards and a fishing village. If you are planning a trip to Bahrain, the dhow yards there are far more interesting and easier to get to. The fishers' shacks lie along the road, beyond the concrete walls of the dhow yards. Also note that security is very tight throughout the Doha area because of the more-or-less permanent US military base adjacent to the fishing community.

To reach Doha Village, take the Al-Jahra Rd west from Kuwait City and follow the signs for Entertainment City. When you reach the roundabout just before the entrance to Entertainment City make a left-hand turn. The Exhibition of Sailing Ships will be on your left after approximately 3.5km. Another 700m brings you to a fork in the road; keep left at the fork and you will almost immediately find yourself in the Doha dhow yard.

Qatar

The thumb-shaped Qatar peninsula is not exactly one of the world's major tourist destinations. Qatar only started issuing visas to tourists in 1989, and while it does little to attract visitors, and it's a far cry from the tourist centres of the United Arab Emirates (UAE), there's enough to see and do to justify a stopover for a few days.

Facts about Qatar

HISTORY
Beginnings

Archaeological digs have shown that the Qatar peninsula was inhabited during the Stone Age when the region's climate was milder than it is today. But the archaeologists have found little evidence of habitation between the most ancient of times and the modern era. Qatar does have its share of ancient grave mounds, but there are no known sites connecting it to the Bahrain-based Dilmun Empire.

Qatar is the only significant place in the Gulf to have no Portuguese ruins of any sort. Since the Portuguese conquered, or at least attacked, just about everywhere else in the Gulf this strongly implies that Qatar in the 16th-century was either uninhabited or very nearly so. Qatar is not mentioned in any substantial way by the various European travellers who reached the Gulf between the 16th and early 18th centuries.

For most of its recent history, Qatar has been dominated by the Al-Thani family who arrived in the mid-18th century and became the peninsula's rulers some 100 years later. The Al-Thani are a branch of the Tamim tribe and are thought to have arrived in Qatar from southern Najd in central Arabia. Originally they were nomadic Bedouins, but the region's sparse vegetation led them to settle in the peninsula's coastal areas where they became fishers and pearl divers.

By the mid-18th century, Qatar was well established as a pearling centre. Activity was then centred on Al-Zubara, in the northwest, which was under the control of the Al-Khalifa family (who are now the rulers of Bahrain). Qatar's current capital, Doha, was never a trading port of the importance of Kuwait or Manama (Bahrain). Throughout the 19th and early 20th centuries, Qatar remained shockingly poor, even by pre-oil Gulf standards. Seemingly bleak and remote places like Al-Zubara were hotly contested because they controlled access to the one thing that provided enough money to feed the local populace: the pearl beds.

The Rise of the Al-Thani

Qatar's first Al-Thani emir was Sheikh Mohammed bin Thani, who took effective control of most of the peninsula from the

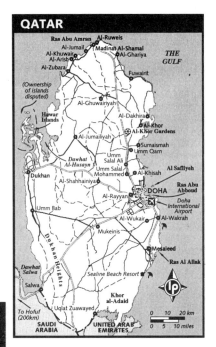

QATAR

early 20th centuries, exercising significant influence, though not quite sovereignty over the region's tribes.

Jasim's successor, Sheikh Abdullah oversaw the withdrawal of the Ottoman garrison in 1915 after Turkey entered WWI on the side of Germany. The British almost certainly had a hand in this withdrawal, and in 1916 they signed an Exclusive Agreement with Abdullah modelled on the agreements they already had in place around the Gulf. According to the agreements, Britain undertook to protect the local ruler in exchange for a promise that the ruler would not have any dealings with other foreign powers without British permission. The 1916 agreement was extended and modified by another treaty signed in 1934.

Oil

Even before the pearl market collapsed, around 1930, life in Qatar was rough. With poverty, hunger and disease all widespread, the emir welcomed the oil prospectors who first arrived in the early 1930s. In 1935, he granted a concession to Petroleum Development (Qatar), or PDQ, the forerunner of today's state-run Qatar General Petroleum Corporation (QGPC). (PDQ was a subsidiary of the Iraq Petroleum Company, which, in turn, was owned by a collection of US, British and French oil interests.)

The prospectors struck oil in 1939 but, because of WWII, production did not begin for another 10 years. It was only then, in 1949, that the British finally posted a political agent to Doha. Until that time the country had been covered by the political agent based in Bahrain.

At that point, things began to move very quickly. The new British agent was followed, a few years later, by a financial adviser sent to help the emir deal with the unprecedented sums of money he suddenly found himself holding. Even then, the Qataris were shrewd enough to maintain some balance. In addition to his British adviser, Abdullah hired an Egyptian named Hassan Kamil to give him financial advice. Kamil stayed on as an adviser to subsequent emirs for several decades.

Al-Khalifa and established his capital at Al-Bida (now Doha), in the mid-19th century. To strengthen his position vis-a-vis the other tribes in the area, he signed a treaty with Britain in 1867. At the time, he was almost certainly seeking British protection from the Al-Khalifa clan.

Sheikh Mohammed died later that year and was succeeded by his son, Jasim. From the 1870s onward, Jasim, who reigned until his death in 1913, became a master at maintaining his own independence by playing the British off against the Turks.

In 1872, he signed a treaty with the Turks allowing them to place a garrison in Doha, though he never allowed it to grow very large and, reportedly, refused to take any money from the Ottomans. The presence of Turkish troops did, however, provide Jasim with a certain amount of prestige locally. As the nominal representative of the Ottoman sultan, Jasim was a powerful figure in eastern Arabia during the late 19th and

Abdullah abdicated because of his advancing age in 1949, and was succeeded by is son Ali who reigned until 1960. Ali resided over the first stages of Qatar's oil oom. The quantity of oil produced in Qatar vas not huge, but the country's tiny population became instantly wealthy on a per apita basis. Much of the early revenue was evoted to establishing the basics of modrn life: Qatar's first school opened in 1952 nd health-care facilities were immediately pgraded, though a full-scale hospital did ot open until 1959.

Sheikh Ali had little interest in the day-to-ay business of government with the result hat by the mid-'50s his nephew, Khalifa bin Hamad al-Thani, was, to a great extent, runaing the country. At the beginning of the 1960s, Ali abdicated in favour of his son, Ahmed, but the new emir was as uninterested n the government as his father had been.

Between local politics and the development of the country, Khalifa was very active. Qatar was not entirely spared from the urmoil which swept the Arab world during the 1960s, including a general strike in 1963, but the ever-increasing flow of oil money seemed to blunt many people's poltical ambitions. Attempts by some Qataris to form leftist political groups in the 1970s never really gained significant support, and the country has been generally stable ever since.

Independence

When the British announced that they would leave the region by the end of 1971, Qatar entered talks with Bahrain and the Trucial States (now the UAE) about forming a confederation. Bahrain eventually pulled out of the talks because it thought it was not being offered a sufficiently central role in the new confederation. Qatar followed suit, withdrawing from the talks almost immediately.

It was indicative of his style of government that Sheikh Ahmed proclaimed Qatar's independence, on 1 September 1971, in Geneva rather than Doha. At that point his demise probably became inevitable: Khalifa took power in a palace coup on 22 February 1972.

Khalifa was well prepared to take over. By the time of the coup, he had been Qatar's de facto ruler for more than 15 years and had, at one time or another, run the departments of foreign affairs, oil and finance, and education and culture. He had also headed both the police force and the secret police. One of his first moves as emir was to crack down on the extravagant ways of certain members of the royal family.

The years following Khalifa's coup were marked by political stability. As was the case throughout the Gulf, the dramatic rise in oil prices after 1974 gave the government more than enough money to build one of the world's great all-encompassing welfare states.

Still, Qatar has been affected by the political turbulence of its neighbours. Like the other small states of the Gulf, Qatar viewed Iran's 1979 revolution with great alarm. In 1983, the government announced that it had discovered a cache of weapons and foiled a plot to overthrow it.

The 1990s

Since independence, Qatar has retained its close defence ties with Britain and has increased defence cooperation with the USA and France. US and Canadian troops were stationed in Doha during the Gulf War.

For many years, Qatar's foreign policy closely followed the lead of Saudi Arabia, but in the 1990s that began to change. Early in the decade Doha ruffled some feathers around the Gulf (including those of Riyadh) by seeking closer ties with Iran. In 1991 the Qataris and Iranians signed an agreement under which Iran would supply Qatar with fresh water via an undersea pipeline, a project which has been viewed with some reservations by Doha's Gulf Cooperation Council (GCC) neighbours. In 1993, following the peace agreement between Israel and the Palestine Liberation Organization, Qatar became the first Gulf country to have open diplomatic contact with the Jewish state. In late 1995, Qatar became the first Gulf State to start an economic relationship with Israel, agreeing to supply Tel Aviv with natural gas, albeit through a third party.

An Israeli trade office was opened in Doha, but at the time of research it was in the process of being closed down.

In June 1995, Sheikh Khalifa, holidaying in Switzerland, was unexpectedly replaced as emir by his son Sheikh Hamad bin Khalifa al-Thani, until then the crown prince and defence minister. This caused a furore at the time, with many GCC countries refusing to recognise the new emir. The government says the former emir has at least US$3 billion tucked away in foreign bank accounts which his son, the current emir, is still trying to claim.

In many ways, Qatar remains a sleepy backwater, but it is becoming more liberal compared to other Gulf countries: the press has relative freedom, and Qatar became the first country in the Gulf to allow women to vote in municipal elections in early 1999.

GEOGRAPHY
The Qatar peninsula juts northward into the Gulf from the east coast of the Arabian peninsula. Qatar is about 160km long, and 55km to 80km wide. The country's total area (including its small islands) is 11,437 sq km. The desert tends to be flat (the highest elevation in the country is only about 98m above sea level) and gravelly, and there is virtually no natural vegetation.

CLIMATE
Temperatures in the warmer months (May to September) generally average 35°C, but it's not uncommon to get up to 50°C. The 90% humidity also means that Qatari summers can be very uncomfortable. The cooler months (November to February) are much milder with pleasant, cool evenings. Sandstorms are common throughout the year, especially in the spring. Although it doesn't rain much in Qatar, the few weeks of wet, or wettish, weather in December and January can be pretty miserable.

ECOLOGY & ENVIRONMENT
One continuing problem is the level of the water table in Qatar. Persistent geological uplift over the centuries means that the country is now 2m 'higher' than it was 400 years ago, so access to underground water supplies is difficult and, in some places, impossible. The result: incredible aridity, very sparse vegetation and a paucity in the quantity and variety of indigenous animals. The encroaching desert sands and the *sabkhas* or salty mud pans that are both a common part of the Qatari landscape are also causing huge environmental problems.

In addition, rampant development, air pollution and seepage from oil and gas drilling and production, are seriously affecting marine and bird life, and precious mangroves. On the land, several species of animals and birds have been hunted to extinction, or placed on the endangered list because of local hunting practices (see the boxed text 'Falconry').

Qatar's government is making some effort to safeguard the country's environment by setting up reserves to protect the Arabian oryx (Qatar's national animal) in Al-Shahhainiya (see the Around Qatar section later in this chapter for details); goats on Halul Island, a remote oil-producing area; and deer on Ras Ishairik Island. During Qatar Environment Day (February 26), loads of school children throughout the country collect litter and plant trees.

Falconry

During the cooler months, around October to March, visitors can witness the local tradition of falconry or hawking (though animal lovers may want to do something else). Once a popular pastime, falconry can now only be enjoyed by the wealthy because the cost of prized birds, such as the hardy and reliable grey falcon can be as much as QR30,000.

The cost is so high because catching and training the birds is very time consuming. Hawks, peregrines and falcons are trapped using nets, with a pigeon as bait. The birds of prey are then trained using complicated schedules of food and sleep deprivation. All sorts of birds are put on sale at specific markets in Doha – ask locally for the exact times and locations.

Qatar possesses some extraordinary sand dunes, perfect for overnight safaris.

Doha's Corniche is a particularly pleasant jogging spot – in the cooler winter months, at least.

One of the Gulf's best-kept secrets, Doha features some pleasant views and an appealing bay.

CHRISTINE OSBORNE

Boats at low tide at Qatar's northernmost point, Al-Ruweis

CHRIS MELLOR

The Pearl, Doha, Qatar

CHRISTINE OSBORNE

Parasailing in Qatar

CHRISTINE OSBORNE

Khor al-Adaid, Qatar's inland sea

CHRISTINE OSBORNE

Twin towers at the east end of Doha's delightful Corniche

The Qatar National Museum has a small, but informative, display about local environmental issues. For further information about Qatar's environment, and its key en-problems, contact the Friends of the Environment group (☎ 888 114) in Doha.

GOVERNMENT & POLITICS

Qatar is ruled by an emir, Sheikh Hamad bin Khalifa al-Thani. Sheikh Hamad is one of the region's more tolerant and forward-thinking rulers, and reasonably well liked by Qataris. He is also minister of defence and commander-in-chief of the armed forces. His third son, Sheikh Jasim bin Hamad al-Thani, is the official heir apparent. The emir's brother, Sheikh Abdullah bin Khalifa al-Thani, is prime minister and minister of the interior.

The emir can appoint and dismiss cabinet ministers at will, though turnover in the cabinet doesn't often occur. Laws are announced in emiri decrees. Although he is, in theory, an absolute monarch, the emir must always retain the support and confidence of the other members of the ruling family. Retaining this support requires not only good government, but ongoing and wide-ranging consultation with the cabinet, other members of the ruling family and representatives of the country's larger merchant families.

Much of this consultation is informal, but some of it takes place at the regular *majlis* (court) which the emir and other members of the ruling family hold. Any member of the public can address the emir, or some other senior figure, about any issue during these sessions. Regular, formalised consultation also takes place through an advisory council whose 30 (male) members are appointed by the emir. The council can comment on proposed laws though it cannot change the proposals or propose new laws on its own.

In 1999 Qatar held elections for municipal councils. In the Gulf, where voting of any sort is rare, this was a major event. Although the councils have little real power the election was closely watched as the first in the Gulf in which women were allowed to participate, a fact which clearly displeased some of Qatar's neighbours.

ECONOMY

Qatar is a member of the Organization of Petroleum Exporting Countries (OPEC), and produces about 600,000 barrels of oil a day. Although Qatar is still essentially an oil-based economy, natural gas has been moving to the fore. Qatar now has the third largest natural gas reserves in the world (3,700 trillion barrels are officially available), which is lucky because the country's oil reserves may run out early this century.

The government has tried to diversify the economy but, as elsewhere in the Gulf, this has met with only limited success. Steel, fertilisers and petrochemicals are the country's main non-oil products, and Qatar is also trying to encourage tourism. Recently, the Qatari tourist authorities have focused attention on big-spending tourists interested in international tennis, motor racing and golf tournaments, as well as business-people.

Qatar has one of the most all-embracing welfare state systems in the world. Qataris are entitled to free education and health care and free, or nearly free, housing. The prices of food, electricity and water are also heavily subsidised.

POPULATION & PEOPLE

About 640,000 people live in Qatar, making it one of the smallest countries in the Arab world by population. Only about 25% are indigenous Qataris, most of whom are of Najdi (central Arabian) ancestry, or of Persian descent.

The foreign population is an eclectic mixture of people from Asia (mainly Thailand and the Philippines), the Indian subcontinent (Pakistan, India – particularly southern India – and Bangladesh) and the Arab world (ie, Egypt, Palestine, Syria, Jordan and Lebanon). Britons make up the largest contingent among the country's Western expatriate population.

EDUCATION

The country's first school opened in 1952, but progress since then has been fast. The University of Qatar was established in 1977, but before then hundreds of Qataris were sent to Egypt, Lebanon and the West to further their education. All education, including tertiary studies, is free for Qataris. Foreign children living in Qatar usually attend international schools which teach a particular national curriculum.

ARTS

The recent modernisation of Qatar has resulted in a decline in both the popularity and variety of traditional arts and crafts, but Qatari music retains some favour among the populace.

Traditional Music & Dance

Qatari music is essentially the same as that found in other GCC countries. Traditional instruments include drums, tambourine, flute and, often, the *rebaba*, a violin-like instrument with only one string.

On Friday afternoon (from about 5 pm) during the summer (May to September) various troops performing traditional dances can be seen around Doha and Al-Khor. In traditional dances, the men and women wear costumes resplendent with jewellery. There is lots of singing, handclapping (by dancers and the audience) and solos by accomplished instrumentalists.

Montazah Park, just south of central Doha, is a good place to go on an early summer evening to see traditional music and, maybe, some dancing. Some of the museums around Qatar have fine displays, with captions in English, about traditional music and dance. For more information contact the Qatari Fine Arts Society (☎ 899 868) in Doha.

Theatre

There is not a lot in the way of traditional Qatari theatre, but performances are sometimes held at the Qatar National Theatre in Doha – see Entertainment in the Doha section later in this chapter for details. Theatre involves spirited acting in well known (to locals) stories of love, betrayal and loyalty. Everything is in Arabic, but there is enough singing, dancing and colourful costumes to entertain anyone who doesn't understand a word.

Arts & Crafts

The Bedouin have always been great weavers of carpets, tents, rugs and curtains, but the traditional weaving practices used only two decades ago have virtually disappeared, supplanted by machinery and cheaper imports. Wool used for carpets is still often prepared in a traditional way: it is washed and soaked in lemon juice and a crystalline mixture to remove impurities and oil, boiled for about 10 hours, dried in the sun and then dyed (often with imported dyes from India and other Gulf States).

In some parts of Qatar, goat's hair is still used to make tents and camel hair is used for ropes and bags. Rope-making is still practised to a lesser degree, often using the *al-gallad* and *al-kahal* methods of plaiting with both hands, one foot and a strangely shaped piece of wood. A form of basketweaving, called *al-safaf*, using palm leaves and cane, is still practised in the villages.

Qatari women like to wear traditional jewellery, particularly on special occasions, and men use precious jewels to decorate ceremonial swords, so expert jewellers and goldsmiths are still in demand, and engage in centuries-old practices, mainly in the *souqs* (markets) outside of Doha. Traditional *burda* cloaks are still worn in Qatar, and the cuffs and sleeves are decorated by hand using thin gold and silver threads.

SOCIETY & CONDUCT

Qatar is certainly more liberal than Saudi Arabia, but still a far cry from Bahrain and the UAE. Although Qataris are quite accustomed to the presence of large numbers of foreigners in their midst, Qatar remains a very conservative place by Western standards, especially in the villages. Dress conservatively and do not wear shorts in public, except at the beach or at a hotel swimming pool. Women should always cover their shoulders, and avoid clothing that is tight or revealing.

Refer to the Society & Conduct section of the Facts about the Region chapter earlier in this book for a rundown of the general dos and don'ts of visiting an Islamic country.

RELIGION

Most Qataris adhere to the austere Wahhabi sect of Islam which also dominates in Saudi Arabia. Qatari Wahhabism, however, is less strict than the Saudi variety. For example alcohol, which is strictly prohibited in Saudi Arabia, is available in Qatar (although hard to find, and expensive), and there is no prohibition on women driving cars. For more information, see Wahhabis under Religion in the Facts about the Region chapter.

Facts for the Visitor

SUGGESTED ITINERARIES

Although visas are possible for up to 14 days, you really only need about four days to see what Qatar has to offer. In Doha, you can visit the Qatar National Museum (preferably more than once), pop into the Ethnographic Museum and Doha Fort, and take a boat trip to Palm Tree Island. Then hire a car for the day and visit some of the better beaches, and the old forts and burial mounds dotted around the countryside. Finish off with an organised, overnight desert safari to really appreciate the grandeur of the landscape at Khor al-Adaid.

PLANNING
When to Go

Because the heat is so fierce in the summer, and sandstorms are so common in the spring and winter, the best time to visit is in November, or late February and early March. During these times the temperatures are more bearable, and there's a minimum of wind. In December and January, there might also be some rain. The rains are not all that heavy, but they often cause problems on the roads. It rarely rains for more than a few days, however, so this need not be much of a consideration in planning your trip.

Maps

If you limit your sightseeing to Doha the maps in this guidebook will be more than adequate, but if you're travelling around the countryside in a rented car it's a good idea to buy a detailed map. The best is the dual-language (ie, Arabic and English) *Qatar & Doha City Maps*, published by Dallah, and available in good bookshops in Doha for QR35. The maps of Qatar and Doha are detailed, but the map of Doha is strictly a street map – no attractions or important buildings are listed.

TOURIST OFFICES

Qatar is poorly set up for the ordinary traveller: the Qatari tourist authorities seem interested only in visitors from other Gulf States, big-spending foreigners who follow the international sporting events held in Doha, and high-flying businesspeople from anywhere. There is no dedicated tourist office in Qatar, so the only way to get any information is to ask the travel agencies who arrange tours (see Organised Tours in the Getting Around section later in this chapter), or possibly your hotel. Qatar's embassies and consulates overseas aren't set up to provide any general information to tourists.

VISAS & DOCUMENTS
Visas

Residents of, and expatriates living in, other countries of the Gulf Cooperation Council (GCC) can enter Qatar without a sponsor or visa, but it's still prudent to check this before coming. A 14-day visa will cost QR120.

UK citizens can get a visa at a Qatari embassy/consulate without a sponsor. Americans can obtain a visa at a Qatari embassy/consulate, but still need a confirmed hotel reservation (but no sponsor). Almost all other nationalities need a sponsor from within Qatar – and for most, this means arranging a hotel to sponsor you.

From an Embassy If you can get a visa at a Qatari embassy/consulate, you must fill out three forms and provide three passport-sized photos. Anyone requesting a business visa may be asked to supply a letter of introduction from the company they will be visiting. Visas will normally take about one week to process.

QATAR

From a Hotel Most tourists will need to be sponsored by a hotel, and only mid-range and top-end places are permitted to act as sponsors. The following hotels sponsor visas, and charge a fee of between QR50 and QR100 (in addition to the official government fee): the Ramada Hotel, Sofitel Doha Palace, Gulf Sheraton, Doha Sheraton, New Capital Hotel, Doha Palace Hotel (which promises to arrange visas in three working days), and the Oasis Hotel.

Contact one of these hotels (preferably by fax or email), book a room and then request sponsorship. Send them your passport details, reason for visit, arrival and departure dates, and flight numbers. Legally speaking, the hotel 'controls' your visa and stay, so it's almost impossible to change hotels after you arrive.

The hotel must send you a letter or fax (email probably won't be accepted by the immigration authorities) acknowledging your reservation, *and quoting a visa number*. Give this letter/fax to the immigration counter at Doha International Airport, and you should be issued a visa for the length of your stay (maximum of 14 days). The official government visa fee, and the fee for arranging the sponsorship, will probably be added to your hotel bill. Allow at *least* six working days, bearing in mind that nothing will get done on Thursday afternoons and Friday.

Visa Extensions Tourist visas can be extended for an additional 14 days, and business visas for seven days. The charges for overstaying are very high: between QR200 and QR500 per *day* for any type of visa. If you were originally sponsored by a hotel, the hotel must arrange your visa extension, which will cost QR300, plus whatever fee the hotel charges for this service. If you obtained your visa through a Qatari embassy/consulate, go to the Department for Passports, Nationality & Residence in Doha (☎ 882 882).

Other Documents

No other special permits are required for travelling to, or around, Qatar. Visitors who are staying less than a week can rent a car using their licence from home, ie, without an International Driving Permit. Refer to Car & Motorcycle in the Getting Around section later in this chapter.

Student, youth and senior cards are of little, if any, use.

EMBASSIES & CONSULATES
Qatari Embassies & Consulates

The addresses of some Qatari embassies and consulates around the world are listed below. (NB: There is no Qatari embassy in Bahrain.)

France
Embassy: (☎ 01-45 51 90 71) 57 Quai D'Orsay, 75007, Paris
Germany
Embassy: (☎ 228-957 520) Brunnen alle 6, 53177 Bonn
Kuwait
Embassy: (☎ 965-251 3606, fax 251 3604) Istiglal St, Diplomatic Area, south of the centre off Arabian Gulf St, Kuwait City
Oman
Embassy: (☎ 691152, fax 691156) Jameat ad-Duwal al-Arabiyya St, Al-Khuwair
Saudi Arabia
Embassy: (☎ 966-1-482 5544) Diplomatic Quarter, Riyadh
UAE
Embassy: (☎ 971-2-435 900) Al-Muntasser St, Abu Dhabi
Consulate-General: (☎ 971-4-452 888) Trade Centre Rd, Al-Mankook District, Bur Dubai, near the Bur Juman Centre
UK
Embassy: (☎ 020-7370 6871; visa info ☎ 0891-633 233) 1 South Audley St, London, W1Y 5DQ
USA
Embassy: (☎ 202-274 1600; fax 237-0061) 4200 Wisconsin Ave, NW, Suite 200, Washington DC 20016
Consulate: (☎ 212-486 9355) 747 3rd Ave, 22nd floor, New York, NY 10017

Embassies in Qatar

Most embassies in Doha are located in the Diplomatic Area, north of the Doha Sheraton – none of these buildings have specific addresses, so the best idea is to charter a taxi. All embassies are open from about 8 am to

pm, Saturday to Wednesday. (NB: There
₃ no Bahraini embassy in Qatar.)

₊rance (☎ 832 283, fax 832 254) Diplomatic
Area
₊ermany (☎ 876 959, fax 876 949) Al-Jazira
al-Arabiya St
₊uwait (☎ 832 111, fax 832 042) Diplomatic
Area
₊man (☎ 670 744, fax 670 747) 41 Ibn al-
Qassem St, Villa 7, Hilal district
₊audi Arabia (☎ 832 722, fax 832 720) Diplo-
matic Area
₊AE (☎ 885 111, fax 882 837)
off Al-Khor St, Khalifa Town district
₊K (☎ 421 991, fax 438 692) Al-Istiqlal St,
Rumailiah district
₊SA (☎ 864 701, fax 861 669) 149 Ahmed bin
Ali St
₊emen (☎ 432 555, fax 429 400) near the Al-
Sadd roundabout, Al-Jazira district

₊USTOMS
₊ustoms procedures can be slow at the
₊oha International Airport, but they are
₊arely intrusive. No alcohol or pork prod-
₊cts can be brought into Qatar. Books, pho-
₊ographs and, especially, videos often come
₊n for careful scrutiny and may be confis-
₊cated for further investigation. Duty-free al-
₊owances are: 800 cigarettes, 100 cigars or
₊00g of tobacco; and 250mL of perfume.

₊MONEY
₊Currency
The Qatari riyal (QR) is divided into 100
dirhams. Notes come in QR1, 5, 10, 50, 100
and 500 denominations. Dirham coins no
longer exist, though some prices are still
quoted in dirhams. If you're charged, for
example, QR1.25 for a (soft) drink, the
amount will be rounded down to QR1;
something costing QR1.5, for example, is
rounded up to QR2.
   The Qatari riyal is fully convertible so
there's no black market or exchange controls. Many shops also accept Saudi riyals
at par for small transactions.

Exchange Rates
The Qatari riyal is fixed against the US dollar. The other exchange rates for the major
currencies are:

country	unit		riyal
Australia	A$1	=	QR2.32
Canada	C$1	=	QR2.42
euro	€1	=	QR0.61
France	1FF	=	QR0.54
Germany	DM1	=	QR2.09
Japan	¥100	=	QR2.99
New Zealand	NZ$1	=	QR1.99
UK	UK£1	=	QR5.86
USA	US$1	=	QR3.65

Exchanging Money
Most major currencies (cash and travellers
cheques) can be changed into Qatari riyals,
though UK pounds and US dollars are the
easiest to exchange. Moneychangers will
offer a slightly better rate than the banks.
The difference is not worth worrying about
unless you're changing a large amount. The
top-end hotels offer about US$1 = QR3.50.
Currencies from Bahrain, Saudi Arabia and
the UAE are easy to buy and sell at banks
and moneychangers.

Credit Cards All major credit cards are accepted in large shops, upmarket restaurants,
mid-range and top-end hotels and most
travel agencies, and many can be used in automatic teller machines (ATMs). The Commercial Bank of Qatar accepts American
Express, Diner's Club, and credit cards on
the Cirrus system. British Bank of the Middle East and Qatar National Bank's ATMs
also accept Cirrus-system cards. (Check the
back of your Visa or MasterCard for the Cirrus logo.) There are also ATMs at the airport, some top-end hotels and upmarket
shopping centres – refer to Money in the
Doha section later in this chapter for details.

Costs
Food is inexpensive. In a cheap Indian/Pak-
istani eatery, meals cost about QR10. Western fast food costs about QR15; and tastier
meals in a comfortable restaurant, at least
QR20. Cheap beds are almost impossible to
find because most visitors must be sponsored by a mid-range or top-end hotel. The
cheapest place that will sponsor visas costs
QR125/150 for singles/doubles; a top-end
place can cost five to ten times more.

QATAR

To stay in the cheapest hotel that can sponsor visas, eat in the cheapest restaurants and walk everywhere will cost about QR150/100 per person per day if travelling as a single/double. A budget of QR180/130 allows for better food, a few taxis and some souvenirs. Add to this the price of hiring a car, and alcoholic drinks.

Tipping & Bargaining

A service charge is usually added to restaurant (and top-end hotel) bills, but this rarely goes to the staff. Local custom does not require that you leave a tip, though it would certainly be appreciated – 10% is fine.

These days, little real bargaining goes on in Qatar. Prices are mainly fixed, although small discounts are sometimes offered in modern clothing stores, and you can often negotiate a bit off the price of electronic goods, rental cars and hotel rooms.

POST & COMMUNICATIONS
Postal Rates

Postal rates are standard for Australia, New Zealand, the UK, Europe, Canada and the US: postcards cost QR1, and letters weighing 10gm or less, QR2. The first kg for parcels sent by sea costs QR73 to USA/Canada and UK/Europe, and QR88 to Australia/New Zealand. Every subsequent kg costs QR57 to USA/Canada, QR27 to UK/Europe and QR50 to Australia/New Zealand.

Sending Mail

The General Post Office is in northern Doha, but there's a more convenient branch on Abdullah bin Jasim St in central Doha – refer to the Doha section later in this chapter for details. Many mid-range and top-end hotels also sell stamps. Most international express post and parcel service companies are represented in Doha.

Receiving Mail

Poste restante is not available in Qatar, and the American Express representative does not hold clients' mail. If you're staying in a mid-range or top-end hotel it will probably be willing to hold mail for a short time prior

to your arrival (assuming, of course, that you have a reservation).

Telephone

The telephone system in Qatar is excellent and direct-dialling overseas calls rarely takes more than one attempt. All services are provided by the national Qatar Public Telecommunications Corporation (Q-Tel).

Calls within Qatar from public telephones cost about 50 dirhams, but these phones do not accept coins, so you have to buy a phonecard worth QR30, QR50 or QR100. These phonecards are available from the Main Telecommunications Centre (MTC) in Doha and from grocery shops around the country. There are several help lines, with English-speaking staff:

International directory assistance	☎ 180
International calls via an operator	☎ 150
Local directory inquiries	☎ 100

The MTC in Doha has a three-minute minimum charge for international calls; any call from the MTC, or any call which uses an operator, is more expensive than dialling directly using a phonecard. The cost of a direct-dial call during the day to the USA/Canada and UK/Europe is about QR7 per minute; and to Australia/New Zealand, about QR9. Direct-dial international calls are about 30% cheaper every day from 8 pm to 7 am, and all day Friday and public holidays.

When calling Qatar from abroad the country code is 974. There are no area or city codes within the country.

Fax

Fax services are available at the MTC in Doha, and at business centres in most top-end hotels. As with the telephones, the service is very good. Costs are based on the time it takes to send the fax, and are the same as a telephone call.

Email & Internet Access

There are email facilities at the business centres in most top-end hotels, and Internet centres in Doha and Al-Khor – refer to those sections later in the chapter for de-

...ils. The only Internet Service Provider is ...nternet Qatar (☎ 329 999), part of the na-...onal Qatar Public Telecommunications ...orporation.

INTERNET RESOURCES

There isn't much about Qatar on the Inter-...et, but the following Web sites provide ...ome useful information:

American Cultural Center Good links.
www.qatar.net.qa/usisdoha
Arab Net Reasonably informative.
www.arab.net/qatar
Gulf Times Current affairs from a local
English-language newspaper.
www.gulf-times.com
Ministry of Foreign Affairs Nice graphics and
useful information.
www.mofa.gov.qa

BOOKS

Anyone intending to stay in Qatar for a while should pick up one or both of the following guidebooks available at major bookshops in Doha. *Qatar – A MEED Practical Guide*, second edition, 1997 (QR45) has a very 'official' feel about it, but is readable and compact. *Welcome to Qatar* (QR35), published in late 1997 by the American Women's Association of Qatar, is very practical for potential residents, but caters mainly to US expats.

One of the few works of literature which focuses entirely on Qatar is Helga Graham's *Arabian Time Machine*. Subtitled 'Self-Portrait of an Oil State', the book is a collection of interviews with Qataris about their lives and traditions, before and after the oil boom, and about how Qatari society has coped with its sudden wealth.

The Merchants, by Michael Field, has lots of good general information on the Gulf in pre-oil days. It also has a chapter devoted to the Darwish family, one of Qatar's more prominent merchant clans. *Regards Qatar*, by Michele Barrault, is the only coffee-table book about Qatar in French. It has some excellent photos and is available in Doha, but it's expensive (QR120).

'The Day Before Tomorrow', the chapter about Qatar in Jonathan Raban's *Arabia*

Through the Looking Glass, is probably the best section of that wonderful book. During a short visit in 1979, Raban managed to speak to a particularly interesting cross section of people: Qatar's leading playwright, a local TV producer and a Jordanian officer working for the Qatari army, in addition to the usual collection of jaded Western expats.

See the Books section in the Regional Facts for the Visitor chapter earlier in this book for a more general list of books about the Gulf and the Middle East.

NEWSPAPERS & MAGAZINES

Two quite readable English-language newspapers are published every day (except Friday), and both cost QR2. The older *Gulf Times* is bright and colourful, but *The Peninsula* is often more informative. The current day's editions of the Dubai-based papers *Gulf News* and *Khaleej Times* are also widely available. International newspapers and magazines, mostly from the UK, can be bought one or two days after publication at major bookshops in Doha. The local Arabic-language newspapers are *Al-Watan*, *Al-Sharq* and *Al-Rayah*.

RADIO & TV

QBS (Qatar Broadcasting Service) offers radio programs in English every day, from early morning until late evening, and has an eclectic musical selection. Its signal goes out on 97.5FM and 102.6FM, and short news bulletins are broadcast every few hours. QBS also has a French-language service on 100.8FM. The BBC World Service, Voice of America and other short-wave services are easy to find.

Channel 37 on QTV (Qatar Television) broadcasts programs in English from late afternoon until about midnight every day. With a good antenna, English-language stations broadcasting from Saudi Arabia, Bahrain and the UAE can also be easily picked up. They all show a selection of British and US entertainment programs, movies and documentaries. Most mid-range and top-end hotels have satellite dishes, and pipe programs by satellite into every room.

QATAR

PHOTOGRAPHY & VIDEO

Colour print film is easy to buy in top-end hotels, shopping centres and specialised photo developers all over Doha. A roll of 24/36 colour print film costs about QR6/8. The charge for developing is a fairly standard QR31/43 for a roll of 24/36 colour print film, which usually includes a free roll of film. Slide film is hard to find, so bring your own. It's also very difficult to get developed. Many photo developers also arrange passport photos.

Refer to the Photography & Video section in the Regional Facts for the Visitor chapter earlier in this book for general information about what not to photograph.

LAUNDRY

There are no do-it-yourself laundrettes in Qatar, but most hotels offer laundry service for guests, and there are some small laundries around central Doha. Hotel laundries charge about QR5 for a shirt, and QR6 for trousers or a skirt. Smaller, independent laundries charge QR2 to QR3 for a shirt, and QR4 to QR5 for trousers or a skirt. Refer to Information in the Doha section later in this chapter for the location of some reliable laundries in the capital.

TOILETS

Most visitors have to stay in mid-range and top-end hotels, all of which have modern, Western-style toilets. Public toilets are invariably the hole-in-the-ground variety. Toilet paper is widely available in supermarkets and smaller grocery stores.

HEALTH

Unless you're arriving from an area where cholera, yellow fever or some similar disease is endemic, vaccination certificates are not required for tourists coming to Qatar. The only disease which local authorities consider to be a 'health risk' is rabies. Anyone wishing to become a resident of Qatar may need to undertake a full medical exam, including an AIDS test. Refer to the Health section in the Regional Facts for the Visitor chapter earlier in this book for a general overview about health issues in the region.

Qatar's tap water is generally OK to drink, but it is usually desalinated seawater without fluoride, so it does taste a little strange. Anyone with a sensitive stomach should probably stick to bottled water.

Like other Gulf States, the standard of health and health care in Qatar is very high, and hospital care is free for residents and usually, visitors. A current list of hospitals and 24-hour pharmacists and their telephone numbers is printed every day in the two English-language newspapers. See under Information in the Doha section later in this chapter for more details.

TRAVEL WITH CHILDREN

The major attraction for children is undoubtedly Aladdin's Kingdom – see the Doha section later in this chapter for details. Doha also has several large, shady and grassy parks, some with playgrounds: one is just north of the Qatar National Museum; Montazah Park sometimes holds traditional music and dance concerts, and Al-Bida Park, near the Qatar National Theatre, is spacious and well laid out.

Other places to take the kids in Doha include the Corniche, which is particularly pleasant in the cooler evenings, and Palm Tree Island – details about both are in the Doha section later in this chapter. Around the countryside, the camel races at Al-Shahhainiya are a lot of fun – see the Around Qatar section later in this chapter.

The most convenient beach is near the Oasis Hotel in Doha, and families can usually use a hotel swimming pool for a small fee if they aren't guests. There are plenty of well-known, Western fast-food restaurants (see Places to Eat in the Doha section later in this chapter).

Most top-end hotels cater well for families: they often have children's playgrounds, and can squeeze in a small bed in the parent's room for an extra charge. Mid-range hotels, however, usually cater to businesspeople, and are not well set up for families.

DANGERS & ANNOYANCES

Qatar is a very safe country. The main thing to watch out for is the traffic, especially in Doha. Much of the capital's traffic system is defined by a series of roundabouts. There are often no lights to control entry to these roundabouts with the result that, when traffic is heavy, people have to force their way into a moving stream of vehicles. When traffic is light the situation is worse; many drivers simply sail straight into the roundabout without slowing down at all. Refer to Car & Motorcycle in the Getting Around section later in this chapter for tips about driving around Doha and Qatar.

LEGAL MATTERS

Most of the normal crimes in your home country are also illegal in Qatar. If you get arrested, contact your embassy immediately (if there is one), but you will receive no sympathy if you have broken an obvious law.

The Qatari authorities are keen to enforce the road rules. Radars are common, and fines for speeding can be up to QR500. Gambling is illegal, and while alcohol is available, rules are strict: alcohol must not be brought into Qatar, sold or offered to a Muslim, carried in a car (except between the place of purchase and your place of residence) and cannot be bought for love or money during Ramadan. Public drunkenness will result in deportation – or worse.

BUSINESS HOURS

Qataris love their midday siesta, and Doha resembles a ghost town in early afternoon – especially in summer. Shops and offices are open from around 8 am until midday, and then reopen from 4 until 7 pm in winter; and sometimes from about 5 to 8 pm in summer. The modern Western-style shopping centres are open every day from about 9 am to 9 pm.

PUBLIC HOLIDAYS & SPECIAL EVENTS

In addition to the main Islamic holidays described in Public Holidays in the Regional Facts for the Visitor chapter, Qatar observes its National Day on 3 September.

ACTIVITIES
Sports

The 155-hectare Doha Golf Club (☎ 832 338, fax 834 790, ✉ dohagolf@qatar.net.qa) is a huge mass of greenery carved out of the desert. Costs are high: QR200/360 for 9/18 holes, and QR80/150 for club hire. No caddies are available, so you'll have to carry your own gear, or hire a buggy. The course is a short drive north of the Diplomatic Area; look for the signs at the roundabouts heading along the Corniche towards the Doha Sheraton.

There are squash courts at the Gulf Sheraton; a putting range at the Doha Sheraton;

QATAR

Bird-Watching

Because of the heat, lack of water and sparse vegetation, Qatar has few indigenous birds. The crested and hoopoe lark are relatively common, but more interesting for bird enthusiasts are the temporary flocks which migrate to Qatar from colder climates, mostly in spring (March to May) and autumn (September to November).

Most are water birds, such as seagulls, which come from all over Asia. Flamingoes also roost in winter along the coast between Al-Wakrah and Mesaieed, and further south towards the Sealine Beach Resort. The south-east coast is popular with migratory spoonbills, as well as various species of duck, swallow and swift.

Most of the year, the nearby Hawar Islands (which are claimed by Bahrain) are home to flocks of flamingoes and one of the world's largest flocks of cormorants. However, the Hawars are in a strict military zone so bird-watching is difficult, but they are protected because much of the Hawars is an 'environmental protection area'.

There are no bird-watching clubs in Qatar, nor any agencies which organise bird-watching tours, so enthusiasts must take pot luck to find the best sites, and will have to travel around independently.

and tennis courts at most top-end hotels. Horse riding is available at the Al-Rayyan Equestrian Centre (☎ 805 901), just off Al-Furousiya St, and more modest horse rides are possible on Palm Tree Island (see the Doha section later in this chapter). Qatar also hosts major international competitions for tennis, squash, golf and, occasionally, soccer (football). See Spectator Sports later in this chapter for more information.

Swimming

The best beaches are off the main road between Doha and Mesaieed to the south, though the quality of these beaches does vary and the best has been commandeered by the Sealine Beach Resort, near Mesaieed (see Around Qatar later in this chapter). If swimming around these areas, beware of strong currents.

The most accessible stretch of beach near Doha is between the Doha Club and the Oasis Hotel. But remember bikinis and immodest swimming gear are frowned upon in public areas. Nonguests can often use hotel swimming pools for a fee of about QR20.

Scuba Diving

Diving is not readily available to tourists. It is mainly enjoyed by, and arranged within, the Western expatriate community – and is not that great anyway because the water is so shallow, and there is little marine life because of high salinity. If you go diving, beware of sea snakes and jellyfish, and the poisonous barbs of the dragonfish and stonefish. If you're still keen, contact Pearl Divers (☎ 449 553) or British Sub-Aqua Club (☎ 446 835).

Water Sports

Some of the private clubs organise water sports, but for members only. The hotels which offer water sports – for guests – are the Sealine Beach Resort (see the Around Qatar section later in this chapter), and the Doha Sheraton. Expect to pay about QR25 (per 15 minutes) for a banana boat ride; QR25 (15 minutes) for water-skiing; and QR20 (30 minutes) for windsurfing. A fishing trip will cost about QR360 per person for three hours (minimum of six people). Sailing

is also popular among expats. Contact the Doha Sailing Association (☎/fax 439 995, ✉ sailing@qatar.net.qa) in Mesaieed.

Desert Activities

Desert excursions are a popular pastime. If you don't have any friends or acquaintances to invite you along, desert outings can be booked through a local tour company – see Organised Tours in the Getting Around section later in this chapter.

Most excursions head for areas southwest of Doha, ie, along the road to Salwa, or the magnificent 'inland sea' of Khor al-Adaid (see the Around Qatar section later in this chapter). But before you hire a 4WD and head into the desert, make sure the vehicle is well equipped and you have plenty of water and a very detailed map. And *never* underestimate the possibility of getting bogged, stranded or lost. Taking a knowledgeable driver or guide is a good idea.

The sand dunes around Mesaieed are perfect for 'sand-skiing' – a local version of snow-skiing complete with skis and poles. There is nowhere to rent equipment, however. Qatar Holidays (see Organised Tours in the Getting Around section later in this chapter) organise trips.

Clubs

Although there are several private clubs in and around Doha where members can play squash, racquetball, tennis etc, they're of little use to tourists because most do not offer day or temporary memberships. One of the more popular clubs, which is sometimes open to overseas visitors for a small temporary membership fee, is the Doha Club (☎ 418 822).

For the visitor, the best options are the health clubs at the top-end hotels. These tend to be scaled-down versions of the bigger clubs, though some, notably the health club at the Doha Sheraton, are large.

WORK

Qatar is not the sort of place where Westerners can expect to pick up a few months of casual work waiting tables or teaching English. Employment agencies do exist in

Qatar, but they deal almost exclusively in cheap labour from the Indian subcontinent and South-East Asia. Almost all working expatriates arrange their job through a work agency *before* coming to Qatar.

If you're in Qatar and want to find work, check out the classifieds in the two English-language newspapers, and ask around the Western expat community because jobs are often 'advertised' by word of mouth. It is possible to arrive in Qatar on a tourist visa, look for a job and then arrange for your employer to convert the tourist visa into a residence visa. This is usually an option only for people with specialised professional skills, and will involve masses of paperwork.

ACCOMMODATION
Camping
There are a few designated camp sites around the countryside, but they're for official school or boy scout trips, and not available to tourists. There is plenty of desert which belongs to no-one, but camping in the desert is not a lot of fun because of fierce sandstorms, lack of water and bumpy ground.

The best place for camping is at the Khor al-Adaid 'inland sea' (see the Around Qatar section later in this chapter), but you may come to the attention of some unsympathetic military and police officials, so it's best to go on an organised camping tour.

Hotels
The range of hotels is limited, but most are clean. There are no youth hostels, and visa rules make most budget-range places inaccessible to tourists. Most tourists have to be sponsored by a hotel – something the cheapest places are unable to do. However, if you are not tied to any hotel, the prices of most mid-range and top-end places are very negotiable, and weekend (Thursday-Friday) specials are commonly offered.

FOOD
Qatar does not have an indigenous cuisine worth mentioning, and restaurants serving good Arabic food are surprisingly scarce. Anyone interested in local delicacies should try some fungus grown in the desert, but to

---

Edible Local Flora

The University of Qatar continues to research local flora to determine which are edible, and which can be used for medicinal purposes. Many of the 300 or so catalogued plants – many of which only grow during, or just after, the brief rains – include *jaad*, a type of mint used for stomach ailments and rheumatism; *ephedra*, used for nasal problems; and *gith-gath*, which has a range of medicinal uses. Perhaps the most delicious, and therefore the most popular and expensive, local plant is the fungus *fafafa*, known in the west as a truffle.

---

avoid becoming ill it *must* be cooked correctly. Some other desert plants are also edible, and collecting these plants and fungi is a popular local pastime.

Central Doha is filled with small Indian/Pakistani eateries which offer curries and biryanis for less than QR10. The cheapest places to eat are the 'cafeterias', which sell sandwiches and *ta'amiyya*, and the juice stalls, which often also sell sandwiches and burgers. The small grocery stores (called 'cold stores') are open all day every day, and sell most basic items.

There are plenty of Western-style fast food joints in Doha, such as McDonald's, KFC and Pizza Hut, but they're mostly in the suburbs, so you'll need to charter a taxi or have your own transport. A hamburger, chips (French fries) and soft drink meal starts at QR15.

Meals at good restaurants, and in the big hotels, cost at least QR20, and usually closer to QR30. Hotel restaurants often hold 'theme nights' with all-you-can-eat buffets from QR40 to QR75 per person. Most restaurants have 'family sections' where families, mixed couples and women unaccompanied by men can enjoy some relative seclusion.

DRINKS
You can't bring alcohol into Qatar, but you can buy it legally if you're staying in a large hotel, or if you're a non-Muslim expatriate and your employer/sponsor agrees.

QATAR

All of the larger hotels have at least one bar and one restaurant that serve liquor. These operate according to fairly strict rules. The hotels are not allowed to advertise the availability of alcohol or the location of the bar. A sign in the lobby advertising 'entertainment in the something-or-other lounge' is usually an ad for the bar.

The bars and 'wet' restaurants are only open to hotel guests and outsiders who have purchased memberships. Nonmembers or nonguests just may be able to talk their way in, but that depends entirely on how accommodating the people checking IDs are feeling. Memberships cost about QR100 for one year, which is reasonably cost-effective for residents, but not for the ordinary tourist.

SPECTATOR SPORTS

Qatar hosts several top international sporting events. These are advertised internationally, and publicised in the local English-language media.

The Qatar Masters is (somehow) part of the PGA European Tour golf circuit. It attracts top-name players, and is held annually at the Doha Golf Club (see Activities earlier in this chapter). The annual Qatar Open tennis tournament is held in January, and the prize money of about US$1,000,000 attracts an impressive number of top players. Some of the older players come for the Seniors Tour of Champions in April. The Qatar International Squash Championship is a major event on the calendar, and is held at different times. All tennis and squash events take place at the Khalifa International Tennis & Squash Complex, just off Khalifa St.

Qatar was the site of some of the Asia qualifying rounds for the 1994 and 1998 (soccer) World Cup.

In 1998, Qatar hosted an international grand prix athletics meeting at the 45,000-seat Khalifa Stadium. Qatar became the first country in the Gulf to allow foreign and local females to participate in an athletics competition, though all women had to wear very modest attire. Qatar hopes to host the Asian Games in the future.

Other major competitions include the Qatar International Desert Marathon (held in March); the Qatar International Regatta; the associated Gulf Open Masters Regatta, organised by the Doha Sailing Association (see Activities earlier in this chapter); and several car rallies.

Local sports (which are all held in winter) include: camel racing (see Al-Shahhainiya in the Around Qatar section later in this chapter); horse racing at the Al-Rayyan Equestrian Centre; and dhow races – check the local English-language daily newspapers for details.

SHOPPING

You're not likely to find much in the way of Arabian souvenirs in Doha, and Qatar is not somewhere to pick up some handicrafts. If you are flush with money there are a couple of stores in central Doha, and in the large hotels, which specialise in carpets, mostly imported from Iran. Many of the ostensibly 'Arabian' souvenirs (eg, incense burners) are actually made in Pakistan or Syria.

Any shop offering genuine discounts or sales promotions is advertised in the local English-language newspapers, and even listed under 'Events' in the newspapers. Refer to the Doha section later in this chapter for information about souqs, markets and shopping centres in the capital.

Getting There & Away

AIR

Qatar is one of the four part-owners of Gulf Air, which has one or more flights a week from Doha to Frankfurt, London and Paris; several each day to major cities on the Indian subcontinent; many every day to other Middle Eastern cities; and weekly services elsewhere around the world, often via Bahrain or Abu Dhabi (UAE). Qatar's own national carrier, Qatar Airways (www.qatarairways.com), also has services from Doha to London and Munich, and to most cities in the Middle East.

The country's only airport, Doha International Airport, is on the edge of central Doha.

is small but adequate (inquiries: ☎ 622
⁑9). Services include a cafeteria, an ATM
⁑nich accepts most major credit cards, a
⁑ty-free shop, gift shop and a couple of
⁑ack bars.

⁑eparture Tax

departure tax of QR20 must be paid in
⁑sh at the airport.

⁑he USA & Canada

⁑here are no direct flights between Doha
⁑d North America. The only option is to
⁑avel via Europe, or another Middle East-
⁑n city such as Amman (Jordan), Abu
⁑habi (UAE), Kuwait or Cairo.

⁑ustralia & New Zealand

⁑he best way to reach Qatar from Australia
⁑to fly to Bahrain on Gulf Air or to Dubai
⁑n Emirates. There are regular connections
⁑ Doha from both Bahrain and Dubai. New
⁑ealanders have to get a connection in Aus-
⁑alia or Asia.

⁑he UK & Continental Europe

⁑atar Airways only flies to Doha from two
⁑ities in Europe: from London (for about
⁑JK£419 return) every day, and from Lon-
⁑on, via Munich, twice a week. Gulf Air
⁑lso has direct flights to Doha from Frank-
⁑urt, London and Paris. Gulf Air has more
⁑requent services from Europe to Bahrain
⁑see the Getting There & Away section in
⁑he Bahrain chapter for details), with very
⁑requent connections to Doha.

⁑sia

⁑ large percentage of Qatari residents are of
⁑akistani, Indian and Bangladeshi origin,
⁑o Qatar Airways and Gulf Air fly most
⁑lays from Doha to Karachi, Mumbai (Bom-
⁑ay), Trivandrum (India), and Dhaka. Air
⁑ndia, Pakistan International Airlines (PIA)
⁑nd Biman Bangladesh also serve the same
⁑outes.

⁑iddle East

⁑any major regional airlines – eg, Saudia,
⁑gypt Air, Gulf Air, Qatar Airways, Oman
⁑ir and Yemenia – link Doha with all major
cities in the Gulf and the Middle East. Some
examples of fares to nearby countries are:

destination	one way/return (QR)
Abu Dhabi (UAE)	480/400
Manama (Bahrain)	370/270
Amman (Jordan)	1180/1610
Cairo (Egypt)	1420/2114
Dubai (UAE)	590/540
Kuwait City	600/820
Muscat (Oman)	1010/900

To some destinations – notably Manama,
Abu Dhabi and Dubai – the one-way fare
can actually be higher than the cheapest return, so if you want a one-way ticket it may
prove more cost-effective to buy a return
ticket and throw away the second coupon.
Always look out for promotional fares: on
Wednesday, Thursday or Friday, the regional airlines sometimes offer 'weekend
fares' to popular 'watering holes' like
Bahrain and Dubai.

LAND
Border Crossings

There are no international bus or taxi services from Qatar to Saudi Arabia or the
UAE. It's worth noting here that Saudi Arabian bus timetables have long listed an international line from Hofuf, Saudi Arabia to
Doha: there is no evidence that this bus has
actually run at any time in the last ten years.

Residents of Qatar, Saudi Arabia and the
UAE – along with all Gulf Cooperation
Council (GCC) citizens – can drive across
the Qatar-Saudi border, but other foreigners
are normally not allowed to. This is because
sponsored visas must be collected at Doha
International Airport and rental companies
are not keen for foreigners to drive hire cars
across the border.

SEA

Despite the proximity of Bahrain, the UAE
and Saudi Arabia, there is currently no passenger ferry or boat service to or from Qatar
– although there is talk about introducing
services between Qatar, the other Gulf
States and Iran.

QATAR

ORGANISED TOURS

Very few international travel agencies organise tours specifically to Qatar. The best place to organise a local tour from outside Qatar is other Gulf States, particularly the UAE. Sharjah-based Orient Tours organises weekend packages to Doha, including accommodation and tours, but these are primarily for residents of countries in the GCC who don't need to bother with visas for Qatar.

Getting Around

Qatar does not have a proper bus or service-taxi system, so rented cars are the only real option for getting around the countryside. Central Doha is small enough to get around on foot with an occasional taxi ride.

CAR & MOTORCYCLE

Driving in Qatar is on the right-hand side of the road. Police are always keen to levy fines on anyone speeding or not wearing a seat belt. There are two grades of petrol: regular (90 octane) is called *mumtaz* and costs 65 dirhams per litre; super (97 octane) costs 70 dirhams. Qatar was built with the car firmly in mind, so there are numerous reputable service stations where repairs and spare parts are readily available.

If you're driving around Doha and Qatar, here are a few things you should know:

- Roundabouts in Doha are common, disorientating and large; few cars stop or give way.
- Finding the right way out of Doha can be confusing. If you're heading south towards Al-Wakrah or Mesaieed, take the airport road (Al-Matar Rd); the main road to all points north is 22nd February Rd (north from Al-Rayyan Rd). To go west, continue along Al-Rayyan Rd.
- Many turn-offs are strangely positioned,so drivers must make a lot of U-turns.

Car Rental

Cars can be rented using your own driving licence (ie, an International Driving Permit is not needed) within seven days of arriving in Qatar. After that, a temporary licence issued by the Traffic Licence Office is re-

quired, which involves an eye test and short verbal exam. The licence costs QR5 and lasts three months. Most of the larg car rental agencies, and a few of the top-e hotels, will take care of this for you – thoug they will probably charge an extra fee.

The minimum rental period for all age cies is 24 hours, which is enough to see t limited number of sights around the cou tryside. Drivers must have a credit card f the deposit, but can pay in cash. Agencie will only rent to someone over 21 years ol There is nowhere to rent motorbikes.

Most car rental agencies have booths the airport or offices in the top-end hotel and will often offer discounts of up to 25 to guests. Prices usually include unlimite kilometres but not petrol, and they do var so shop around. Expect to pay aroun QR110/700 per day/week for the smalle sedan, and at least QR240/1250 for a 4WL Most agencies add a compulsory Collisio Damage Waiver to all bills at QR20 QR40 per day (depending on the size of th vehicle). A few agencies also add a com pulsory Personal Accident Insurance Fee c about QR15 per day. If you want a chau feur, add another QR125 or so per day.

Many agencies around Doha offer ca rentals, but it's better to use a reputabl agency, even if it costs more. All of the mai agencies have rental desks at the airport.

Avis (☎ 447 766, fax 441 626, 🖂 avis@qatar.net.qa) with offices at the Gulf Sheraton (☎ 495 578) and Ramada Hotel (☎ 444 167)
Budget (☎ 419 500, fax 419 077)
Europcar (☎ 411 982) with an office at the Hotel Sofitel Doha Palace (☎ 322 194)
Hertz (☎ 622 891, fax 621 291)

LOCAL TRANSPORT
Taxi

Taxis are plentiful, modern and cheap: trip across town costs about QR5. Driver are supposed to use the meter, but some times need a little encouragement. The flag-fall is QR2 during the day (QR3 at night) and then 10 dirhams per 100m. For trave outside the capital you may want to negoti ate a fixed fare.

ORGANISED TOURS

Very few of the travel agencies around Doha arrange tours. The only agency dealing almost exclusively with organised tours Qatar Holidays, which has offices at the Gulf Sheraton (☎ 495 585) and Doha Sheraton (☎ 854 829). It runs tours around Doha, and to places that independent travellers cannot visit easily, eg, Khor al-Adaid and the oil fields around Dukhan. Tours with a German-speaking guide can also be arranged. Prices range from QR75/200 for a half-day/full-day tour to QR450 for an overnight 'desert safari'.

Two other companies in Doha which also arrange interesting tours are Arabian Adventures (☎ 431 879) and Orient Tours (☎ 417 184).

Refer to Organised Tours in the Getting Around the Region chapter for more information.

Doha

Around the Gulf, Doha (where about 80% of Qatar's population lives) has earned the unenviable reputation of being the dullest place on earth, and you'll be hard-pressed to find anyone who'll claim the place is exciting. However, there's nothing *wrong* with Doha: the bay is charming, and there are enough interesting sights around town to keep most travellers occupied for a few days.

Orientation

The older section of Doha lies between the A Ring Rd and the coast. The city centre begins with the string of large buildings along the Corniche, between the Qatar National Bank and the Emir's Office and extends several blocks inland, taking in the souq and the main business district. The oldest and most interesting part of town, and the best focal point for budget travellers, is the area around the Clock Tower and Grand Mosque. This is where the cheapest restaurants and hotels are located (though most visitors won't be able to stay here because their visas will be sponsored by expensive hotels).

The streets around Doha are well signposted, but the signs are often so small that it's almost impossible to read them while trying to manoeuvre through a chaotic roundabout. Places of interest to the visitor, eg, shopping centres, tourist attractions and sporting arenas, are poorly signed, or not at all. If you're staying for a while, pick up a detailed street map – see Planning in the Facts for the Visitor section earlier in this chapter.

Information

Money All major currencies can be exchanged at the larger banks, and at the moneychangers dotted around central Doha. (The small collection of moneychangers just south of Doha Fort offer good rates.) ATMs for most major credit cards can be found at Commercial Bank of Qatar, British Bank of the Middle East; and Qatar National Bank. See Money in the Facts for the Visitor section earlier in this chapter for more details.

American Express is represented by Darwish Travel & Tourism (☎ 422 411) on Al-Rayyan Rd. It's open Saturday to Thursday from 8 am to midday, and about 3 to 7 pm. Travellers cheques are cashed for AmEx card holders, but the office won't hold mail for clients.

Post The General Post Office is along the Corniche in northern Doha. The post office on Abdullah bin Jasim St is more convenient, and is open Saturday to Thursday, from 7 am to 1 pm, and 4 to 7 pm; and Friday, 8 to 10 am. There's also a small post office in The Centre shopping complex on Salwa Rd, open Saturday to Thursday, from 9 am to midday, and 4 to 8 pm.

Telephone The Main Telecommunications Centre on Al-Musheireb St is easy to find, and is open 24 hours a day. It offers complete telephone, fax, telex and telegram services – refer to Post & Communications in the Facts for the Visitor section earlier in this chapter for more information.

Email & Internet Access At the business centres at the two Sheraton hotels, and at the Ramada Hotel (see Places to Stay later in this

QATAR

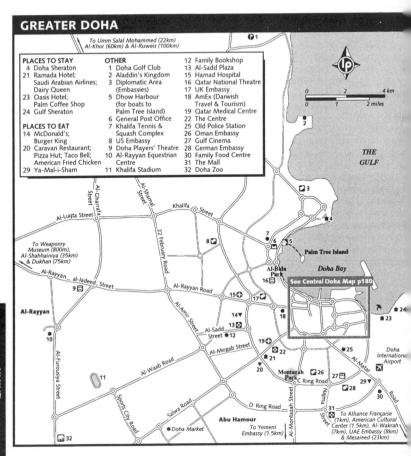

GREATER DOHA

To Umm Salal Mohammed (22km)
Al-Khor (60km) & Al-Ruweis (100km)

PLACES TO STAY
4   Doha Sheraton
21 Ramada Hotel;
    Saudi Arabian Airlines;
    Dairy Queen
23 Oasis Hotel;
    Palm Coffee Shop
24 Gulf Sheraton

PLACES TO EAT
14 McDonald's;
    Burger King
20 Caravan Restaurant;
    Pizza Hut; Taco Bell;
    American Fried Chicken
29 Ya-Mal-i-Sham

OTHER
1   Doha Golf Club
2   Aladdin's Kingdom
3   Diplomatic Area
    (Embassies)
5   Dhow Harbour
    (for boats to
    Palm Tree Island)
6   General Post Office
7   Khalifa Tennis &
    Squash Complex
8   US Embassy
9   Doha Players' Theatre
10 Al-Rayyan Equestrian
    Centre
11 Khalifa Stadium

12 Family Bookshop
13 Al-Sadd Plaza
15 Hamad Hospital
16 Qatar National Theatre
17 UK Embassy
18 AmEx (Darwish
    Travel & Tourism)
19 Qatar Medical Centre
22 The Centre
25 Old Police Station
26 Oman Embassy
27 Gulf Cinema
28 German Embassy
30 Family Food Centre
31 The Mall
32 Doha Zoo

THE GULF

To Weaponry
Museum (800m),
Al-Shahhainiya (35km)
& Dukhan (75km)

Al-Rayyan

Palm Tree Island

Doha Bay

See Central Doha Map p180

Al-Bida Park

Doha International Airport

Montazah Park

Abu Hamour

Doha Market

To Yemeni
Embassy (1.5km)

To Alliance Française
(1km), American Cultural
Center (1.5km), Al-Wakrah
(7km), UAE Embassy (8km)
& Mesaieed (23km)

QATAR

chapter), access to the Internet costs about QR60 per hour. Down Gulf St, in the Gulf Commercial Centre, the Internet Cafe (☎ 350 711, ✉ sales@ig.com), charges a more reasonable QR15 per hour. Take a taxi there.

Travel Agencies A number of travel agencies are dotted around town; several with good reputations are located along Al-Musheireb St, opposite the New Capital and Qatar International hotels. Most of the travel agencies in Doha only sell airline tickets, but if you are buying a ticket or confirming a flight, it's safer to deal directly

with the airline. The Getting There & Away section later in this chapter has a list of airline offices. For more information see Organised Tours in the Getting Around section earlier in this chapter.

Bookshops Doha has a few well-stocked bookshops, such as the Abu Karbal on Al-Musheireb St, and Al-Hijaz next to Thai Noodles on Al-Bareed St. The Centre (on Salwa Rd) and The Mall (on D Ring Rd) shopping complexes sell English-language books, novels and magazines, and the Journal Bookshop in the Gulf Sheraton is also pretty good. The best range of books in Qatar can be found in the Family Book-shop, down the road from the Al-Sadd Plaza. Another good selection can be found in the lobby of the Doha Sheraton – and not just because it offers an impressive range of Lonely Planet guidebooks!·

Libraries The Qatar National Library on the corner of Jabr bin Mohammed and Ras Abu Abboud streets has a small collection of books in Arabic, French and English. The books can be borrowed by residents, and read by visitors in the library. It is open Saturday to Thursday, from midday to 7.30 pm.

Cultural Centres Some of the foreign cultural centres in Doha include:

Alliance Française (☎ 417 548) Ibn Naeem St, just off Ibn Seena St. Open Saturday to Wednesday, from 9 am to midday, and 5 to 7 pm.
American Cultural Center (☎ 351 279, ✉ usis doha@qatar.net.qa) Muaither St, just off Suhaim bin Hamad St. Open Saturday to Wednesday, from 8 am to 4 pm.
British Council (☎ 426 193) Ras Abu Abboud St. Open Saturday to Wednesday, from 10 am to midday, and 4 to 7 pm.

Laundry Some of the better laundries around town include the cheap, but ponderous Al-Baker Laundry; the more expensive Ramada Laundry, which is linked to the hotel of the same name, but located in the car park of The Centre shopping complex; and Al-Rayes Laundry & Dry Cleaning. See under Laundry in the Facts for the Visitor section earlier in this chapter for an idea about general laundry costs.

Medical Services Medical care is free for residents, and usually for visitors. If you get sick or injured, ask your hotel to refer you to a doctor, hospital or medical centre. The major public hospital is the Hamad Hospital (☎ 392 222) on Al-Rayyan Rd, which offers treatment for tourists on a walk-in basis. The Qatar Medical Centre (☎ 440 606), opposite The Centre shopping complex on Salwa Rd, is a modern and private clinic, with dental facilities.

Emergency An emergency (free-call) number for fire, police and ambulance services is ☎ 999.

Qatar National Museum

The highlight of Doha is unquestionably the Qatar National Museum (☎ 442 191), a grand building opposite the Corniche. The large number of varied exhibits are well labelled in English, and it's worth visiting more than once. Before entering the museum, take a moment to look at the building: most of the museum complex once served as a palace for Sheikh Abdullah bin Mohammed, Qatar's ruler from 1913 to 1949.

The courtyard inside the museum complex is surrounded by a series of rooms displaying artefacts, such as medals and jewellery, which show the traditional lifestyle of the Qatari people. Also in the courtyard are three residential buildings, once inhabited by Sheikh Abdullah's family and entourage and added to the complex at different points over the last 80 years.

The **main museum** houses various exhibits about Qatar's climate, environment, industries and archaeology, and several short films about various aspects of Qatar and its history run continuously. The archaeological display, which occupies most of the ground floor, includes a collection of arrowheads, potsherds, flint etc, but the section on seafaring, and traditional celestial navigation methods, is more interesting. The lower level is a jumbled collection of displays on desert life, Islam and astronomy, as well as an exhibit on the oil industry.

Next to the large artificial 'lagoon' (with a dhow or two), the **marine museum** has informative displays about fishing, pearling and boat building – all ancient industries recently supplanted in importance by oil and gas. Underneath is a small but impressive **aquarium** with plenty of turtles and other marine life, all carefully labelled and well lit.

The museum complex is open every day except Saturday, from 9 am to midday, and 3 to 6 pm (winter) or 4 to 7 pm (summer); and 4 to 7 pm only on Friday (all year). Admission costs QR2. A pleasant outdoor *cafeteria* sells drinks, but little else.

QATAR

Ethnographic Museum

The Ethnographic Museum (☎ 436 008) is in a restored traditional Qatari house from the early 20th century, and provides a look at what life in Qatar was like before the oil era. Signs explain the function of the various rooms in the house, and their importance in the life of the family.

Of particular interest is the building's well-restored wind tower, one of Qatar's few remaining examples of this form of traditional Gulf architecture. (See Traditional Architecture under Arts in the Facts about the Region chapter.) When inside the museum spend a few minutes sitting under the wind tower to appreciate the ingenuity involved in designing this pre-electricity form of air-conditioning.

The museum is pleasantly located in the middle of the central courtyard of the yet currently unfinished Al-Nayad Shopping Centre on Grand Hamad St, and is open Sunday to Thursday, from 9 am to midday, and 3 to 6 pm (winter) or 4 to 7 pm (summer). Admission is free.

Doha Fort

Doha Fort (☎ 412 742), also known as Al-Koot Fort, was built in the 19th century to house Doha's Turkish garrison. On Jasim bin Mohammed St, the fort is worth a look if you're in this part of town and not pressed for time, but many of the topics on display are covered much more thoroughly in the Qatar National Museum.

The interior of the fort consists of a large, paved courtyard with a fountain. The displays run the gamut from model dhows to paintings of Qatari life. To the right from the entrance, the first of the rooms surrounding the courtyard contains weavings, paintings with Qatari themes and several examples of stone and wood carvings. The rooms on the opposite side of the courtyard have displays on goldsmiths, rope-making, stone carving, textiles, weaving and other traditional crafts – all of these exhibits are particularly well laid out, and labelled in English. There is also a small separate exhibit on fishing, shipbuilding and seafaring. The roof provides a picturesque view of the courtyard.

Officially, Doha Fort is open Sunday to Friday, from 9 am to midday, and 3 to 6 pm (winter) and 4 to 7 pm (summer), but opening hours are erratic. Admission is free.

Other Museums

If you're a stamp collector, the **Postal Museum** should figure near the top of your list of must-sees. The museum is part of the old (but still functioning) post office on Abdullah bin Jasim St, but the door to the museum is along Al-Bareed St. It is officially open Saturday to Thursday from 4 to 6 pm, though these hours are loosely interpreted and don't be surprised if you never find it open.

The **Weaponry Museum** in the Al-Laqta district, on the outskirts of Doha, is a private collection of swords, guns and other traditional Qatari and Arabic weapons. However, visitors are only welcome if they're on an organised tour of Doha. The three agencies mentioned in Organised Tours in the Getting Around section earlier in this chapter can arrange a visit as part of their tours.

Old Police Station

This tiny fort-like building was once a police station on the outskirts of Doha, but is now little more than a curiosity within the city's urban sprawl. It's not open to the public, and a peek through the windows confirms that you're not missing much anyway: the interior is empty. The small whitewashed building is on the corner of Al-Matar Rd and Al-Waab St.

The Corniche

The Corniche, which is about 7km long, is delightful and one of the prettiest in the Gulf. It starts at the Layali Zaman restaurant, almost opposite the Qatar National Museum, and finishes at the Doha Sheraton hotel. A **walkway** parallels the main road most of the way, and there's plenty of greenery and shade, bicycle and jogging tracks and lovely views, especially further north near the General Post Office. From several different, seemingly temporary, spots along the Corniche, speedboats and dhows take passengers on **boat trips**. The rips start from about 4 pm, and fares are negotiable.

Doha Zoo
The Doha Zoo is pleasant, well designed and has some nice gardens. The animals are caged, but do not seem worse off than animals in most zoos around the world, though some species undoubtedly suffer in the heat. There is a playground for the kids, and a *cafeteria* on the grounds.

The zoo is open Sunday to Friday, from 2 to 7 pm (winter) or 3 to 9 pm (summer). The general public is admitted only on Thursday, Friday and Sunday. Monday and Wednesday are for families, and Tuesday is for women and children. Admission is QR7 for adults, and QR5 for children under nine. The zoo is a long way south-west of central Doha, and only accessible by private car or taxi.

Aladdin's Kingdom
Aladdin's Kingdom (☎ 831 001), set grandly on a peninsula north of Doha, has the distinction of being the only amusement park in the Gulf with a serious roller coaster. It also boasts a huge ferris wheel, video games and go-karts for which drivers need to show their driving licences! During family days, plenty of enjoyable games and other fun things are available for the kids, and there are often fireworks at night.

The park is open Sunday to Friday, from about 3.30 to 9 pm. Some days are allocated for women or families only, so it's best to ring first. Admission is QR40 for both adults and children. It is only accessible by private car or taxi. If driving, take the Corniche towards the Doha Sheraton, and look for the sign to the West Bay Lagoon at a roundabout.

Palm Tree Island
Palm Tree Island (☎ 269 151) is a tiny (2.5 sq km) haven pleasantly located in the middle of Doha Bay, and very popular on Fridays and public holidays. The island is still being developed, but currently boasts a tiny **corniche**, **swimming pool**, **beach** and activities such as **horse riding** and **water sports**. The expensive *Fish Market Restaurant* is also there.

Palm Tree island is 'open' every day from 9 am to 11 pm, but only families are allowed to visit on Thursday and Friday. Transport is on official quasi-dhows, which currently leave from a spot next to an American Fried Chicken stand along the Corniche – but the point of departure does change regularly so check with your hotel or taxi driver first. Return tickets to the island on the cheaper boats cost about QR10 per person. A return trip on the better boats costs QR25, which includes a voucher for some junk food and access to some of the activities.

The island is run by the Qatar National Hotels Company (☎ 495 912), and further information is also available from the two Sheraton hotels (see Places to Stay below) and the Qatar Holidays travel agencies (see Organised Tours in the Getting Around section earlier in this chapter).

Places to Stay
For general information about accommodation in Qatar, see the Accommodation section in the Facts for the Visitor section earlier in this chapter. For a list of hotels that will sponsor visas for tourists, see the Visa & Documents section earlier in this chapter.

Places to Stay – Budget & Mid-Range
All of the rooms at the hotels listed below (except the Al-Zahra) have air-con, a TV (normally with satellite programs), fridge and private bathroom with hot water.

Al-Zahra Hotel (Al-Najada St) is one of Doha's better cheap hotels. The manager claims that it will sponsor visas sometime in the future, but don't count on it. The rooms are simple, but still comfortable and well furnished, and a comparative bargain at QR80/120 for singles/doubles. However, contacting them about visas will be very difficult, because there is no telephone or fax number.

Safeer Hotel (☎ 353 999, fax 353 888, Al-Muthaf St) is conveniently next to the Qatar National Museum. It has large, well-furnished rooms for QR130/180, which is very good value.

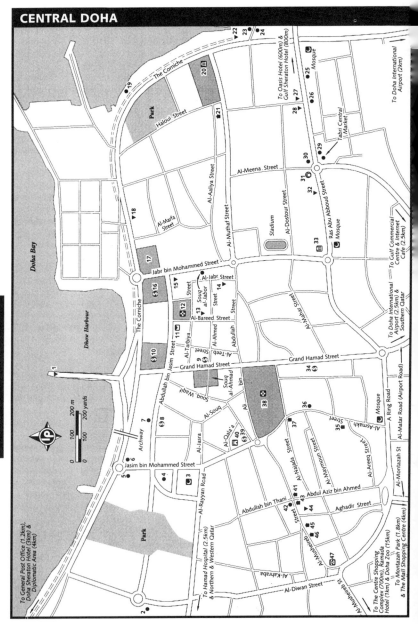

CENTRAL DOHA

CENTRAL DOHA

New Capital Hotel (☎ 445 445, fax 442 233, Al-Musheireb St) is the cheapest place in town for those who crave a swimming pool, and the cheapest option for anyone who needs a visa sponsored by a hotel. The clean and comfortable rooms look a little dated, but are good value for QR125/150, and there are panoramic city views from the balcony.

Qatar International Hotel (☎ 361 222, fax 442 413, Al-Musheireb St) is reasonable, but not as good as the New Capital next door. The rooms are fine, but a little musty, and cost QR120/150. It's a favoured haunt for Russian tourists and traders.

Qatar Palace Hotel (☎ 421 515, fax 321 515, Al-Asmakh St) falls somewhere between the New Capital and the Qatar International in terms of quality. It has large, well-furnished and quiet rooms in a central location for QR176/220. Surprisingly, the managers don't sponsor visas for guests.

Doha Palace Hotel (☎ 360 101, fax 423 955, ✉ dpalace@qatar.net.qa, Al-Musheireb St) is probably the best mid-range place. It has helpful staff, and a large number of comfortable rooms for QR150/180 in a most convenient (but noisy) location.

Places to Stay – Top End

All of these places add 17% in taxes and service charges to the bill (included in the prices listed below). The glut of hotel space means that most places will readily offer discounts on the rates listed here.

Doha Sheraton (☎ 854 444, fax 832 323), built for the Gulf Summit in 1984, dominates the northern side of Doha Bay, and has become the country's main architectural landmark. The lobby is incredibly opulent, and has a small, but well laid-out, display of 17th- and 18th-century Islamic antiquities. Singles/doubles cost a whopping QR1170/ 1287, and suites start at QR2106/ 2340, but the management should be able to reduce this a little. If you can't afford to stay here, at least drop by and take in the sweeping view of Doha and the bay from the foyer, or the (expensive) rooftop restaurant.

Gulf Sheraton (☎ 432 432, fax 418 784, Ras Abu Abboud St) is large, comfortable and has good service. It is reasonable value compared to some of the others in this range: rooms start from QR761/878, but cost more for a sea view.

Oasis Hotel (☎ 424 424, fax 327 096, Ras Abu Abboud St) is also large, but has better

QATAR

views and is better value than the nearby Gulf Sheraton. The rooms, which cost QR350/470, could do with some modernisation, but they are well furnished. Fans of Jonathan Raban should note that he stayed at the Oasis while researching his book on Arabia (see Books in the Facts for the Visitor section earlier in this chapter). The Gulf Sheraton and Oasis are inconvenient, however, and under the airport's flight path.

Hotel Sofitel Doha Palace (☎ 435 222, fax 439 186, @ sofisale@qatar.net.qa, Abdul Aziz bin Ahmed St) is upstairs in a commercial building, and in a central location. It charges QR702/819, which is not great value, so you're probably better off somewhere else. It's popular with all sorts of Qatari and foreign military personnel.

Ramada Hotel (☎ 417 417, fax 410 941), at the intersection of Salwa and the C Ring roads, is an unmistakable orange building. It has all the luxuries you would expect for QR643/761, and is very convenient to The Centre shopping complex and a number of fast food outlets.

Places to Stay – Rentals
Check the classified sections of the two English-language daily newspapers for a list of places to rent, but tourists probably won't be able to rent a property without sponsorship from an employer in Qatar. Most Western expatriates have accommodation pre-arranged through their employer.

Places to Eat
Restaurants In the older part of the city, just south of the Postal Museum, there are a few cheap Indian/Pakistani eateries where tasty and filling curries and biryanis cost about QR10. *Thai Noodles (Al-Bareed St)* is small, popular and serves some interesting Middle Eastern versions of Thai cuisine.

Elsewhere, *Desman Restaurant*, near the Doha Palace Hotel, offers good and cheap Chinese and Indian food; and *Dreamland Restaurant*, on the corner of Masafi and Aghadir Sts, has a selection of biryanis and curries for about QR8.

Red Rose (☎ 413 807, Al-Jabr St) is a pleasant surprise in the older part of the city.

The restaurant upstairs is cool, if a little dark, and the menu has a wide range of Chinese, Indian, Filipino and Western food though some items are not always available Soup costs about QR7; Chinese dishes about QR12; and the soft drink prices are cheap.

Gulf Broasted Restaurant (Ras Abu Abboud St) is reasonably close to the Oasis and Gulf Sheraton hotels, and serves tasty burgers for around QR6, and filling chicken meals from QR12.

Ya Mal-i-Sham (Al-Matar Rd), directly opposite the main entrance to the airport, has great but expensive Lebanese food (about QR35 per main meal), including the usual Lebanese mix of chicken, kebabs, mixed grill and pigeon, plus delicious fish from the Gulf.

Caravan Restaurant (☎ 412 277), almost lost among the plethora of fast food joints at the intersection of C Ring and Salwa Rds, has popular all-you-can-eat buffets for about QR45 per person. Most of the dishes are also available à la carte, but cost at least QR35, so you might as well enjoy the buffet. *Green Ribbon (Abdullah bin Jasim St)* is similar to the Caravan but, unlike all other restaurants listed here, is not open for lunch.

Layali Zaman (☎ 351 413, The Corniche) is an extraordinary place with wind towers in a building known locally as *al-qalla*. It is an expensive restaurant, which caters primarily to large groups, but the adjoining *Cafe Royal* is a pleasant place to enjoy a soft or hot drink on a pontoon, overlooking the jetties.

Al-Bandar is a collection of atmospheric restaurants specialising in seafood, overlooking the bay and at the end of the main pier. At the major restaurants, such as the *Al-Sharqui (☎ 311 414)* and the *Al-Gharbi (☎ 311 616)*, starters cost from QR15, and main dishes about QR40. The informal, outdoor *Terrace Restaurant*, in the same complex, is far better value: burgers cost QR12; pizzas, QR18; and Lebanese-style entrees, about QR6.

Maharaja Restaurant (☎ 421 642, Qatar Palace Hotel) is a popular place where locals enjoy some fine, reasonably priced, Indian food, in pleasant surroundings; biryanis cost about QR13, and huge curries about QR15. *Palm Coffee Shop (Oasis Hotel)* is one of the city's best-value hotel restaurants for Western food: eg, burgers cost about QR18 and omelettes about QR12.

If you want an alcoholic drink with dinner, you'll have to stay in one of the hotels large enough to have a bar. The restaurant serving booze is usually hidden away on an upper floor, along with the bar. The best, and certainly most expensive restaurants, are located in the two Sheraton hotels. The Doha Sheraton, for example, has the more informal, and reasonably priced, *Al-Hubara Restaurant* on the ground floor, and the expensive *Pirate's Cove* overlooking the sea. The Ramada Hotel has *Maxim's* for Asian food, and theme nights at the *Hyde Park*.

Fast Food The Centre shopping complex on Salwa Rd has *KFC*, *Hardee's*, *Chicken Tikka* and an excellent *bakery*. The Mall shopping centre on D Ring Rd has several more fast food joints. Junk food junkies will be in heaven at the intersection of the C Ring and Salwa Rds, where *Pizza Hut*, *American Fried Chicken* and *Taco Bell*, among others, are located; and opposite, *Dairy Queen* is one of the few places to serve breakfast (QR15). *McDonald's* and *Burger King* are also along the C Ring Rd.

The cheapest places for a snack are the cafeterias dotted around town, such as *Alanfal Cafeteria*, along the Corniche. *Petra Restaurant (☎ 412 720, Ras Abu Abboud St)* is mainly a takeaway, but sells excellent tamiy'ya (QR3) and *shwarma* (grilled meat sliced from a spit and served in pita bread with salad) (QR4), and is particularly good for roast chicken meals. *Kebab King (☎ 444 215)*, next door, is small, clean and good value.

Self-Catering Unless you have cooking facilities, self-catering is not likely to save a lot of money over the cafeterias or cheaper Indian/Pakistani eateries. There are plenty of grocery stores (called 'cold stores') all over Doha, and well-stocked supermarkets at the Tabri Central Market on Ras Abu Abboud St, The Centre on Salwa Rd, The Mall on D Ring Rd and the Family Food Centre on Al-Matar St.

Entertainment

Doha is the kind of place where going out means dinner out, and that's about it. Some of the big hotels, such as the Doha Sheraton with its *Hospitality Lounge*, offer light entertainment (ie, live background music). Check the 'Events' sections in the two English-language daily newspapers to find out what's going on, or ask at the reception desks of the larger hotels.

Cinema Two cinemas show modern, Western (mainly English-language) films, sometimes with Arabic subtitles: the Gulf Cinema (☎ 671 811) on C Ring Rd, and the theatre at The Mall shopping centre on D Ring Rd. Tickets cost about QR15, and programs are advertised in the two English-language daily newspapers.

Theatre The 500-seat Qatar National Theatre (☎ 832 021) on the Corniche hosts occasional performances of plays in Arabic. Depending on the event, tickets cost about QR50 and can be obtained from the box office at the theatre. The Doha Players (☎ 871 196), run by amateur but very enthusiastic expatriate thespians, put on some impressive shows at their small theatre on Al-Rayyan al-Jadeed St. The British Council (see Cultural Centres earlier in this chapter) sometimes sponsors shows from the UK.

Bars & Nightclubs Bars are only open to guests and 'members' – refer to Drinks in the Facts for the Visitor section earlier in this chapter for details about visiting a bar. One of the few genuine nightclubs, where alcohol is available and the public are welcome, is Al-Qalla, part of the Layali Zaman complex on the Corniche. The two Sheraton hotels also offer taped music and alcoholic drinks in a Qatari version of a nightclub.

Arabic Teahouses There are a few pleasant teahouses around Doha. *Forda Teahouse*, at the back of the Laffin Marine

QATAR

Service building along the Corniche, has views, breezes, simple meals and hot and cold drinks in an authentic atmosphere.

Shopping

Souqs The places regarded as 'souqs' in Doha are disappointing, and rarely more than Western-style, air-conditioned and undercover groups of small, individual shops. The prices in the souqs are cheaper than in the modern shopping centres and the staff are friendlier, but they lack the atmosphere of the traditional souqs found elsewhere in the Gulf. Some of the better souqs in Doha are Souq al-Ahmad on Grand Hamad St, for electrical and household goods, and Souq al-Jabor on Jabr bin Mohammed St for leather goods. A good area for clothes is near the Gulf Finance & Exchange Company building on Grand Hamad St.

Markets The Doha Market on Salwa Rd is open every day, but is best during the cooler and busier early mornings. This market caters mostly to locals, and sells mainly fruit, vegetables, meat and fish, but the produce is fresh and cheap, and it's a fascinating place to watch the locals haggling.

Shopping Centres The two main shopping centres are The Centre on Salwa Rd and The Mall on D Ring Rd. The Centre is a mishmash of stalls, but boasts a supermarket, an excellent bakery and a decent bookshop. Larger and newer is The Mall, with its international chain stores such as JC Penny. Both are open from about 9 am to 9 pm, every day, but close earlier on Friday evening.

The Al-Nayad Shopping Centre on Grand Hamad St is central and built in a more authentically 'Middle Eastern' style, and will be pleasant when it's finished; the City Centre, and the Al-Sadd Plaza on Al-Sadd St has a few modern shops, but is inconvenient.

Getting There & Away

Air For information about flights into Doha International Airport, see the Getting There & Away section earlier this chapter.

Most airline offices are located in the Airline Centre on Ras Abu Abboud St, in the Al-Sadd Plaza, or at the airport. The main airlines flying to and from Doha was are:

British Airways (☎ 323 258) Airline Centre
Emirates Airlines (☎ 418 877) Abdullah bin Jasim St
Gulf Air (☎ 455 444) Airport building
KLM (☎ 321 208) Airline Centre
Kuwait Airways (☎ 422 392) Airline Centre
Lufthansa Airlines (☎ 428 008) Next to the Emir's Office, off Jasim bin Mohammed St
Pakistan International Airlines (PIA) (☎ 426 290) Airline Centre
Qatar Airways (☎ 621 681) Airport building
Royal Jordanian (☎ 431 431) Airline Centre
Saudi Arabian Airlines (☎ 432 200) Salwa Rd, near the Ramada Hotel

Car Refer to Car & Motorcycle in the Getting Around section earlier in this chapter for information about renting a car in Doha.

Getting Around

To/From the Airport If a top-end hotel has sponsored your visa, it should provide free transport to and from the airport in a hotel bus. A taxi between the airport and central Doha will cost about QR10. There are lots of taxis in the city so you won't have too much trouble finding one, but remember to remind the driver to use the meter.

Around Qatar

AL-SHAHHAINIYA

Camel racing is a popular sport – and business – in Qatar. Races are held at Al-Shahhainiya, which is also the place to see plenty of camels roaming around the countryside at other times. With some local knowledge, visitors can get a good position at the start or finish of the purpose-built stadium, but it's more fun to follow the camels along the 18km track in a car. A 4WD is best, but not totally necessary. As one reader observed, the 'spectacle of dozens of landcruisers and jeeps chasing alongside the racing camels is almost as impressive as the camels themselves'. Races are held in winter. Check the two English-language daily newspapers for the race times.

The village also has an **oryx farm**, a small reserve which protects a few lucky members of the endangered species of Arabian oryx. It is a private concern, and is normally open only to organised tours. If you want to visit, contact Arabian Adventures. (See Organised Tours in the Getting Around section earlier in this chapter for details.)

Al-Shahhainiya is about 35km west of Doha. The village, stadium and oryx farm are well signed from the main road towards Dukhan.

AL-WAKRAH

The fishing village of Al-Wakrah, and the nearby village of Al-Wukair, have several interesting **mosques** and **traditional houses**. Al-Wakrah also has a small **museum** (☎ 643 201), which keeps somewhat unpredictable hours: officially Sunday to Friday, 8 am to midday, and 3 to 6 pm, but it rarely opens in winter. Behind the museum are the **ruins** of what is thought to be a palace.

Along the coast between Al-Wakrah and Mesaieed there are several spectacular, but often inaccessible, **beaches**. If you go swimming, beware of strong currents. Many **flamingoes** roost along this coast during winter. (Also see the 'Bird-Watching' boxed text in the Facts for the Visitor section earlier in this chapter.)

Al-Wakrah is about 17km south of Doha. Follow Al-Matar Rd past the airport and look for the signs.

MESAIEED

Mesaieed (formerly known as Umm Said) is mainly an industrial zone, but it does boast some of the finest beaches in Qatar – and the best has, of course, been commandeered by a new resort. The sand dunes in the area are perfect for 'sand-skiing' – see Activities in the Facts for the Visitor section earlier in the chapter for details.

Sealine Beach Resort (☎ 772 722, fax 772 733) has about 75 luxurious villas, chalets and rooms, and is a short drive south of Mesaieed. The resort has a wonderful location on a pleasant beach near some awesome sand

dunes, and it's a great base from which to explore Khor al-Adaid. The resort caters mainly to locals, but foreigners and their children are welcome. Ring for current rates, and ask about special offers. Nonguests can use the swimming pool for QR20 per person, and water sports are also available.

Mesaieed is about 38km south of Doha, and easy to reach by car. From Doha, drive along Al-Matar Rd, past Al-Wakrah, and follow the signs to Mesaieed. If you can't find the signs to the resort from Mesaieed, ask directions.

KHOR AL-ADAID

Understandably touted as the major attraction in Qatar is the 'inland sea' of Khor al-Adaid, with a huge lake jutting into the desert and surrounded by extraordinary sand dunes. There has been some discussion about making the region a protected area.

The best time to visit is in the late afternoon, but to appreciate the area fully it's best to camp overnight and marvel at the changes in the landscape between day and night.

Getting There & Away

This region is only accessible by 4WD, and independent travellers should travel with someone who both knows the area and can really drive a 4WD. Note that if you camp independently you may come to the attention of some unsympathetic military and police officials. From Doha, head towards Salwa for about 60km, and look for the turn-offs south, and then east, to Khor al-Adaid. The area is located near the border with Saudi Arabia, so don't venture too far off the main trails. Khor al-Adaid is popular on weekends (Thursday and Friday), but the region is empty and very serene during the rest of the week.

Refer to Car & Motorcycle in the Getting Around section earlier in this chapter for information about renting a 4WD. You can day trip from Doha or the Sealine Beach Resort in nearby Mesaieed, or go on an organised tour (see Organised Tours in the Getting Around section), allowing you to stay overnight in some relative comfort and safety.

QATAR

SALWA

Right on the border with Saudi Arabia is the tiny fishing village, and immigration post, of Salwa. Its other main claim to fame is the attractive **beach**, but it's only worth visiting if you're driving to or from Saudi Arabia.

UMM BAB

The village of Umm Bab has an ugly cement factory, but there's a clean **beach** at the end of the road continuing south towards the coast from the village. The beach is easier to reach than Salwa, but there are better beaches closer to Doha, around Mesaieed. Umm Bab is about 80km west of Doha, and is accessible via Dukhan or the direct road west from the highway to Salwa.

UMM SALAL MOHAMMED

Umm Salal Mohammed village has a small **fort**, but it's normally only open when someone is around to unlock the door (mornings are your best bet). It's a whitewashed rectangular building with two towers, one of which rises to a height of about four storeys. Near the fort is a small **mosque** with an old minaret that has been restored to its original state.

The village is about 22km north of Doha, just west of the main road to Al-Ruweis. To find the fort, drive through the village for about 1.5km, and look for the signs. If in doubt, ask directions.

UMM SALAL ALI

The village of Umm Salal Ali is flanked by the only field of **burial mounds** in Qatar. They probably date from the 3rd millennium BC. (All of the region's burial mounds, whatever their age, are pre-Islamic in origin. Islam forbids cairn burials.) The site is not on the scale of the mounds in Bahrain, but if you haven't seen a mound field yet, Umm Salal Ali is worth a quick diversion.

Umm Salal Ali is about 27km north of Doha, not far from the main road to Al-Ruweis. One small mound field lies just north of the village, and more mounds are scattered in among Umm Salal Ali's buildings – you'll probably have to ask directions to find the better ones. The village has

two small *restaurants*, and several shops near the main road.

AL-KHOR

The pleasant town of Al-Khor, with its charming **corniche**, is an easy day trip from Doha. (The tranquillity may change, however, with the proposed development of a resort boasting world-class sailing facilities.)

The former police station along the corniche has been turned into a small **museum** (☎ 721 866) displaying some archaeological and cultural artefacts from the region. The museum is officially open every day, except Saturday, from 9 am to midday, and 3 to 6 pm (winter) or 4 to 7 pm (summer), but seems always to be closed.

Al-Khor has a number of old **watchtowers** scattered around the centre, several of which have been restored to their original form. It's impossible to date the construction of the watchtowers with any precision: they weren't built before the 20th century, though the towers visible today were probably built on the ruins of earlier, similar, structures.

According to an Arabic inscription, the ruined **mosque** in the town was built in Ramadan 1372 AH (AD 1953). From the mosque, the **view** of the ocean is splendid, and the setting is peaceful.

There's nowhere to stay in Al-Khor, but the *Ain Helaitan Restaurant & Coffee-shop*, on the Corniche, between the ruined mosque and museum, is a good place for a snack. *Pearl of Asea*, along the Corniche and closer to the museum, serves cheapish Chinese and Filipino food. There are several ATMs and grocery stores around town, and the Al-Khour Internet Cafe is in a group of shops near the stadium.

Al-Khor is nearly 60km north of Doha, and easy to reach from the main highway heading towards Al-Ruweis. From the road into Al-Khor, follow the signs to the Corniche. The road then passes the museum, and the mosque about 700m further along the coast.

AL-KHOR GARDENS

The new Al-Khor Gardens are a pleasant respite from the seemingly endless desert landscape. There's plenty of greenery, several places to eat and a children's playground. The main turn-off to the gardens is along the main highway north from Doha, about 2km north of the turn-off to Al-Khor. Admission is free.

AL-DAKHIRA (AL-THAKHIRA)

From the main roundabout in Al-Khor, a road leads to the small village of Al-Dakhira (also listed as Al-Thakhira on some maps). A short distance north of the village is a picturesque **beach**, but access is difficult without a 4WD and knowledgeable driver.

FUWAIRIT & AL-GHARIYA

Fuwairit village is about 90km north of Doha, and some 15km east of the main highway north to Al-Ruweis. The main beach, a few kilometres north of the village, is rocky and not worth a special effort, but the **sea views** from some points are superb. It's easy to reach with a 4WD, but normal cars should take care to avoid getting bogged.

The next village north, Al-Ghariya, has a better **beach**, but the road between Fuwairit and Al-Ghariya is not that great, so anyone without a 4WD will probably have to backtrack to the main highway.

AL-ZUBARA

Al-Zubara occupies a special place in Qatari history. For almost 200 years, it was controlled by the Al-Khalifa clan, Bahrain's ruling family, but hotly contested by them and Qatar's Al-Thani family. Al-Zubara was a large commercial area in the 18th century, but all that remains is the fort, built shortly after the Al-Thani family wrested the settlement from Bahraini control. The fort was used as a border police and military post until 1986, when it was restored as the **Al-Zubara Regional Museum** (☎ 701 252).

Several of the rooms around the fort's courtyard have displays of various items, mostly archaeological, as well as pottery, coins and maps found at or near the fort.

The towers provide a rather bleak view of the surrounding desert, and there's a well in the fort's courtyard.

Admission is officially free, but the caretaker offers visitors a small pamphlet, with limited information in English, and expects a 'donation' in return: QR2 is enough. The fort is open every day, except Saturday, from 9 am to midday, and 3 to 6 pm (winter) or 4 to 7 pm (summer).

About 2km beyond the fort, and along a rough road, are the ruins of some much older **coastal fortifications**. Low brick walls and the excavated remains of a city are clearly visible, but there are no explanatory signs of any sort. The fortifications were probably built directly on coastal rocks, indicating that they were the site's first and only level of occupation. The buildings are possibly from the 18th century, but may have been occupied a century or so earlier.

The fort is at the intersection of a road from Doha and Al-Ruweis. From Doha, follow the signs to Al-Zubara from the main northern highway; from Al-Ruweis, follow the road to Abu Dhalouf and keep going. You can't miss the fort: on a clear day you'll see it from a distance of about 7km, because there's absolutely nothing around it.

AL-RUWEIS

The Qatar peninsula's northernmost point offers little to the traveller. There are a few small grocery stores and *restaurants*, and a causeway out to the fishing village on **Ras Abu Amran** island but that's about it.

If you have a car, an hour or so to kill and it's not too hot, the road between Al-Ruweis and Al-Zubara passes several abandoned coastal villages, most notably **Al-Khuwair** and **Al-Arish**. The abandoned villages are easy to see from the main road, and can be reached without a 4WD. The towns were abandoned in the 1970s for economic reasons. The shells of the houses and shops clustered around a ruined central mosque can be a bit spooky.

Language

English is widely spoken throughout the Gulf, but a few words of Arabic can do a lot to ease your passage through the region.

There are several different varieties of Arabic. Classical Arabic, the language of the Quran, is the root of all of today's dialects of spoken and written Arabic. A modernised and somewhat simplified form of classical Arabic is the common language of the educated classes in the Middle East. This language, usually known as Modern Standard Arabic (MSA), is used in newspapers and by TV and radio newsreaders. It's also used as a medium of conversation by well-educated Arabs from different parts of the region. Such a written language is necessary because the dialects of spoken colloquial Arabic differ to the point where a few of them are mutually unintelligible. Mercifully, the words and phrases a traveller is most likely to use are fairly standard throughout the Gulf. The words and phrases in this chapter should be understood anywhere in the region.

Transliteration

It's worth noting here that transliterating from Arabic script into English is at best an approximate science. The presence of sounds unknown in European languages, and the fact that the script is 'incomplete' (most vowels are not written), combine to

The Transliteration Dilemma

TE Lawrence, when asked by his publishers to clarify 'inconsistencies in the spelling of proper names' in *Seven Pillars of Wisdom* – his account of the Arab Revolt in WWI – wrote back:

Arabic names won't go into English. There are some 'scientific systems' of transliteration, helpful to people who know enough Arabic not to need helping, but a washout for the world. I spell my names anyhow, to show what rot the systems are.

make it nearly impossible to settle on one method of transliteration. A wide variety of spellings is therefore possible for words when they appear in roman script – and that goes for places and people's names as well.

The matter is further complicated by the wide variety of dialects and the imaginative ideas Arabs themselves often have on appropriate spelling in, say, English: words spelt one way in a Gulf country may look very different in Syria, heavily influenced by French (not even the most venerable of western Arabists have been able to come up with an ideal solution).

Pronunciation

Pronunciation of Arabic can be tongue-tying for someone unfamiliar with the intonation and combination of sounds. Pronounce the transliterated words slowly and clearly.

This language guide should help, but bear in mind that the myriad rules governing pronunciation and vowel use are too extensive to be covered here.

Vowels

a	as in 'had'
e	as in 'bet'
i	as in 'hit'
o	as in 'hot'
u	as in 'put'

A macron over a vowel indicates that the vowel has a long sound:

ā	as the 'a' in 'father'
ē	as in 'ten', but lengthened
ī	as the 'e' in 'ear', only softer
ō	as in 'for'
ū	as the 'oo' in 'food'

You may also see long vowels transliterated as double vowels, eg, 'aa' (ā), 'ee' (ī) and 'oo' (ū).

The Arabic Alphabet

Final	Medial	Initial	Alone	Transliteration	Pronunciation
ﺎ			ا	ā	as the 'a' in 'father'
ﺐ	ﺒ	ﺑ	ب	b	as in 'bet'
ﺖ	ﺘ	ﺗ	ت	t	as in 'ten'
ﺚ	ﺜ	ﺛ	ث	th	as in 'thin'
ﺞ	ﺠ	ﺟ	ج	g	as in 'go'
ﺢ	ﺤ	ﺣ	ح	H	a strongly whispered 'h', almost like a sigh of relief
ﺦ	ﺨ	ﺧ	خ	kh	as the 'ch' in Scottish *loch*
ﺪ			د	d	as in 'dim'
ﺬ			ذ	dh	as the 'th' in 'this'
ﺮ			ر	r	a rolled 'r', as in the Spanish word *caro*
ﺰ			ز	z	as in 'zip'
ﺲ	ﺴ	ﺳ	س	s	as in 'so', never as in 'wisdom'
ﺶ	ﺸ	ﺷ	ش	sh	as in 'ship'
ﺺ	ﺼ	ﺻ	ص	ş	emphatic 's'
ﺾ	ﻀ	ﺿ	ض	ḍ	emphatic 'd'
ﻂ	ﻄ	ﻃ	ط	ṭ	emphatic 't'
ﻆ	ﻈ	ﻇ	ظ	ẓ	emphatic 'z'
ﻊ	ﻌ	ﻋ	ع	'	the Arabic letter 'ayn; pronounce as a glottal stop – like the closing of the throat before saying 'Oh oh!' (see Other Sounds on p.190)
ﻎ	ﻐ	ﻏ	غ	gh	a guttural sound like Parisian 'r'
ﻒ	ﻔ	ﻓ	ف	f	as in 'far'
ﻖ	ﻘ	ﻗ	ق	q	a strongly guttural 'k' sound; in Egyptian Arabic often pronounced as a glottal stop
ﻚ	ﻜ	ﻛ	ك	k	as in 'king'
ﻞ	ﻠ	ﻟ	ل	l	as in 'lamb'
ﻢ	ﻤ	ﻣ	م	m	as in 'me'
ﻦ	ﻨ	ﻧ	ن	n	as in 'name'
ﻪ	ﻬ	ﻫ	ه	h	as in 'ham'
ﻮ			و	w	as in 'wet'; or
				ū	long, as the 'oo' on 'food'; or
				aw	as the 'ow' in 'how'
ﻲ	ﻴ	ﻳ	ي	y	as in 'yes'; or
				ī	as the 'e' in 'ear', only softer; or
				ay	as the 'y' in 'by' or as the 'ay' in 'way'

Vowels Not all Arabic vowel sounds are represented in the alphabet. See Pronunciation on p.188 for a list of all Arabic vowel sounds.

Emphatic Consonants To simplify the transliteration system used in this book, the emphatic consonants have not been included.

Consonants

Pronunciation for all Arabic consonants is covered in the alphabet table on the preceding page. Note that when double consonants occur in transliterations, both are pronounced. For example, al-Hammam (toilet/bath), is pronounced 'al-ham-mam'.

Other Sounds

Arabic has two sounds that are very tricky for non-Arabs to produce: the 'ayn and the glottal stop. The letter 'ayn represents a sound with no English equivalent that comes even close. It is similar to the glottal stop (which is not actually represented in the alphabet) but the muscles at the back of the throat are gagged more forcefully – it has been described as the sound of someone being strangled. In many transliteration systems, 'ayn is represented by an opening quotation mark, and the glottal stop by a closing quotation mark. To make the transliterations in this language guide (and throughout the rest of the book) easier to use, we have not distinguished between the glottal stop and the 'ayn, using the closing quotation mark to represent both sounds. You'll find that Arabic speakers will still understand you.

Pronouns

I	*ānē*
you (sg)	*inta/inti* (m/f)
he	*huwa*
she	*hiya*
we	*nahnu*
you (pl)	*untum/inti* (m/f)
they	*uhum*

Greetings & Civilities

Hello.	*as-salāma alaykum*
Hello. (response)	*wa alaykum e-salām*
Goodbye. (person leaving)	*ma'al salāma*
Goodbye. (person staying)	*alla ysalmak* (to a man)
	alla ysalmich (to a woman)
	alla ysallimkum (to a group)

Goodbye.	*Hayyākallah* (to a man)
	Hayyachallah (to a woman)
	Hayyakumallah (to a group)
Goodbye. (response)	*alla yHai'īk* (to a man)
	alla yHai'īch (to a woman)
	alla yHai'īkum (to a group)
Good morning.	*sabaH al-kheir*
Good morning. (response)	*sabaH an-nur*
Good afternoon/ evening.	*masa' al-kheir*
Good afternoon/ evening. (response)	*masa' an-nur*
Good night.	*tisbaH ala-kheir* (to a man)
	tisbiHin ala-kheir (to a woman)
	tisbuHun ala-kheir (to a group)
Good night. (response)	*wa inta min ahlil-kheir* (to a man)
	wa inti min ahlil-kheir (to a woman)
	wa intu min ahlil-kheir (to a group)
Welcome.	*ahlan wa sahlan* or *marHaba*
Welcome to you.	*ahlan fik* (to a man)
	ahlan fich (to a woman)
	ahlan fikum (to a group)
Pleased to meet you. (also said on leaving)	*fursa sa'ida*
Pleased to meet you. (response)	*wa ana as'ad* (by an individual)
	wa iHna as'ad (by a group)

Basics

Yes.	*aiwa/na'am*
No.	*lā*

Maybe.	*mumkin*
Please.	*min fadhlik* or
	lō tsimaH
	(to a man)
	min fadhlich or
	lō tsimiHīn
	(to a woman)
	min fadhelkum or
	lō tsimiHūn
	(to a group)
Thank you.	*shukran* or
	mashkur
	(to a man)
	mashkura
	(to a woman)
	mashkurin
	(to a group)
You're welcome.	*afwan/al-afu*
Excuse me.	*lō tsimaH*
	(to a man)
	lō tsimiHīn
	(to a woman)
	lō tsimiHūn
	(to a group)
I'm sorry/	*ānē āsef*
Forgive me.	
After you.	*atfaddal* or
	min badik
	(to a man)
	min badak
	(to a woman)
OK.	*zein/kwayyis/tayib*
No problem.	*mafi mushkila*
Impossible.	*mish mumkin*
It doesn't matter/	*ma'alish*
I don't mind.	

Small Talk

How are you?	*kef Halak?*
	(to a man)
	kef Halik?
	(to a woman)
	kef Halkum?
	(to a group)
Fine, thanks.	*(zein) al-Hamdulillah*
	(by a man)
	(zeina) al-Hamdulillah
	(by a woman)
	(zeinin) al-Hamdulillah
	(by a group)

What's your name?	*shismak?*
	(to a man)
	shismich?
	(to a woman)
	shisimkum?
	(to a group)
My name is ...	*ismi ...*
Do you like ...?	*tahabi ...?*
I like ...	*ahib ...*
I don't like ...	*la ahib ...*
God willing.	*inshallah*

I'm from ...	*ana min ...*
Australia	*usturālyē*
Canada	*kanadē*
Egypt	*masur*
Ethiopia	*ithyūbyē*
Europe	*ōrobba*
France	*faransa*
Germany	*almania*
Jordan	*elerdon*
Netherlands	*holanda*
New Zealand	*nyūzilande*
South Africa	*jinūb afrīqye*
Switzerland	*swissra*
Syria	*sūriye*
Tunisia	*tūnis*
UK	*britania*
USA	*amrika*

Language Difficulties

I understand.	*ana fahim*
	(by a man)
	ana fahma
	(by a woman)
We understand.	*iHna fahmīn*
I don't understand.	*ana afHām*
We don't	*iHna nafHām*
understand.	
Please repeat that.	*lō simaHt ti'id hādtha*
I speak ...	*ana atkallam ...*
Do you speak ...?	*titkallam ...?*
English	*inglīzi*
French	*fransawi*
German	*almāni*
I don't speak	*ma-atkallam arabi*
Arabic.	

I speak a little Arabic.	*atkallam arabi shwayē*
What does this mean?	*shu ya'ani?*
How do you say ... in Arabic?	*kef igūl ... bila'arabi?*
I want an interpreter.	*urīd mutarjem*

Getting Around

I want to go to ...	*abga arouH li ...*
When does the ... leave?	*mata yamshi il ...?* *muta yamshi il ...?* (in Kuwait)
When does the ... arrive?	*mata tosal il ...?* *muta tosal il ...?* (in Kuwait)
What is the fare to ...?	*cham il tadhkara li ...?*
Which bus/taxi goes to ...?	*ai bas/tax youH il ...?*
Does this bus/taxi go to ...?	*Hadhal bas youH il ...?*
How many buses go to ...?	*cham bas youH li ...?*
Please tell me when we arrive at ...	*lau samaHtit goul li mata nosal li ...*
May I sit here?	*mumkin ag'id hina?*
May we sit here?	*mumkin nag'id hina?*
Stop here, please.	*'ogaf hina, law samaHt*
Please wait for me.	*law samaHt, intidherni*

Where is (the) ...?	*wein (al-) ...?*
How far is the ...?	*cham yibe'id ...?*
airport	*al-matār*
bus stop	*mokaf al-bas*
bus station	*maHattat al-bas*
taxi stand	*maHattat tax/ maHattat ajara*

boat	*markab*
bus	*bas*
camel	*jamal*
car	*sayyara*
donkey	*Hmār*
horse	*Hsan*
taxi	*tax/ajara*

daily	*kil yōm*
ticket office	*maktab al-tadhāker*
ticket	*tadhkara/bitāq*
first class	*daraje ūlā*
second class	*daraje thānye*
crowded	*zaHme/matrūs*

Where can I rent a ...?	*min wein agdar asta'ajir ...?*
bicycle	*saikel*
motorcycle	*motorsaikel*

Directions

Where is the ...?	*wein al ...?*
Is it near?	*uhwe girīb?*
Is it far?	*uhwe bi'īb?*
How many kilometres?	*kam kilometer?*
Can you show me the way to ...?	*mumkin tdallini mukān ...?*

address	*onwān*
street	*shāri'*
number	*raqam*
city	*madina*
village	*qaria*

here	*hnī*
there	*hnāk*
next to	*yam*
opposite	*gbāl/mgābel*
behind	*warā/khaif*
to	*min*

Signs

ENTRY *dukhūl*	مدخل
EXIT *khurūj*	خروج
TOILETS (Men) *Hammam lirrijal*	حمام للرجال
TOILETS (Women) *Hammam linnisa'a*	حمام للنساء
HOSPITAL *mustashfa*	مستشفى
POLICE *shurta*	الشرطة
PROHIBITED *mamnu'u*	ممنوع

from	*ile*
left	*yasār*
right	*yimīn*
straight	*ala tūl*
	sīda (in Kuwait)
north	*shimāl*
south	*jinūb*
east	*sharug*
west	*gharub*

Around Town

I'm looking for the ...	*ga'ed adawwēr ala ...*
Where is the ...?	*wein ...?*
bank	*al-bank*
barber	*al-Hallaq*
beach	*il-shatt/il-shāt'i*
city centre	*wasat al-balād*
customs	*al-jamarek*
embassy	*al-safara*
mosque	*al-masjid*
museum	*al-matHaf*
old city	*al-madina il qadima*
palace	*al-qasr*
passport & immigration office	*markaz aljawazat welhijrā*
police station	*al-makhfar*
post office	*maktab al-barīd*
telephone	*al-telefon/al-hataf*
telephone centre	*maqsam al-hatef*
toilet	*al-Hammam*
tourist office	*isti'ilāmāt alsuyyaH*
university	*al-jam'a*
zoo	*Hadiqat il-Haywan*

What time does it open?	*mita tiftaH?*
What time does it close?	*mita tsaker?*
I'd like to make a telephone call.	*abgyi attisel telefōn/ abi akhaber*
I want to change money.	*abga asrif flūs*
I want to change travellers cheques.	*abga asrif sheikat syaHīa*

Accommodation

Where is the hotel?	*wein al-funduq/el-ōtel?*
I'd like to book a ...	*abgyi aHjiz ...*

bed	*sarīr/frāsh*
cheap room	*ghurfa rikhīsa*
single room	*ghurfa mifred*
double room	*ghurfa mijwīz*
room with a bathroom	*ghurfa ma'Hammam*
room with air-con	*ghurfa mukhayyafa*

for one night	*la leila wiHdē*
for two nights	*la leiltein thintein*
May I see the room?	*mumkin ashuf al-ghurfah?*
May I see other rooms?	*mumkin ashuf ghuraf dhānia?*
How much is this room per night?	*cham ujrat hādhil ghurfah fil-leila?*
How much is it per person?	*shtiswa ala eshshakhs al-āhed?*
Do you have any cheaper rooms?	*fīh ghuraf arkhas?*
This is fine.	*hadha zein.*

This is very ...	*hādhi wāhed ...*
noisy	*muzi'ije*
dirty	*waskha*
expensive	*ghalye*

address	*al-unwān*
blanket	*battaniyye*
camp site	*emakan al-mukhayyam*
electricity	*kahruba*
hotel	*funduq/ōtel*
hot water	*māi Hār*
key	*miftaH*
manager	*al-mudīr*
shower	*al-dūsh*
soap	*sābūn*
toilet	*Hammam*

Food

I'm hungry.	*āne jūda'ān*
I'm thirsty.	*āne atshān*
I'd like ...	*aHib/abghi ...*
Is service included in the bill?	*al-fatūra fihā qīmat al-khidma?*
What is this?	*shinū hādhe?*
Another one, please.	*ba'ad wiHde min fadhlik*

breakfast	*riyūg/ftūr*
lunch	*al-ghade*

Emergencies

Call the police!	*khaber eshurta!*
Call a doctor!	*khaber ettabīb!*
Help me, please!	*sa'idnī lō simaHt!*
Where is the toilet?	*wein al-Hammam?*
Go away!	*rūh wallī!/isref!*
Go/Get lost!	*imshi!*
Thief!	*Harāmi!/bawwāg!*
They robbed me!	*bagonī!*
Shame on you!	*yā eibak!/yal mā*
(woman to man)	*tistiHi!*

dinner	*al-ashe*
restaurant	*mata'ām*
set menu	*qa'imat al-akel muHaddada*
bread	*khubz*
chicken	*dajaj*
coffee	*qahwa*
fish	*samak*
meat	*laHma*
milk	*laban/halīb*
pepper	*felfel*
potatoes	*batatas*
rice	*roz*
salt	*sel/melaH*
sugar	*suker*
tea	*chai*
water	*mayya*

Shopping

I want ...	*abga ...*
	abi ... (in Kuwait & Bahrain)
Do you have ...?	*indik ...?* (to a man)
	indich ...? (to a woman)
Where can I buy ...?	*wein agdar ashtiri ...?*
How much is this?	*kam hadha?*
How much is that?	*kam hadhak?*
How much are those?	*kam hadhol?*
How much ...?	*kam ...?*
It costs too much.	*ghalia wai'd*

bookshop	*al-maktaba*
chemist/pharmacy	*saydaliyya*
laundry	*masbagha*

Numbers

Arabic numerals are simple to learn and, unlike the written language, run from left to right. Note the order of the words in numbers from 21 to 99.

0	٠	*sifir*
1	١	*waHid*
2	٢	*idhnīn*
3	٣	*dhaladha*
4	٤	*arba'a*
5	٥	*khamsa*
6	٦	*sitta*
7	٧	*sab'a*
8	٨	*dhimania*
9	٩	*tis'a*
10	١٠	*ashra*
11	١١	*Hda'ash*
12	١٢	*dhna'ash*
13	١٣	*dhaladhta'ash*
14	١٤	*arba'ata'ash*
15	١٥	*khamista'ash*
16	١٦	*sitta'ash*
17	١٧	*sabi'ta'ashr*
18	١٨	*dhimanta'ash*
19	١٩	*tisi'ta'ash*
20	٢٠	*'ishrīn*
21	٢١	*waHid wa 'ishrīn*
22	٢٢	*idhnīn wa 'ishrīn*
30	٣٠	*dhaladhīn*
40	٤٠	*arbi'īn*
50	٥٠	*khamsīn*
60	٦٠	*sittīn*
70	٧٠	*saba'īn*
80	٨٠	*dhimanīn*
90	٩٠	*tis'īn*
100	١٠٠	*imia*
101	١٠١	*imia wa-waHid*
200	٢٠٠	*imiatayn*
300	٣٠٠	*dhaladha imia*
1000	١٠٠٠	*alf*
2000	٢٠٠٠	*alfayn*
3000	٣٠٠٠	*dhaladha-alaf*

Ordinal Numbers

first	*awwal*
second	*dhānī*
third	*dhālidh*
fourth	*rābi'*
fifth	*khāmis*

market	*souq*
newsagents/ stationers	*maktabet-al-qurtāsiyye*
big	*chibīr*
bigger	*akbar*
small	*sighīr*
smaller	*asghar*
cheap	*rikhīs*
cheaper	*arkhas*
expensive	*ghāli*
open	*āmaftūH*
closed	*msakkar/mughlaq*
money	*flūs*

Health

I need a doctor.	*abi tabīb*
My friend is ill.	*sidiji marīd/ayyān*
hospital	*mustashfa*
pharmacy	*saydaliyye*
prescription	*wasfa tibbiyā*
tampons	*fuwat siHiyya lalHarīm*
headache	*wija' rās*
stomachache	*wija' batun*

Time & Dates

What time is it?	*as-sa'a kam?*
It is ...	*as-sa'a ...*
one o'clock	*waHda*
1.15	*waHda wa rob'*
1.20	*waHda wa tilt*
1.30	*waHda wa nus*
1.45	*idhnīn illa rob'* (lit: 'quarter to two')

When?	*mita?*
now	*alHīn*
after	*ba'ad*
daily	*kil yom*
today	*al-yom*
yesterday	*ams*

tomorrow	*bukra*
morning	*es-subāH*
afternoon	*ba'ad ezzuhur/ edhuhur*
evening	*al-masa*
day	*nahār*
night	*leil*
week	*esbū'u*
month	*shahar*
year	*sine*
early	*mbach'ir/badri*
late	*mit'akhir*
on time	*alwaqit*

Monday	*yom al-idhnīn*
Tuesday	*yom al-dhaladh*
Wednesday	*yom al-arbā'*
Thursday	*yom al-khamis*
Friday	*yom al-jama'a*
Saturday	*yom as-sabt*
Sunday	*yom al-Had*

The names of the months are virtually the same as their European counterparts and are easily recognisable.

January	*yanāyir*
February	*fibrāyir*
March	*māris*
April	*abrīl*
May	*māyu*
June	*yunyu*
July	*yulyu*
August	*aghustus*
September	*sibtimbir*
October	*'uktūbir*
November	*nufimbir*
December	*disimbir*

Glossary

Here, with definitions, are some words and abbreviations you might meet in this book or while you are in Bahrain, Kuwait and Qatar.

abaya – woman's full-length black robe
abba – black or gold cloak worn over the *dishdasha* on formal occasions
abu – father; saint
agal – (also *'iqal*) headropes used to hold a *gutra* in place
ahwa – see *kahwa*
ain – spring
Allah – God
azzan – call to prayer

bab – gate
bait – see *beit*
barjeel – wind towers
Bedouin – (also Bedu) desert dweller of Arabia
beit – (also *bait*) house
burda – traditional Qatari cloak
burj – tower

caliph – Islamic ruler
chai – tea

dalla – (also dallah) traditional copper coffeepot
dhow – traditional sailing vessel of the Gulf
dishdasha – name of men's shirt-dress worn in Kuwait and the UAE
diwan – meeting or reception room, sometimes ruler's office
diwaniya – Kuwaiti gatherings, usually at someone's home, where men discuss politics and other events of the day

Eid al-Adha – Feast of Sacrifice marking the pilgrimage to Mecca
Eid al-Fitr – Festival of Breaking the Fast; celebrated at the end of *Ramadan*
emir – Islamic ruler, military commander or governor; literally, prince

fuul – dish made from stewed fava beans mostly eaten at breakfast
GCC – Gulf Cooperation Council; members are Saudi Arabia, Kuwait, Bahrain, Qatar, Oman and the UAE; sometimes referred to as the AGCC or Arab Gulf Cooperation Council
gutra – white headcloth worn by men in the Gulf States

haj – (also hajj) annual Muslim pilgrimage to Mecca
halal – religiously acceptable or permitted under Islam
haram – forbidden by Islam; religiously unacceptable
hareem – the women of the household or family
Hejira – migration; also name of Islamic calendar
hibb – ceramic pot used to keep water cold
hubble bubble – see *sheesha*

ikhwan – brotherhood/army of *Bedouin* soldiers
imam – prayer leader, *Muslim* cleric
inshallah – 'god willing'
'iqal – see *agal*
iqama – residence permit
iwan – vaulted hall, opening into a central court in the *madrassa* of a *mosque*

jebel – hill, mountain
jihad – literally: striving in the way of the faith; holy war

Kaaba – (also *Qaaba*) the rectangular structure at the centre of the Grand Mosque in Mecca (containing the Black Stone) around which pilgrims circle
kahwa – (also *ahwa*) coffee; coffeehouse
kandoura – casual shirt-dress worn by men and women
KOC – Kuwait Oil Company
Koran – see *Quran*
kufic – a type of stylised old Arabic script

madrassa – *Muslim* theological seminary; also modern Arabic word for school

majlis – formal meeting room or reception area; also parliament

medina – old walled centre of any Islamic city

mihrab – (also mihrib) nichè in a *mosque* indicating the direction of Mecca

minbar – pulpit used for sermons in a *mosque*

mosque – the *Muslim* place of worship

muezzin – cantor who sings the *azzan*

Muslim – one who submits to God's will; follower of Islam

nargila – see *sheesha*

OPEC – Organization of Petroleum Exporting Countries

PDQ – Petroleum Development (Qatar); forerunner of today's state-run QGPC

Qaaba – see *Kaaba*

qala'at – (also qal'at) castle or fort

QGPC – Qatar General Petroleum Corporation

Quran – (also *Koran*) the holy book of Islam

rakats – (also rakahs) cycles of prayer during which the *Quran* is read and a series of bows are performed

Ramadan – the *Muslim* month of fasting

salat – prayer

sawm – fasting

shahadah – a Muslim's profession of his or her faith

shaikh – see *sheikh*

Sharia'a – Islamic law

sheesha – tall, glass-bottomed smoking implement, also known as a *hubble bubble* or *nargila*

sheikh – (also *shaikh*) a venerated religious scholar. In Bahrain, Kuwait and

Qatar this is also a title for all members of the ruling family.

Shi'ite – (also Shi'ia) sect of Islam which believes that the leadership of the Muslim community should descend through the Prophet Mohammed's son-in-law, Ali

shwarma – grilled meat sliced from a spit and served in a pita bread with salad

sirwal – women's trousers, worn under the *kandoura*

souq – market or shopping centre

Sunnah – body of works recording the sayings and doings of the Prophet and his family

Sunni – follower of the faction of Islam that believes that any *Muslim* who exercises justice according to the *Sharia'a* can become a ruler

ta'amiyyah – deep-fried balls of crushed chickpeas with spices served in flat bread with pickled vegetables

talli – different coloured cotton, silver and gold threads interwoven to make decorative ankle, wrist and neck bands

taqia – men's lace skull cap worn under the *gutra*

tatrees – traditional Bahraini embroidery

tell – an ancient mound created by centuries of urban rebuilding

thobe – floor-length shirt-dress worn by men in Bahrain and Qatar

Trucial States – now the United Arab Emirates (UAE)

umm – mother

umrah – any pilgrimage to Mecca that is not *haj*

wadi – dried-up river bed; seasonal river

Wahhabi – back to basics religious movement which predominates in Saudi Arabia and, in a less severe form, in Qatar

wasta – influence high up

zakat – alms or charity

LONELY PLANET

Phrasebooks

L onely Planet phrasebooks are packed with essential words and phrases to help travellers communicate with the locals. With colour tabs for quick reference, an extensive vocabulary and use of script, these handy pocket-sized language guides cover day-to-day travel situations.

- handy pocket-sized books
- easy to understand Pronunciation chapter
- clear & comprehensive Grammar chapter
- romanisation alongside script to allow ease of pronunciation
- script throughout so users can point to phrases for every situation
- full of cultural information and tips for the traveller

'... vital for a real DIY spirit and attitude in language learning'
— *Backpacker*

'the phrasebooks have good cultural backgrounders and offer solid advice for challenging situations in remote locations'
— *San Francisco Examiner*

Arabic (Egyptian) • Arabic (Moroccan) • Australian *(Australian English, Aboriginal and Torres Strait languages)* • Baltic States *(Estonian, Latvian, Lithuanian)* • Bengali • Brazilian • British • Burmese • Cantonese • Central Asia (Uyghur, Uzbek, Kyrghiz, Kazak, Pashto, Tadjik • Central Europe *(Czech, French, German, Hungarian, Italian, Slovak)* • Eastern Europe *(Bulgarian, Czech, Hungarian, Polish, Romanian, Slovak)* • Ethiopian (Amharic) • Fijian • French • German • Greek • Hebrew • Hill Tribes • Hindi & Urdu • Indonesian • Italian • Japanese • Korean • Lao • Latin American Spanish • Malay • Mandarin • Mediterranean Europe *(Albanian, Croatian, Greek, Italian, Macedonian, Maltese, Serbian, Slovene)* • Mongolian • Nepali • Pidgin • Pilipino (Tagalog) • Portugese • Quechua • Russian • Scandinavian Europe *(Danish, Finnish, Icelandic, Norwegian, Swedish)* • South-East Asia *(Burmese, Indonesian, Khmer, Lao, Malay, Tagalog Pilipino, Thai, Vietnamese)* • South Pacific Languages • Spanish (Castilian) *(also includes Catalan, Galician and Basque)* • Sri Lanka • Swahili • Thai • Tibetan • Turkish • Ukrainian • USA *(US English, Vernacular, Native American languages, Hawaiian)* • Vietnamese • Western Europe *(Basque, Catalan, Dutch, French, German, Greek, Irish, Italian, Portuguese, Scottish Gaelic, Spanish (Castilian), Welsh)*

LONELY PLANET

Lonely Planet Journeys

Journeys is a unique collection of travel writing – published by the company that understands travel better than anyone else. It is a series for anyone who has ever experienced – or dreamed of – the magical moment when they encountered a strange culture or saw a place for the first time. They are tales to read while you're planning a trip, while you're on the road or while you're in an armchair in front of a fire.

These outstanding titles explore our planet through the eyes of a diverse group of international writers. JOURNEYS books catch the spirit of a place, illuminate a culture, recount a crazy adventure or introduce a fascinating way of life. They always entertain, and always enrich the experience of travel.

MALI BLUES
Traveling to an African Beat
Lieve Joris (translated by Sam Garrett)

Drought, rebel uprisings, ethnic conflict: these are the predominant images of West Africa. But as Lieve Joris travels in Senegal, Mauritania and Mali, she meets survivors, fascinating individuals charting new ways of living between tradition and modernity. With her remarkable gift for drawing out people's stories, Joris brilliantly captures the rhythms of a world that refuses to give in.

THE GATES OF DAMASCUS
Lieve Joris (translated by Sam Garrett)

This best-selling book is a beautifully drawn portrait of day-to-day life in modern Syria. Through her intimate contact with local people, Lieve Joris draws us into the fascinating world that lies behind the gates of Damascus. Hala's husband is a political prisoner, jailed for his opposition to the Assad regime; through the author's friendship with Hala we see how Syrian politics impacts on the lives of ordinary people.

THE OLIVE GROVE
Travels in Greece
Katherine Kizilos

Katherine Kizilos travels to fabled islands, troubled border zones and her family's village deep in the mountains. She vividly evokes breathtaking landscapes, generous people and passionate politics, capturing the complexities of a country she loves.

'beautifully captures the real tensions of Greece' – *Sunday Times*

KINGDOM OF THE FILM STARS
Journey into Jordan
Annie Caulfield

Kingdom of the Film Stars is a travel book and a love story. With honesty and humour, Annie Caulfield writes of travelling in Jordan and falling in love with a Bedouin with film-star looks.

She offers fascinating insights into the country – from the tent life of traditional women to the hustle of downtown Amman – and unpicks tight-woven western myths about the Arab world.

Lonely Planet Travel Atlases

L onely Planet has long been famous for the number and quality of its guidebook maps. Now we've gone one step further and produced a handy companion series: Lonely Planet trave atlases – maps of a country produced in book form.

Unlike other maps, which look good but lead travellers astray, our travel atlases have been researched on the road by Lonely Planet's experienced team of writers. All details are carefully checked to ensure the atlas corresponds with the equivalent Lonely Planet guidebook.

- full-colour throughout
- maps researched and checked by Lonely Planet authors
- place names correspond with Lonely Planet guidebooks
- no confusing spelling differences
- legend and travelling information in English, French, German, Japanese and Spanish
- size: 230 x 160 mm

Available now: Chile & Easter Island ● Egypt ● India & Bangladesh ● Israel & the Palestinian Territories ● Jordan, Syria & Lebanon ● Kenya ● Laos ● Portugal ● South Africa, Lesotho & Swaziland ● Thailand ● Turkey ● Vietnam ● Zimbabwe, Botswana & Namibia

---

Lonely Planet TV Series & Videos

L onely Planet travel guides have been brought to life on television screens around the world. Like our guides, the programs are based on the joy of independent travel and look honestly at some of the most exciting, picturesque and frustrating places in the world. Each show is presented by one of three travellers from Australia, England or the USA and combines an innovative mixture of video, Super-8 film, atmospheric soundscapes and original music.

Videos of each episode – containing additional footage not shown on television – are available from good book and video shops, but the availability of individual videos varies with regional screening schedules.

Video destinations include: Alaska ● American Rockies ● Argentina ● Australia – The South-East ● Baja California & the Copper Canyon ● Brazil ● Central Asia ● Chile & Easter Island ● Corsica, Sicily & Sardinia – The Mediterranean Islands ● East Africa (Tanzania & Zanzibar) ● Cuba ● Ecuador & the Galapagos Islands ● Ethiopia ● Greenland & Iceland ● Hungary & Romania ● Indonesia ● Israel & the Sinai Desert ● Jamaica ● Japan ● La Ruta Maya ● London ● The Middle East (Syria, Jordan & Lebanon ● Morocco ● New York City ● Northern Spain ● North India ● Outback Australia ● Pacific Islands (Fiji, Solomon Islands & Vanuatu) ● Pakistan ● Peru ● The Philippines ● South Africa & Lesotho ● South India ● South West China ● South West USA ● Trekking in Uganda & Congo ● Turkey ● Vietnam ● West Africa ● Zimbabwe, Botswana & Namibia

The Lonely Planet TV series is produced by: Pilot Productions
The Old Studio
18 Middle Row
London W10 5AT, UK

Lonely Planet Online

Whether you've just begun planning your next trip, or you're chasing down specific info on currency regulations or visa requirements, check out Lonely Planet Online for up-to-the-minute travel information.

As well as miniguides to more than 250 destinations, you'll find maps, photos, travel news, health and visa updates, travel advisories and discussion of the ecological and political issues you need to be aware of as you travel. You'll also find timely upgrades to popular guidebooks that you can print out and stick in the back of your book.

There's an online travellers' forum (The Thorn Tree) where you can share your experience of life on the road, meet travel companions and ask other travellers for their recommendations and advice.

There's also a complete and up-to-date list of all Lonely Planet travel products including travel guides, diving and snorkeling guides, phrasebooks, atlases, travel literature and videos, and a simple online ordering facility if you can't find the book you want elsewhere.

Lonely Planet Diving & Snorkeling Guides

Beautifully illustrated with full-colour photos throughout, Lonely Planet's Pisces books explore the world's best diving and snorkeling areas and prepare divers for what to expect when they get there, both topside and underwater.

Dive sites are described in detail with specifics on depths, visibility, level of difficulty, special conditions, underwater photography tips and common and unusual marine life present. You'll also find practical logistical information and coverage on topside activities and attractions, sections on diving health and safety, plus listings for diving services, live-aboards, dive resorts and tourist offices.

LONELY PLANET

Guides by Region

Lonely Planet is known worldwide for publishing practical, reliable and no-nonsense travel information in our guides and on our Web site. The Lonely Planet list covers just about every accessible part of the world. Currently there are thirteen series: travel guides, shoestring guides, walking guides, city guides, phrasebooks, audio packs, city maps, travel atlases, diving & snorkeling guides, restaurant guides, first-time travel guides, healthy travel and travel literature.

AFRICA Africa on a shoestring • Africa – the South • Arabic (Egyptian) phrasebook • Arabic (Moroccan) phrasebook • Cairo • Cape Town • Cape Town city map • Central Africa • East Africa • Egypt • Egypt travel atlas • Ethiopian (Amharic) phrasebook • The Gambia & Senegal • Healthy Travel Africa • Kenya • Kenya travel atlas • Malawi, Mozambique & Zambia • Morocco • North Africa • Read This First Africa • South Africa, Lesotho & Swaziland • South Africa, Lesotho & Swaziland travel atlas • Swahili phrasebook • Tanzania, Zanzibar & Pemba • Trekking in East Africa • Tunisia • West Africa • Zimbabwe, Botswana & Namibia • Zimbabwe, Botswana & Nambia Travel Atlas • World Food Morocco
Travel Literature: The Rainbird: A Central African Journey • Songs to an African Sunset: A Zimbabwean Story • Mali Blues: Traveling to an African Beat

AUSTRALIA & THE PACIFIC Auckland • Australia • Australian phrasebook • Bushwalking in Australia • Bushwalking in Papua New Guinea • Fiji • Fijian phrasebook • Healthy Travel Australia, NZ and the Pacific • Islands of Australia's Great Barrier Reef • Melbourne • Melbourne city map • Micronesia • New Caledonia • New South Wales & the ACT • New Zealand • Northern Territory • Outback Australia • Out To Eat – Melbourne • Out to Eat – Sydney • Papua New Guinea • Pidgin phrasebook • Queensland • Rarotonga & the Cook Islands • Samoa • Solomon Islands • South Australia • South Pacific • South Pacific Languages phrasebook • Sydney • Sydney city map • Sydney Condensed • Tahiti & French Polynesia • Tasmania • Tonga • Tramping in New Zealand • Vanuatu • Victoria • Western Australia
Travel Literature: Islands in the Clouds • Kiwi Tracks: A New Zealand Journey • Sean & David's Long Drive

CENTRAL AMERICA & THE CARIBBEAN Bahamas, Turks & Caicos • Bermuda • Central America on a shoestring • Costa Rica • Cuba • Dominican Republic & Haiti • Eastern Caribbean • Guatemala, Belize & Yucatán: La Ruta Maya • Jamaica • Mexico • Mexico City • Panama • Puerto Rico • Read This First Central & South America • World Food Mexico
Travel Literature: Green Dreams: Travels in Central America

EUROPE Amsterdam • Amsterdam city map • Andalucía • Austria • Baltic States phrasebook • Barcelona • Berlin • Berlin city map • Britain • British phrasebook • Brussels, Bruges & Antwerp • Budapest city map • Canary Islands • Central Europe • Central Europe phrasebook • Corfu & Ionians • Corsica • Crete • Crete Condensed • Croatia • Cyprus • Czech & Slovak Republics • Denmark • Dublin • Eastern Europe • Eastern Europe phrasebook • Edinburgh • Estonia, Latvia & Lithuania • Europe on a shoestring • Finland • Florence • France • French phrasebook • Germany • German phrasebook • Greece • Greek Islands • Greek phrasebook • Hungary • Iceland, Greenland & the Faroe Islands • Istanbul City Map • Ireland • Italian phrasebook • Italy • Krakow •Lisbon • London • London city map • London Condensed • Mediterranean Europe • Mediterranean Europe phrasebook • Munich • Norway • Paris • Paris city map • Paris Condensed • Poland • Portugal • Portugese phrasebook • Portugal travel atlas • Prague • Prague city map • Provence & the Côte d'Azur • Read This First Europe • Romania & Moldova • Rome • Russia, Ukraine & Belarus • Russian phrasebook • Scandinavian & Baltic Europe • Scandinavian Europe phrasebook • Scotland • Slovenia • Spain • Spanish phrasebook • St Petersburg • Switzerland • Trekking in Spain • Ukrainian phrasebook • Venice • Vienna • Walking in Britain • Walking in Ireland • Walking in Italy • Walking in Spain • Walking in Switzerland • Western Europe • Western Europe phrasebook • World Food Italy • World Food Spain
Travel Literature: The Olive Grove: Travels in Greece

INDIAN SUBCONTINENT Bangladesh • Bengali phrasebook • Bhutan • Delhi • Goa • Hindi & Urdu phrasebook • India • India & Bangladesh travel atlas • Indian Himalaya • Karakoram Highway • Kerala • Mumbai (Bombay) • Nepal • Nepali phrasebook • Pakistan • Rajasthan • Read This First: Asia & India • South India • Sri Lanka • Sri Lanka phrasebook • Trekking in the Indian Himalaya • Trekking in the Karakoram & Hindukush • Trekking in the Nepal Himalaya
Travel Literature: In Rajasthan • Shopping for Buddhas • The Age Of Kali

LONELY PLANET

Mail Order

L onely Planet products are distributed worldwide. They are also available by mail order from Lonely Planet, so if you have difficulty finding a title please write to us. North and South American residents should write to 150 Linden St, Oakland, CA 94607, USA; European and African residents should write to 10a Spring Place, London NW5 3BH, UK; and residents of other countries to PO Box 617, Hawthorn, Victoria 3122, Australia.

ISLANDS OF THE INDIAN OCEAN Madagascar & Comoros • Maldives • Mauritius, Réunion & Seychelles

MIDDLE EAST & CENTRAL ASIA Bahrain, Kuwait & Qatar • Central Asia • Central Asia phrasebook • Dubai • Hebrew phrasebook • Iran • Israel & the Palestinian Territories • Israel & the Palestinian Territories travel atlas • Istanbul • Istanbul to Cairo on a shoestring • Jerusalem • Jerusalem City Map • Jordan • Jordan, Syria & Lebanon travel atlas • Lebanon • Middle East • Oman & the United Arab Emirates • Syria • Turkey • Turkey travel atlas • Turkish phrasebook • Yemen
Travel Literature: The Gates of Damascus • Kingdom of the Film Stars: Journey into Jordan • Black on Black: Iran Revisited

NORTH AMERICA Alaska • Backpacking in Alaska • Baja California • California & Nevada • California Condensed • Canada • Chicago • Chicago city map • Deep South • Florida • Hawaii • Honolulu • Las Vegas • Los Angeles • Miami • New England • New Orleans • New York City • New York city map • New York Condensed • New York, New Jersey & Pennsylvania • Oahu • Pacific Northwest USA • Puerto Rico • Rocky Mountain • San Francisco • San Francisco city map • Seattle • Southwest USA • Texas • USA • USA phrasebook • Vancouver • Washington, DC & the Capital Region • Washington DC city map
Travel Literature: Drive Thru America

NORTH-EAST ASIA Beijing • Cantonese phrasebook • China • Hong Kong • Hong Kong city map • Hong Kong, Macau & Guangzhou • Japan • Japanese phrasebook • Japanese audio pack • Korea • Korean phrasebook • Kyoto • Mandarin phrasebook • Mongolia • Mongolian phrasebook • North-East Asia on a shoestring • Seoul • South-West China • Taiwan • Tibet • Tibetan phrasebook • Tokyo
Travel Literature: Lost Japan • In Xanadu

SOUTH AMERICA Argentina, Uruguay & Paraguay • Bolivia • Brazil • Brazilian phrasebook • Buenos Aires • Chile & Easter Island • Chile & Easter Island travel atlas • Colombia • Ecuador & the Galapagos Islands • Healthy Travel Central & South America • Latin American Spanish phrasebook • Peru •Quechua phrasebook • Rio de Janeiro • Rio de Janeiro city map • South America on a shoestring • Trekking in the Patagonian Andes • Venezuela
Travel Literature: Full Circle: A South American Journey

SOUTH-EAST ASIA Bali & Lombok • Bangkok • Bangkok city map • Burmese phrasebook • Cambodia • Hanoi • Healthy Travel Asia & India • Hill Tribes phrasebook • Ho Chi Minh City • Indonesia • Indonesia's Eastern Islands • Indonesian phrasebook • Indonesian audio pack • Jakarta • Java • Laos • Lao phrasebook • Laos travel atlas • Malay phrasebook • Malaysia, Singapore & Brunei • Myanmar (Burma) • Philippines • Pilipino (Tagalog) phrasebook • Read This First Asia & India • Singapore • South-East Asia on a shoestring • South-East Asia phrasebook • Thailand • Thailand's Islands & Beaches • Thailand travel atlas • Thai phrasebook • Thai audio pack • Vietnam • Vietnamese phrasebook • Vietnam travel atlas • World Food Thailand • World Food Vietnam

ALSO AVAILABLE: Antarctica • The Arctic • Brief Encounters: Stories of Love, Sex & Travel • Chasing Rickshaws • Lonely Planet Unpacked • Not the Only Planet: Travel Stories from Science Fiction • Sacred India • Travel with Children • Traveller's Tales

Index

Abbreviations

Text

Bold indicates maps.

Bold indicates maps.

Boxed Text

MAP LEGEND

CITY ROUTES

Freeway .... Freeway	Street .... Street	= = = = ... Unsealed Road
Highway .... Primary Road	Lane .... Lane	========= .... Pedestrian Street
Road .... Secondary Road	========= .... On/Off Ramp	========= .... Footbridge

REGIONAL ROUTES

========= .... Primary Road
========= .... Secondary Road
========= .... Minor Road

HYDROGRAPHY

.... Wadi

TRANSPORT ROUTES & STATIONS

----- .... Ferry
- - - - - .... Walking Trail

BOUNDARIES

.... International
— — — .... Disputed

AREA FEATURES

.... Building	.... Market	.... Beach
.... Park, Gardens	.... Sports Ground	.... Cemetery

.... Plaza

POPULATION SYMBOLS

✪ CAPITAL .... National Capital	● CITY .... City
	● Town .... Town

● Village .... Village
.... Urban Area

MAP SYMBOLS

✿ .... Place to Stay	▼ .... Place to Eat	● .... Point of Interest

✕ .... Airport	🏰 .... Castle	🛆 .... Monument	🔲 .... Ruins
❸ .... Bank	🎬 .... Cinema	☪ .... Mosque	✕ .... Shopping Centre
◉ .... Border Crossing	🛄 .... Embassy/Consulate	🏛 .... Museum	🏛 .... Stately Home
🚏 .... Bus Stop	⛽ .... Fuel	🅿 .... Parking	☎ .... Telephone
🚌 .... Bus Terminal	⛳ .... Golf Course	✚ .... Police Station	🎭 .... Theatre
☕ .... Cafe	✚ .... Hospital	✉ .... Post Office	❶ .... Tourist Information

Note: not all symbols displayed above appear in this book

LONELY PLANET OFFICES

Australia
PO Box 617, Hawthorn, Victoria 3122
☎ 03 9819 1877 fax 03 9819 6459
email: talk2us@lonelyplanet.com.au

UK
10a Spring Place, London NW5 3BH
☎ 020 7428 4800 fax 020 7428 4828
email: go@lonelyplanet.co.uk

USA
150 Linden St, Oakland, CA 94607
☎ 510 893 8555 TOLL FREE: 800 275 8555
fax 510 893 8572
email: info@lonelyplanet.com

France
1 rue du Dahomey, 75011 Paris
☎ 01 55 25 33 00 fax 01 55 25 33 01
email: bip@lonelyplanet.fr
www.lonelyplanet.fr

World Wide Web: www.lonelyplanet.com *or* AOL keyword: lp
Lonely Planet Images: lpi@lonelyplanet.com.au